Grace Livingston Hill

Because of Stephen, Grace Livin[gston Hill] [...] Margaret Halstead, left alone foll[...] to live with her estranged half-broth[...] [...]y goods with her and sets up house [...] in hopes of winning his love for her and for her God. Not always welcome, she decides to begin a Sunday school class for Stephen, his roommate Philip and their drinking buddies. Soon this motley crew undergoes a transformation no one can believe. . .and Margaret undergoes a transformation of her own. But Stephen's heart is still hardened to the Lord. Is there any way Margaret can help him find salvation?

Lone Point, Grace Livingston Hill
Maria is only happy when she is seen with the "right" people. She is mortified when the family finances fail and her sister Rachel suggests that their parents rent out their comfortable home for the summer—for a sizable amount—and they move to an inexpensive cottage at Lone Point. She is so unhappy with the arrangements that she weaves a miserable web around herself. But while she is there, she meets Howard, a young minister who believes she is a model of selflessness and virtue. Can she ever live up to his unrealistic view of her character?

The Story of a Whim, Grace Livingston Hill
College girls on a holiday spy battered furniture at a train station. Hazel Winship takes pity on the owner, whom she supposes to be a woman, and sends a care package that includes an organ and a picture. But the owner is a man, living alone among his orange trees in Florida. He cannot return the gifts and finds his life somehow changed by them for the better. But a year later he must face the consequences of deceiving the one girl to whom he owes his changed life.

An Interrupted Night, Isabella Alden
Isabella Alden had keen insight into human nature. *An Interrupted Night,* her last published novel, is a book for our times, exposing the hurts and horrors of infidelity. She also shows how someone can confront an angry person in the wrong with calmness and confidence—and communicate the truth with clarity. And she demonstrates through her characters the love and faithfulness of God.

Grace Livingston Hill

COLLECTION NO. 2

FOUR COMPLETE NOVELS

Updated for today's reader

BARBOUR
PUBLISHING, INC.
Uhrichsville, Ohio

Edited and updated for today's reader by Deborah Cole

ISBN 1-57748-444-4

Published by Barbour Publishing, Inc., P.O. Box 719, Uhrichsville, Ohio 44683 http://www.barbourbooks.com

Member of the
Evangelical Christian
Publishers Association

Printed in the United States of America.

Because of
Stephen

Chapter 1

T he room was full of blue smoke from bacon sizzling on the stove when Philip Earle walked in. He was hungry, but the odor of the bacon took the edge off his appetite; it reminded him in a strangely monotonous way of past meals.

The lamp was doing its best to help the smoke and the odor that filled the room, while the smoke was delaying any other function it might have had. The lamp sat on a little shelf on the wall, and under it, half hidden by the smoke, stood another young man bending over the stove.

The room was not attractive. The walls, floor and ceiling were made of rough boards. The furniture consisted of an old extension table, several chairs, a cheap cot covered with a gray army blanket and a desk that showed hard use, piled high with papers and a few books. A wooden bench next to the stove held a tin washbasin and cooking utensils close by.

Several coats and hats and a horse blanket hung on nails in the walls. A line of boots and shoes stood against the baseboard. Nothing else but a barrel and several boxes was in the room.

The table was set for supper with a loaf of bread, two cups, knives and spoons, a bag of crackers, a paper of cheese, a pitcher of water and an open can of baked beans.

Philip added to the table's confusion by throwing his bundles down at one end. Then he stood his whip in one corner and tossed his felt hat across the room to the cot.

"A letter for you, Steve!" he said as he sat down at the table and ran his hands wearily through his thick, black hair.

Stephen Halstead emerged from the cloud of smoke by the stove and examined the postmark on the letter.

"Well, I guess it can wait till we've had supper," he said. "It's not likely to be important. I'm hungry!" He put a large plate of smoking bacon and shriveled, blackened fried eggs on the table beside the coffeepot and sat down.

They began to eat in silence but with sharp appetites, for both had been in the open air all day. Stephen knew that his partner would presently report about the cattle he sold and about searching for several stray animals that had wandered off. But that could wait.

Philip, however, was thinking of something else. Perhaps it was the texture of the envelope he'd just laid down, or the whiff of violet he breathed from it as he took it from his pocket, that reminded him of old days; or perhaps he was just hungry and dissatisfied.

"Say, Steve," he said, setting down his empty cup, "do you remember the banquet in 1895?"

A cloud crossed Stephen's face. He had reasons to remember it that his friend didn't know.

"What of it?" he growled.

"Nothing. I was just thinking I'd like to have the squabs and a few other little things I didn't eat that night. They wouldn't taste bad after a day like the one we've had."

He helped himself to another piece of cheese and dished out more baked beans.

Stephen laughed harshly. He didn't like to be reminded of that banquet night. To create a diversion, he reached out for the letter.

"This is from that precious sister of mine, I suppose, who isn't my sister at all and yet insists on keeping up the appearance," he said. "I don't know what she expects to get from it. I have nothing to leave her in my will. Besides, I rarely answer her letters."

"You're an ungrateful dog," said Philip. "You should be glad to have someone in the world to write you. I've often thought of advertising for somebody who'd be a sister to me, at least enough to write to me. It would add a little zest to my life. I don't see why you're so prejudiced against her. She never did anything. She couldn't help it that her mother was your father's second wife. When did you last see her?"

"Never saw her but once in my life, and then she was a little, bawling, red thing with long clothes and everybody waiting on her."

"How old were you?"

"About ten," said Stephen doggedly, not joining in Philip's laughter at his expense. "I was old enough to resent her being in my home, where I should have been, and her mother managing things and sending me off to boarding school to get rid of me. I could remember my own mother, Phil. She wasn't dead a year when Father married again."

"Well, it wasn't your fault anyway, that I can see," Philip said with amusement. "After all, she's your sister. She's as much your father's child as you are."

"She's nothing but a half-sister," said Stephen, "and of no interest to me. Why on earth she writes me long letters I can't figure out. She's done it only since Father died. I suppose her mother thought it would be good to appease me, lest I make trouble about the will. But I knew Father wouldn't have much for me. His precious second wife did me out from the minute she saw me. And she's dead now, too. If it hadn't been for what my mother left, I wouldn't have a cent."

"Who's the girl living with?" asked Philip.

"Oh, with an aunt—her mother's sister—an old woman up in New England."

Then Stephen tore open the letter and shoved his chair back closer to the lamp. The room was silent while he read his letter. Philip, emptying the coffeepot, mused over the life of an orphan girl in the home of a New England maiden aunt.

Suddenly Stephen's chair jerked about with a sharp thud on the bare floor, and he stood up, uttering some strong language.

He had light hair, originally a golden brown, but bleached by the sun to a tawny shade. He was a slender fellow, well built, tanned, with deep, unhappy blue eyes. He would have been handsome but for a weakness about his mouth.

He was angry now and perplexed. His yellow brows were knit together in a frown, his head up, his eyes darker than usual. Philip watched him in mild amusement and waited for an explanation.

"Well, is she too sisterly this time?" he asked.

"Altogether!" said Stephen. "She's coming to see us."

The amusement left Philip's face. He sprang to his feet, while the color rolled up under his dark skin.

"Coming to see us?" he exclaimed, looking around and seeing as if for the first time the room's faults.

"Coming to see us?" he repeated as if uncertain of the sound of his own words. *"Here?"*

"Here!" Stephen said, spreading out his hands. The two gazed about in sudden awareness of the desolation of the place they had called "home" for three years.

"When?" Philip managed to murmur weakly, trying to think of a way of escape for himself without deserting his partner.

Stephen stooped to pick up the letter he'd thrown on the floor in his excitement.

"I don't know," he said dejectedly. "Here, read the thing, and see if you can find out." He handed the letter to Phil, who received it eagerly and settled into the chair under the light.

"She'll have to be stopped," said Stephen, sitting down on the cot to study it out, "or sent back if it's too late for stopping. She can't come here, of course."

"Of course!" agreed Philip.

Then he read: *"My dear brother Stephen—"*

Philip suddenly felt jealous of his friend. It would be nice to get a letter like that.

> *It's been a long time since I've written to you, but you've never been out of my thoughts for long. Aunt Priscilla was taken ill the day after I wrote you the last time. She was confined to her room all winter and some of the time a little flighty. She got odd ideas. One was that I was going to run away and marry a Spaniard. She couldn't stand for me to be out of her sight. This tied me down a lot, even*

though we had a nurse who took care of her. I couldn't even write when I was in her sight, because she imagined I was plotting to put her in an old folks' home, and she was terrified.

I don't like to think of those long, dreary months, but they're over now. Aunt Priscilla died a month ago, and now I'm alone except for you. Stephen, I wonder if you have any idea how dear you've grown to me. Sometimes it's seemed as if I just couldn't wait any longer to see you. It's cheered me up to know I have a lovely, big, grown-up brother to turn to.

Philip's eyes grew moist, and he stopped to clear his throat as he turned the page and glanced at the unloving brother, who sat darkly with his elbows on his knees and his chin in his hands.

So now, Stephen, I'm going to do just what I've wanted to do ever since Mother died and I left college and came home to Aunt Priscilla. I'm coming to see you! I've sold the old house. I had a good offer, and I can't bear the place. It's so desolate here.

Philip wondered what she would think of her brother's home.

I can't bear the thought of staying here alone, and I know I couldn't coax you away from your beloved West. So I'm packed now and am starting at once. Maybe you won't like it or not want me; in that case of course I can come back. But anyway I'll see you first. I couldn't stand it without seeing you. I keep thinking of what Father said to me just before he died. I never told you. I've always thought I'd rather wait till I could say it to you, but now I'll send it on to you as my plea for a welcome. It was the last afternoon we had together. Mother was lying down, and I was alone with him. He'd been asleep, and he suddenly opened his eyes and called me to him. "Don't forget you have a brother when I'm gone," he said. "Tell him I'm afraid I wasn't always wise in my treatment of him. Tell him I loved him, and I love you, and I want you two to love each other."

I began to love you then, Stephen, and the longing to know you and see you has grown with the years, five years, since Father died. I never told Mother about it. She wasn't well enough to talk much, and she didn't live long after that. I've only sought to claim that love in writing you letters occasionally, and sometimes I've been afraid you didn't care to get them. But now I'm coming to see for myself. I won't be a burden to you, brother. I have enough, you know, to take care of myself. And if I'm not welcome, all you have to do is tell me so, and I

*can go away again. But I hope you'll be able to love me a little for
Father's sake.*

"Have you read all of this, Steve?" asked Philip, suddenly looking up as he
reached the end of one sheet of paper and was starting on another.

"No," said Stephen gruffly. "I read enough."

"Read the rest," commanded Philip, handing over the first sheet while he
went on with the second.

> *Now I've burned my bridges behind me, Stephen, and I haven't let
> you know until the last minute. This letter will reach you only a few
> days before I do; so it won't be any use to telegraph me not to come if
> you don't want me. Please forgive me. I did this purposely because I
> felt I must at least see you before I gave up my plan, or I'd never give
> it up. And I'm hoping you'll be glad to see me and that maybe I can be
> of some use to you and put a little comfort into your life. You've never
> told me whether you're boarding or housekeeping or what. It's strange
> not to know more about one's brother than I do about mine, but I'll
> soon know. I'm bringing all the little things I care about with me. So, if
> you let me stay, I'll have nothing to send for; and if I have to go back,
> they can, too.*
>
> *I shall reach your odd-sounding station at eight o'clock Friday
> evening, and I hope you'll be able to meet me at the train. Forgive me
> for surprising you this way. I know Aunt Priscilla would think I was
> doing a dreadful thing. I can't feel that way about it myself, and any-
> way I have myself to look out for now. So good-bye until Friday
> evening of next week, and please make up your mind to be a little
> glad to see your sister,*
>
> *Margaret Halstead.*

Philip handed over the last sheet to Stephen and sat up, looking blankly at
the wall for a minute. He couldn't deny he was won over to the enemy's cause.
There was something so fresh and appealing in her letter and something so
brave in her hunting up a renegade brother who showed no wish to be brotherly,
that he could only admire her. But what could they do with her here? Of course
she must go back. A pity, too, when she seemed to have her heart set. But if she
stayed, she'd be disappointed. Philip looked at Stephen sadly. It was a good
thing she must go back and wouldn't need to know how little worthy of her love
and admiration her unknown brother was. He was a good-hearted fellow, too.
A pity for the girl she had no one to care for her.

Suddenly a new thought came to him as he glanced down at the envelope
of the letter Stephen had flung aside. The date on it was a week old.

He picked it up excitedly.

"Steve, what day was that letter written?"

"The twenty-eighth," said Stephen, looking up to see what caused the unusual tone in Philip's voice.

"Man alive!" exclaimed Philip. "That letter's lain in the office for more than a week now, or else it's gone up to Humstead's ranch, lying around till someone had time to bring it back to the office. Such a postmaster as they have out here anyway! Get up, Steve, and do something! This is Friday night! Don't you realize your sister's almost here? If the Northern Central wasn't always at least an hour late, she'd be standing alone down there on the platform in the dark this minute, with all those deadbeats hanging around. What are you going to do?"

"I don't know," said Stephen, dazed.

Philip towered over him. "Well, you better know. Get up. It's five miles away, and the express is due now if it's on time."

Chapter 2

Margaret Halstead stood alone on the narrow board platform that seemed to float like a tiny raft in a sea of plains and darkness.

The train had discharged her trunks, picked up some freight and wound its snakelike way out into the darkness. Until now even the last glimmer of its red lights had faded from the mist.

The night winds swept about her, touching her hair and cheek and dress and peering solicitously into her face as if to inquire who this strange, sweet thing might be that had dropped, alien, among them.

A few lights dotted the gloom about her, and loud, rowdy voices sounded from the shanty that served, she supposed, as a station. She dreaded to walk over to it, for a new terror had seized her in the darkness since the friendly train disappeared.

She remembered that the porter had been concerned about leaving before her brother arrived to claim her. He paused beside her until the last car began to pass; then he finally touched his cap and swung himself onto the last car, calling back to her that he hoped she would be all right. She didn't realize till then what it would be like to be left alone at night in this strange place, with no assurance, except her undaunted faith, that her brother received her letter, much less would meet her.

Apprehension and alarm clamored for attention, while she suddenly realized how rash she was to follow her fancy across half a continent, only to end up in this wild way.

She guessed she ought to go over to those rough men and ask some questions. What if she'd been put off at the wrong station? She turned to walk in that direction, when a wild shriek followed by a gunshot rang out. She stopped, frightened, a whispered prayer on her lips. Had she come all this way on what her heart told her was a mission, to be forsaken now?

Philip heard the commotion as he rode through the night.

Stephen heard it also and urged his horse on.

Then out of the grim terror the young girl's ears picked up the soft, regular thud of horses' hoofs. Almost at once two dark shapes loomed before her out of the mist.

She started back again, her heart beating wildly. But suddenly she heard a strong, pleasant voice.

"Don't be afraid. We're coming!"

What seemed like a giant landed in front of her. With a gasp she cried, "Oh, Stephen, you've come!" and put her hands in Philip Earle's, hiding her face against his shoulder with a shudder.

Philip was suddenly glad of his strength and realized there were sweeter things in life than those he'd counted on.

Instinctively his arm supported her for just an instant, and a great wave of jealousy toward her brother swept over him. His impulse was to stoop and give her the welcoming kiss she was evidently expecting. But he held himself back, though his blood rushed in hot waves over his face in the darkness.

To have this unexpected and most unwelcome guest of his partner thus suddenly thrown upon him, and find she wasn't altogether undesirable, was embarrassing and delicate to handle. He blessed the darkness for what it hid, and Stephen was beside them in an instant. Philip managed somehow—he never could describe it to himself afterward—to face the young woman toward the real brother and turn her attention in that direction. Then he watched while Stephen welcomed the new sister with open arms.

Though he grumbled all the way to the railroad about what a nuisance she would be, it was like Stephen to succumb to a sweet voice and a trusting way.

Philip's lips were dry, and he swallowed with difficulty. He had felt the pressure of soft gloved hands in his coarse ones. He turned away, angry with himself that he should be so easily affected and by someone he'd never met except in the pitch dark. Yet even as he said this to himself he knew the face would fit the voice and the hands when he saw them.

So, though Philip on the faster horse was the first to greet her, and though he had the cool head and expected to have to explain why they were so late to meet her, it was Stephen's eager voice that made the explanations.

"You see, I never got your letter until an hour ago. It was misdelivered or something, and then we don't get to the office often when we're busy. So when I understood you were really coming and looked at the time, your train was already overdue. If they weren't always two hours late, you might have stood here alone all this time."

Stephen said it cheerfully. He was beginning to think it was nice to have a sister, after all. He'd forgotten how Philip had to insist on his coming at once to meet her and that he'd been rude and reluctant.

It occurred to him at this point to introduce his partner.

Philip stirred as he heard his name mentioned and was glad again for the darkness.

Margaret Halstead blushed and wondered whether he knew how close she came to greeting him with a kiss. And she hoped he hadn't noticed how her head rested against his shoulder for an instant when she was frightened. What would he think of her?

Her voice quivered a little as she acknowledged the introduction. But her words were so few and cold that Philip felt as if she suddenly held him at arm's length.

"I didn't know you had a partner, Stephen. You never said anything about it in your letters. I'm afraid I was wrong in coming without waiting to hear from you before I started."

But Philip had noticed the tremble in her voice, and he hurried to make her feel welcome.

Nevertheless, a stiffness hung about the trio and made it hard for them to be natural. If it hadn't been for another gunshot from the shanty down the road and another tumult of voices, they might have stayed there longer.

"Oh! What can be wrong?" Margaret exclaimed. "What a dreadful place!"

"We must get your sister out of this, Steve," he said, sensing a need to protect. "We must take her home."

And somehow the word *home* sounded like a haven as he pronounced it. The two young men had thought only of arriving on time as they galloped to the station. They made no plans.

But now they recalled the manners they'd learned some years earlier, which this young woman still practiced, and recognized at once the wretchedness of their situation.

"It isn't much of a place to call home," said the brother, apologetically, "but I guess it's better than this. If we'd only known before, we'd have fixed things up."

He made the statement lightly and probably thought it was true. Philip wondered how. There wasn't a house within fifty miles where she might have lodged comfortably.

"How do you think we'd better arrange the trip?" asked Stephen, suddenly encountering one problem.

"You see," he said to his sister, "we didn't have time to hitch up, though I'm blamed if it occurred to me how we could carry you in our pockets. Say, Phil, guess I'll go over and see if I can get Foxy's buckboard."

"Foxy's gone over to Butte in his buckboard with his mother. I saw him go this afternoon," answered Philip.

Stephen whistled. "I'll ask Dunn for his wagon," he said, starting off.

"Hold on!" said Philip. "I'll go myself. You stay here."

"Couldn't we go down to the station and see about my trunk, Mr. Earle?" Margaret asked timidly.

To his ears the name had never sounded so sweet.

"Give me your checks and stay here, please," he said in quite a different tone from the one he'd used with Stephen. He left them standing in the dark, while the mist closed in behind him.

Alone with her brother, Margaret asked, "You're a little bit glad I've come, aren't you, Stephen?"

"Indeed I am," he answered, rousing out of his sulkiness that Philip wouldn't let him go. He knew he had good reason for making him stay. "But we're a rough lot out here. I don't know how you'll stand it."

His voice had lost a shade of the lightness, and she thought it was touched with anxiety. She hastened to assure him.

"Oh, I won't mind a bit. And I'll try to make things a little pleasanter for you. You think I can, don't you?"

"I'm sure you can," said Stephen. Something in her voice appealed to his better self and reminded him strangely of his childhood. It couldn't be his father. His father had always been silent and serious, and this voice was sweet and enthusiastic and flowed out as if it loved to speak. And yet it must be the likeness to his father's voice he noticed.

"I'm so anxious to get you in the light and see how you look," she said, and then added softly, "my dear brother."

Stephen slid his arm about her awkwardly and kissed her on the forehead. He felt embarrassed in doing this; yet it certainly wasn't the first time he'd kissed a girl. It might have been the memory of those other kisses that embarrassed him now. He was glad to hear Philip's step coming toward them.

"Dunn's wagon was broken down, and both the front wheels are off for repairs. We can't get a thing in town tonight," Philip said anxiously. "Miss Halstead, can you ride? Horseback, I mean."

"Why, I can try," said Margaret. This was a rather startling proposal even to her courage. Involuntarily she glanced down at her city-made dress in the darkness. She felt restricted by it.

"It's too bad, Miss Halstead," he said apologetically, while Stephen wondered at his tone and manner. "But there's no other way, and I think you'll enjoy getting out of this, anyway. There's going to be a big row over there," he added quietly to Stephen. "Jim Peters is on his high horse. Hurry!"

Then he said cheerfully, "It won't be so bad. You can rest your foot in the stirrup, and Steve and I'll take turns walking beside the horse. She'd better ride your horse, Steve. He's gentler."

Margaret felt herself suddenly lifted in the dark by strong arms and seated on a horse. She clung to the saddle and left her foot obediently in the stirrup where it was placed by a firm hand, but she wasn't certain whether her brother or his friend had put her there. It was bewildering, all in the dark, and neither of them spoke till both were standing by her side. She was glad the horse stood still. She felt timid about Western horses, having heard they were wild. But it was Stephen who after a moment of quiet talk came and stood by her side and placed his arm about her as they started.

"My suitcase and my bag," she murmured.

"Phil has them all safe," said her brother.

"And the trunks?"

"They're locked safe in the station, Miss Halstead, and we'll get them early in the morning," said a voice out of the mist before her.

Then she was silent as she looked anxiously into the darkness. The road was rough and her seat unsteady. A man's saddle is not the surest thing for riding sidesaddle on. She put her hand timidly on her brother's shoulder and seemed to gain courage. It gave Stephen a new sense of his power to protect.

They traveled slowly on the rough road, for the night was dark and the mist lay thick about them. The sounds of chaos grew fainter, but now and then a shriek or a fragment of an oath would reach them through the night air.

Margaret shuddered when this happened. "What awful people they must be, Stephen! Isn't it unpleasant to live in their neighborhood?"

"Oh, they never bother us. They've got a little too much tonight, that's all. When they get like that, they can't stand a difference of opinion."

"How dreadful!" said Margaret. Then after a minute she added, "I'm so glad my brother isn't like that. Of course, it wouldn't be likely, but they must be somebody's brothers, and how their sisters must feel—and their mothers!"

Stephen felt his face grow hot. He said nothing for a long time. His throat felt strange, and he tried to clear it. And the mist kept getting in his eyes. He was glad when his sister talked about her aunt's illness and the long months she was chained to the sickroom at the beck and call of a wandering mind.

She didn't say much about herself, but he felt touched by her sacrifice and loneliness. It reminded him of his own lonely boyhood, and his heart went out in sympathy to her. He decided it was nice, after all, to have a sister. And, as was his way, he forgot about the end of their journey and the poor accommodations he had to offer her. He grew cheerful, talking more freely with her as they traveled. When Philip appeared out of the darkness ahead of them and said it was time to change guides, he was almost loath to leave his sister.

Margaret, too, preferred not to change, but she could scarcely ask her brother to walk the whole five miles. Something about him reminded her, even in the dark, of their father, and so he didn't seem strange. But this other man, who had taken control of the entire expedition, frightened her a little. She wished she could get a glimpse of his face and know what kind of man he was. She didn't know what to say to him but was even more embarrassed to say nothing.

But the road was getting rougher and rising in front of them now. The new guide had to give his attention to the horse, and she to staying in the saddle.

Once she slipped and almost fell from the saddle, but Philip caught her. After that he placed his arm about her and steadied her. She couldn't object, for there was nothing intimate or personal in the touch. She concluded that Philip was a gentleman, whatever else he might not be.

Margaret gripped the saddle in front of her a little tighter and peered into the darkness, wondering whether the journey would ever end. She attempted one or two sentences of conversation, but the young man beside her was distressed and more interested in guiding the horse.

The road was even steeper now, and she wondered if they were climbing the Rocky Mountains. By her vague idea of the geography of the land, she thought they must have come far enough to have reached them.

"Wouldn't it be better if I were to get off and walk?" she asked timidly, after the horse had almost stumbled to his knees.

"No," answered Philip. "We'll soon be over this. Put your arm around my neck and hold on now. Don't be afraid! Steady, there, steady, Jack!"

The horse scrambled and, from where Margaret sat, seemed to be walking on his hind legs up into the air. She gasped and threw her arm about Philip's neck, but he held her steady. Finally they reached upper ground, and she was sitting firmly on the horse's back, with Philip walking calmly beside her, his arm no longer about her.

It was lighter here too. The mist had dropped away and melted at their feet.

"It's all over now," Philip said with relief in his voice, quite different from the silent, distracted man who had walked beside her. "I hope you weren't frightened too much. I was afraid how Jack would act there. That's an ugly place. It must be fixed before you come this way again. You see, the bridge was broken down the way we usually go, and we had to come around another way. You were perfectly safe, but it wasn't good to frighten you when you've just come, and you're tired too. We're almost there now, though. And look! Look ahead!"

Margaret saw before her a blaze of light flare up till it made a great half-circle on the edge of the horizon. Not until it rose still higher did the girl recognize the moon.

"Oh, it's the moon!" she exclaimed. "Is it always so big out here?"

Philip watched her as she looked. For the first time in his life he felt that he was sharing this magnificent sight he never tired of with a companion.

"It's always different," he said thoughtfully, "and yet always the same." He felt as he said it that she would understand. He'd never talked about the moon to Stephen, who didn't care for such things unless they added to his personal convenience or pleasure. Moonlight might be interesting if one had to take a long ride, but not for sentimental purposes.

"I see," said Margaret. "Yes, I recognize my old friend now. It seems as if it's wearing a smile of welcome."

"Do you mean the man in the moon or the lady? Which do you claim?"

"Oh, both!" laughed Margaret, turning toward him for the first time since they'd had any light. She could see his profile against the moon, the firm chin, the well-molded forehead and nose, and the expressive lips.

"Now look down there, back where we've come!" said Philip.

"Oh!" breathed the girl in wonder. "You can almost see the darkness flee away!"

"So you can," said Philip, looking off. "I never noticed that before."

And they started forward round the bend in the road where Stephen was waiting impatiently for them. Almost at once they saw before them the outline of the crude building the two young men called home, bathed in the newly risen moonlight.

Chapter 3

The moonlight gilded the place with something like beauty to welcome the stranger. But it worked only outside. The two young men were painfully conscious of the state in which they left the inside of their house, as they helped their guest from the horse and prepared to take her in.

Stephen took on his sulky look, which didn't suit him, while he opened the door and lit the oil lamp. He had no desire to welcome his sister here. What did he want of a sister anyway? As he threw the match down, he crushed a piece of crisp paper under his foot; he knew it was her letter lying on the floor. The same mood that seized him when he read it took hold again. He scowled, determined to show her she had made a serious mistake by rushing out here uninvited.

Margaret Halstead turned from the brilliant moonlight to the blinking lamplight bravely and faced the scene of her self-chosen mission.

Something in her brother's half-defiant attitude dissuaded her from taking a long look at him and making sure of her welcome. She may have realized she hadn't yet won her way into his heart, and wisdom or intuition led her to break the embarrassment of this first moment in the light with a simple remark.

Her eyes scanned the bleak room for something cheerful. They fell upon the old desk in the corner.

"Oh, Stephen! There's the desk from your old room!" she cried, stepping over to it and touching it. "I used to go up into your room and sit by it to study my lessons. And sometimes I'd put your picture on top—the one you sent Father when you were in military school—and sit and admire you and think how nice it was to have a straight, strong brother dressed in a military suit."

Stephen turned toward her with astonishment and admiration. His ugly mood was already exorcised. The soft rustle of hidden silk created a new world in the rough place. She stood by the old desk, loosening the hat pin and taking off her hat. He saw the grace in every movement. And this beautiful girl cared for him enough to look at his picture once in a while when he was just a boy! He wished he'd known it then; it might have made some things in his life different.

His voice was husky as he said, "You don't mean you ever thought of me then and called me your brother!"

"Yes, of course," she said with a bright smile. She ran her fingers through the soft hair over her forehead and settled it easily into a fitting frame for her face. "Oh, you don't know how I idealized you! I used to go to sleep at night with stories of how brave and good you were and how you did great things for me—I'll tell you about them someday. But now do you know you haven't welcomed me home yet? You're sure you'll be glad I came?"

She looked up with a pleading in her eyes as she came over to him and held up her face. Stephen bent over her awkwardly and kissed her forehead; then, stepping away quickly, he knocked the tin washbasin off the bench. But Margaret felt she had her welcome and set out to win the brother.

Philip would have escaped to the barn from the confusion of the first few minutes. But he was drawn back to the door—he felt ashamed to desert his partner in time of need—and overheard the brief dialogue.

He slipped away from the door and returned to the horses thoughtfully. He'd never seen that look on Stephen's face before or heard his voice so tender. Maybe, after all, there was something in a sister.

Margaret folded her veil as carefully as if she'd just come home from a concert in the East, instead of being dropped off in a strange land. Meanwhile, she was making mental notes of the place—its desolation, its need for her, its paucity of materials with which to work—and wondering how these two men had lived and been comfortable.

"You must be hungry," she said, as if her brother were the guest and she the hostess. "What can we get for supper?"

"Not much except bacon and beans, the same old stuff. We have it morning, noon and night."

Margaret walked over to the table and gathered the dishes together. It was a strange assortment, and she felt like laughing as she pulled the hammer out from under the paper of cheese and looked about for a place to lay it. But she kept a straight face and acted as if that were the right place for hammers and cheese.

"Do you have any eggs? I think you mentioned poultry in one of your letters."

"Oh, yes, we have eggs. We always have eggs and bacon. They'd taste good if they weren't always the same."

"How would you like an omelet? Do you ever make them?"

"Yes, we've tried, but they lie around in little heaps and won't 'om' for us," said Stephen, laughing at last. "I'll go out and get some eggs if you think you could make one."

"Yes, indeed!" said Margaret. "Just show me how this stove works first, and fill the teakettle. I always use boiling water for my omelets; it makes them fluffier than milk. Where do you keep your eggbeater?"

"Eggbeater!" said Stephen with a shrug. "Don't ask me. I wouldn't know one if I met him on the street. Can't you make an omelet without an eggbeater?"

"Oh, yes," said Margaret, laughing. "A fork is slower, but it'll do. Bring me the eggs now. I'll have them ready by the time the kettle boils and the frying pan is hot."

Margaret worked rapidly while he was gone and managed to clear the table and wash three plates and cups before he returned. Then she searched through her bag and pulled out four large clean handkerchiefs; she usually carried a supply with her on a journey. She spread one under each plate and one in the center. At least it wouldn't seem quite as uncivilized as the bare table had.

In her lunch box she found a glass of jelly untouched and half a dozen sugar doughnuts, the farewell gift of an old neighbor of her aunt's. She arranged these on the table with a plate of bread cut in slices and was just searching for coffee when she heard the voices of the two young men.

Stephen went whistling out to the barn for the eggs. "Guess what, Phil! She knows how to make omelets! Hustle there, and help me get a lot of eggs. We'll have something worth eating again if it takes every egg on the place."

Philip had been wondering if he could be excused from going back to the house that night at all. But an omelet sounded too appetizing for him to stay away, so he eagerly helped gather eggs.

They stopped in amazement at the door, stared at the table as though it were enchanted and then at the cook. They'd left her a fashionably dressed young woman from a world that was no longer theirs. They found her now a busy woman, with dress tucked up; a white towel pinned about her waist like an apron; her sleeves rolled up, revealing white, rounded arms; and her cheeks pink with interest in her work.

"That lamp smokes horribly," she remarked, looking up at it. Something about her voice and words caused both young men to laugh.

That broke the stiffness, and it didn't return. Their relations were established with the guest in charge. She told her hosts what to do, and they did it. She broke the eggs—the whites into one dish, the yolks into another—and handed Stephen one dish with a fork to beat them. She took the other herself while telling Philip to find the coffee and make it.

They had fun while they worked and watched the puffy omelet swell and take on a golden brown coat. By the time they drew up to the table, their appetites were sharp.

While they ate, Margaret told about her journey and described some of the people she met.

It was late when they finished their meal and put the room into what could be loosely defined as order. Now they must face the problem of the night, and Margaret wondered what would become of her. She suddenly realized how tired she was and that her nerves, worn out by new experiences, were ready to give way to tears.

Stephen knew they had to do something about sleeping now, but he had no idea what to do with the new sister. He turned helplessly to Philip, who always knew what to do in emergencies, though he didn't like to admit he depended upon him.

Philip had already thought about the problem while he stood by the horses in the moonlight. A log lean-to opened off their large one-roomed cottage, and a board partition divided it into two fair-sized rooms. Philip had one room and Stephen the other. Each room had only a bunk with heavy blankets. In fact, blankets were the only bedclothes in the house, and beds were easily made with them.

Philip entered his room now and in the dark grabbed clothing from the nails driven into the logs and threw them out the window. Then he struck a match, picked up a few things thrown here and there and decided that was the best he could do toward cleaning up.

He explained to Stephen quietly that he was to give his sister that room, and he himself would sleep in the hay. Then, saying good night, he went out.

Margaret almost laughed out loud when she surveyed her primitive bedroom by the light of the blinking lamp a few minutes later. Then her eye caught a photograph pinned to the wall, and she crossed the room to study it. It was Philip's one prized possession, and he'd forgotten it in his haste. It showed a kind-looking woman with white hair and eyes like Philip's that followed one about the room sadly.

Prepared as she was for primitive living, Margaret was shocked to find her brother among such rough surroundings. Nevertheless, she was determined. She came to help her brother, and now that she'd seen him she wouldn't turn back. Hardships might come, but in the end, with God's help, she would win. She felt shy toward Philip and almost wished him away. Maybe he didn't have a good influence over Stephen. He seemed to be very domineering, and the strange part was that Stephen yielded to him. She may complicate matters.

She knelt down beside the hard gray cot and laid the work she came to do at the foot of the cross, asking for help and guidance. She wondered as she prayed whether she'd been rash and had gone her own way, instead of waiting for heavenly guidance, in coming to this strange land where evidently, to say the least, her presence had not been desired. Then she added, *Oh, Jesus Christ, if this work is Yours, bless me in it. And if it was merely my own wild impulse, send me back where You want me.*

Then with contentment she lay down, wrapped in the gray blankets, and was soon asleep.

Philip lay out in the hay wide awake. Plans needed to be made for tomorrow. Would the guest choose to stay, or would she flee from them at the morning light? Could she stand it there, so rough and devoid of all she was accustomed to? Of course not. She came only out of curiosity. She'd probably give it up and go back in a few days. But in the meantime, unless she came to her senses by morning and returned to civilization at once, what should they do?

In the first place, a woman of some sort must be found, a servant, so to speak. She would be called a chaperone back in the East. Such things may not be necessary here, especially since she was really Stephen's sister, but it would be better to have a woman around. The girl mustn't be allowed to cook, and surely they couldn't cook for her. It was bad enough for them to eat what they cooked. How good that supper tasted! The omelet reminded him of his mother, and he drew his hand quickly across his eyes. What would his mother think of his staying out here in the wilds so long? And all because a pretty girl had chosen to flirt with him for a while and then throw him aside. But was it that? Didn't he stay for Stephen's sake? What would become of Stephen without him?

But maybe Stephen's sister here meant he was free to go. He might pretend to have some business call him away and leave them together. Then a vision of the frightened hands that greeted him through the mist at the station recalled him sharply. No! He couldn't leave her alone with her brother! It wouldn't do. At once he knew that his mother, if she could know what went on in this life, would approve of his staying here.

But where would they find a woman to be a fit servant for Miss Halstead? He mentally searched around the country and at last reached a conclusion.

The hay settled and crackled about him, and the hens clucked nearby. Now and then the horses pushed against the stall, and away in the distance the sharp, vigilant bark of a dog was heard. Philip dropped asleep and dreamed of a small hand clinging to his neck and a wisp of soft hair blowing across his face. A short while later he awoke to find the hay touching his cheek and a warm ray of morning lighting the sky.

The dawn was cool and fresh with sleep yet when he rose and saddled his horse, then hurried along the dew-covered trail. He wondered what Stephen's sister would say to this or that view or the woodland that he passed, and then he checked his thoughts angrily. She was nothing to him, even if she did understand his thoughts about the moon. Women were all alike, heartless—with the possible exception of mothers.

With these thoughts he flung his horse's bridle over the saddlehorn and sprang down at the door of a crude dwelling. After much ado he brought a dark-faced woman with black hair, of Mexican and Indian blood, to the door.

What arguments he used or rewards he offered to get her to promise to come, he never told. But a half-hour later, with a large bundle fastened to his saddle, he started home, smiling faintly to himself and wondering why he did it. After all, by this time their guest may have prepared to leave. And what would this woman with her sullen looks add to their already curiously assorted family?

A familiar rebellion rose up within him against the Power, whether God or what, that made a universe filled with lives so awry and hearts of bitterness and sorrow. Not even the breath of the morning or the rich notes of wild birds could dispel this from his heart. The peerless sky above him and the matchless earth around him—and only lives like his and Stephen's and that dark-faced old woman's to enjoy them. He thought about the rough friends who sometimes gathered with them, but he saw no good in any of them.

Still, there was Margaret Halstead. She seemed a fitting one to place amid beautiful surroundings. He doubted she would mar a scene like the one this morning with anything her heart or life contained.

Yes, there was Margaret. But it might be only on the surface. No doubt she was like the rest of them. They had yet to find out what she was really like. But what were they all made for anyway?

That was the lonely question that had troubled Philip for a long time, and he frowned as he stopped before the only home he now owned.

Chapter 4

Margaret Halstead stood at the door and looked out in the bright morning light at the new land she had come to as a stranger and a pilgrim. The atmosphere of her Eastern home still lingered about her. She had changed her long, dark traveling dress for a simple dress of light percale which she had wisely brought in her bag. The garment was plain and walking length, and it occupied little space in the bag. Yet it hung with a grace and finish unknown in that part of the country.

She opened the door wide and stood there for a moment. The dark woman huddled on the steps sprang up and stared at her. She had never seen anything like this before: golden hair touched with sunshine, blue eyes like brilliant jewels, the fair face, the pleasant mouth, the graceful form in the soft blue cotton gown.

Margaret stared back at the woman in amazement and then at the bundle on the steps at her feet.

"Who are you?" she asked after they surveyed each other for a moment.

"Man come get. Say heap work. Man say big pay."

"Oh, my brother went after you. I see. He brought you here this morning before I was awake. That was kind of him. And I thought he was asleep yet."

She was thinking out loud rather than speaking to the woman. Just then Philip rounded the corner of the house, heard what she said and stopped; his lips settled in a stern line, and a curious expression crossed his face. Then he turned and went back to the other side of the house without being seen. Let her think this was her brother's work; it should have been. It was as well for her to think so.

But Margaret was wrestling with the problem of breakfast and with the addition of this unknown person who had come to assist her. She hit upon a plan of setting the newcomer to scrubbing the doors and windows until breakfast was out of the way. Then she could decide what to do after that.

She smiled to herself as she set the table. It was nice of Stephen to go out so early in the morning and get a woman to help. She felt sure he would justify her highest ideal of him.

During breakfast they felt some embarrassment, for the morning light displayed the crudities of the small home. Margaret's beauty showed in stronger contrast as she moved about in her soft blue and white dress and seemed like a rare bird of paradise dropped into their midst. The two young men in their dark flannel shirts were ill at ease, and all were perplexed about what to do next.

Margaret felt that the crucial moment was coming and she must walk carefully. She realized, even more than they did, the changes her remaining here would make in their lives. As for the men, it seemed also in the morning light impossible for her to stay. They discovered to their surprise that they were disappointed. She had given them a glimpse into the way they used to live, and it would be harder for them to relinquish it now.

At last Margaret ventured.

"I don't intend to be a bit of trouble when I get settled," she said brightly, "and I'll be as patient now as possible. But I'd like to know when you think my things could be brought up."

The silence was heavy. Stephen looked at Philip, and Philip stared at his plate. Margaret watched them anxiously from the corners of her eyes. At last Philip spoke.

"How many things are there?" he asked, simply to stall and give Stephen a chance to tell her what he must, that this was no place for her to stay.

Margaret wished her brother had taken the initiative. It was awkward to ask a stranger for favors. She wondered how much of a partner he was anyway and what right he had in the house. Could he be part owner? If so, it was more complicated than she expected.

"Oh, I'm afraid there are a good many," she answered humbly. "You see, I had to bring them or sell them. There wasn't a good place in town to store them where they'd be safe. It's just a little country town, you know. And some of the things I love. They belonged to my old home. I thought Stephen would like having them around again too." She glanced wistfully over at her brother. These old things were part of the ammunition she'd brought for fighting the battle to win her brother.

"Of course!" said Philip brusquely, scowling at Stephen. He was disgusted with Stephen for not being more of a brother.

"And there's my piano!" said Margaret, brightening at this slight encouragement. "I couldn't leave that!"

"Certainly not!" said Philip, wondering more and more about what was coming to the crude room. How impossible! A piano in the wilderness!

"Oh!" exclaimed Stephen, glancing up at last and struggling to express his feelings. "Why did you do it? You can't put a piano or other things in here. Think of a piano in this barn!" he said, waving his hands toward the bleak walls.

"Oh, we'll make something of it besides a barn, Stephen," said Margaret, laughing. She was glad he'd spoken at last, if only to veto her plans. "I figured it all out this morning when I woke up. This room is pleasant and large. It may need a few more windows and a fireplace to make it perfect. But unless you're attached to this primitive simplicity, you won't know this place after I fix it up. Just wait till my materials come, and we'll have a real home here. Couldn't you boys build a fireplace, the old-fashioned kind, with a wide chimney in the room? Isn't there any rough stone around here? It would be wonderful to sit around winter evenings reading out loud or singing. It could go right over there!" She indicated a space between two windows rather far apart and opposite the front door.

"No doubt," said Philip, staring blankly at the wooden box that occupied the position and trying to imagine a stone fireplace in its place. His imagination failed him, however. But the picture of reading aloud and music around an open fire on winter evenings was alluring.

"Interesting," he added, seeing that the weight of the answers fell upon him. "I've never built stone chimneys for a living, but I think I could assist if you'd be so good as to direct the job, Miss Halstead. I can't imagine anything in this room being pleasant, but if you say so I suppose it's possible."

Stephen stared in amazement. He wasn't certain whether Philip was sincere or not.

"And the piano ought to stand there," said Margaret after the laugh had subsided.

"Certainly," answered Philip again, more amazed than ever. "But may I ask what you would do with the stove? You couldn't cook on the piano, could you? Or would you expect to use the fireplace?"

The old woman peered in through the windows she was washing to see what all the laughter and shouts meant. This seemed to be a lighthearted household the man brought her to; she hadn't heard sounds like these, free from the bitterness that tinged most of the humor in the region, since she was a child playing with the other children.

"The stove," said Margaret, "must go in the kitchen, of course."

"Ah!" said Philip meekly. "Strange I didn't think of that. Now where, may I ask, is the kitchen?"

Margaret stood up and walked over to the back window, and the two men followed her. "It ought to be right here," she said, "and this window could be made into a door leading to it. What's that little square building out there? Can't we use that for a kitchen?"

"That building, madam, was originally intended for other purposes, the housing of cattle or smaller animals—I forget just what. It isn't much use for anything in its run-down condition. But if your magic wand can transform it into a kitchen, so it shall be."

"Say, now, that's an idea, Phil!" said Stephen with sudden interest.

"Then we could use a corner of this room for a dining room, you know," said Margaret, turning back to the house again. "I have a pretty little cupboard with glass doors that will fit into that corner, and some screens and draperies. It'll be perfect. I've always wanted to fix up a lovely big room that way. Can't you imagine the firelight playing over the tablecloth and dishes?"

"We haven't seen a tablecloth in so long it would strain our minds," said Stephen with a hint of bitterness. All this talk was tempting, but impossible. Long ago he'd given up expecting such things in life. A look of despair crossed his face, and Philip saw it and wondered. He'd felt that way himself, but he never thought his partner would understand such feelings.

"But what would you do with the roughness on everything?" asked Philip. "Pianos and corner cupboards wouldn't like to associate with forests of splinters."

"Oh, cover them," Margaret said easily. "I brought a whole bolt of burlap for such things. It's leaf-green and will be just right for a background. I don't suppose I have enough; but I can send a sample to New York and have it here before we need it. I've been thinking this morning about what a beautiful molding those smooth, dry cornstalks would make tacked on next to the ceiling. When the walls are covered with something that makes a good background, this will look like a different place."

"You see, Steve—that's what's the matter with us. We've never had a suitable background," said Philip.

Thus, with laughter and questions, Margaret got her wish and finally saw Philip head out with two horses and a large wagon. She was disturbed that Stephen didn't go with him. It seemed strange when he was her brother and she was sure Philip would need help loading the furniture. Philip certainly was an odd man. Why did he presume to dictate to Stephen, and, strangest of all, why did Stephen sulkily submit? When she knew her brother better, she would find out and spur him on to act independently. Again she wondered if Philip would hinder her plans. A man who could so easily command her brother was one whose influence was to be feared.

So Stephen stayed behind, followed his sister about and did what she asked him to do. In the course of the morning much scrubbing and straightening up were done, and a savory dinner was under way in spite of the absence of necessary culinary utensils.

Philip Earle drove away into the sunshine at high speed. He was determined to get there and back as soon as he could. He felt uneasy about Stephen, lest he should follow on his horse, in spite of his instructions to stay around the house and take care of his sister until they got things into some sort of shape. There were more reasons than one why Philip should feel uneasy about Stephen today. Nothing must startle the newcomer on her first day. Maybe she could make things much better. Who knew? It certainly would be great to have something homelike there—though it would be worse when she got tired of it, as of course she would sooner or later, and take her things and leave them desolate again. But Philip wouldn't let himself think of that. With the energy of a boy of fifteen he whistled to his horses and hurried to town.

Meanwhile, Margaret and Stephen walked around the house, planning how the kitchen could be brought close enough for use. Margaret suggested, too, that another bedroom should be built on the other side of the house. She tried to find out how much of a share Philip owned, but her brother was noncommittal and morose when she talked about it. He didn't seem interested in any changes she wanted to make in the house, so she didn't pursue them.

She wondered why he acted this way. Was he short of money? She knew he had a good sum left to him by his mother, and their father had also left certain properties which had gone to him at her mother's death. Were they tied up so that he couldn't get at the interest, or had he lost some of his money by speculation? Young men were sometimes foolish; maybe that was it, and he didn't want to tell her.

Well, she would be quiet on the subjects she realized he didn't wish to talk about and work her way slowly into his confidence. She accomplished even more than she hoped for right at the first, for Stephen's letters hadn't led her to think she would be welcome. Margaret had come with high hopes of winning first his love for her and then his life for God.

For several years she had prayed for this estranged brother. Now that she was left alone in the world, she'd come to feel that God had a special mission for her concerning him. So she dared to come out here by herself, uninvited. She wasn't going to be daunted by any little thing. She would try to be as wise as a serpent and harmless as a dove. Meanwhile, she thought she understood Philip Earle somewhat and wished he didn't live in the same house with her brother. He might be interesting by himself to try to help, but she was afraid he wouldn't help her with her brother.

Margaret wondered how it would fare when Philip saw her luggage. She had planned well. Knowing the ways of railroad delays, she had shipped her household goods out ahead of her own arrival time. Then, when she came, they wouldn't be as likely to send her away—at least, not until she had an opportunity to try her experiment. A girl with more experience in the world, especially in the West, wouldn't have dared attempt what she had.

In town, Philip succeeded more easily than he expected in getting help to bring the freight that was waiting at the station. He enlisted two stalwart ranchmen with their team of horses to help him. Wild men, they drank heavily, gambled recklessly and didn't care that man's days are as grass and he will soon be cut off. Instead, they lived as if they expected to survive forever against the odds and gain all the evil from it.

Philip said nothing to them about Stephen's sister. Something inside held him back. They were the kind of men he wouldn't want his own sister to know—not that he objected to them himself; they were good fellows in their way. They could tell a story well, though not always the cleanest, and were fearless. But they possessed no moral principles.

As Philip drove home, silent for the most part while the men talked, he reflected on his own life; he was not faultless. In the three years since he'd come to this region and become a part of it, his own moral principles had lowered considerably. He hadn't noticed it until today. That girl's arrival had shown him where he stood. He still knew what those principles were, how-ever. And these two men must, if possible, be kept from knowing Miss Halstead had come.

But how could he manage that? He should have warned Steve. What a fool he was not to take him out to the barn and have a good talk with him before he went away. Steve would never think to be careful. He had no idea of the part he needed to play in protecting his sister.

The two men joked about the amount and kind of furniture they were load-ing into the wagons, but Philip only laughed them off with other jokes. They accepted that for the moment and asked no more questions. They knew Steve would tell them what they wanted to know; he couldn't keep a thing to himself when he got among his companions. They were curious to know why Steve didn't come along when he was expecting such an important shipment, and they were even more curious about the piano. They felt sure that either Stephen or Philip was about to be married and was trying to keep the matter quiet. But they were obliged to content themselves with Philip's dry answer, "Steve couldn't get away this morning."

As they came within sight of the house, Stephen went out to meet them, still nursing a grudge that Philip had insisted on going by himself. Philip said a few quiet words to him as he halted the first wagon; the other two men were following on their own wagon just behind. Stephen demurred, but Philip's insistent tones meant business, he knew. Without waiting to do more than wave a greeting to the two in the other wagon, he walked reluctantly back into the house.

He was resisting Philip as well as his sister's presence again. He could see plainly that it was going to hamper his own movements. His friends were good enough for him, so why should his sister be too good to meet them? If she wanted to stay here, she must take what comes. But he did as Philip told him. He told his sister he thought she should go into her room and shut the door until the wagons were unloaded; Phil had brought rough fellows with him to help, and she wouldn't want to be around them. He said it gruffly. He didn't relish saying it at all. The men were his special friends. If he hadn't known in his heart that Philip was right, he wouldn't have done it at all.

Margaret did as he suggested, also reluctantly, but on her way looked out the window.

She was right, then. Philip was wild. Stephen knew it. Her brother was try-ing to help him, perhaps, to reform him or something, and that was why he was so hesitant to speak about Philip's share in the household. And now Philip had brought to the house some of his rough friends Stephen didn't approve of and didn't wish her to meet, and he was trying to protect her.

It was dear of Stephen to care for her that way, and she appreciated it, but she felt that it was wholly unnecessary. She thought her womanhood was enough to protect her from insult here in her brother's house. She wasn't in the least afraid to be out there and direct where things should go. If Stephen was trying to help Philip be a better man, then she ought to help too. Helping what her brother was interested in was another way of helping him. And these friends of his, couldn't they be helped too? She wished she'd had time to argue with him, for she really ought to be out there to tell them where to place things. It would save a lot of trouble later.

She stood thinking about these things as she heard the horses' feet stamping around the front door, the wagon wheels creaking as they ground upon the steps, and then the heavy footsteps, the men's voices and the thud of heavy weights being set down.

She grew restless with her imprisonment even more because the room had no window from which she could watch the operations. At last, when she heard them discussing the best way of getting the piano out of the wagon, she could stand it no longer. She felt that she was needed, for they'd made absurd suggestions, and her piano was very dear to her. She must tell them how the piano men in the East always did it. It was ridiculous for her to be shut up here, anyway. Stephen might as well learn that now as anytime. For an instant, she knelt beside the gray cot and lifted a hurried prayer—why, she didn't know, for she was sure there was nothing to be afraid of. With a firm hand she turned the knob of her door and went out among the boxes and barrels scattered all over the room. She reached the door and stood there framed, with the brilliant noonday sun shining on her golden hair and full into her eyes. Her ruffled sleeve fell away from her white wrist as she raised her hand to shield her eyes.

"Stephen, wait a minute," she called. "I can tell you just how to move that. I watched the men put it in the wagon when I started out. It's very easy. You want two rollers. Broomsticks will do."

Chapter 5

Silence fell outside the front door. The two strangers turned and stared in frank admiration. Stephen looked sheepishly triumphant toward Philip, and Philip frowned with displeasure.

"My sister!" said Stephen airily, recovering first and waving his hand toward the two men. He felt rather proud of this new possession of a sister. His own eyes glowed with admiration as he noticed her trim form in its blue and white dress framed in the rough doorway, one hand shading her eyes and eager interest on her face.

But now Margaret was surprised. Why did Stephen introduce her if he considered these men too rough for her even to appear in their presence? Was he afraid of Philip? Ah! They must be Philip's friends whom Stephen didn't like. He had to introduce them on his partner's account, but had wanted to avoid it by keeping her out of sight. Well, what did it matter? A mere introduction was nothing. She would show them by her manner that they were still strangers.

So she acknowledged Stephen's naming of them as "Bennett" and "Byron" with a brief nod that only served to increase their admiration. Perhaps the coolness of her manner was an added charm to them. Stephen rose in their estimation, being the possessor of such an attractive sister.

After she gave her directions—which they had to admit were quite sensible — she vanished into the house again, but not, as they supposed, from hearing. She went quickly into Stephen's bedroom and watched them from the small window. She intended to see that her directions were carried out and the piano safely landed in the proper place.

For one instant she was out of hearing as she opened the door to the other room, closed it softly after her and pushed aside the torn paper that served as a window shade. During that instant Byron, who was known for his terrible oaths and daring remarks, burst forth with a comment to Stephen, prefacing it with an oath. He meant to convey with the comment his intense admiration for Stephen's sister, and Stephen himself would have been inclined to take it in the spirit in which it was meant.

But Philip was standing close by with a dark expression on his face and laid a heavy hand on Byron's shoulder. "That kind of talk doesn't go down here!" he said in a low, menacing voice.

At that moment Margaret was within hearing, and her intuition told her she was the subject of the conversation.

"What's the matter with you, man?" said Byron, shaking off the hand. "Can't you bear to hear a woman praised? Maybe you want a monopoly on her. But she don't belong to you—," he said with another oath. "I say it again, Steve, she's a—"

But Philip's hands were at Byron's throat, and the word was smothered before it came out. Margaret dropped the paper shade and stood back pale and trembling; she didn't know why. Was Philip against her? Did he hate to hear her praised and wish her away, or was he defending her? She couldn't tell, though she saw something strong and true in the flash of Philip's eye as he sprang toward the other man; the look and action made her afraid lest she misjudge him.

What kind of a country had she come to, anyway? And why, if she needed to be defended, hadn't Stephen done it, since he warned her to keep away?

She sat on the hard little cot, thinking and looking around the dismal room. The pity of her brother's life touched her even more than it had. She resolved to put away any foolish misgivings and make a home here to help him live his life the best he could. She knelt down beside her brother's bed and asked help of her unseen Guide, in some sense consecrating herself to the mission that had brought her to this strange country.

Then she crossed over to the window and looked out. The men were unloading the wagons as calmly as if nothing had happened. Philip's mouth and chin had a firmness about them that wasn't to be trifled with, and he seemed distracted and distant from the rest. But the others were working cheerfully, whistling and calling out to one another. Margaret watched them awhile. The one called Byron had a handsome face with heavy, dark waving hair and round black eyes that darted about but were interesting. She shuddered as she remembered the oath he used with Philip and Stephen, a much milder one than the first, which she hadn't heard. The name of her Savior, Jesus Christ! She'd never heard it spoken in that way. It seemed to come from the depth of evil.

A wave of pity and sorrow washed over her as she watched the muscular arms lift her furniture, saw the fun and daring on the handsome features, and thought it was the name of his Savior, as well as her own, he had used. His Savior, and he didn't know Him or recognize, perhaps, what he was doing. Oh, if he might be shown! If she might help show him! There might be a way.

Suddenly her mission broadened to include Byron, Bennett, Philip and an unknown host of similar companions. And her heart swelled with the possibility that God might have chosen her to help all these as well as Stephen.

She watched a long time and listened, too, but there were no more oaths and no more fights. She studied the faces of the four men as they worked, especially the man who had spoken that awful word, and she prayed as she watched. It was a habit she'd acquired during her last three or four years of loneliness. And soon a plan formed in her mind.

Then she went quietly out to see that the dinner she started was progressing as it should and set the table for five instead of three.

By this time some packing boxes and trunks were within reach, and with Stephen's help she opened one containing some table linen. It gave her great satisfaction to have a tablecloth the first time she gave a dinner party in her new home.

The goods were unloaded from the wagons and put under cover, and the two helpers were mopping the perspiration from their brows. Philip was driving his own wagon to the barn when Margaret came to the door again.

"Dinner is ready now," she remarked, quite as if they'd all been invited. "I suppose you'd like to wash your hands before you come in. You'll find the basin and towels out by the pump at the back door, Mr. Byron and Mr. Bennett." She'd watched long enough from the window to know which was which; with a slight glance she recognized each now, but it was a glance that kept them at an immeasurable distance. "And, Stephen, please hurry, because everything will get cold."

Stephen's eyes lit up with pleasure. He liked this kind of thing; but Philip wouldn't, and he knew it. Philip would probably pitch the two guests out the door and down the hill when he came in and saw them about to sit down at the table.

They drew a long whistle at the same time when they entered the door together and saw the table draped in snowy white. They weren't used to tablecloths.

Margaret had cleared a space around the table and arranged boxes for seats where there weren't enough chairs, so there was room for all. Before each place she had laid a snowy napkin. The young fellows so unused to this custom of civilization were dazzled by the whiteness, and each one became immediately aware of his own poor appearance. She had set the table with silver knives, forks and spoons from her trunk as she would have in the East for a luncheon with a few friends. She knew no other way. This was enough to awe the two wild cowboys, who under other circumstances might have proved to be unwelcome guests.

Margaret had also added a touch of refinement in the few green leaves and blossoms she gathered in her morning tour around the house. They were wild blossoms, it's true, and nothing but weeds in the eyes of the men who daily stepped on similar ones without noticing. But here, on this snowy linen, in a tiny crystal vase carefully unpacked from Margaret's trunk, they took on a new beauty and weren't recognized as belonging to the world in which they lived.

It was like the girl, impulsive and poetical, that she kept the whole dinner waiting a minute while she found the vase and added the touch of beauty to the already inviting table. Who knew but the flowers might speak to those men of the God who made them?

And the flowers, with their delicate pink faces and faint scent, created a kind of embarrassment among the strange company at the table.

Just as they were sitting down, Philip entered and paused in the doorway at the sight, his brow furrowing.

"Please sit over there, Mr. Earle," said Margaret, passing a plate of steaming soup to the place indicated.

Philip hesitated, half-reluctant, and sat down silently. But his eye ran sharply around the table in one warning glance, like the threat of lightning.

Philip's look, however, wasn't needed. The spoons and napkins and flowers, and above all the young woman, had awed the men known in that region for their fearlessness and cunning. Margaret had rummaged among the tin cans on the shelf of the cupboard in the corner and compounded a most delicious soup with the aid of a jar of beef extract, a can of baked beans and another of tomatoes. To be sure, its recipe wasn't found in any cookbook ever published; but it was nonetheless appreciated.

She had toasted half a loaf of stale baker's bread and cut it into crisp little squares for the soup. From cornmeal she made a johnny-cake, or cornbread, that only New England cooks knew how to make so flaky and delicious.

It wasn't exactly a menu for a luncheon in the East. But another glass of jelly from a box hastily pried open made it seem like a feast to the hungry young men who had been their own cooks for long months of famine.

Bennett was tall and lanky, with a freckled face, straight red hair and white eyelashes heavily shading light-blue eyes. He had a hard, straight mouth and a scar over his left eye, and he was known among his associates as a dead shot. His voice had a harsh, cruel ring when he spoke. Margaret did not like his face.

She sat at her end of the table, pouring coffee, or slipped quietly over to the stove, waiting on their needs. Her presence diffused a soft, quiet influence about the table.

The old woman crept from her duties in the new kitchen she was scrubbing and purifying to peep inside the door. The strange hush that hovered over the usually boisterous group puzzled her. She knew the reputation of those young men and couldn't understand their silence. Then she looked at the sweet presence of the girl as she presided over the meal and shook her head, wondering again as she slipped away.

After the last crumb was finished and they'd risen from the table, with a mixed expression on their faces of satisfaction in the meal and relief that it was over, Margaret dared her part.

She had decided to do it while she was preparing dinner, and her heart thumped so hard at times she could scarcely eat. Some rebuke must be given to the man who uttered the name of Jesus Christ in that awful way. What she should say she didn't know.

Lord, give me courage; give me words; give me opportunity! she pleaded silently during dinner.

And now, as she lifted her eyes, intent on her purpose, she met Byron's bold, handsome eyes. He was trying to think up something appropriate to say to the hostess for giving them this delightful dinner. He was noted for his funny speeches; but the usual language in which he framed them would not match Philip's ideas, and he didn't care to rouse Philip twice in a day. Engaging in a free fight with Philip Earle in front of the young woman would scarcely put him in her good graces.

Something in her troubled gaze embarrassed him as he strode across the room to where she stood. He was also conscious of Philip's piercing glance on his back. Yet, he swaggered a little more and held his head higher. He wouldn't be put to shame before a girl. He ran his fingers through his abundant black hair and tightened the knotted silk handkerchief about his bronzed throat. Then he stepped forward gallantly with a few pleasant words of thanks on his lips which were, for him, unusually free from profane extras.

He even reached out to shake hands with her, hoping to hold the small white hand in his brown one.

But Margaret looked at his hand and then faced him squarely, putting her own hand behind her back.

They didn't notice Philip, his eyes like a panther's, unconsciously moving toward them. Bennett and Stephen stood over by the door to see what would happen.

Her voice was very low, but clear. Philip, standing behind Byron, could hear every word she said, but the two by the door could not.

"Mr. Byron," she said, with pain in her voice, "I cannot shake hands with you. You have insulted my best friend."

A red flush appeared under the bronze in the young man's cheek, and he drew back as if struck.

He stammered and tried to find words. He'd said only a word in passing, he explained; he and Philip were as good friends as ever. He didn't know, or he wouldn't have spoken. He would apologize to Philip.

Margaret caught her breath. She didn't expect to be misunderstood.

"I don't mean Mr. Earle," she answered quietly. "He's only a new acquaintance. I mean my best friend. I mean Jesus Christ, my Savior. I heard you speak his name in an awful way, Mr. Byron."

She lifted her eyes to his now, and they were full of tears.

The man was silent before her. The flash of anger and embarrassment changed to deep, overpowering shame. He had nothing to say. He had never encountered anything like this. He couldn't point the barrel of his revolver at it, nor could he wrestle with it and overcome. It was shame, and he had never met real shame before.

The fire in Philip's eyes died, and he turned away, as if it were something too holy to look upon. He saw the tears in the girl's eyes and heard the real trouble in her voice. Into his own heart rebuke sent a shaft as it passed to meet this other man, whose guilt was greater.

At last the rough man, void of his usual lighthearted words, spoke.

"I didn't know—," he said, then turned and stumbled out of the room, without looking back.

And Margaret, with tears blinding her, took refuge in her room.

Chapter 6

The next few days were strenuous ones in the house with the unbidden guest. Philip and Stephen rose early and retired late. They did their regular work at odd times when they got a chance and entered like two young boys into the plans of their young commander.

They moved the cattle shed next to the house and floored it with some lumber that had been lying idle for some time. They took down the cookstove and set it up in the new kitchen, where it soon shone out in a coat of black under Margaret's direction and the old woman's hand.

A box of kitchen utensils Margaret had considered indispensable to her career as a housekeeper—and was thankful she hadn't left behind—was unpacked. Soon wonderful concoctions in the shape of waffles and muffins began to appear on the table, making each meal the rival of the last one and keeping the two young men and the old woman in a continual state of amazement.

Into the midst of all this work came the first Sabbath of Margaret's new life.

A storm had burst in the night and seemed to have made up its mind to stay all day; so there was nothing to do but remain in the house as much as possible.

At the breakfast table Stephen talked about the work they would do that day and said what a shame it was raining. Now they couldn't work on a little room to accommodate the old woman, who had to hobble home at night to her shanty a mile and a half away.

"You forget what day it is, Stephen," said Margaret, smiling. "You wouldn't work if it didn't rain. It's Sunday, you know."

Stephen looked up in surprise. He'd almost forgotten that Sunday was different from any other day, but he didn't wish to confess this to his sister. He scowled and answered, "Oh, bother, so it is!"

Then Philip scowled too, but for a different reason, and looked anxiously at the sky to see whether it would really be a rainy Sunday. He grew suddenly thankful for the rain. But what would he do with Stephen all day?

They were compelled to do some work, after all, for the old woman did not hobble over at all that day, and no wonder: the rain came down in sheets, thunder rumbled and lightning flashed across the heavens. And Philip blessed the rain again.

"Go into the kitchen, Steve, and wash those dishes," said Philip laughingly, "and I'll help. We're a lazy lot if we can't do the work one day out of seven for our board. It's enough for Miss Halstead to do the cooking." So they worked together, and Philip hunted around and managed to make work, little things that Stephen must do at once. Margaret kept telling them they could wait until tomorrow. But Philip insisted on keeping Stephen helping him till dinner was out of the way and it was nearly five o'clock.

The sky was lighting up and showed some signs of clearing.

Stephen wandered restlessly to the door and looked down the road and then at his watch.

Philip was on the alert, though he didn't show it. He glanced at the large piano case still unopened.

"Miss Halstead," he ventured, "why didn't we open that piano yesterday? If we should knock off a couple of those front boards and get at that keyboard, don't you think you might play for us a little and while away the rest of this day? Steve will be off to livelier company than ours if you don't amuse him."

He laughed lightly, but something troubling in his voice caused Margaret to follow his glance toward her brother. She saw the restlessness in his whole attitude and took alarm. Was it for one or both of the young men she was anxious? She couldn't have told.

"Oh, yes, if you can do it easily," said Margaret. She would be delighted to touch the keys of her piano again, and it would drive away any lingering homesickness.

Philip's voice again called back Stephen's wandering attention, and soon their united efforts brought the row of ivory and black keys into view.

Margaret, seated on a kitchen chair, picked out some strong, sweet chords while the two young men settled down to listen.

From memory she played Sabbath music, a bit from some of the old masters, a page from an oratorio, a strain from the minor of a funeral march, a grand triumphant hymn. Then she touched the keys more softly and began to sing quietly. Eventually a rich tenor and a grumbling bass issued forth from the two listeners as she wandered into familiar hymns they had sung as little boys.

The rain poured down again, and it grew darker. Still they sang, until at last Philip sighed with relief and realized it was bedtime and Stephen hadn't gone to the village. Then Margaret stopped playing, and they all went to get a snack before retiring.

Margaret, before she slept that night, asked a blessing again on the work she hoped to do. She never dreamed she had already been used to keep the brother for whose sake she came on this long journey.

After they finished the old woman's room, Philip came in with his arms full of huge rough stones and announced that he was ready to begin the fireplace. He thought it best to get the muss and dirt of plaster out of the way before they put things to rights in the living room.

Margaret had almost forgotten the doubts she had about Philip when she first came, along with his strange actions on the morning after her arrival; she was prepared to accept both the men as good comrades, or brothers. They all went to work. Margaret drew the outline of the fireplace she thought should be built, and Stephen mixed mortar while Philip carried in stones from a great pile the former owner of the place had collected to build a fence.

"There's nothing like being a jack of all trades," said Stephen as he slapped on some mortar with the blade of a broken hoe and settled into it a large stone Philip had just brought in.

Margaret's eyes shone as she watched the chimney being built. She saw in her mind's eye a charming room, and she was anxious to get it into shape before another Sabbath, so they might have a quiet, restful time. While she played and sang the night before, ideas for how she might point the way to her Savior were revealed to her, and she longed to begin.

The young woman also had a lot to do in teaching the other woman new customs and in keeping clean the things they used every day. But Margaret was one of those whose hands are never idle, and she had put her whole soul into the making over of her brother's home. So she accomplished much in her own way while the young men worked at masonry and the stone fireplace grew into attractive proportions.

By the time it was finished, she had rooted out from the boxes and barrels most of the things she needed in arranging the living room. She also cut and sewed cushions and trim ready to put into place when the time came, so that the refurbishing moved forward rapidly. Indeed, the two helpers became as eager to see the room finished as the young architect.

Before she left the East, Margaret bought a number of items she thought she would likely need in arranging her own room; she wanted to make it as pretty as possible to keep her from getting homesick. She abandoned this plan now and used the items to adorn the large, bare living room which she intended to be the scene of her labors.

Among other things were bright materials for cushions and enough rolls of paper to hang on the walls of a reasonably large room. Careful calculating and measuring soon revealed that the paper would cover most of the walls of this room, which was the size of an ordinary whole house without any partitions. She puzzled a while about whether she should risk sending for more; but finally a bright idea occurred to her as she looked at the large bundle of green burlap lying in the box with the paper. This she'd intended for draperies, or floor covering, if necessary, or maybe a cover for a chest or cushion. Now it was clear to her.

The paper had an ivory background on which great palms seemed to be growing, as though a myriad of hothouses had let forth their glories of greenery. There was enough of this paper to cover the two sides and front of the room. It would look as if the room opened on three sides into a palm grove. On the back end, in the center of which was the great stone fireplace, she would put the plain leaf-green burlap, fastened along its breadths with brass tacks. Two or three good coats of whitewash would give the ceiling a creamy tint, and she could cut out a few of the palms from the paper to apply in a delicate design only in the center and corners.

The two young men looked bewildered when she tried to explain, and she finally stopped trying and simply issued her directions.

They covered the back of the room first. When the mossy breadths were smoothed on over the rough boards, fastened at intervals with the gleaming tacks, the old stone fireplace stood out sharply against the dark background.

"Now if you have any guns and things, that's the place to put them," said Margaret, pointing to the wall beside the fireplace.

Philip proudly brought out a couple of guns and crossed them on the wall to the right, while Stephen fastened a pair of buffalo horns over the door to the left that led into the new kitchen. That side of the room was at once named the dining room, and Margaret unwrapped a handsome four-panel screen of unusual size, wrought in black and gold, and stood it across that corner.

They turned eagerly to follow her next directions, having more faith in the result than before. And another day or two saw the walls papered and the ceiling smiling white with its greenery traced here and there.

It didn't take long after that to unpack rugs and furniture. Margaret had brought many items, including rare mahogany furniture and Oriental rugs, from the old home. A wiser person might have advised her to leave them behind until she was sure of making a home in this distant land. But the girl rejoiced in the beauty of the things she could give to her "life work," as she liked to call it, and had brought everything with her that she intended to keep at all.

The rough old floor with its wide cracks and unoiled boards didn't look too bad when a great, soft rug of rich, dark coloring nearly covered it, and it was set off here and there by the skin of a tiger or black bear or a strip of white goatskin.

A wide, low seat, covered with green and piled with bright cushions, ran along the wall to the right of the fireplace. In the corner beyond the window was a low bookcase, which Margaret had intended for her own room, and again beyond her bedroom door another low bookcase ran along to the other bedroom door. These doors were hidden by dark-green curtains of soft, velvety material, and no one would have suspected the rough, cheap doors behind them. By each one on the top of the bookcase, half against the green of the curtain and half mingling with the lifelike palms on the wall, stood a living palm in a terra-cotta jardiniere, which made the pictured ones seem even more real.

The piano stood near the front of the room, across the right-hand corner, and a wide, low couch invited one to rest and listen to the music.

The rest of the room that was not the dining room was filled with easy chairs, a large round mahogany table with a delightful reading lamp in the middle, and more books. Stephen's old writing desk stood across the left-hand front corner.

The finished room was charming to look upon, when at last the weary workers sat down to a belated Saturday evening supper and realized what they had accomplished during the week.

There was still much to be done. As Margaret ate her supper, she glanced around and planned for a row of little brass hooks against the wall, where she could hang her tiny teacups and wondered how she should manage a plate rail for the saucers without moldings. The little glass-faced buffet that was to hold the china still stood on the floor in the corner, waiting to be hung, and the pictures were as yet unpacked; but there was time enough for that. There was a room in which to spend the Sabbath, and she prayed that her work might now begin.

Softly there crept up through the darkness of the sky the dawn of another Sabbath day, and Margaret rose with eager anticipation. In the first place, she meant to get Stephen, and Philip, too, if possible, to go with her to church. That, of course, was the right place to begin the Sabbath.

Before she left her room she laid out on her bed the things she would wear to church. She chose them with care so she might be neatly dressed in the Lord's house and as winsome as possible to those she wished to influence.

She didn't acknowledge even to herself that she had some doubt as to whether she would get Stephen and Philip to attend church, for she meant to accomplish it in spite of all obstacles.

Nevertheless, she went about her self-appointed task with great care and deliberation, prefacing her request with their most delectable breakfast yet.

Just as they finished she brought up the subject that was so near to her heart and about which she had prayed all morning.

"Stephen, what time do we have to start for church? Is it far from here? You don't go on horseback, do you?"

Stephen dropped his knife and fork on his plate with a clatter and sat back in astonishment. A blank silence filled the room for some seconds.

Chapter 7

To church!" Stephen uttered the words half mockingly. "What time do we start! Well, now, Phil, how far would you say it is to the nearest church?"

A mirthless laugh broke from Philip. It was involuntary. A wave of bitterness rolled over him as the highest ocean wave might break over the head of someone trying bravely to breast the tide. As soon as he laughed he was sorry, for he sensed the shock it would be to Margaret even before he saw her start at his harsh laughter.

These two young men both carried bitterness in their hearts. Stephen's was caused by the hardness of his heart toward his earthly father, while Philip had hardened his heart, for what he considered just cause, toward his Father in heaven. Of the two, his bitterness was the more galling.

Philip checked the laugh, which was really only the semblance of one, and answered steadily with his eyes on his plate: "About forty miles by the nearest way, I'd judge."

Stephen's eyes twinkled merrily as he tipped his chair back against the wall and watched his sister. He had no inkling of the desolation this would bring her and couldn't understand, or perhaps didn't notice, the whiteness of her face as she stared at him, only half comprehending. So Philip, the stranger, felt with her the appalling emptiness of a country without a church. Dismay covered her face.

"But what do you do?" she faltered. "Where do you go to service on Sunday?"

"Same as any other day," laughed Stephen. "'The groves were God's first temples,'" he quoted with a feigned air of piety. "Suppose we go out in search of one. This will be a first-rate day for your first lesson in riding horseback. It won't do for you to stay in the house working all the time."

But Margaret's face was flushed and troubled.

"Do you mean you don't go anywhere to church?" she asked. "Is there no service in town? Are there no missionaries even, out here?"

"There isn't even a town worth speaking of, Miss Halstead," answered Philip, feeling that someone must answer her earnestly. "You don't know what a God-forsaken country you've come to. Churches and missionaries wouldn't flourish here if they came. You won't find it a pleasant place to stay. Men get used to it, but women find it hard."

She lifted her troubled eyes to his, wondering subconsciously whether he was hinting that she should go back where she came from. But she saw in his kind face no eagerness to get rid of her, as his eyes met hers. She turned sadly toward the window and gazed out on the stretch of level country below the hill and in the distance. She thought in despair of the place she'd come to and the hopelessness of carrying out her plans without the aid of a church and a minister.

She thought her part would be simply to make a good home for her brother, speak a quiet word when the opportunity arose and influence him to lay hold of the power of the gospel. But out here it seemed there was no gospel, unless she preached it. For this she wasn't prepared.

Baffled, she hardly knew what words she used to decline her brother's urgent request to go riding with him. His partner added his earnest solicitations when he saw that Stephen wasn't going to succeed. She wondered afterward at the anxiety and annoyance in Philip's eyes when she told him firmly that she did not ride on Sunday and would rather stay quietly at home. It seemed strange to her that he should try to interfere between her and her brother. Then she went into her little log room, shut the door and knelt in discouraged prayer beside her bed. Had she, then, come out on a fruitless mission? What good was there in bringing pianos, books and palm-covered walls into her brother's life, if there were no means for bringing him to see the love of the Lord Jesus Christ?

The sound of a rider leaving the dooryard scarcely roused her from her disappointed petitions. She wondered idly whether it were Philip, but soon she heard another horse's quick tread. Crossing to the window, she was just in time to see Philip fling himself upon his horse and ride at a furious pace down the road.

Quiet settled down on the house, and Margaret realized with disappointment that both young men had left. Why didn't she try to keep Stephen with her? Perhaps he would have listened to her while she read something, or she might have sung. Evidently Philip intended going off all the time and was only anxious to get her and Stephen out of the way so he could do as he pleased. The tears came into her eyes and spilled over onto her cheeks. How shamefully she failed! Even the little she might have done she let slip because of her disappointment that God hadn't arranged things according to her expectations. Perhaps it might have been better for her to go on the ride with Stephen rather than for him to go off with some friends who never had a thought of God or His holy day.

Thus reflecting, she read herself some bitter lessons. She forgot to ask for the Spirit's guidance and went in her own strength, or she might have been shown a better way and been blessed in her efforts.

Eventually she went out where the old woman sat outside the kitchen door, mumbling and glowering at the sun-clad landscape. Perhaps she might attempt a humble effort with this poor woman.

"Marna, do you know God?" she asked, sitting down beside the old woman and speaking tenderly.

The woman looked at her curiously and shook her head.

"God never come here," she answered. "Missie, you—*you* know God?"

"Yes," answered Margaret earnestly. "God is my Father."

"God your Father! No. You not come off here; you stay where your Father at. God, your Father, angry with you?"

"No, my Father loves me. He sent His Son to die for me. God is your Father, too, Marna."

The old woman shook her head decidedly. "Marna have no father. Fathers all bad. Fathers no love anybody but selves. Brothers no much good, too. All go off, leave. All drink. I say, stay 'way. No come back drunk. Knock! Scold! Hate! I say stay 'way! Drink self dead!"

Marna was gesticulating wildly to make up for her lack of words. Suddenly she turned to the girl, with a gleam of something like motherliness in her wrinkled old face.

"What for Missie come way here? Brothers no good. All go own way. Make cry!" Marna's work-worn finger traced down the delicate cheek, which was still flushed with the recently shed tears.

Margaret instinctively drew back, but she did not wish to hurt the old woman's feelings, so she answered in as bright a tone as she could summon.

"Brothers are not all bad, Marna. Some are good. My brother was lonely here, and I came to take care of him."

"Take care! Take care!" muttered the old woman. "And who 'take care' of Missie? Men go off—stay all day. Drink. Come home drunk! Ach! No, no, Missie go back. Missie go off while men gone. Not see brothers anymore."

Margaret was half frightened over this harangue. But she tried to be brave and answer the poor woman, though her heart misgave her as a great fear began to rise.

"No, Marna," she said, smiling through her fear. "I cannot go back. God sent me, and until He tells me to go back I cannot go."

"God love you and send you here? Then He never come here. He don't know—"

"Yes, He knows, Marna, and He is here, too," she answered softly, as if reassuring herself. "Listen!"

Then Margaret started at the beginning of the story of the cross and told it to the wondering old woman as simply as she knew how.

But, when she finished, the listener only shook her head and murmured, "No, God never love Marna. Marna have bad heart. No love for good in heart. No heavenly Father love."

It was time to get dinner ready, and Margaret arose with a sigh, a great depression settling on her heart. Not even to this poor old woman could she show the light of Christ.

She gave herself to preparing the noon meal for a while, thinking she would soon hear the sound of horses coming up the road. But when the dinner was ready and sent forth savory odors into the air, Margaret stood shading her anxious, wistful eyes with a hand that had grown cold with a new fear, and no sound of horses came.

The girl ate a few mouthfuls and had the dinner put away.

The old woman went about muttering, "Men no come. Men off. Have good time. Missie cry. Missie go home. Not stay."

The stars came out thickly like sky blossoms unfolding all at once, and the sky drew close about the earth. But still no sound of travelers came along the long, dark road.

Margaret went in at last from her vigil on the doorstep and lit the great lamp. It was a disappointing Sabbath. In fact, it seemed to be a wasted Sabbath. She might as well have been riding with Stephen if perchance she might have said some helpful thing to him. And the old woman rocking and muttering to herself in the back doorway—what good had she done for her?

At last she could bear the silence and her fears no longer.

She called to Marna to come in. "Sit down," she said gently. "I will sing to you about Jesus."

Marna sat down on a wooden stool with her hands folded and listened while Margaret sang. She chose the songs that used simple language, that told of Jesus and His love; songs that spoke to weary, burdened souls and bade them rest; songs that told of forgiveness and a Father's love.

She sang for a long time. Then, yearning for some kind of help and feeling as if she must have companionship in her need, she walked over to the old woman, took her hand and drew her down beside the fireplace seat.

"Come," she said. "We'll talk to God."

The old woman knelt with her eyes open wide, watching the girl.

Margaret closed her eyes and said, "Oh, God, show Marna how her Father loves her. Help Marna love God. Help Marna be good, for Jesus' sake."

Dazed, the old woman stood up. She fixed her eyes on the girl's face in both fear and fascination.

Margaret smiled and said good night, but Marna went out under the stars and muttered, "Help Marna be good?" as if it were a thing that had to be and she couldn't see how.

Then Margaret locked the door, turned out the light and sat down by the window to watch and pray. During that time part of what she might do in this land without a God or a temple was revealed to her. A strength not her own came out of her darkness, fear and feebleness.

It must have been long past midnight—her watch had run down and she couldn't tell—faint sounds at last drifted up the hill. Two horsemen, strangely close together, crept past her window and wound around the house to the barn. One seemed to be supporting the other. They spoke no words, but one turned his head as he passed her window and looked, though she couldn't tell which one.

Neither of them came to the house that night, though she lighted the lamp and waited for them awhile. She concluded they didn't wish to disturb her.

Then, not caring enough to remove her clothes, she lay down and wept. After the long day the tension was loosened at last, but what did she know? Was one of her newfound fears dissipated? Was she sure Stephen came home with Philip and was in the barn lying in the hay? Was she sure it was Philip? They might have been two tramps—but no. Tramps wouldn't come to a desolate land like this. They would tramp to more profitable places for plying their beggarly trade. A strange peace settled on her. She wasn't afraid anything would happen to her. She feared only for her brother—and, yes, she must admit it—for his friend. After all, he was her brother too, in a broader sense, but still the son of her heavenly Father.

And Marna's words—what did they mean? Did the two with whom she came to make her home drink? If so, how could she hope to help save them, just she alone in that country without a church? For the absence of a Christian church and a Christian minister left her feeling inexpressibly alone.

Yet not alone, for out of the darkness of her room came the words to her heart, *And lo, I am with you always.*

Then she prayed as she'd never prayed before, until her soul seemed drawn up to meet the loving Comforter, Strengthener and Guide. In that hour she laid down herself, her fears and wishes, and agreed to do what God would have her do in this lonely place, against such fearful odds as might be—just her alone with God.

Out in the hay Philip lay, body and mind weary with the fight of the day, which he had not won; yet, he was too troubled to sleep now that he had the chance.

He peered anxiously through the darkness toward the house and wondered how it fared with the one who waited all day while he was on the battlefront. Was she frightened at being left alone so late? Did she see them when they came in? Did she guess what the trouble was, or had she coupled them both in deserting her?

Philip's heart was bitter against God tonight. He felt like cursing a god who would let a woman suffer, especially one so fair. Poor, straying child of God, who didn't know the comfort of trusting and leaning on the everlasting arms or that even suffering may bring a beautiful reward!

Chapter 8

Stephen slept late the next morning. When he came heavy-eyed and cross to the breakfast table, he complained of a headache. But Philip sat silent, with grave lines drawn about his forehead and mouth. He was too strong a man to show the signs of fatigue or loss of sleep in any other way.

Margaret came through the night's horror with peace on her brow, but her face looked pale from lack of sleep. Philip gave her a long look while she was pouring the coffee and saw this. It angered him to think she had suffered.

Margaret was sweetness itself to her brother. She insisted upon his lying down on the long seat by the chimney, while she shaded his eyes from the morning glare, pulled a chair close and read to him. He turned his head away from her, too ashamed to face her kindness and knowing in his heart what he really was. Then she laid the book aside and, bringing a bowl of water, dipped her cool, soft hand in it and stroked the throbbing temples.

Something was at work in his easily stirred heart, something that went beyond the mere surface where most emotions were born and died. As her hand passed back and forth, comforting his sick nerves, he reached up a shaking hand and caught hers.

"You are a good girl—a good sister!" he said, his voice choking.

Then Margaret stooped over and kissed his cheek, murmuring softly, "Dear brother, now go to sleep. When you wake up, you'll feel better."

Stephen had to work hard to hold back the moisture that kept creeping into his eyes. And he was glad when she finally thought he was asleep and tiptoed away. It had been many years since he felt a lump like the one growing in his throat till it seemed as if it would burst. But eventually the quiet and the darkness brought sleep. Philip looked in anxiously and left with a relieved sigh.

Dinner was late that day, for Stephen slept a long time, and Margaret would not have him disturbed. But when it came it was delicious: strong soup seasoned just right, homemade bread, delicious coffee and a mound of raspberry jelly, cool and luscious with the flavor of raspberries from the old New England preserve-closet. It was marvelous how many things this sister could make from canned goods and boxes of gelatin.

But Stephen was restless as dinner neared the end, and Philip looked uneasily toward him.

Stephen shoved his chair back with a creak on the floor and said crossly that he believed he would ride down to the village for the mail. He needed to get outdoors; it would do his head good. Philip frowned deeply and opened his mouth to reply. But before he could speak Margaret's sweet voice broke in eagerly.

"Oh, then, give me my lesson in riding, Stephen, please. It's a lovely afternoon and will soon be cool. I don't want to be left behind again. I was sorry I didn't go with you yesterday. Please do. I'm in a great hurry to learn to ride so I can go all about and see this country."

Philip's face relaxed. He waited to see what Stephen would do, and after a bit of coaxing Stephen consented, although Philip still felt uneasy.

The horses were saddled and brought to the door. Philip held the bridle of the gentler horse, while Stephen helped his sister mount, advising her elaborately on how to hold the reins and how to sit. Then they were off.

"Take the east road, Steve!" called Philip as they rode away from him.

But Stephen drew his head up haughtily and didn't answer. Then Philip knew he'd made a mistake and bit his lip as he turned quickly toward the barn. There was still another horse on the place, though it wasn't a good riding horse and had some disagreeable habits. It was usually left behind when any pleasure riding was to be done. Philip flung his own saddle across her back now and, hardly waiting to pull the girths tight, sprang into it and after the two. They were turning westward, as he was sure Stephen would do after his unfortunate remark.

He urged the reluctant old horse into a trot and soon caught up with the riders, calling pleasantly, "Made up my mind I'd come along too. It was lonely staying by myself."

Stephen's only answer was a frown. He knew what Philip meant by following. His anger was roused at Philip's constant care for him. Did Philip think he was a fool that he couldn't take care of himself with his sister along?

Margaret, too, was a little disappointed. She hoped to get closer to her brother during this ride. She thought she might find out where he was the day before and have a heart-to-heart talk with him. But now here was this third presence that always stood between her and her brother, hindering the talk.

Philip, however, was unobtrusive. He rode behind them or galloped on ahead, dismounting to gather a flaming bunch of flowers. Then he would ride up to fasten them in the bridle of the lady's horse and ride on again. Stephen ignored him utterly, and Philip ignored the fact that he was ignored. Margaret came to feel that his presence wasn't troublesome and, in fact, was rather pleasant, as he hovered about like a guardian angel. Then she laughed to herself to think of her using that simile. To think of an angel in a flannel shirt, buckskins and a sombrero!

Philip suggested quietly that a certain turn would bring them to a view of the river. As a result Margaret pleaded for going that way just as they came to a critical turn in the road. Stephen, unsuspecting, turned willingly, thinking they'd return soon and find their way to the village. But wary Philip led them on still further until the town with its dangers was far behind them. Then Stephen woke up to the plot that was laid for him and rode his horse sulkily home. But the deadly fiend that slumbered within him was allayed for the time, and he went to his room and slept soundly that night.

There was plenty of work yet to be done upon the house. Philip surprised them all a few days later by driving up to the door before breakfast with a load of logs, several men and another load of logs following after him. The sound of the axe, saw and hammer rang through the air that day, and by night a good-sized addition of logs, divided into two nice rooms, was added to the right-hand side of the living room.

Margaret's eyes shone. It was just the addition she'd spoken of to Stephen, to which he was so opposed. Her heart swelled with gratitude toward him. It seemed she didn't understand her brother yet, who was sometimes so cold, but who was still trying to do all in his power to please her. She watched the work some of the time and was surprised to find that, while Stephen worked with the rest, he took his orders from Philip, as the others did; he also seemed to expect Philip to command the whole affair. It was even more strange that the orders were just what she suggested to Stephen on the first walk around the house.

As they were coming to the supper table that evening, she attempted to tell her brother how good it was of him to do the things she suggested. She thought they were alone; but Philip had come in behind them while they were talking, and Stephen saw him.

The back of Stephen's neck grew red, and the color stole up around his golden hair as he said laughingly, "Oh, thank Phil for that. He's the boss carpenter. I couldn't build a house if I had to stay out in the rain the rest of my life."

Margaret looked up brightly and gave Philip the first really warm smile he'd received from her, a smile that included him in the family circle.

"I'll thank him, too," she said and put out her hand to grasp his large one, rough from handling the logs. But she left her other hand lovingly on her brother's shoulder, and Stephen knew she didn't take back the gratitude she gave him. It somehow made him feel strangely uncomfortable.

In a few days the addition to the house was in good order and the windows draped in soft, sheer muslin.

With great cheerfulness all around, the three householders took a final survey of the premises before the sun went down.

"If we could only grow bark on the outside of the old boards on the main part of the house!" said Margaret wistfully.

"Nothing easier," answered Philip quickly. "It shall be done."

"What do you mean?" asked Margaret.

"Why, cover it with bark," answered Philip. "Steve, get up early with me in the morning, and we'll strip enough bark down in the ravine to cover one side of this front before breakfast."

"Won't that be beautiful?" said Margaret, clapping her hands.

The stern lines in Philip's face broke into a pleased smile. He was glad he suggested it. What was it about this girl that always made him feel glad when he did her a favor? Other girls he had known were not that way.

That night he slept in the house for the first time since Margaret came to live there. The front room of the addition was fitted up for him. Margaret had just discovered that his only bed had been in the hay and that he had permanently and quietly given up his room to her. She supposed the barn had a large, comfortable room over it which he called his own, though she'd indeed thought little about it. She took special pains with furnishing Philip's room. She felt it was due him for giving up his own for her. It wasn't difficult to make it beautiful. There was enough fine old mahogany furniture left. She picked out the most handsome pieces and arranged them attractively. She hadn't fixed up her own room yet, other than to have her own bedstead set up instead of the hard little cot, but she wanted to make Philip's as attractive as possible.

As a final touch, she went to her room and unpinned from the wall the photograph of the sweet-looking woman with white hair. Framing it in a small leather case of her own, she set it on the white cover of Philip's bureau. And it was his mother's eyes that looked at Philip in the morning as he opened them for the first time in his new abode. He lay for a moment, looking at the picture, wondering how it got there, then blessing the thoughtfulness that placed it. He wondered what his mother would think of him now in this strange, wild life. He wondered, too, what she would think of the girl who was bringing such miracles of change to pass in this desolate house. He touched the smoothness of the sheet and the pillowcase; he'd missed such things for a long time and hadn't known it.

The days were busy and happy. At times Stephen seemed to be stirred up to the same level of enthusiasm and effort that kept the other two at work. He didn't seem to want to stop even for his meals, until all was finished.

"We ought to have a housewarming when it gets done," he said one night, when they were standing at a distance, surveying the almost completed outside of the house.

"Certainly," said Margaret. "We'll do it by all means. How soon can we have it, and whom will you invite?"

As she turned to go into the house, however, she caught that look of disapproval on Philip's face that she hadn't seen for several days and wondered about it.

"Let's have it next Sunday," said Stephen enthusiastically. "The weather's getting cooler now, and by evening we can have a fire in that great new fireplace of Phil's. And we'll ask all the fellows, of course."

Philip stood still, aghast. If Margaret hadn't been there, he would have fairly thundered. But his tongue was tied. This must be managed, if possible, without letting her know what a precipice she was treading near. She would be overcome if she knew everything.

"Is there no other day but Sunday, Stephen, dear?" asked Margaret, and her troubled voice was soft and pleading. "You know I always make the Sabbath a holy day and not a holiday. I would much, *much* rather have it some other time."

She didn't say no definitely to his proposition, remembering her Sunday's experience when she declined to ride with him. Perhaps there was some better solution to the puzzle than that. She wouldn't antagonize her brother yet and would ask her Guide. There surely would be a way.

"No, there isn't any other time when they can all come," answered Stephen shortly. "But of course if you have your puritanical notions, I suppose it's no use. I can't see what harm it would do for the boys to be here that day more than any other day. You can go off into your room and pray if you want to. The boys won't be doing any worse than they would down in the village carousing around."

Stephen was angry and forgetting himself. Philip's cheeks flamed with indignant sympathy for the girl who winced under her brother's words.

"Oh, Stephen, *don't,* please! Let me think about it. I want to do what you wish if there's a right way," she said in a pleading tone. There were tears in her voice, but her eyes were bright and dry.

"Well, then, do it," said Stephen sulkily. "It won't hurt your Sabbath to give us some tunes on the piano. The boys will like that better than anything else. They don't hear music around here."

Margaret looked up troubled but thoughtful.

"I'll think about it tonight, Stephen, and tell you in the morning. Will that do? I'll really try to see if I can please you."

Stephen assented dismally. He had very little idea she would do it. He remembered her face that Sunday when she declined to ride with him. He considered her bound by prejudices and of very little use in such a country as this.

But Philip, troubled, hovered about the door.

"Miss Halstead," he called after a few moments, "the moon is rising. Have you noticed how bright the stars are? Come out and look at them."

"Come, too, Stephen," said Margaret.

"What do I care for the stars?" Stephen retorted. Then he went into his room and shut the door.

Margaret's eyes filled with tears, but she blinked them back and walked over to the door, anxious to reach the kind starlight that would hide her discomfiture.

"Miss Halstead, I beg you not to think of doing what Steve asks," said Philip in hushed, earnest tones.

"Why not, Mr. Earle? Have you any conscientious scruples against company on Sunday?" Her voice was cold and searching.

"No, of course not."

"Then why? You spent all one Sunday off somewhere, presumably on a pleasure excursion."

"It was anything but a pleasure excursion, Miss Halstead," said Philip, his face growing dark with anger in the starlight. "But that has nothing whatever to do with the matter. I beg you not to do this for your own sake. You don't know what those fellows are. They won't be congenial to you in the least."

"Does that make any difference if they're my brother's friends?" Margaret drew herself up haughtily. "I thank you for your advice, Mr. Earle. But this is my brother's house, and of course I can't stop him from having guests if he wishes. I don't like company on Sunday. But if they must come, I'll do my best to make it a good Sunday for them. More than that I can't promise. Do you think I can?"

Her voice held a mixture of coldness and pleading which would have been amusing at another time. But she had silenced Philip most effectively. He bit his lip and turned away from the house to walk out into the starlight with his vexation.

Chapter 9

Margaret slept little that night. A great plan had come to her, born from anxiety and prayer. At first she thought it seemed preposterous, impossible! She drew back, caught her breath and prayed again; but over and over the idea recurred to her.

It was this. Perhaps God sent her out here into these wilds to witness for Him, yes, even among rough men like the two that had eaten dinner with them that first day after her arrival.

Could she do it? Could she make that proposed Sunday gathering into a holy thing? She, who had never spoken in public in her life, except to read in a low voice an essay from a school platform? She, who always shrank from doing anything publicly and let honors pass her by rather than make herself prominent? She who was never taught the ways of Christian work, other than by her own loving heart?

Could she do it? And *how* could she do it?

The most she knew about Christian work was learned in the class of boys she taught in Sunday school at home. But they were boys, most of them still in knee-trousers and under home discipline. They loved her, it's true, and listened respectfully to her sincere teaching. They even gave up their mischief before her trusting smile. They learned their lessons and found no disgrace in answering her questions. They came to her home occasionally and seemed to enjoy it, and she talked with several of them about holy things. She worked with two of them especially and knelt beside them while she heard their first stumbling acknowledgment that God was their Father and Jesus Christ their Savior.

But that was very different from bringing the gospel to a lot of men who knew little and cared less about God or their own salvation. She shuddered in the dark as she remembered the sound of Byron's awful oath. How could she do it? Was it even right for her to try?

Then out of the night she felt her Savior's eyes upon her and knew that such things mustn't count against the great need of souls when she was the only one at hand to help. And she bowed her head and answered aloud in a clear voice.

"I will do what You want me to do, Jesus. Only let me help save my brother."

The sleeper in the next room stirred at the unusual sounds and thought about the words he heard. He tried to give them meaning but thought he'd dreamed, so he slept again, uneasily.

After Margaret said, "I will," to her Master, the rest came easily. The plan, if it was a plan, was His. The Spirit would guide her. She had asked for such guidance. If it was of God, it would be crowned with some sort of success. She would be helped to understand it was right. If she went her own faulty way, it would fail. It surely could do no harm to try to have a Sunday school class of Stephen's friends who'd come. And if they refused or laughed at her, why, then she could sing. The gospel could always be sung, where no one would listen to it in another form. It would be a question of winning her brother over, and that might be difficult.

Wait! Why did she need to tell him? Why not take them all by surprise and make the afternoon so enjoyable to them that they would want to come again? Could she?

Her breath came quickly as the idea assumed practical proportions and she realized she was really going to carry it out. She had a spirit of strong convictions and impulsive notions; otherwise she would have stopped there. But in saying that, too little weight may be given to the fact that she relinquished herself to the guidance of One wiser than she was.

Just before the stars paled in the eastern sky she lay down to rest, her mind made up and her heart at peace. As for Philip's words of warning, she forgot them entirely. Philip she did not understand, but neither did he understand her.

The two young men were both surprised the next morning when she told them, quietly enough, that she would be glad to help them entertain their friends on Sunday afternoon. But they must allow her to carry out her own plans. She thought she could promise them a pleasant time, and would they trust her for the rest?

She said it sweetly, and her morning dress, with a touch of seashell pink in it that made her look like a flower blossom in the greenery of the room, was gathered neatly about her. Her brother could only admire her as he watched her put the sugar in his coffee.

Stephen was surprised, but he was too frivolous himself to realize the depth of earnestness in anyone else. He concluded that Margaret had decided to let her dreary ideas go and have a good time while she was here; and he resolved to help her with it. She was certainly a beauty. He was glad she had come.

But Philip's face darkened, and the little he ate was quickly gone. After that he excused himself and went out to the barn. He was angry with Margaret and troubled for her. He knew better than she what she was bringing upon herself; furthermore, her brother, who should have protected such a precious sister better, knew even better than he. Why didn't Stephen see and stop it?

But Philip predicted that matters had gone too far for him to say a word to Stephen. Former experience had taught him that Stephen took refuge from direct attacks by escaping to his companions in the village, which always ended in something worse.

Philip was so angry that, after he finished the chores around the barn, he decided to get away for a while. There was enough in the house to keep Stephen occupied for the day. The fear that had caused him to keep guard ever since Margaret Halstead's arrival was dominated for the time by his anger at both brother and sister. So he took his revenge by traveling many miles across the country on business connected with a cattle sale; he'd proposed to make the trip for some time but kept putting it off from week to week.

He didn't stop to explain to the household except in a sentence or two, and then he was off. Margaret noticed the arrogance in his tone as he announced his departure at the door, but she was so full of her plans for Sunday that she took little heed of it. It didn't matter much about Philip anyway. He was only an outsider, and, besides, he would feel different, perhaps, when Sunday came.

Philip's anger boiled within him and grew hotter as he put the miles between him and the cause of it. He wished himself out of this heathen land and back into civilization. He decided to let people take care of themselves after this. Of what use was it to try to save this girl from knowing her brother's true self? She was bound to find it out sooner or later, and she would perhaps only hate him for his effort.

But Stephen, after teasing his sister to discover her plan for entertaining their guests, decided to make the most of Philip's absence and get his guests well invited before that autocrat interfered. It was remarkable he hadn't done so already. So he slipped away to saddle his horse while his sister was busy in her room. Leaving a message with Marna, he rode into the sunlight, as light of heart as the insects that buzzed around his horse, and with less care for tomorrow than they had.

Margaret was disappointed to find her brother gone when she came out, for she had planned to get him to do several things about the house that morning. While he was doing them she'd intended to find out about the friends he wanted to invite. She wondered if there were many and if any among them could help her establish the Sunday school. There must be some good women around there. Surely she could get a helper somewhere.

But perhaps this first time it would be only two or three of Stephen's best friends. He had spoken of "the fellows," and it might be better not to complicate things with womankind till she was well acquainted and knew whom she could count on for help. She admitted to her own heart, too, that she could open up the plan to them and teach a class in her own way; it would be easier then to calm her frightened heart, if no women or girls were watching.

She was disappointed, but after a moment she reflected that perhaps even Stephen's absence was an advantage. She would study a lesson during this quiet hour and plan her program, though it would be much easier if she knew what kind of scholars she was to have. She spent a happy morning and afternoon planning for the Sunday, and only toward night did she begin to feel uneasy and hover near the door looking down the road.

Marna came in, shaking her head and muttering again, and it required all of Margaret's faith and bravery to keep her heart up.

The night closed down like that other night when she kept a vigil, and still neither young man appeared. Margaret wished Philip would come, so that she might reassure herself by asking where he supposed Stephen went and when he would return. She admitted that after all there was something strong and good to lean upon in Philip.

She prayed a great deal that evening and, in time, lay down and tried to sleep. After several hours of restless turnings she finally fell into an uneasy sleep.

But when the morning broke with its serene sunshine, and neither of the two men had returned, she became more restless. She tried in vain to settle into working at a task, for she constantly returned to look down the road.

Marna said little that day. But Margaret remembered her former words, and her old anxieties returned to clutch her till she was driven to her knees. As she prayed, a great, deep love for her newfound brother grew in her soul till she felt she must help save him, for instinctively she knew that he needed saving more than many.

The second day wore away into the night, but still they did not return.

Margaret lived through various states of mind. Now she was alarmed, now indignant that they would treat her so; and now she blamed herself for coming out here at all. Then alarm succeeded all other feelings, and she would fly to her refuge and find strength.

When the third day dawned and seemed likely to be as the others, she asked Marna where she thought they went; but the old woman shut her lips and shook her head. She didn't like to tell. She'd watched the young girl long enough to have a tender, protective feeling toward her.

This third day was Saturday. Margaret entertained some wild ideas of trying to saddle the horse and venture into the unfamiliar territory to find out about her brother, but her good sense told her this would be useless. She must wait a little longer. Some news would surely come soon. Resolutely she sat down to study the Sunday school lesson just as if nothing had disturbed her. She planned out everything for the next day, trying to think that her brother would surely return for Sunday. But her heart sank lower as the night came on once more. She left her supper, which Marna had carefully prepared, untasted on the table while she stood by the dark window looking down the road.

Philip's anger had carried him far toward his destination. When at last it cooled with his fatigue, he reflected on what might happen during his absence. He would have turned back, but his horse was weary and the day far spent. Besides, it would be foolish to go back now when he'd almost accomplished what he came to do. He needed only a few minutes with the man he was looking for; perhaps he could exchange horses, or give his a few hours' rest and then return. He hurried on, annoyed that it was getting so late.

He had some difficulty in finding the place. Several old landmarks had been removed by a fire, and it was quite dark before he reached the desolate ranch.

He didn't know how strong his desire was to return until he discovered he would be hindered. The man he came to see had gone to another ranch a few miles farther on and would probably not return for three or four days. It would be ridiculous to turn back, having taken this long journey for nothing. He must accomplish what he came for. He got a fresh horse and, taking only a quick supper, spurred his horse forward through the darkness, recklessly trusting his own knowledge of the country to bring him to the right place.

Of course he lost his way and pulled up at the place the next morning when the sun was two hours high, only to find that the man he was searching for had started back the afternoon before and must be at home by this time.

Another delay and another fresh horse, and he was on his way back, too weary to realize how long he'd been under a strain. When he reached the first ranch and found his man, he was so worn out that he dared not start home without a few hours' sleep. So, the business disposed of, he lay down to sleep, tormented by thoughts of Stephen and his own discarded trust.

But worn nature will take her revenge, and Philip didn't awaken until almost sunset on the second day. Then his senses returned sharply with a vision of Margaret, a dream perhaps or only his first waking notions. She seemed to be crying out in distress: *My brother! Stephen! Oh, save him, Philip!* And with the dream voice came a longing in his heart to hear her speak his name that way.

But he put this from him. He tried to remember he was angry with her and that this whole thing was her fault anyway for not following his advice. Then he recalled that she had no reason to follow his advice—a stranger. What did she know of him and his reasons for what he said? In some way she must be told, but how could he tell her?

All these thoughts rushed through his mind as he hunted up his own horse and quickly prepared to go home. He wouldn't have stopped to eat except that his host insisted.

During the long miles back, most of it in darkness, Philip was thinking and cursing himself for being so foolish to leave Stephen alone with his sister—and almost cursing God that such a state of things was possible.

Toward morning he approached the handful of buildings that constituted the village near their home. The horse quickened its pace, and familiar things urged the travelers on. Distant discordant sounds filled the air. A gunshot rang out now and again, but that wasn't unusual. Shots were as common as oaths in that neighborhood. They were a nightly occurrence, part of a gentleman's outfit, like his generosity and his pipe. The closer he got, the sounds resolved themselves into human voices, the deep bark of dogs, singing, the clinking of glasses, a slamming shutter, a rider galloping home after a night of revelry to strike terror into the heart of any who waited for him.

The muscles around Philip's heart tightened as a sickening thought came to him, and he put spurs to his willing beast, making the road disappear rapidly behind him.

Near the one open house in the village, where lights were still burning and the sounds were coming from, he drew rein, and the patient horse obeyed, having felt that anxious check to his rein before. He stopped under the window and listened. Then, rising in his saddle, he looked to make sure of what his heavy heart had told him.

There in the middle of the room, on a table, stood Stephen, his hair disheveled, his clothes awry, his blue eyes mad with a joyless mirth and his whole face idiotic without the soul that lived there. He had evidently been entertaining the company, and he was speaking as Philip looked.

"Jes' one more song, boys!" he drawled. "I got a go home to my sister. Poor little girl's all alone, all aloney. Zay, boys, now that's too bad, ain't it?" His voice trailed off into jibberish.

Great anger, horror and pity rose within Philip. Pity for the sister, anger and horror over her brother. He had seen Stephen like this before, sadly taken him away and brought him to himself, excusing him in his heart. But he'd never felt more than a passing disgust over the weakness of the man who put himself into such a condition. He operated on the principle that, if Stephen liked that sort of thing from life, why, of course he had a right to take it. But he always tried to save him from himself. Now, however, the thought of the trusting girl alone in the night waiting for him—how long had she waited?—while the brother she came to help and love bandied her name and her pity about among a set of drunken loafers—Philip stopped his thoughts short and sprang into action.

He usually entered such scenes and took possession of his partner in a quiet, careless way—but not this time. His soul was roused as great men's are when they must perform a deed of valor.

He strode into that maudlin company, tossing men right and left. They rose from the floor in resentment or reeled against the wall and shook trembling fists, reaching for their weapons. But Philip's wrath was powerful, and the men quailed before him.

He uttered one word between set teeth and white lips: "Fiends!"

Then he grabbed the shrinking Stephen firmly and dragged him from the table and from the room before the fiery men around him had realized and drawn their revolvers. One or two wild shots whistled harmlessly into the air after him, but he and Stephen were gone.

He put Stephen, already in a senseless state, on his horse and took him to a shanty he knew was empty. The rest of that night and through the brightness of Saturday he stayed guard over him.

He read to himself some stern lessons of life as he sat there studying the tainted comeliness of the face lying before him. All of Stephen's happy, winning qualities were hidden behind the awfulness of what the man had become. He had never noticed it. He'd simply borne with Stephen till he came out of one of these states and became his lively, companionable self again. Now Philip looked with disgust upon him. And the difference was that up on the hill five miles away sat a young woman whose trust and love the man before him had betrayed.

When Stephen had slept a long time, Philip brought water, washed his face and made him drink. He was determined that Stephen would be perfectly sober and as soon as possible, so they might get home and relieve the anxieties of the girl who waited there. But it was a stern face that Stephen gazed into from time to time, and it was a silent journey they took that night when darkness covered them.

As they neared the house Philip spoke only one sentence, in a tone Stephen would not likely disregard. "Be careful what you say to your sister!"

Stephen wondered what had happened since he left home and how many days he was away as he rode up to the house.

Margaret met them at the door, her face pale.

Philip spoke first, his tone anxious and earnest. "I'm afraid you've been lonely, Miss Halstead. I'm sorry it happened that way. You see, Steve thought he must come after me, and we were delayed because the man we went to see wasn't there. The ride was too much for Steve. He's played out, I'm afraid. He should go right to sleep. If you have any coffee, I'll take a cup to him. It'll do him good. No, he isn't sick, just used up, you know. Nothing to worry about."

Philip's voice was quite cheerful. If Margaret could have seen his face, she'd have wondered at his tone. But Margaret had been sitting in the dark, and it took a few minutes to light the lamp with her trembling fingers, shaking now from the released strain.

"Hope I didn't scare you, Margaret," Stephen said, his easy manner settling on him like an old coat he plucked from its familiar nail and put on. "You know one mustn't wait where duty calls. But I'll take Phil's advice, I guess, and turn in. I feel mighty seedy. All worn out with the long ride."

Philip returned soon from tending the horses and took the steaming coffee from Margaret's hand. As she handed it to him, she looked into his face.

"How about you, Mr. Earle? You look as if you needed the coffee more than Stephen."

The tender tone was almost too much for Philip after his recent grimness. It carried a note of his mother's voice when he used to come home with a bruise from a fall or a fight. He smiled faintly and said with earnestness, "Thank you."

When he stepped out from Stephen's room, he found that she had set him a tempting supper on one end of the table.

She hovered about, waiting on him until he was finished, and told him to sleep late in the morning when she said good night. Then she went to her room, buried her face in the pillow and cried. She didn't know why she was crying. It wasn't from trouble—perhaps relief. When she grew calm, she thanked God for saving her from some nameless trouble that she felt, but didn't understand, and begged Him again for help for tomorrow and the work she was going to try to do for Him.

Chapter 10

Sleep and its healing power settled down upon the little household late that Saturday night and lasted far into the morning.

When Margaret awoke, the sun shone across her floor, and a sense of relief shone into her heart. As she prepared for the day, awe filled her in remembering her plan. She didn't dare think of any words to speak, and she hadn't decided how she would introduce her plan to the expected guests. She hesitated as she recalled Byron's bold, handsome eyes and wondered whether he would be among those invited or if he was just Philip's friend. She shut her eyes and prayed she might think only of the message she would bring.

The two young men did as she told them and didn't wake up until almost noon. Margaret kept their breakfast waiting until it was too late, and then she hastened the dinner preparations; so the first meal they ate together was dinner.

After dinner Philip hurried to tend to the neglected horses and some matters at the barn, and Stephen threw himself on the couch. The day was chilly, and Marna had kindled a fire on the hearth. It crackled pleasantly, and Stephen was feeling the relief that comes after a throbbing headache has ceased. He picked up a book from his sister's case and began to read, as though he'd forgotten about his company. Margaret thought perhaps he didn't invite them after all, and it would be best not to speak about it. He was tired, and it would be much better for him.

She felt immensely relieved that her task, which at times assumed impossible proportions, would be put off indefinitely. Yet, she sensed a strange pang of disappointment, for her careful study of the lesson had revealed hidden, wonderful truths, which the Spirit had stirred a longing in her to impart to others. She wondered whether she could muster courage to suggest to Stephen that the two of them, and perhaps Philip, too, if he liked, study the lesson together. She was sitting shyly by the piano, watching her brother behind his book and contemplating whether she should ask him about it, when the door burst open and three young men stood on the threshold.

To be sure, they knocked loudly on the opening door, and their greeting was noisy and exuberant. Margaret stood up, startled. But they stopped as suddenly as they began and gazed about on the changed place. This room was unfamiliar to them, even though they'd climbed the hill many times to pass a jovial evening with Stephen. And the woman who stood quietly by the piano was a lady, and beautiful beyond question.

It was as if they came expecting summer weather and suddenly plunged into a magnificent snowbank. They were embarrassed and silent for the moment, just as the other two strangers had been. All the audacity of their brave, outlandish

Western apparel deserted them. Instinctively the men thought to defend themselves, and their hands involuntarily sought out their weapons. Not that they meant to draw them, only to feel the cold, hard steel reassuring them.

These three were raised as gentlemen, at least in appearance, but long ago forgot what the word meant. Perhaps it was harder for them, therefore, to understand the beauty of purity and art, having known it and wandered so far from its path, than if they'd never seen it.

They were speechless for a moment, not knowing how to adjust to the new position.

Stephen stepped over to the men. He was glad Philip was out of the way for now and hoped he'd stay away until things were going well.

"Welcome!" he said, waving his arm around the place as if it were his palace and he its king. "My sister, Margaret Halstead, gentlemen. Margaret, Bowman and Fletcher and Banks."

Margaret bowed in a stately way she had; it made her seem much taller than she was and kept at a distance any man she chose to keep so. Nevertheless, a welcoming smile appeared in her manner, which to the three strangers seemed like cool sunshine that had fallen their way and charmed them but didn't belong to them.

They entered and sat down, trying to speak naturally and easily. But a mist of formality surrounded them, and they couldn't drive it away. All but Banks.

Banks was small, slightly hard in his features, with an unfeeling slit of a mouth and hateful, twinkly black eyes that weren't large enough to see anything wonderful. He conveyed a sense of self-satisfaction that belonged to a much larger man. His collegiate career had been cut short by his compulsory graduation to an inebriate asylum and later to the West.

Banks attempted a remark to Margaret which would have caused Philip to sling him out the door if he'd been there. It was complimentary and coarse in the extreme. Fortunately, Margaret didn't understand it and stood in silent amazement at the shout of laughter that followed. She was glad when other guests entered the room, for she sensed something painful in the atmosphere. She looked for Stephen to stand beside her, but he was already slapping shoulders with a newcomer. Her gaze met Byron's bold, admiring eyes as he stepped forward and tried to take her hand in greeting, hoping to show the others his superior acquaintance with the queen of the occasion.

But Margaret drew her hand behind her and held him back with the gentle dignity of her greeting. She hadn't forgotten their last meeting and the words she'd spoken to him, and her glance reminded him reproachfully of it. He realized he mustn't expect to be her friend with that between them. The blood stole up his swarthy cheeks, and he stood back conquered, only to see Bennett—whom he knew to be no better than he was, but whom she didn't know—greeted with a welcoming smile.

Bennett's white eyelashes dropped beneath the radiant smile, and his freckles were submerged in red. He sat down hard in a Morris chair that was several inches lower than he expected, while Banks caroled out a silly song befitting the moment. This happened to be Banks' role—to bring in appropriate songs and sayings at the wrong minute and cause a laugh.

Margaret looked about the room bewildered. The place seemed to be swarming with large, bold, loud men. She remembered Philip's warning and gasped. One moment more, and she thought her head would whirl dizzily. She must get command of the situation or fail. Surely her Strength would not desert her now, even though she'd made a mistake. She lifted her soul to God and wished while she prayed that Philip would come in. Philip somehow seemed so strong.

Only seven men were invited, though they looked like more. They were for the most part the pick of the country thereabout, at least among Stephen's friends. He'd meant to be careful on Philip's account, for he knew Philip wouldn't tolerate anyone outrageous. But his discretion forsook him with his first taste of liquor, and two worse than the rest had crept into the band. Well for Margaret that she was ignorant of this.

"Well," began Stephen, and Margaret saw that now was her opportunity if she wasn't to let this strange gathering slip from her control.

"My brother asked you to come this afternoon because he thought you might enjoy some music and reading," she said in a clear voice that commanded instant attention, "and I'll be very glad if I can help you do so."

Then she smiled on them like an undesired benediction, and each man dropped his eyes to his feet and then raised them, wondering why he dropped them.

"Won't you all sit down and make yourselves comfortable?" she went on pleasantly. "We hope you'll feel at home."

"Be it ever so humble, there's no place like home," sang out Banks flippantly.

"Shut up, Banks!" said Bennett, turning redder and glaring from under his white eyelashes at his neighbor.

"I want to get acquainted with my brother's friends, of course," went on Margaret, not heeding this accompaniment to her words. She suddenly had the feeling she was holding a pack of hounds at bay. She must say the right thing at once and work quickly, or lose her cause.

"I don't know what kind of music you like best, so perhaps you'll excuse me today if I play my own favorites. I'll begin at once, so we'll have plenty of time for them all, because in a while I want you all to sing."

They watched her as they might a new star in a theatre, wondering, awed by the strangeness for the moment, but not permanently. It takes a great deal to awe a Western cowboy.

Margaret turned with a sweep of her white skirt and sat down at the piano.

As she did, she caught a glimpse of Philip standing in the doorway, his rugged face lined with disapproval and anxiety. It spurred her to do her best; laying her fingers upon the keys, she imparted her own spirit to them.

Some music stood on the rack before her. It wasn't what she intended to play first, but it would do as well as anything. She mustn't waste any more time in starting, for Philip's face looked capable of almost any action with sufficient cause.

It was Handel's "Largo" that sounded throughout the room with a swelling, tender strain. She thought perhaps it wasn't the right selection for hypnotizing her audience, but she put her soul into it. If music could express sacred and true things, then her music should do so. But music of any kind was such a rare treat and so unique that, if she'd known it, she might have played a common scale and held her audience until the strangeness wore off.

She gave them no time, however, to grow restless. She glided from one thing to the next, now a great burst of triumph and now a tender, sympathetic melody, and all of them connected with worship in her childhood's church at home. Instrumental music might not convey anything of a Sabbath nature to these untamed men, but it certainly could be no worse than no attempt at it, and she was finding her way.

Philip stood like a grim sentinel in the doorway. The company felt his shadow and resented it, but they were engrossed with the music at first. Philip couldn't let himself enjoy it. He stood as it were above it and let it break like waves about his feet. He felt he must, or some wave might engulf them all.

He watched their faces like a watchdog eyes intruders, mistrusting, glowering, a growl already in his throat.

The dreamlike state the girl had charmed them into hadn't touched him. He was guarding her.

Suddenly she felt the pressure of emotions too strong for her. With a chord or two she dealt "one imperial thunderbolt that scalps your naked soul," as Emily Dickinson has put it, and stopped.

They caught their breath and, emerging from the charm, turned toward Philip to take their revenge for his attitude.

But Margaret was alert now and sensed a growing disturbance in the air. She moved quickly.

"You must be thirsty," she said, unconsciously using a term that meant more to them than she imagined. "I have some tea. Stephen, please call Marna to bring the kettle, and, Philip, will you pass the cups?"

She gently deferred in her tone to Philip, almost as if she asked his pardon and admitted he was right about what he told her.

Something more was in her tone, a pleading for him to stand by and help her out of this scrape into which she allowed herself to go.

Philip's soul heard and responded, and his quiet compliance sustained her throughout the afternoon. It was as if there were some unspoken understanding between them.

The men watched her curiously as she moved about the room, collecting thin, little dishes, the likes of which some had never seen and others had almost forgotten. There was enough unexpected and interesting to keep them moderately subdued, although a muttered oath or coarsely turned expression passed about now and again, and Banks tried a joke about the tea which didn't take very well.

Margaret, however, was happily ignorant of much of this, though she felt the general pulse of the gathering fairly accurately.

The tea came soon, for Marna had obeyed orders implicitly and hovered near the door with a curious, troubled expression and shaking head. With the tea were served sugary cakes, olives, salted almonds and dainty sandwiches.

The whole menu was just what Margaret would have used at home with her own friends. She knew no other way. Extravagant and unusual? Oh, certainly, but she didn't realize this, and the very strangeness of it renewed the charm she broke when she ceased playing and kept the wild, raucous spirits quiet till she had the opportunity for which she prayed.

The delicious treats vanished as dew before the sun. The capacity of the company seemed unlimited. The entire stock of sweet things from Margaret's carefully packed tin boxes would scarcely have been enough to satisfy such boundless appetites.

They eat as if they're at a Sunday school picnic, thought Margaret, laughing behind the screen. She waited a minute to catch her breath before going out to try her hand at the most daring move of her program.

Then she looked across to where Philip stood watching her faithfully and saw that he was eating nothing. She motioned him to her and gave him with her own hands a cup of tea. It was well she gave it behind the screen; if the others had seen it, a bitter rivalry would have begun at once for favors from the lady's hand.

He took it from her as one might take an unexpected blessing and drank it almost reverently. Then he glanced up to thank her, but she was gone. He saw her standing near the piano again, surrounded by palms, her soft white dress setting her apart from the whole room and her golden hair making a halo about her head. The rays of the setting sun barely touched her with its burnished blessing like a benediction upon her work. Philip felt, as he looked, that she was surrounded by some angelic guard and needed no help from him. His stern expression relaxed, and in its place came one of amazement.

She was talking now in low, pleasant tones, as if these men were all her personal friends. Each man felt honored separately and dropped his gaze that the other might not know.

She was telling them in a few words about her home and how she came out there to her brother since she was alone in the world now. She was putting herself at their mercy, but she was also putting them on their honor as men, if they had any such thing as honor. Philip was doubtful about that, but he listened and wondered.

Then she told them about the first Sabbath she spent there and how shocked and disappointed she was to find no church or Sabbath services held nearby. She told them how she missed this. They couldn't help but believe her sincerity, though such a state of mind was beyond their understanding. And she spoke of her Sabbath school class at home and how she loved the hour spent with them, until each man wished he might be a small boy for the time being and offer her a class.

"I haven't asked my brother if I may," she said with a girlish smile, turning toward Stephen as he sat uncomfortably in the corner. She felt intuitively that Stephen would count it a disgrace to be implicated in this manner and thus honorably exonerated him. "But I'm going to ask if you would help me make up for this loss I've felt. Perhaps some of the rest of you have felt it too."

Here she gave a searching glance around the circle of sunburnt faces.

"I wonder if you'll help."

One or two straightened up and looked as if they wanted to assent, but Margaret went quickly on. She didn't want to be interrupted now till she was finished; otherwise she might not have the courage to do so.

"I'm going to ask if you'll help me have a Sunday school, or Bible service, or something of that sort. I'll try to be the teacher unless you know of someone better—"

There was a low growl of dissent at the idea that anyone could equal her, and Margaret flushed a little, knowing it was meant for her encouragement.

"We couldn't do as much as they do at home in the East, but it would be keeping the Sabbath a little bit, and I think it would help us all to be better. Don't you?"

She raised her eyes, at last submitting the question to them. The blood mounted slowly in each face before her, while shame crept up under it. When had anyone there thought he wanted to be helped to be better?

"Now will you help me?" she asked in a sweet, pleading voice and then sat down to await their decision.

Chapter 11

B ut shame does not sit easily upon those like Banks. He roused himself to shake it off; he seldom failed to do so. He saw an opportunity in the intense silence that filled the room.

I am a little Sunday-school scholar, lah, lah,
I dearly love my pa and ma, ma, ma, ma;
I dearly love my teacher, too, too, too, too,
And do whatever she tells me to—to, to, to,
Teacher, teacher, why am I so happy, happy—

He chanted the words rapidly in his most irresistible tone and expected to shake up the audience and turn the whole gathering into a farce. But he sang only so far when strong hands pinioned him from behind, gagged him with a handkerchief and would have removed him swiftly from the place. But Margaret's voice broke the stillness that succeeded the song. Her face was white, for she realized she'd been ridiculed; but her voice was pleasant and earnest.

"Oh, not that, please, Philip. Let him go," she said. "I'm sure he won't do it again, and I don't think he quite understood. I don't want to urge anything you wouldn't all like, of course. I want it very much myself, though, and I thought perhaps you'd enjoy it too. It seems so lonely out here to me, without any church."

She sat down, unable to say more. It must be left with God now, for she'd done all she could.

Then Byron stood up. It was his opportunity to redeem himself.

"My lady," he began gallantly, "I ain't much on Sunday schools myself, never having worked along that line. But I think I can speak for the crowd if I say that this whole shootin' match is at your disposal to do with as you choose. If Sunday school's your game, we'll play at it. I can sit up and hold a book myself, and I'll agree to see that the rest do the same if that'll do you any good. As for any better teacher, I'm sure the fellows'll all agree there's not one to be found within six hundred miles could hold a candle to you, so far as looks goes. As for the rest, we can stand 'most anything if *you* give it to us."

It was a long speech for Byron, and he was nearly distressed three times in the course of it because of some familiar oath he felt he needed to strengthen his words.

Philip, as he held the struggling, sputtering Banks, glared at Byron threateningly during it all and thought he might have to gag the entire crowd before he was through. But Byron stumbled into his chair at last. Margaret wanted to laugh and cry both and wondered what would come next. Then a wild cheer of assent broke out from the five other guests, and Margaret knew she'd won her chance to try.

"Oh, thank you!" was all she could manage to say. But she put meaning into her words, and the men felt they'd done a good thing.

"Then we'll start now," said Margaret, almost choking over the thought that she was really going to try to teach those rough fellows a Bible lesson. "Mr. Byron, will you pass that pile of singing books? And let's sing 'Nearer, My God, to Thee.' You must all have heard that, and I'm sure you can sing. Philip, please give this book to your friend, and release him so he can help us sing." She was even brave enough to smile into Banks' hard eyes.

Philip took the book and let Banks go as he might give a kick and a bone to a vagrant dog, then watched the remarkable Sunday school superintendent in amazement.

And they could sing. Oh, yes, they could sing! A volume of song poured forth that would have shamed many Eastern church choirs. They sang in the same way they would have herded cattle or forded a stream, from the pleasure of the action itself; and they sang because they were trying to help out a lonely, pretty girl, who for some mysterious reason was to be helped by this task.

As she played and listened to the words, Margaret had an overwhelming desire for them to know the meaning of those words and sing them with sincerity.

The lesson, the same she would have taught if she'd been at home with her class of young boys, began with the thrilling statement: "There is therefore no condemnation to them that are in Christ Jesus, who walk not after the flesh, but after the Spirit."

They listened respectfully while she read the lesson, but the words conveyed little to their minds. When she talked about a prisoner condemned to death and a pardon coming just in time to save him, it's doubtful they connected it with the words she read or that they even recognized them as the same when she repeated them later after making the meaning clear.

She used simple language with everyday stories for illustrations, for she was used to teaching the small boys. But a doctor of theology could not have more plainly told the great doctrines of sin and atonement than she did to those men whose lives were steeped in sin and to whom the thought of conviction of sin, or of condemnation, seldom if ever came.

They felt as if they'd suddenly dropped into a new world as they listened. Some of them fidgeted, and some of them wondered, but all were attentive.

She didn't make the lesson too long. For one thing, her rapid heart would have prevented it. She was afraid she wouldn't have enough to make the lesson a respectable length. But when she began, the need of the souls before her appealed to her so strongly that she found words to bring the truth to them.

Philip looked around at the hard faces, softened now by something new and strange that had come over their feelings. He felt her strength and knew her way had been right; yet he feared for her, was jealous for her and hated all who dared to come against her.

What power enabled her to hold them? Was it the mere power of her pure womanhood? Or the fascination of her beauty? No, for that would have affected these men in another way. They would have admired openly, but they wouldn't have been quiet or respectful.

Another thought kept forcing itself into his mind. If the God she was preaching, whom she claimed as her Father, should prove indeed to be the one true God, was he, Philip Earle, condemned? But this thought Philip tossed aside.

"I've been thinking," said the teacher, "as I sat here talking, how beautiful it would be if Jesus Christ were still on the earth so we could see Him. What if He should walk into this room right now?"

Involuntarily each man lifted his eyes to look around, and Philip with the rest.

"He would come in here, just as He used to come into households in those Bible times, and we would make room for Him, and you would all be introduced."

Some of the men shuffled their feet restlessly.

"And you would all see just what kind of a man Jesus is," continued the sweet voice. "You couldn't help admiring Him. You'd see at once how gracious He is. You wouldn't be—I hope—I think—none of you would be like those people who wanted to crucify Him—though we do crucify Him sometimes in our lives, it's true. But if we could see Him and know Him it would be different. He'd call you to be His disciples, just as He called those other disciples of His, Philip and Andrew and Matthew and John and Peter and the rest."

Unconsciously, Philip Earle flushed and started at his name. She'd never called him Philip until that afternoon, and he thought for a moment she was speaking to him now.

Others looked conscious too; for Bennett's name was Peter, and Fletcher's name was Andrew, and two others bore the name of John. Because of these little coincidences they were even more impressed by what she said.

"And what would you answer Him?" She paused, and the room was still for just a minute.

"I'm going to tell you what I want for you all," she said. "It is that you shall know Jesus Christ, for to know Him is to love Him and serve Him. Suppose, as we study in this class, that you try to think of yourselves as men like those disciples of old, whom He has called, and that you're getting acquainted with Him and finding out whether you want to answer His call. Because until you know Him you can't decide if you'd care enough for Him for that. Will you try to carry out my idea?"

She had struggled a great deal about what to do about prayer. It didn't seem right to have a service without it, and she didn't feel that she could pray. It was unlikely that the others would be willing to do so. She had settled on asking them to join in the Lord's Prayer until she saw them, and then she knew that wouldn't do. She even doubted whether many of them knew it. She'd decided to go without prayer, but now in the moment she followed her heart's longing to speak to her Father.

"Please let's all bow our heads for just a minute and stay quiet before God," she said. And the silence of that minute, in which heartbeats counted out seconds, was one whose memory did not fade from the minds of the men present through long years afterward.

Painful stillness! Banks couldn't bear it. It seemed to single out his weak flippancy and hold it in judgment. He wanted to escape, to break forth into something ridiculous, and yet he was held silent by some unseen Power, while the seconds rolled slowly around him.

"Oh, Jesus, let us all feel Your presence here, amen!" said Margaret as if she were talking to a friend.

Then she turned quickly to the piano. And before the raising of eyes, that dared not look their comrades in the face lest they should be discovered in prayer, soft chords filled the room, and Margaret's clear voice rang out in song.

"Abide with me," she sang; "fast falls the eventide."

The room had grown dusky, lighted only by the glowing fire in the fireplace. Philip had quietly replenished it from time to time with pine knots, sending fitful light on the touched faces of the men, while they sat in close attention to the music.

A few more chords, and the melody changed.

Weary of earth, and laden with my sin,
I look at heaven and long to enter in;
But there no evil thing may find a home,
And yet I hear a voice that bids me, "Come,"

So vile I am, how dare I hope to stand
In the pure glory of that holy land?
Before the whiteness of that throne appear?
Yet there are hands stretched out to draw me near.

She played gentle chords here. She had a way with the piano, making it speak from different parts of the room and say the things she was feeling. The listeners half looked up as if they felt hands stretched out to them.

The clear voice went on:

It is the voice of Jesus that I hear,
His are the hands stretched out to draw me near,
And His the blood that can for all atone
And set me faultless there before the throne.

O Jesus Christ, the righteous! live in me,
That, when in glory I Thy face shall see,
Within the Father's house my glorious dress
May be the garment of Thy righteousness.

Then Thou wilt welcome me, O righteous Lord;
Thine all the merit, mine the great reward;
Mine the life won, and Thine the life laid down,
Thine the thorn-plaited, mine the righteous, crown.

"And now will you all sing a few minutes?" asked their leader, turning toward them in the firelight. Her face reflected the feeling of the prayer with which her song had closed.

"Philip, will you give us some light? Now let's sing 'I Need Thee Every Hour' before you go home."

They growled out their bottled-up feelings into that song and made it ring out, till Marna crept around and peered into the window to watch the strange sight. She stood there muttering, for she never saw such a miracle before. Perhaps Missie could work charms on even her, if she could make those wild fellows sit quietly and sing that way.

And then they were dismissed.

"I'll expect you next Sunday at the same time," she said, smiling. "Thank you so much for helping. It's been so good, almost like a Sunday at home. I have a fine story and a new song for you next week."

And they went out quietly beneath the stars, mounting their horses in silence, and rode away. One attempt on Banks' part came to a dismal failure. Philip, standing at the door, heard the silly, swaggering voice rollicking through the night: "I dearly love my teacher, too, too, too, too," and Bennett's unmistakable roar, "Shut up, you fool—can't you?" as the song ended abruptly.

Byron dared to linger a moment by the teacher's side. With an almost earnest expression on his face he asked, "Aren't you ever going to forgive me?"

"You must go to the One you insulted for forgiveness," answered Margaret seriously. "When you've made it right with Him, I'll be your friend."

Then Byron dropped his head and walked away silently.

Philip and Margaret turned then and found themselves alone. They could hear Stephen slamming around in his room, the thud of first one boot and then the other thrown noisily across the floor. He was evidently not in a good humor.

Margaret realized sadly that through the whole afternoon her thoughts were taken up more with the others than with the brother she came to help. Had the message reached him at all?

Seeing Philip standing in the door watching her, with awe still upon his face, her expression changed. She walked over to where he stood and, putting out one hand, touched him gently on the sleeve. "I didn't understand," she said simply. "You were right. I should have listened to you."

He glanced down at the little hand with fingertips just touching the cuff of his sleeve, as if it were some heavenly flower fallen upon him by mistake. Then he said, his voice shaking, "No, I'm the one who didn't understand. You've been *wonderful!*"

Chapter 12

The days passed busily now. The odd little dwelling on the hill grew in beauty and interest with every passing hour. Stephen did his part and seemed pleasant enough about it, although the first few days after the Sunday school he was strangely moody and quiet. Margaret couldn't tell whether or not he was pleased with what she did.

Now she lured the two young men to gather around the hearth in the evenings while she read out loud to them from books that touched their life experiences and made them forget themselves for a little while. Margaret's gift of singing was equalled only by her ability to read well; and no dialect, be it Southern or Scottish, was too difficult for her to enter into its spirit and interpret it for her readers. They'd been out of the world so long that some of the best books people raved about for a few days and then forgot had passed them by entirely. These were among her favorites, and she brought them out and read them, while the two listened and were moved. They said nothing except to laugh appreciatively at some fine bit of humor.

Thus she read *Beside the Bonnie Brier Bush*, *A Singular Life*, *Black Rock* and *The Sky Pilot*, and then went further back to George Macdonald and chose some of his beautiful Scottish stories, *Malcolm*, *The Marquis of Lossie* and *Snow and Heather*. Over this last they were as silent as with the rest, but now and then Margaret noticed that Stephen covered his face with his hand and Philip turned his eyes away from the light while she was reading about the "Bonnie Man."

This was all new to the two lonely fellows, who were used to making companions of the woods and fields and beasts, and letting life go for little. This world of the imagination peopled life more richly. But whenever a book was finished Stephen would grow restless and sometimes go off on his horse, and Philip too would disappear. When they returned—late the same night or perhaps after a day passed—Margaret couldn't tell which of the two, if either, had started first, and her heart grew heavy.

She rode with Stephen or with both of them quite often now and was getting to be an expert horsewoman. She knew the country and had seen some beautiful views. But not once did either escort take her near the railroad station where she arrived or point out what she imagined must be the semblance of a village. When she asked, they always put her off, and she wondered why.

With some trepidation she faced the next Sabbath, half fearful her class would come again, half fearful they wouldn't. But they all came and brought two or three others. Philip didn't much need to stand guard, as he did, at the rear, ready to jump should the slightest insult be given to the teacher.

The rough scholars had odd ways and were as undisciplined as city raga-muffins. But they respected the beautiful girl who chose to amuse herself by amusing them, and they listened quietly enough.

After the newness wore off they had an air of humoring her whimsical wishes. It pleased them to take it this way. It helped them to humble themselves into respectful attention. But once in a while some word would strike home to their hearts. Then would come that restless shuffling of the feet, dropping the eyes and avoiding one another's gaze, as each tucked his own past away within his breast and imagined no one knew.

They grew to love the singing and put their whole souls into the hymns they sang together. But they preferred when Margaret sang to them the songs that sometimes reminded them of the days when they were innocent and pure.

Always, too, there was that solemn hush, that moment of silent prayer, before the one trembling but trustful sentence Margaret spoke to God. At times, as the weeks went by, this or that man would find himself saying over in his own heart that sentence she prayed the week before. She didn't often use the same sentence. But it was always something that touched the heart's experience or impressed the lesson's thought upon the mind.

The first prayer she uttered in that house would always remain with Philip—"Oh, Jesus, let us all feel Your presence here." And, as he looked about the glowing room, it seemed as if a Presence had entered there and come to stay.

He often thought, as he waited for the evening reading to begin, of how that room looked the night her letter came and how much he hated the thought of her coming. Now light would go out of his life if she went away! She didn't know that. She never would, most likely. She was as far above him as the angels of heaven, but her coming there had been like a gift from heaven. Would it last? Would she stay and keep it up? And Stephen, sitting on the other side of the hearth! What were his thoughts as he alternated between his fits of moody silence and lively restlessness?

A day came when Philip and Stephen were mending fences where the cattle had broken them down. In the afternoon Margaret put on a thin white dress with a scarlet jacket and wandered out to where they were working.

The day was bright and warm for late October and hot in the sun. The light scarlet jacket was almost unnecessary, but it intensified the scarlet in the landscape. So she came, a bright bit of color into the routine of their work.

She meant to talk to Stephen. In her heart she was keeping some precious words she meant to say to him as soon as an opportunity offered. She longed to see him give himself to Christ. As yet she saw no sign he even heard the call to become a disciple.

But Stephen was in his most silent mood. He answered her in monosyllables and at last gathered up his tools and said he was going to the other end of the lot. She saw it would do no good to follow him, for he was not in a spirit to talk. Sad and confused, she walked slowly along the fence toward the house. Until she came close to where he stood, she hadn't noticed that Philip was working in the way where she would have to walk.

He stood up, welcomed her with a smile and offered her a seat on a low part of the fence where some of the rails were taken down.

It came to her that perhaps her message today was for Philip rather than Stephen, so she climbed up and sat down.

He stood leaning against the supporting stakes near her, and the breeze caught a fragment of her muslin dress and blew it gently against his hand. It was a pleasant touch, and his heart thrilled with the joy of her presence so near him. The muslin ruffle reminded him, with its touch, of the wisp of hair that had blown across his face in the dark the night she had come.

An overpowering desire to tell her he loved her welled up in him, but he put it aside. She was as cool as a lily dropped here upon this wayside, and she talked with him frankly. But there was something in their conversation this afternoon more like their first brief talk about the moon than there had been since the night she came. She seemed to understand what he was saying, and he to interpret her feeling of the things in nature all about them. He dropped his tools and stood beside her, willing to enjoy this precious moment of her companionship.

She looked across the fields to the valley, the other hills beyond and a purple mountain in the distance, while he followed her gaze.

"You see a picture in all that," he said briefly, as if reading her thoughts.

She smiled. "Was it for this that you gave up your home and friends and came out here to stay?"

His face darkened. "No," he said, "I was a fool. I thought life's happiness was in one bright jewel, and I lost mine."

"Oh," she said. "And when you found out it wasn't so, why didn't you go back?"

"Perhaps I was a fool still," he said drearily. He wouldn't tell her why he stayed.

Each looked at the dreamy mountains in their autumn haze in silence for a few minutes, but neither noticed much of what was to be seen.

"There's one jewel you might have which can't be lost. It's the pearl of great price. Do you know what I mean?"

"Yes, I understand," he answered, deeply moved, "but I'm afraid that would be impossible."

"Oh, why?" said Margaret, with pain in her voice. "Don't you care the least in the world to have it? I thought I saw longing in your face last Sunday when we talked about Jesus Christ. Was I mistaken?"

Then she'd watched him and cared. Last Sunday! The thought throbbed in his throat with joy. He lifted his hand and laid it firmly on the bit of fluttering muslin on the rail beside him. It was the only way he dared to show his joy that she cared even so much.

"No, you weren't mistaken," he said, his voice choking with sincerity. "I would give all I own to feel as you do, but I can't believe your Jesus is more than a man of history. If it were true, and I could believe it, I would be His slave. I would go all around the world searching for Him till I found Him if He were upon earth. But I can't believe. I wouldn't shake your sweet belief. It's good to know you feel it. It makes your life a blessing to everyone you meet. Don't let my skepticism trouble you or make you doubt."

"Oh, it couldn't!" said Margaret quickly. "You couldn't shake my belief in Jesus any more than you could shake my belief in my mother or my father. Because I have known them. If you told me I hadn't had a mother, and she wasn't really good and kind to me, I'd just smile and pity you because you never knew her. But I *have,* you know. I don't blame you, for you've never known Jesus. You haven't felt His help or almost seen Him face to face. You don't know what it is to talk with Him and know in your heart He answers, or to be helped by Him in trouble. You think I imagine all this. I understand. But you see I *know* that I don't imagine it, for I have *felt*. You may feel too, if you will."

"I wish I might," said Philip with a sigh.

" 'And ye shall find me, when ye shall search for me with all your heart,' " quoted Margaret softly. "And there's another promise for someone like you. God knew you would feel so, and He prepared a way. 'He that doeth His will shall know of the doctrine, whether it be of God—' "

"Do you really think that's true?" asked Philip, looking into her eager face.

"I know it is. I've tried it myself," she replied.

There was silence then, broken only by the whisperings of some dying leaves among themselves.

"Won't you take that promise and claim it, just as you'd take a bank bill that promised to pay so much money to you and present it for payment? Won't you do it—Philip?"

She'd never called him that before, except the first day of the Sunday school. She seemed to have done it then as a half-apology to him for not following his advice. After that day she returned to the formal "Mr. Earle" when she addressed him by name at all.

Philip started and crushed the bit of muslin between his fingers.

He was deeply touched.

"How could I?" he asked softly.

Margaret caught her breath. She felt the answer to her prayer coming.

"Just begin to search for Him with all your heart, as if you *knew* He was somewhere. You've never tried to find Him, have you?"

"No."

"Then try. Kneel down tonight, and tell Him just how you feel about it, just as you've told me. Talk to Him as if you could see Him. You may not feel Him right away; but eventually, when your whole heart is in it, you'll begin to know. He'll speak to you in some way, until you're quite sure. Take as many other ways to find out, too, as you can—not that it matters so much, though, about convincing your mere reason. When you've felt Him near, you'll know against any kind of reasoning. But take the way of talking with Him. It's the quickest way to find Him."

"But shouldn't I feel like a hypocrite, talking to One I don't believe in, whose existence I have no assurance of?"

"No, for you said you wanted to find Him. It would be reaching out for what your heart desires, just as the untaught heathen do."

Philip flushed.

"You think I'm a heathen," he said reproachfully.

"No, Philip, only a child of God, lost in the dark. I want you to find the way back."

"But suppose I do this, and nothing comes of it. Then you'll be disappointed."

"What does that have to do with it?" she said, waving her hand as if to put aside any thought of herself. "Something will come of it. No soul ever went to God in that way and nothing came of it. Besides, there's more you can do. There's the promise. 'He that doeth His will.' After you come to Him and tell Him you want to find Him, but you can't believe, and you ask Him to show you how, you can set to work to do His will. For through doing what He wants you to do, part of Himself will be revealed. Now will you go to Him and tell Him all about it, tonight, and begin to try to find Him? Will you?"

Philip had drawn his hat low over his eyes and stood looking off to the crimson sky. The sun had sunk low as they talked, and the air was growing chilly. Margaret, in her intentness, didn't know how grateful she was for the warmth of the little scarlet jacket. She waited silently and prayed while Philip thought.

At last he turned to her and held out his hand with a serious smile.

"I will try," he said.

"With all your heart?" asked Margaret, as she laid her small white hand in his.

"With all my heart," he said reverently, as he looked into her eyes and pressed the hand he held.

Margaret let him know by the quick pressure of her handclasp how glad she was.

"And I shall be praying too," she said softly.

Philip's heart quickened. It seemed to him like a holy tryst.

The young man picked up the idle tools, and they walked slowly toward the house through the twilight. They said little more. They were thinking of what was said and promised. It was enough to walk quietly together thus and know what had passed. Stephen wasn't in sight. He must have gone to the house sometime before.

But when they came in and were ready to sit down to supper, he hadn't come yet. Philip went out to call him.

Margaret listened to his full, deep shouts, with purpose in them. They grew more distant, and she thought he must have gone back to the lot to see what was keeping Stephen. She waited a long time by the door, and they didn't come. Then she went in to search out the book she wanted to read to them that evening. Marna was keeping supper hot in the kitchen.

Suddenly the sound of rapid horse hoofs was heard down the road. She ran to the door and looked out. Down against the western sky, which still kept a faint blush from the sunset, she saw a hatless rider, galloping, etched for a moment against the sky. Then he was gone.

A sudden fear filled her heart. She put her hand to her throat and rushed to the kitchen.

"Marna," she cried, "did my brother come to the house before we did?"

The old woman shook her head.

"Brother rode off fast 'for dark," she said doggedly.

"Marna," said the girl, catching the old woman's arm in a grasp that must have been painful, "you talked about brothers drinking. I want you to tell me the truth if you know anything about it. Does my brother go where they drink?"

The old woman shut her lips, and a stubborn look came into her eye. She didn't reply.

"Quick! Tell me at once," said Margaret, stamping her foot in her excitement. "Do they both drink? Is that why Stephen and Philip go away so suddenly sometimes? Do they both drink?"

"No!" said the old woman quickly. "Not both drink. One all right. Pretty good man. He take care. Bring other home. Heap good man."

"Which one, Marna?"

"Big man, heap good," answered Marna.

"And my brother drinks?" demanded Margaret, the sad truth hers now. "Answer me."

The old woman hung her head and nodded. It was as if she felt responsible.

Margaret let the woman's arm fall and stood still for one brief minute with her hand upon her heart, too frightened to cry out, too bewildered even to frame a prayer. But her heart was waiting before God to know what to do. Then swiftly she turned and, snatching up her scarlet jacket as she ran, fled toward the barn.

The old woman looked up to try to say something comforting and saw her vanish through the open door. She hobbled after her, some faint idea of protection coming to her withered senses. She found her in the barn with white, set face, struggling with the buckles of the saddle girth. The two empty stalls beside the one remaining horse had confirmed her fears.

The poor old horse was left, for Philip needed the best in his chase through the night. Margaret had never ridden this horse, but she didn't stop to think of that.

"Buckle this!" she ordered, as Marna entered the barn, and she held the lantern that Philip had left lighted to find his own saddle.

"Missie no go out 'lone," pleaded Marna after she did the bidding of the stern little voice. "Missie get lost. Big man find brother. Bring home. Missie stay with Marna."

"I must go," said Margaret quietly with terrible intensity in her voice. She swung herself into the saddle without stopping to think, as she usually did, how she was ever to get up to that great height. And she was doing it alone now.

"Now hand me the lantern!" she exclaimed, and Marna obeyed, her hand trembling. Tears from the long-dried fountains of her soul were running down her cheeks.

The old horse seemed to catch her spirit and started off snorting as if he felt battle in the air. Some instinct carried him after the others who had sped along that road only a few minutes before. Or perhaps he'd gone that way before so many times he could think of only one direction to take as he flew along.

Margaret held her seat firmly, grasping the lantern and the bridle with one hand, and tried to think and pray. The night wind gently swept about her, protectingly, as if it thought she needed guarding.

Chapter 13

Margaret forgot her fears of former rides, that the horse might stumble or be frightened, or the saddle slip or she be thrown. Even the dark had lost its terror.

Somewhere the road cut away at its outer edge and fell sharply down to a great depth. She might even be near it now, and any moment the horse's feet might slip over the precipice. But her heart was steady. The Father was watching. She must find her brother.

Why she felt strongly impressed that she must go herself and not wait for Philip to find Stephen, Margaret perhaps couldn't have told. It may have been a wish to see Stephen's danger for herself. Possibly, too, it was fear for Philip. Were Marna's words true? "The big man no drink." Oh, what comfort if she might be sure of that! What a tower of strength Philip would then become!

Riding and praying and trusting God, she was carried safely through a dangerous shortcut that Philip, knowing and fearing, had avoided. She galloped onto the main road only a moment after Philip passed the spot.

The moon stood out like a silver thread hung low and useless against the horizon. It made little difference in the darkness.

Margaret was anxious to catch up with Philip if possible, or at least get within sight of him. It wouldn't do to catch him too soon or he would send her back, and that she couldn't bear. So she pushed on and after a short time heard the sound of his horse and caught glimpses of a dark form riding hard.

Eventually she emerged on a bridge across a deep gully; how deep she couldn't see as she peered down for one awful glimpse, then closed her eyes and didn't look again. It was too late to turn back. The way was scarcely wide enough for that, and the bridge swayed back and forth with the horse upon it.

She held her breath as if to lessen her weight and dared not think until she felt the horse's feet touch solid ground. Then behind her she heard a snap, as sharp as if some giant tree had parted, and something, a bit of timber from the rail, perhaps, fell far below.

If the bridge had been one foot longer, or the horse going a little slower, horse and rider might have been lying down below in that sea of dark trees. The lantern slipped from her trembling hand and crashed on the road. But the horse flew on, frightened, perhaps, by the danger he must have felt.

But Philip didn't cross the swaying bridge that was discarded sometime ago. Further down the road he crossed by the new bridge and didn't know of the rider rushing through such profound dangers.

He heard the crashing of the falling rail and the sound of flying hoofs a moment later. He checked his horse, wondering who could be riding behind him. For a moment the possibility that Stephen didn't get ahead of him, after all, but tried to trick him by going another way, passed through his mind. But he looked back and saw only the darkness and heard the steady thud of the horse's feet. It wasn't like the gait of Stephen's horse. He pushed on, but occasionally he halted, pursued by the feeling that he should wait till that rider caught up with him.

Then in the darkness the lights of the village twinkled below him. In a few minutes he would reach his journey's end. He could see the glare of the saloon lights and almost hear the tinkle of glasses and the sliding of wooden chairs on the wooden floor. He paused again, for the other horse was very near now.

Out of the night he heard his name called once, in a wild, frightened cry, like a sob, as if someone's breath was almost gone.

"Philip!"

He stopped and waited as the horse raced toward him, something white taking shape upon its back. Then he saw the girl, her face white like her dress, her hair loosened by the ride, no hat to hold it back.

One word he spoke.

"Margaret!"

He'd never used her name before in speaking to her. He didn't know he used it now. But she did, even in her fear, and it gave her courage and renewed her strength.

"Don't stop! Keep going!" she cried. Her horse almost swept by him, and he was forced to start his own horse again to stay beside her. "Don't lose time. I know all about it now. Let's hurry!"

"But, Margaret, you mustn't go!" he cried, putting out his hand to catch the bridle. "Why did you come? And how? You didn't cross the broken bridge!"

"It broke just after we got across, I think," she shuddered. "But don't think about it now. I'm here. I can't go back alone, and you mustn't turn back with me. Let's hurry on to save Stephen."

"But you can't go down there. It isn't safe for a woman."

"I'm going, Philip. I'm going to help my brother. And God is with us. There's no danger." In some way she imparted her eagerness to the old horse, and before Philip knew what she was doing she flew down the road far ahead of him.

It took only a minute for him to catch her again. But their gait was too rapid now for them to talk, and the lights of the saloon were straight ahead.

They stopped by the open window, where coarse laughter was spilling out into the night, with foul words and oaths. Margaret looked through the window and saw what she was searching for—her brother, Stephen, standing by the bar, a glass of something raised to his smiling lips.

Forgetting about her unbound hair and the rough men staring at her, she slid from the horse, threw the bridle down and ran to the open door.

Like a heavenly Nemesis she appeared in the lighted doorway. Some of the men who had already drunk deeply that night thought she was the angel of the Lord sent to strike them dead.

She stood there in her limp white dress, with long golden hair and arms outstretched, and the vivid scarlet of the jacket gleaming here and there like a flame in the glory of her hair.

She rushed to her brother and struck the glass from his hand, even as he held it to his lips. Then, turning to the roomful, she looked at them with one long, mournful glance. There standing before her was the Sabbath class to a man. They weren't drunk, for most of them could hold a great deal of liquor.

She said nothing to them but searched each face with a quick, heart-rending glance; then she turned and pulled her brother away.

Philip tried to stop her as she flew from her horse to the open door. But she vanished from his hand like a wisp of air, and now he stood behind her ready to protect or help, even with his life. But she needed no help. Like darkness before the light they backed away from her; and no one, not even Banks, raised a word or a laugh at her expense.

Even Stephen yielded unwillingly and followed her from the room. She led him silently to Philip, with no one to hinder or scoff. It was as if a messenger from God had walked into that saloon and plucked Stephen away, searching each soul that stood there with one flaming glance.

The little cavalcade started out into the night. As the sound of their going died away, each man inside the lighted room drew apart from the rest of the silenced throng, moving noiselessly into the darkness, and went his way by himself. The saloon was deserted except for one or two old drunkards too sodden with drink to understand. The barkeeper thus cursed the girl who entered and stopped business for that evening. But he soon put up his shutters and turned out his lights.

Stephen rode ahead with his head bowed, whether in anger or shame they couldn't tell. Margaret and Philip rode abreast. No one spoke a word as the horses moved slowly through the dark. Once Philip turned and looked at the girl beside him, her white face and dress lighting up the darkness. He saw her shivering so he took off his coat and buttoned it around her. She tried to protest by lifting her hand, but he wouldn't be put off; so she smiled wanly and let him fasten it around her. By common consent they communicated without words. Stephen was just in front.

When they emerged onto the road near where Philip first heard Margaret's call, he reached out for her cold, white hand that lay limp on the saddle and held it in his warm, strong one the rest of the ride. Again she let him and was comforted by the reassuring pressure.

When they arrived at the house, she didn't burst into tears and hang about

Stephen's neck, pleading and condemning. She was too wise for that, and her trouble went too deep.

She told him to lie down on the couch by the fire. She brought strong coffee that Marna had made, along with an inviting supper, and tried to make him eat. But when she bent over him to ask if he would sit up, she saw that on his face were tears he had turned away to hide. Then she stooped and kissed him. And kneeling there beside him with her face next to his, she prayed: "Oh, Jesus Christ, save my dear brother!"

She kissed him again and drew a little table close to him with the supper upon it, leaving him to eat it when he would, while she prepared something for herself and Philip.

Without being reproached by any words, Stephen went to his room a little later and lay down, more miserable than he'd ever been in his whole reckless life. Thoughts that until now were too serious for him to entertain forced their way into his mind, along with searching questions he'd never asked himself. Through them all he could not keep from hearing his sister's voice on the other side of the thin board partition as she prayed and pleaded for her brother's salvation.

All night long he wrestled with the two spirits battling over him: the spirit of the demon that cried for drink, aroused by the few drops that had wet his lips before the glass was struck from them, and the Spirit of God's Holy One who strove to have him for eternity.

He sat dejectedly beside the fire the next morning after breakfast. His young face showed the strain of the night in deep creases. He looked up as Margaret came over to him and smiled wearily.

"I'm not worth it," he said. "You'd better give me up."

Margaret sat down beside him.

"I will never give you up, Stephen, until you are safe."

He reached out and took her hand.

"You are a good sister," he said. That was all, but she felt that hereafter he would not be against any effort she made on his behalf.

He could scarcely let her out of his sight during the next few days. If she left the room, he followed her, and when he closed his eyes he saw a vision of his sister in white with burnished golden hair like an angel of mercy come to save.

When the Sabbath came, Margaret doubted she would have any class but Stephen and Philip. Her heart was heavy because of them all. She had hoped more than anything that they were being led close to Christ. Now her hopes were dashed. Of what use was it to pray and preach and sing to men like these? Men who could stand about and watch quietly or help in the downfall of one of their own. She had read profound lessons of the morals of that region ever since she came, but not until that night in the saloon had she realized how little she had to build upon with any of them. She even looked at Philip doubtfully sometimes. How could he be different from the rest, since he was one of them?

Philip hadn't presumed upon the intimacy of that night's wild ride. He was the same quiet, respectful gentleman, only with this difference: there was a promise between them. And when he looked at her, his eyes let her know he hadn't forgotten it.

Contrary to her expectations, however, the entire company of men trooped in at the regular hour and seated themselves, perhaps a little more ostentatious than usual.

Margaret welcomed them quietly. She wasn't sure of them, even though they came. Marna had told her just before dinner about a circus and a painted lady who was to dance in the saloon that afternoon.

"Men no come today," she said. "If come, no stay late. Go see dance-woman."

Margaret's heart had sunk. Of what use was it for her to try to help these men if they were going straight to perdition as soon as she was through?

Margaret's fingers trembled as she played; she had chosen minor melodies with dirge-like, wailing movements. Even the singing was solemn, for the men only growled instead of letting out their usual voices.

They turned to the lesson, and Margaret read the text. But then she pushed the Bible from her and raised her troubled eyes to them, eyes in which tears were not a stranger.

"You came here because I asked you to help me start a Sunday school, but I'm afraid I've done you more harm than good," she said.

"You've studied for a good many weeks now about Jesus Christ. I've told you how He loves you and wants you, and how He left His home and came down here to suffer so you might be saved from sin and come home to live with Him. It hasn't seemed to make a bit of difference. You've listened just to humor me, but you haven't done anything to please Him, my dearest friend, for whom I did it all. You've kept on doing wrong things. You've gone to places you knew He wouldn't like. Some of you may be planning to go to a wicked place this after-noon after we finish the lesson. I've been showing you the right way, and you've chosen the wrong. It would be better for you that you didn't know the right than, knowing it, that you shouldn't take it. I've made a great mistake. I've shown you the loveliness of Christ, and you've treated it with indifference."

She turned away to hide the tears. Anxious nights and stressful days were telling on her nerves.

The silence was profound.

Then Bennett, with the white eyelashes and red hair, stood up before them. His face was also red, but his voice held a true ring.

"My lady," he said. "We're pretty rough, I know, and maybe you can't say anything too bad about us. But we ain't so bad that we're ungrateful. We promised to stick by this thing, and we're a-going to do it. I don't know just what you want, and I don't think the other fellows do either. But if you just speak up, we're with you. If it's the drinking you mean, we'll shut up that saloon if you say so, though it'll be a dry spot for some of us without it. And if it's that dancing woman, if a single feller goes out of this room with intentions of visiting her show, he goes with a bullet in him."

Bennett paused and waved his pistol slowly around the room. Banks started back in terror, then recovered himself and laughed nervously. But the other men faced Bennett steadily, and their silence lent consent. Bennett took it as such, for he put the revolver back in its holster and resumed his labored speech.

"As for treating anyone with indifference, we ain't meant to. It's just our way. We've listened respectful-like to what you said about Him and ain't questioned but what it's all so. But we ain't just up to this Sunday school thing and don't know what to do. If you'd say plain what 'tis you want, we might be able to please."

Margaret turned her moist eyes to the young man and said earnestly: "I want you to be like Him, Mr. Bennett, to live like Him, to love Him, to grow to look like Him. That is what He wants. That's why He sent the message to you."

Bennett stood abashed at the awful disparity between the One spoken of and him. He looked at her helplessly.

"I'll be dashed if I know what you mean," he replied with fervor. "But if you'll make it all out easy for us, we'll try."

Later that night she sent them away. She had prolonged the lesson and singing and then read them a tender story, full of the tragedy, love and salvation of life.

Their magnificent voices burst forth with their closing song as if they meant it:

Just as I am, without one plea,
But that Thy blood was shed for me,
And that Thou bidst me come to Thee,
O Lamb of God, I come, I come.

They were still all there. Not one stole away to the revelries in the village. If Banks had entertained thoughts of doing so, he didn't dare.

She'd asked them to sing the words as a prayer if they could. Each man sang with his eyes on his book, and a startled look of new purpose dawned in some faces.

Before they walked out into the starlight silently, each man paused and shook hands with Margaret as she stood by the door. They'd never done this before, and they wouldn't have dared to touch her lily hand unless she extended it to them now.

Some of the handclasps were awkward, but each one was a kind of pledge of new loyalty to her.

Last of all came Byron, looking down at the floor. He didn't know if she would shake his hand. He hesitated before her. It was a new experience for him to be embarrassed.

"Will you take Christ for your own?" she asked, understanding his hesitation.

"If I know how," he answered brokenly.

Then her eager hand reached out, sealing the promise with a warm grasp of friendliness. And Byron walked out that door with honor awakening in his breast.

She turned back to the room with a bright smile. Stephen, standing behind her, leaned over and kissed her on the forehead. Then he walked quickly into his room and shut the door behind him.

Margaret stood alone then with Philip.

Chapter 14

Had I the grace to win the grace
Of maiden living all above,
My soul would trample down the base
That she might have a man to love.

A grace I had no grace to win
Knocks now at my half-opened door;
Ah! Lord of glory, come Thou in;
Thy grace divine is all, and more!

—George MacDonald

I've been thinking," said Philip, with a new light in his eyes. He turned to her from watching the firelight. "How much is unbelief worth? It doesn't change facts. I'll throw mine away. I'll take your Christ. If there isn't a Christ, I'll lose nothing. If there is, I'll gain everything. Margaret, I'm taking your Jesus tonight to be my Savior."

He said it solemnly, as someone utters a vow for eternity. And the girl stood looking up at him, the radiance in her face reflected in his own.

When he went to his room that night, he closed the door and knelt down. A strange joy filled his heart. He didn't shrink from praying but longed to record his vow to begin his new life.

"Oh, Christ!" he murmured, reaching out his arms as if to grasp his heart's desire. "Christ, come to me! Let me know You're here. Keep me from ever doubting again. I'll give You my whole self, though it's worth little. Only come to me! Jesus! I take You as my Savior!"

He might have prayed a different prayer if he didn't know Margaret. Even if his will and desire were stirred to praying at all without her influence, he wouldn't have used such language or spoken to Jesus, the Christ, if he hadn't heard Margaret's simple, earnest talks of Him every Sunday. He would have spoken to God more distantly, with less insistence, and he may not have received the blessing so soon.

Someone has said prayer is throwing the arms of the soul about the neck of God.

Philip had laid his soul before Christ, and tenderly, as if the great arms of God had folded about him, a sense of the presence of Jesus entered his soul.

"How sweet the name of Jesus sounds in a believer's ear!" they sang in the Sunday class once. In his corner behind the piano, Philip had curled his lip over the sentiment. How could the name of One who has never been seen be dear, no matter how much someone believed?

But now in the dawn of his own second birth the name "Jesus" was sweet to him. How it came about, he couldn't explain. He said it over and over, gently at first, for he feared the sweetness might depart, and then more confidently, as his soul rang with the joy of it. One could truly feel Jesus' presence, after all, as Margaret said.

With a sense of great peace he lay down, but before he closed his eyes to sleep he murmured, "Thank You for sending—Margaret!" He spoke the name reverently.

Philip and Margaret didn't say much to each other about the wonderful change in his heart. But a secret understanding passed between them when their eyes met across the room, and Margaret's heart sang a song as she worked. It was several days before Philip told her he was getting the answer to his prayer she promised and how he knew now that what she said was true.

The days went by in much the same way, except that both Margaret and Philip watched over Stephen more carefully. They spent the evenings with delightful readings, and Margaret invented all sorts of things she wanted made, which the young men could work at while she read.

Margaret was becoming a better rider since her night adventure. It seemed to have freed her from fear, and the three rode about the country together, enjoying the clear, crisp days as winter hastened on.

About this time a young minister arrived in the region. He had broken down in his first charge and come West to a cattle ranch to find rest for his nerves. He was a sincere fellow without any foolish ideas, and before long he made friends of the men at the ranch. He wanted to do them some good, though he saw little hope for it. He didn't feel well enough to preach, even if there was any encouragement for starting religious services on Sunday. Apparently no church was within reach. He thought a lot as he rode and laughed and learned from the rough men; they gave him no easy lessons on how to rub off the "tenderfoot" look and ways.

At last, one day he asked a man from the ranch if there wasn't a service held in that whole region? Didn't they know of even a Sunday school? Surely some Christian people lived around there.

The man he asked was Banks.

Now Banks was growing very unpopular among the Sunday class members who met with Margaret Halstead. He didn't care for the extreme principles she taught or yield his rights in drinking and gambling as some of the others were considering. He tried once or twice to oppose the power of the young teacher but didn't succeed. He felt he'd lost his influence. So seeking revenge by getting the minister on his side and against the young woman, he told him about Sunday school.

Banks had a gift for imitation and a vein of what he supposed was humor.

He used them both and not to the Sunday school's advantage. The young theologian wasn't blind to his character, however, and didn't believe all Banks told him. When Banks offered to take him the next Sunday, he accepted. It would at least give him a chance to study the men and see what influence could hold them. It also was the neighborhood's only opening for a religious service.

"But you gotta wear your regular clothes, or the boys'll get on to you bein' a preacher an' make it hot for you," said Banks. "They won't have any snobs around. The teacher might think you come to break up the meeting, and Earle'll take a notion to throw you out the back door."

The minister wondered what kind of a strange Sunday school he was to be taken to, but he quietly accepted the advice. The next Sunday as they were singing the opening hymn—Banks had timed his coming, when everyone would be occupied and wouldn't dispute the newcomer's appearance—they walked into the room and sat down.

The minister stared about on the beauty and refinement everywhere, but his attention was held at once by the lovely girl who, dressed in soft white, presided over the motley gathering. He glanced from the men's hard faces to her pure profile again and again.

Philip noticed at once an ease and mark of the world about the minister, even in his cowboy garb. He frowned with displeasure almost as he used to, was jealous of the newcomer's looks at Margaret and of his easy way of smiling and accepting the open book Banks handed him. But the name "Jesus," repeated in a chorus they were singing, reached Philip's heart and felt for that resonating chord that was learning to thrill at the name of his Master. Then he realized an ugly feeling toward the stranger had sprung up inside him uninvited. He tried to dismiss it and searched about for some hospitality to offer the visitor; in spite of himself, however, he felt dismayed at the man's presence. He was different from the other fellows, and Margaret would see it at once.

Fortunately for Margaret, she had no time to scrutinize the stranger until after the lesson was finished; otherwise she might have been disconcerted. She overcame long ago her fear of the men she taught every Sabbath, through her intense desire to lead them to the Savior. But if she'd known her audience contained a full-fledged minister fresh from theological training, she would have hesitated and perhaps had no message to deliver that day.

She did everything as usual, including the silent waiting and the earnest prayer. The young minister decided he had more to learn about preaching than might be learned in a seminary.

She found him out as soon as he spoke to her, however, after the lesson while they were passing the tea and cakes. She recognized him as one of her world and welcomed him pleasantly.

Now the minister was small and slight. In contrast to Philip and Stephen and the others he looked insignificant to Margaret, who had grown accustomed to the larger Western men. So when he asked permission to come to the class some-times, she didn't feel intimidated as she would have felt before. He refused to teach; his physician forbade it, but he thanked her warmly for the help she gave him that afternoon. He left her with the impression that he needed help, too, for he didn't seem to have the same idea about a personal friendship with Jesus Christ that had become so dear to her.

She felt strengthened, however, at the thought of another Christian to help in the work; she began at once to plan how to ask him to explain deep points in the lessons that she might in turn explain to the class. He seemed a bright, interest-ing young man. Margaret was glad he'd come. He was from near her own home, also, and knew many of her close friends. That made him doubly interesting.

As winter progressed, the minister dropped in on them at sunset, occasion-ally, to spend the evening. Stephen liked him and encouraged his visits. Margaret rejoiced at this and made the minister more welcome because of it.

During the long evenings they read and talked and enjoyed music, much as when they were alone.

The minister naturally gravitated to a seat beside Margaret. He turned the music for her when she played, and his voice joined in the duets they sang, for he was something of a musician as well as a theologian.

He was also a good reader and often took the book from Margaret and read while she rested or worked a bit of embroidery.

Sometimes the entire Sunday class would be invited for an evening of read-ing and song. At such times the minister proved to be an admirable helper ready with some witticism or good recitation. He could imitate different birds and would whistle wild, sweet tunes to a running accompaniment on the piano.

He was not altogether unpopular among the men. He kept any extra self-esteem he might have brought out West locked away inside and carried with him a hearty friendliness. The men couldn't help liking him, and Margaret more and more turned to him for advice and looked for his help in planning for her different gatherings. But when he was present, Philip was silent and gloomy.

Three times during that winter Stephen grew restless and slipped away. Twice his faithful guardians galloped after him when he was scarcely out of sight of the house and took him on a long ride that didn't end until late at night, when all were worn out. But they brought him safely back, sober. The third time he met Bennett on the way. Bennett was immediately suspicious and shadowed him till he made sure—whereupon he laid hands on Stephen and insisted on riding home with him.

Margaret had hoped and prayed. She even ventured to talk with Stephen at dusk sometimes, when he came in and threw himself on the couch by the fire. He always listened, but he said very little. She had never received much hope from him that he was heeding her earnest pleading to come to Jesus Christ and be a new man.

And winter wore away into spring.

Chapter 15

All I could never be,
All, men ignored in me,
This, I was worth to God.

—ROBERT BROWNING

One day in early summer the minister and Stephen set out on a long ride. They were to return in time for supper, and Margaret had planned a pleasant evening for everyone. "The boys," as the Sunday class was called, were all coming.

She watched them ride away in the afternoon light and wondered whether the minister would have an opportunity to speak to Stephen. She felt very sad about her brother. He didn't seem to get any closer to eternal life.

Philip was to have gone with the riding party. But a message in the morning had called him in another direction on business, and he wouldn't return till evening.

Margaret watched the two riders disappear and then went in to finish her plans for the evening. She often thought of new things to win these men into another world besides their own.

The two men rode to a distant ranch famous for its superior cattle. They passed some beautiful spots on the way and stopped to marvel at them. And the minister did have an opportunity to speak a few sincere words to Stephen.

Stephen answered half wistfully but wouldn't commit himself. He didn't repel the words and seemed to like his companion even more because he dared to speak them.

They rode about the ranch for a while and late in the afternoon turned their horses homeward.

They were about halfway home when a messenger overtook them to beg the minister to return. It was whispered around the ranch that one of the visitors was a minister. The mother of one of the men was lying ill, not likely to live, and she begged that he would return to pray with her. The kind-hearted minister could hardly refuse.

Stephen insisted upon going back with him, but Mr. Owen wouldn't allow this. He told Stephen to go home and tell his sister the circumstances. He'd come as soon as possible. The messenger offered a fresh horse and an escort for returning, and the minister said he would be with them before the evening was over. It wouldn't do for Stephen to go with him, since his sister would hold supper and it would spoil their plans.

The young minister was disappointed. All day as he rode through the fresh air his heart rejoiced over the evening. He'd formed a plan during the past week, that tonight he'd ask Margaret to ride with him soon. Then he could be alone with her and perhaps—that was as far as he let his thoughts go in the presence of others. He liked to be alone when he thought of Margaret.

Miles away another man rode thinking of Margaret and of the minister. Sometimes he rejoiced over the girl's smile and farewell wave as he left that morning, and other times he felt sad and uneasy as a vision of the minister's face rose before him. For Philip had known for a long time that he loved Margaret better than his own life. Now and then he lifted up his eyes to the clear blue sky and called out from his heart to his Father, and her Father. He didn't pray or ask anything for himself but sought to assure himself that a heavenly Father belonged to them both, loved them both and would do well.

Stephen sat in his saddle, watching his friend go back on the road. He felt a strong impulse to turn and follow him. Something whispered to him it would be better, that here was his safety. He almost called to them as they disappeared around a knoll. Then he remembered that Margaret would be watching anxiously for them. So he determined for once to show he was a man and could be trusted and reluctantly started on alone.

But the devil went also. He hadn't had such a good chance at Stephen for nearly a year. He'd all but given up this soul that had been firmly in his clutches. But now he came swiftly with his old tricks and more.

"You'd better ride through town," he whispered, "and then you can tell Margaret how strong you are."

That was the first thought. Ride through town, not go into the saloon or stop to talk to anyone! He'd enjoy knowing he could do that. He might even try to be the Christian Margaret and the minister wanted him to be if he could do that once. He wouldn't be so ashamed. He half decided he'd do it and turned it over in his mind, but for him the thought of going through town was almost as much of a temptation as going. He could see the saloon keeper standing at the door, calling to him. He could smell the odor of the familiar room as it floated out through the swinging door.

Something seized him with the thought of that odor—a spirit that would not be overcome. He forgot his intention to ride safely through town to please his sister with his strength. He forgot his near-desire to be a Christian. He forgot the minister's words, which had indeed taken hold on his wavering nature. He forgot everything except that one fiendish thirst for strong drink. He spurred his horse deeply and rode like mad, with his breath coming in great waves through his lungs. His eyes grew bloodshot, and all the demons in the service of the arch-fiend flew to urge him on. He had miles yet to cover, but they were nothing. He was alone and unsuspected. He had time to get there and get all he wanted. All he wanted! For once no one could stop him, for no one would know until the minister came back, and that might not be tonight.

He turned on a road that wouldn't lead past home and galloped on. It was the road his sister took in her wild night ride after him and Philip.

At dusk he reached the bridge she had crossed in safety, barely escaping with her life. He knew the bridge hadn't been used for a long time and was considered unsafe. He didn't know that the great supporting timber had fallen into the ravine below on the night Margaret crossed. But he knew enough about it that even in his most daring moods, before this, he'd rather not try to cross it.

But something stronger than reason was urging him tonight. This bridge would lead to a crossroads where he wouldn't meet any of the fellows coming to Margaret's gathering. Lately they'd been sort of self-appointed watch-guards. He couldn't shake them off. They kept him many times from himself. He would escape them all tonight. The fever in his blood had caught fire through his veins.

Jerking the bridle he turned his frightened horse and put him at the bridge, not letting him slacken his pace. He sensed—even in his wildness—that his safety lay in getting over quickly, if safety there was. And so under full gallop the panting horse flew at the bridge in the oncoming darkness.

It wavered, cracked and wavered again. Then suddenly, too late, the horse drew back on his haunches with a terrified snort almost human in its anguish and poised a moment in mid-air. The bridge did not reach across the chasm. One whole section had fallen. The last support was tottering in decay.

In one awful second Stephen realized his position and saw in vivid panorama the follies of his life and the sins of his heart. He saw and cried out in one wild cry to God, in acknowledgment and late submission. The cry rang through the upper air and down into the dark ravine. Then Stephen lost consciousness as bridge, horse and rider fell crashing below.

Supper had been ready for some time when Philip came. Margaret was growing restless and was glad to see him. He became anxious when he heard that the riders hadn't returned, though he tried to laugh it off and say the minister wasn't used to long rides. Maybe it was too much for him, and they stopped to rest. But in another half-hour Mr. Owen, his horse covered with froth, rode cheerfully up to the door and dismounted.

He made his apologies, explained his lateness and then looked around for Stephen.

"Isn't he here yet?" he asked in surprise.

But more than surprise was reflected in the faces of the other two. Philip excused himself and headed to the barn. His own horse was weary with the long, hard day. He saddled the other horse and quickly led it out into the darkness. But Margaret stood at the door, with her face white and drawn and purpose in her eyes. Philip could see it shining through the starlight like another star. She had followed him to the barn, intending to ride with him after Stephen.

He dropped the horse's bridle and walked over to her. Taking her small cold hands in his strong ones, he gazed down into her face.

"Margaret," he said tenderly. "I know what you want to do, but you mustn't. You must promise me you'll stay here and pray. You can't go out into the night. There's no need, and I won't let you. I won't go until you promise."

She caught her breath and dropped her face on his hands that held hers so firmly.

He drew her to him in the shadow of the great, dark barn and, bending over her, reverently kissed her silken hair. "Margaret, I love you. Will you do this for me? Will you promise to stay at home and pray?"

He was half-frightened afterward that he spoke to her so, but she didn't pull away. Instead, she stood very still, held her breath a moment, then answered softly, "Yes, Philip!"

He longed to take her in his arms but didn't dare. He gave her hands a long, tender clasp and sprang into his saddle. But Margaret's pale face looked up now, and she ran a step or two beside the horse.

"You'll be careful, Philip—for yourself," she said brokenly. His heart leaped with joy as he promised. Yet, after all, he told himself it might be only a sisterly care.

She watched him ride away through the dark, her hand at her throat to still the wild, sweet joy that thrilled her soul. For a moment she almost forgot her fears for Stephen in love and fear for Philip. She stood still several minutes and let the memory of his kiss flow over her and cover her with its glory. Then she hurried in and tried to entertain the minister, who was rejoicing that he had her to himself for a while. Poor soul, he didn't know her thoughts were far down the dark road, following a rider through the night.

As Philip rode along, he couldn't believe he told Margaret he loved her. And it seemed too strange and wonderful that she didn't repulse him when he kissed her. As the tumult in his heart quieted enough for him to think, he told himself that perhaps she was excited about Stephen and needed comfort. She didn't realize what his words of love meant. She might have thought he meant it as a kind and brotherly feeling. If so, he would never take advantage of her. That moment they spent together should be a sacred thing between them. He would always rejoice in that kiss and the chance to hold her dear hands.

But throughout those thoughts the joy of loving her sang a song of hope in his heart. For every now and then something assured him that she loved him.

So Philip rode through the dark into town. Finding no trace of Stephen or anyone who saw him, he turned his horse back to the house to see if he'd come. He was anxious, canvassing every possible way to look for Stephen. Then he remembered and prayed for guidance and help.

Stephen's wild cry had reached the ears of two men traveling in a wagon along the upper road above the ravine. They stopped, listened and heard the crashing timbers and the fall of horse and man.

By instinct they knew what the accident must be and went to find out who had fallen to their death. They carried a lantern. The night was dark, and one man was old; and the road they had to travel was treacherous in some places. So now, when they could see only the blackness below, they climbed down another way, leaving their horse tied above, and found the place where Stephen lay.

The horse was dead and lay motionless with all four legs broken and a great beam of rotten timber across one temple, where it struck and mercifully ended his life.

But Stephen lay a little farther off, perhaps flung there partly by his horse's struggles, or he may have leaped on his own in the moment of falling. He was stretched on a grassy place and lay unscratched apparently, the damp gold waves of hair lying loose upon his forehead, his hands out as if he were asleep. He was profoundly unconscious.

The men held the lantern to his face, and one muttered with a great oath. "Steve Halstead! Drunk again!"

They tore his shirt open and felt for his heart but couldn't tell if he was dead or alive. Finally they carried him with great difficulty up a sloping, circuitous path and put him in the wagon.

Bennett and Byron and two or three others had just arrived at the house when the two men brought him in. Margaret turned away in sick horror. She had never seen her brother drunk. She couldn't bear to look now. They motioned her away from the door and laid him on his bed. But something in his face made Byron stoop down. There was no smell of liquor on him. They listened with shocked faces as the two who found him told their story. Then Byron jumped on his horse and galloped off into the night for the doctor, while the others worked desperately to revive him, with the door closed to his sister.

Bennett told Margaret that her brother fell on the way home and hadn't been to the village at all but was found on his way there. Her face lighted at that. She understood his meaning. She was glad Stephen hadn't been drinking. They sent the minister to stay with her. She was wide-eyed and brave and talked little, looking anxiously through the open front door.

She heard the sound of horses presently and rushed out into the night. Mr. Owen thought she was looking for the doctor and let her go. He thought it might be well for her to have something to do, even if only to watch for the doctor, who couldn't possibly have come so soon.

It was Philip who had come.

She ran out to him and looked anxiously through the dark.

"Oh, Philip, is it you? Are you safe?"

Philip's heart warmed with hope.

"They brought him home, Philip. He fell through the bridge. I was afraid you fell too. I don't know how badly he's hurt, but, Philip, he hadn't been drinking!"

Her last words held a ring of triumph, as if whatever might come couldn't be all bad. Then together they went into the house.

"She's a wonderful girl, isn't she?" said the minister to Philip in subdued tones a little later, as he watched her making a cup of tea for Philip. "It seems so strange I had to come out here to find her, when our native towns were only twenty miles apart." His voice carried a tone of possession and pride, and Philip's heart sank as he listened.

Chapter 16

The doctor arrived eventually and was able to bring back the spirit into the body that had lain so still and deathlike. Stephen opened his eyes and gazed about him in bewilderment. He looked first at his sister, who had come into the room with the doctor, and then he smiled.

"I didn't get there, though, Margaret," he murmured. "God stopped me. It was the only way He could save me."

He closed his eyes, and they thought he had fainted again. But he opened them with his old, careless, mischievous smile and looked around on the boys, his eyes lingering lovingly on Philip's face.

"I've been a coward, boys," he said, "and I've tried to get away from Him all the time. But still He kept drawing me, and you all helped. And now He's going to take me to Himself. There won't be any more drinks up there, and maybe I can start over again."

The words were faint, and the doctor bent over him and administered a stimulant.

He examined him thoroughly and told them Stephen was hurt internally and couldn't live long. They thought he was unconscious, but he opened his eyes and smiled at them.

"It's all right, doctor. It's better this way," he said feebly. "But can't you give me something to make me stronger for a few hours? I want to say a few words to the boys."

The doctor turned away to rub his hand across his eyes. The men moved, choking, away from the bed and over to the window or slipped into the other room.

"I'll try!" said the doctor huskily. "If you'll lie quiet and rest a little, you may live through the night."

Stephen took the medicine and lay quiet for a few minutes. But as soon as he felt strength from the artificial means he started to talk. The reckless tongue that had been the life of so many gatherings had only a little while longer to speak.

Philip stepped over to him first and tried to quiet him with the strong personality that had so often saved him from himself.

But Stephen's mind was unusually active. He was thinking of things he'd neglected all his life. He spoke of this and that he wanted Philip to do for him, and he talked tenderly of his sister.

"You'll look after her, Phil?" he asked anxiously. "You know she'll have no one now when I'm gone. She'll be sad. You like her, don't you?"

Philip's eyes filled with tears.

"I love her, Steve, with all my soul," he said. "I'll care for her as far as she will let me. I will make her my wife if she'll consent."

"Consent?" said Stephen, his voice rising and his old petulant manner coming back to him, as always when his will was crossed in the slightest. "Consent! Of course she will! Why shouldn't she? No one could help admiring you, Phil. Why can't you be married right away, before I go? I'd like to see it. I'd like to give you my blessing."

He looked up eagerly into Philip's face.

Philip almost groaned.

"Why can't you, Phil?" he urged again.

"I haven't asked her yet," said Philip. "She may not love me at all. Sometimes I think she loves the minister."

"Then ask her now," said Stephen. He called out in the high, thin voice of those who are at the end of life: "Margaret!"

She heard his cry through the board partitions and came at once.

Stephen had almost exhausted his breath with his eagerness and lay breathing weakly, looking up first at Philip, then at his sister.

"Phil—has something—to tell you," he gasped. Then he swallowed the spoonful Philip gave him from the glass the doctor left and closed his eyes.

Philip scarcely dared to look at Margaret. It seemed almost a desecration in this hour of death to speak of what meant life and joy to him.

"I've been telling Steve of my love for you," he said, trying to control the tremble in his voice. "I told him I would like to make you my wife. I wouldn't dare put this on you now, but he longs to know how you feel about it."

Philip had come near her, and they both stood close to Stephen's side. Philip's voice conveyed an undertone of pity for her as he spoke and a slight touch of formality in his words because of the presence of a third person, making it sound like a contract in writing. But Margaret remembered his impassioned tones a little while before in the shadow of the night and didn't doubt his deep love for her.

With tears filling her eyes she looked up to Philip and tried to smile. Her lips were trembling, but she said simply, "I love you, Philip!" And she put out her hands to his.

Then Stephen's large brown hand, so weak now, reached out to them and clasped them both, and the two with one accord knelt down beside his bed.

"Be married now, while I'm here," he whispered. "I can leave you better that way." He looked pleadingly at them.

Margaret caught her breath with a sob, and Philip put his arm tenderly about her.

"Can you bear to—dear?" he asked.

She was quiet a moment with her face sad and eyes downcast, and then she whispered softly, "Yes."

Philip stooped and kissed her forehead, and Stephen smiled his old joyous smile. For a minute the shadow of death that hovered over his face was chased away.

"Where are the boys?" he asked. "I want the boys and the minister. I'll tell them. No, it won't be too hard. I'd like to. Go and get ready."

They came trooping in, the great, rough men who loved him and tried so hard to ruin him and save him both. The minister came behind them, and the doctor hurried in and felt Stephen's pulse. But he was too excited to notice the doctor.

"Boys, we're going to have a wedding!" he said in a cheerful, yet weak voice. They thought his mind was wandering and looked sadly at one another.

"That's all right, boys," he said as he saw they didn't understand. "It's sure enough. I want you to carry me into the other room for the ceremony. No, don't say they can't, Doc. I'll stay alive long enough to say all I need to say. I must go out there where we've had so many good times. I'd rather die out there. Take me out, boys. We have no time to waste. Philip and Margaret are out there waiting, and the minister will marry them."

His old impatience was using up his strength fast. The doctor said in a low voice, "Take him out. It can't make much difference."

The fellows gathered up the mattress tenderly and carried it out to a cot placed in front of the fireplace. They almost thought he was gone when they laid him down. But he rallied and, smiling, whispered, "Go on."

Philip and Margaret, quiet and pale, stood together, hand in hand, in front of the mass of summer blossoms Margaret had arranged a few hours before for the expected evening gathering. She had sat there to teach their first Sunday class, and she was wearing white as then. The light in her eyes defied even the sadness of death. Stephen wondered as he watched her whether she was looking up to and speaking with the unseen presence of Christ.

The room was beautiful. Only Stephen, as he lay with partly closed eyes and watched them, impatient for the ceremony to be over, remembered the bare old room. They brought his sister into that room filled with the odor of lamp smoke and bacon the night of her arrival. And in his heart he thanked God for her coming.

The minister performed the ceremony, despite his stricken demeanor and shaking voice. Life was taking away his love just as death was stealing a good friend. He had begun to mourn and would learn his lesson; but it was bitter at the start.

There in the "chill before the dawning, between the night and morning," while the angel of death delayed a little, watching, they were married. The night was black around the little house, and the stars kept watch above.

As soon as it was over and the short prayer ended, Stephen moved as if to rise and then, remembering, dropped his head again.

"Boys, I can't stay long," he said, smiling in his old, reckless way. "I only stayed for the wedding." Then, growing serious, with an honest ring to his voice that sometimes made his speech convincing, he said, "I want you to do something, boys. You can if you only will. I want you to promise me before I go. I want you to build a church here and get the minister to run it. You can do it well enough if you don't go to the saloon. It's the saloon, boys, and the gambling, that have taken all our money and made us into such beasts. The saloon ruined me. You all know that. You know how I came here and bought this place and then drank it up and everything else I had. I would have gone to the devil at once if it hadn't been for Philip coming out and buying back the place and keeping me halfway straight."

His breath was growing short. His sentences became more broken.

"You all know what my sister's done for me," he went on. "God bless her. But even she couldn't save me. The devil had too tight a hold. I'm sorry I didn't do as she wanted me to and take Jesus Christ—it might have done some good—but now it's too late—He'll just have to take me. I guess He'll do it. I've made a clean breast of it—but it's been a wasted life. Don't wait any longer, boys. I've thought if there'd been a church here when I came—and a minister—who lived right up to what he said—it might not have been that way with me. Now, boys, will you build the church?"

They turned away to hide the tears that were running down their bronzed faces. But one by one they went solemnly, grasped his cold hand and promised in hoarse, broken murmurs.

"That's all right then, boys. I know you'll do it," said Stephen. "And, boys," he said with almost a twinkle of the old mischief in his eyes, "I want them to put me on the hill here under the big tree and mark the place so you'll remember your promise. Maybe I can help a little by reminding you and make up that way for all I've wasted."

He was quiet a moment. His voice kept its strength.

"Sing, boys," he said, opening his eyes. "Sing all the old songs. It will make me feel more at home where I'm going if I hear your voices on the way."

They looked helplessly at one another. They didn't know what to sing.

"Sing 'Jesus, Savior, Pilot Me,' boys," he said. "I didn't live for Him, but maybe I can die with Him."

Trembling, the deep voices started, like some grand organ that has lost its player and creaks on feebly at the touch of sorrow with a broken heart.

"Sing 'Safe Home in Port,' " he said when they finished. "I always liked that. And, boys, sing it as if you were glad. Sing it as you always do."

Then they controlled themselves and sang:

Safe home, safe home, in port!
Rent cordage, shattered deck,

Torn sails, provisions short,
And only not a wreck:
But, O, the joy upon the shore,
to tell the voyage perils o'er!

They sang as they used to sing it on those first bright Sundays. Something of the spirit of the triumph in the song had caught them.

No more the foe can harm!
No more the leaguered camp,
And cry of night alarm,
And need of ready lamp;
And yet how nearly had he failed,
How nearly had the foe prevailed!

"That's right, boys! That's me! It's all true," Stephen called out to them. They could see the shadow deepening about his eyes now.

Their voices grew softer with tenderness, but they sang on. They would sing him grandly into heaven if he wanted that, even if their hearts broke. Their voices should not fail him while he could listen.

The exile is at home!
Oh, nights and days of tears!

At these words Stephen pressed Margaret's hand that lay in his, and she kissed him tenderly.

Oh, longings not to roam!
Oh, sins and doubts and fears!
What matters now grief's darkest day
When God has wiped all tears away?

The minister started other hymns he heard them singing in their gatherings. They needed no books, nor could they have seen the words through their tears.

Stephen was sinking fast. He didn't talk anymore or look at them. Once he opened his eyes and, looking at Margaret, murmured, "Dear sister!"

He lay still for so long they thought he stopped breathing. But suddenly he opened his eyes and, with strength born of his flight into another world, raised himself from the pillow and called in a loud, clear voice: "Did you call, Father? Yes, Sir, I'm coming!"

Then he fell back dead.

Was it some memory of his boyhood that came to him at last, or did he hear his heavenly Father's voice?

The minister started to sing,

Safe in the arms of Jesus,
Safe on His gentle breast . . .

With choking sobs the men joined in the song Stephen loved. Just then the sun shot up behind the hills and laid a touch of glory on the gold of Stephen's hair.

"He is safe home," said the minister. "Let's pray."

They knelt about the minister in their grief and heard him pray for them. Then the men stepped out of the house, leaving Philip and Margaret with their sorrow and their joy.

They departed into a new world in which vows were to be kept and a goal attained. Each man was resolved to do his best to keep the sacred trust Stephen left to them.

They visited Stephen's friends and gathered a good sum of money. They brought it to Margaret on the day of the funeral service and told her it was for the church and that it should be built at once. Margaret, smiling through her tears, thanked God and knew her prayers were being answered.

They laid him in the place he spoke of under the magnificent tree that crowned the hill. To mark it they placed a stone with Stephen's name, the date and the simple words engraved: "*Safe Home.*"

Beside the grave the church was built, its spire pointing heavenward, its doors open day and night, its bell pealing over the lonely country for times of worship, and over the door, cut into the stone, the words "*Stephen Halstead Memorial.*"

The minister found his church. And Stephen's life, though gathered safely home, is going on in the memory of those he is helping.

Lone Point

Chapter 1

Rachel Hammond sat by the open window with her Bible on her knee. The muslin curtains didn't blow with the breeze, for no breeze was blowing that hot June morning. The air seemed breathless. Rachel had put her room in order, finished her morning duties and was sitting quietly with her Bible before she began the day.

Her sister, Maria, two years older, sat in the adjoining room, her door open for the air to circulate. In fact, the door between the sisters' rooms was scarcely ever shut, day or night. Maria was trimming a hat at that moment, instead of reading her Bible. Not that she didn't read her Bible, for she did, but she didn't have a set quiet time for doing it as her sister did.

The hat was a white sailor, stylish and thus expensive earlier in the season. But now most people were supplied with hats for the summer, and, because of the reduced prices, poorer people could indulge their taste for pretty things. It went against the grain for Maria Hammond to have to wait until late for the pretty summer things she wanted; even then she was obliged to buy carefully from her savings—for until recently she was used to buying when and what she pleased.

Maria took her father's change of fortune more bitterly than any of the other family members. The others looked on the bright side of things and cheerfully told each other how good that matters weren't any worse; that the father didn't fall ill under the burden a trusted partner's fraud placed on him; that the beautiful home where the three children were born was still theirs, with a little left to keep things going; and, best of all, that all the creditors were fully paid.

But Maria could see only the dark side. From a rich man, who could do what he pleased, who intended soon to build a home lovelier than their present one and who could afford to place his daughters in the best society, her father had become a poor man. Thus to her the present home lost even its charm before she looked forward to the finer one.

The present home was by no means an undesirable one. It was located on a quiet, pleasant street where the neighbors were dignified and old-fashioned and of fine old families. The house was built of stone with ample room and broad porches, vines peeping in the windows in summer and lawn enough around to give the feeling of space. It was in the plainest end of a fashionable suburb, but it wasn't fashionable. The house had none of the modern twists and turns that art and fashion decreed should adorn a modern handsome dwelling. For this reason Maria despised it and pitied herself for having to live in it. A look of discontent had settled on her pretty forehead and was little by little changing her expression permanently.

"Oh, dear!" sighed Maria, jerking a loop of white ribbon into place behind the cheap white wings she was arranging on her hat. "What's the use of fixing up things to wear after all? The only place to wear them will be church, and all the people we know or care about will be out of town by another month. We might as well wear our old rags after all."

Rachel looked up from her Bible, through the open door where she could see her sister working.

"Oh, yes, there'll be plenty of places. Don't be so disheartened, dear," she answered brightly. "How pretty that hat will be, 'Ri! It looks just like you."

"Does it, indeed?" responded the elder sister. "Then my face must be badly snarled, for this ribbon is. I can't get the right twist to it. I wish I could afford to take it down to Haskins' and have our old milliner trim it. It's frustrating to have to do everything ourselves or go without. But I'd be willing to do it myself if we could only go out of town for a little while, Ray. It's so horribly common to stay in the city all year round. Everybody else is going."

"You forget, 'Ri—we don't live in the city; we live in the suburbs. Plenty of people stay all summer in the suburbs. Some people prefer to take their trips away from home in the winter. Look at the Adamses and Monteiths—they don't go away at all. Even Mrs. Burbank told me the other day they didn't care to take any vacation because they enjoyed their home in the summer so much."

"Oh, yes, I should think they would. They have a park surrounding them, a great, cool house with plenty of servants and all the guests they want, and they're up on a high hill besides, with shade around. Besides, it's nonsense for them to talk about not going away. They're hardly at home two weeks in succession all year. Mrs. Burbank and Tilly spend a week at a time at Atlantic City every time they sneeze or have a headache, and Mr. and Mrs. Burbank took a trip to California last winter, while Tom and his aunt went to Florida. When they don't run up to New York or out to Pittsburgh for a few days they go up to that sanitarium in the mountains for their health for a month or take a trip to Bermuda. I wouldn't care about going away in the summer either if I knew I could go whenever I pleased and, what's more, knew that everybody else knew it. I tell you, Ray, the hardest thing is to feel that folks are saying we can't go anywhere now and pitying us! I just can't stand it." And Maria threw her half-finished hat on the bed beside her and lay back on one of the downy pillows in discouragement.

Rachel knew it was of no use to argue with her sister, so she tried to cheer her as best she could, sighing a little as she closed her Bible and walked into her sister's room. She had just read the verse "For me to live is Christ" and wondered if she'd ever know what that meant; she wished Maria felt more of the spirit of it, so her life wouldn't seem so hard to her.

"If you want to go away so much, perhaps we might go to the same place Marvie Parker told me about yesterday," said Rachel, seating herself on the foot of Maria's bed and resting her chin thoughtfully in her hand.

"No, thanks!" said Maria. "I wouldn't care for anyplace where Marvie Parker goes. I don't know what you find in that girl, Ray. She's the dowdiest thing I've seen in a long time. Her father is nothing but a clerk in his brother-in-law's store. There are plenty of nice girls for you to be with without choosing her for a friend."

"But she's nice, 'Ri," said the younger sister, her eyes flashing in her eagerness to defend her friend. "You don't know her, or you wouldn't talk that way. She's very bright and has read and studied far more than either of us. The whole family is bright. I never enjoyed myself more than the evening I spent with them last week. She has a brother just home from college who's full of life, and Marvie is the sweetest girl I know, next to you."

"She may be sweet enough," answered Maria, ignoring the earnest compliment, "but she's not of the same social standing as you. It's much wiser not to try to upset the world and drag people out of their circles." She said this with an air of having long experience with the world.

"Well, I think you might wait until you've known them before you judge them. But listen. Let me tell you where they're going. It sounds very interesting. The place is an island right between the bay and the ocean, not very wide either, so you get a view of both. Marvie says it's beautiful there and the sunsets are gorgeous. It's a real, old-time beach with no boardwalks or merry-go-rounds, and everybody does as he pleases. They have a lot of bathing and boating and fishing and sailing. I think it would be delightful. Marvie says there are cottages down there for seventy-five dollars for the season—just think of that! They're not fine, of course, but real comfortable, with big rooms and lots of corners and shelves to fix up. I think I'd like it immensely."

"Now, Rachel Weldon Hammond, what in the world do you mean?" said Maria, sitting upright on the bed and looking at her. "Seventy-five dollars for the season! The idea of our living in a cottage that costs only seventy-five dollars for the season! You must be crazy. Why, the cottage the Johnses lived in last year at Atlantic City was twelve hundred, and even the Pattersons paid a thousand. I think you're nothing but a child, in spite of your seventeen years."

Just then a servant came to announce that a young lady was in the parlor to see Miss Ray, and Rachel with a bright spot on each cheek went down to find her friend Marvie.

Not until dinner that evening was the subject renewed. Maria had spent the afternoon in town hunting among the bargain tables and came home thoroughly tired. A disappointing day of shopping can exasperate some people's nerves. Every subject that came to Maria's mind seemed to produce discomfort. At last something was said about Rachel's morning caller.

Then Maria exclaimed: "Was that Marvie Parker here again? I think she's running things into the ground. Mama, do you know what kind of girl is influencing Rachel? I think the friendship ought to be stopped. She isn't in our set at all, and Rachel will feel uncomfortable in a year or two if she makes a special friend of a girl like that. She can't invite her or go with her anyplace, of course, when she gets old enough to care."

"What's the matter with Miss Parker?" asked Mr. Hammond, turning his sad gray eyes to his elder daughter's face. "Just because she isn't in your set doesn't seem to be a good reason for objecting to her. If she isn't, bring her in—that is, if the set is worth her coming. If it isn't, it might be a good thing for Rachel to have a few friends outside it, in case of an emergency. Miss Parker ought to be a good girl. Her father's a fine man, and I used to know her mother years ago when we were children. The girl ought to be well brought up. What's the matter with her, besides that senseless idea?"

Maria's face grew red. She didn't like to have her father against her, neither was she prepared to face his sharp eyes or his searching questions. She was on the point of reminding him that she and Rachel were no longer in a position to say who should or shouldn't belong in their set and that their own footing there might at any time grow insecure. But she remembered just in time to save herself this disgrace and her father the pain of such a remark. Instead she flew at once to defend her own statements.

"She may be a good girl, Papa. I presume she is," she replied. "But you'll surely acknowledge that she's putting strange ideas into Ray's head. Why, this morning she actually told me she'd enjoy going to some out-of-the-way place, on an almost desert island. The Parkers are seeking solitude there for the summer and living in a shanty at seventy-five dollars for the season. Just think of it! I don't know where she thought even the seventy-five dollars was to come from, with the railroad fares and all, but she wants us to go. Did you ever hear of such an idea?"

Rachel's fair face had grown red during the conversation. She was a sensitive girl and shrank from being the center of observation, even in her own family. Now as the glance of father, mother and brother were turned upon her, she could hardly keep tears from rushing into her eyes. But she tried to smile in answer to her father's encouraging look as he asked for an explanation.

"Why, Papa, I didn't really say I wanted to do it," said Rachel, her cheeks flushing redder. "I only said I thought it would be real nice. Of course I'm perfectly happy where I am. But if we were to do it I suppose we'd have to the same way the Parkers do. They rent their house here and get $250 for the season for it. Some people have to stay in town all summer for business; they have to be at their stores at seven o'clock, so they can't get far away from the city. Marvie said her father knew a lot of men who wanted homes just like ours for the summer, where they could bring their families out of the brick row houses. I thought someone might want our house that way. It ought to bring more than the Parkers' since ours is larger and is on a nicer street. But 'Ri seemed to think it was all so dreadful that I didn't say anything about it or mention renting our house."

Rachel dropped her eyes to avoid the exclamations she knew would follow.

"Rent our house!" said Maria, aghast. "Whatever can you be thinking about? Are you crazy? I guess we haven't quite come to that state of disgrace!"

"My dear child!" exclaimed the mother, astonished. "How could we have people using our carpets and our dishes?" A distressed pucker formed between her eyes, showing that the idea didn't seem impossible to her after all and she was really considering it.

"And what did you propose to do with Father and me, Ray?" asked her brother Winthrop, who was a little older than Maria and in business with his father; they were struggling to restore the name the former firm had lost through the treachery of one of its members. "You know we're obliged to be in town at a set hour every day, as well as some other folks."

Rachel's cheeks flushed anew at the implication that she, the quietest member of the household, had taken the family affairs into consideration and presumed to make the plans. But she answered shyly: "I hadn't thought it all out, but Mr. Parker and his son go into town every day. Marvie said a train leaves the island early enough to get here before nine, I think. They have special season tickets for businessmen, so it doesn't cost much. The store closes early during the summer anyway, doesn't it? But I didn't mean to plan. I'm happy where I am. I wouldn't have said a word, only 'Ri was worrying because we had to stay in town all summer, and I thought maybe Mother would enjoy the coolness by the shore."

"She's nothing but an absurd child!" exclaimed her sister. "Papa, surely you're not going to encourage her in such notions. I'm sure I'd rather die respectably than go away for the summer in such a disgraceful manner." She sat back in her chair with a sneer.

"Maria," said Mr. Hammond, looking straight at his daughter, "I'm ashamed if a child of mine has come to the place where she can say such a thing as that. You don't mean it. And as for this 'notion,' as you called it, it's nothing new to me. I've thought for a long time I could save a good deal and repair our finances much more quickly if I could rent this house. In fact, I had an offer last week of four hundred dollars for this place, stable and all, from now till the first of October. I declined the offer, not because of the frivolous reasons you've expressed, but simply because I knew of no cheaper place where my family could be comfortable while the house was earning the four hundred dollars."

"I should think not!" put in Maria. The fashion question and what her little world of "they" would think and say meant a great deal to her. It meant all that she now cared for in life, though she wouldn't have believed it if someone told her it was true.

But her father continued in his calm tone: "Now if the Parkers have found a place for seventy-five dollars where they can be comfortable, I think we might also. They're respectable people and used to having the necessities of life, if not the luxuries. It might be worth looking into at least. Don't you think so, Mother?"

And the wife, with a troubled look at her eldest daughter's face and a sigh of longing for the cool air of the ocean, agreed they should ask, at least.

Maria, with tears of chagrin in her eyes, suddenly left the table, and Rachel, whose tender heart was sorely distressed at having caused trouble to her sister, soon went to her own room. There for once she found the connecting door between her room and her sister's closed, and upon turning the knob softly a few minutes later she discovered it was also locked. This hadn't happened since the two girls were very little and first had rooms to themselves, and Rachel couldn't keep the tears back. She sought out her Bible for comfort and, finding it, resolved to try to make Maria happy that summer no matter what happened, seashore or home, heat or cool breezes, pleasure or disagreeableness. And so she slept.

Chapter 2

Maria Hammond had a very determined nature. When she liked or wanted a thing, she liked or wanted it intensely and bent all her energies to get it. What she disliked she was equally persistent in opposing. And when her plans and desires were frustrated, as they often were, a great struggle of her will ensued before she would give up and yield to the inevitable.

Even then, at the slightest opportunity, she would try for her way again. She insisted, however, that it wasn't her way she desired but merely to have things right about her; if the way were another person's and it seemed right to her, she would be just as eager to have it as her own. With such sophistry she excused herself to herself and to others for being so headstrong and willful. And because of her discontented nature, which was always desiring the unattainable, she was constantly in trouble.

When she went to her room after her stormy speeches at the dinner table, tears of anger, defeat, chagrin and disappointment swelled into her throat and eyes. She locked her door and threw herself on her bed weeping. She wouldn't for the world have let anyone, even a member of her own family, see her this way. But she had such an uncontrolled nature that when it burst out like this, she gave way to it.

Furthermore, in her eyes very small things often seemed important, so that what might simply be an annoyance to someone else became an overwhelming grief to her. It was, as it were, her very life that hung in the balance. For what else was life to her but the world's good opinion?

Maria lay on her bed crying for a long time. It wasn't simply what occurred at the dinner table that caused her trouble. Nor was it the prospect of spending the summer in an unfashionable retreat, though that seemed unlikely to her, even after what her father and mother said.

For surely, she thought, *they'll see it would be simply dreadful.*

But it seemed like a climax of all the disappointments that had come since her father lost his money. As a result, she mourned and pitied herself and perhaps pitied the rest of the family a little with what heart she had left after her own need was lavishly supplied.

Eventually she grew more calm. Then a shadow of her religion questioned why it couldn't help her in this trying time; for this stormy-natured girl had a religion, in spite of her will and her fear of what "they" would say. With the thought of her religion she also reflected on all she meant to do to help in the church work during the summer—of the class of delightfully bad little boys she promised to take in the Sunday school; of the young people's meeting she promised to lead; and of the tennis picnic in the park she was planning for those same young people. The picnic was to close in the dusk of evening with a short prayer meeting under the trees, and she hoped it would do a lot of good. Then she told herself she couldn't truly be removed to an out-of-the-way place where she would have no opportunity for anything of the kind when she planned to do so much. Thus she magnified her own projected goodness until she seemed like a martyr.

Now a nature like Maria's doesn't remain under a cloud for long. In time she persuaded herself that things couldn't be as bad as they seemed and silenced her uneasy conscience, which was reproaching her for the way she spoke to her father and sister. Conscious of her martyrdom, she sighed and resolved to go to her father the next morning and tell him she was resigned to being a hermit if it would contribute to his financial comfort. She thought her father would most likely not accept her sacrifice and, thus comforted, went to sleep.

Meanwhile the father and mother were discussing what to do. Money matters had come to a crisis during the last few weeks. Business was slow at the store. Mr. Hammond hoped he could tide affairs over until fall and so weather the gale. He felt that a serious talk with his wife was necessary, even though she was frail and he spared her all he could because she worried too much. Their talk, however, resulted in his eating breakfast a half-hour earlier than usual so he might stop and speak to his friend Mr. Parker on his way to the office. So Maria didn't speak to her father until evening.

The dinner bell rang throughout the house, and Maria hurried downstairs to talk to her father as he entered the dining room. Just then she heard her mother's voice speaking to him as she passed the door of the library.

"Yes, it would be very nice and just the thing," she said with an anxious sigh. "I would do it in a minute if it weren't for the girls' sake. I hate to do it when they're so opposed."

Her father's voice sounded weary. "It's Maria who's opposed, not both of them, remember, and things are as they are. Maria may come to worse trouble if we don't do this."

"Yes," said the mother sadly, "but Maria is the oldest, you know, and just at the age when everything like this makes so much difference to her. It might hurt her future, dear."

"Nonsense!" said her father rather sharply, although he felt the truth of what his wife was saying. "If Maria's future is to be hurt because her father rented his home to good, respectable people for a few months and went to a quiet, unfashionable place to stay during that time, I think it had better be hurt. Friends who are affected by such things are not worth having." But he sighed again as he walked downstairs.

Maria caught her breath, and tears filled her eyes. She hadn't realized she was causing so much trouble for her beloved father. She immediately forgot about any personal sacrifices and rushed up to him. Pulling him into the sitting room, she threw her arms around his neck and begged him to forgive her for what she said; she told him not to mind her in what he wished to do and that she'd try to be as helpful as she could.

So, after all, through Maria, the Hammond home was rented to a family who would pay well for four months' use of it, and the Hammonds themselves migrated to the seashore.

Maria didn't change in a moment. Many evenings she wept over the inevitable, but the memory of her father's weary face and her mother's anxious tones kept her from demurring any further to the family plans. Only to her sister, Rachel, and her brother, Winthrop, did she grumble. Win had long ago said his sisters were well named: Rachel was like a ray of sunlight everywhere, always cheery, never cross; while Maria, or 'Ri, as they called her, "always took things awry and kept a wry face much of the time."

"I say, 'Ri, do let up a little, can't you?" said her brother one day when Maria had finished one of her sarcastic speeches about their summer outing. "It's too late now to give up, so you'd better make the best of it. Where's the Christian fortitude I hear church members talk so much about? Can't you summon up a little to help you through this? You've taken every grain of pleasure out of the summer for Rachel and me, so be satisfied. You surely can't wish Father and Mother to suffer."

This somewhat caustic speech from her usually good-natured brother sent Maria to her room weeping. The days had already been hard for her. She imagined coming home to find the treasures in her room spoiled by ruthless alien hands and begged that certain articles necessary to the thorough furnishing of the house be locked away. But she was told this couldn't be.

While she cleared out her bureau drawers and closet and her private cubbyholes, she realized these places would be filled with some other girl's belongings. She thought she could never feel the same toward the little corners after strangers called them their own. She was also obliged to help pack cushions and cretonne draperies that could be spared from the home, along with curtains, pictures, screens and other essentials, to make the summer cottage habitable.

This went against the grain too. To think of spending the summer amid things fit only for a bedroom! It was humiliating. If they were to have a cottage, why couldn't they at least have it look comfortable and cheery and furnish it with taste?

Maria was the artist of the family and was thus called upon to select the draperies they should take. But she chose the silk-chenille portieres, satin embroidered sofa pillows and a plush hand-painted screen. So her mother decided to make the selections herself or quietly put it into Rachel's hands, for Rachel had already gone down to the little beach cottage.

Marvie Parker had invited Rachel over for a Sunday, and her father thought this would be a good opportunity for a family member to judge the fitness of the cottage. Before this Rachel was considered the child of the family, but her judgment was usually good. Her parents thought she would be less prejudiced than her sister, for she would tell both the best and the worst.

So Rachel accepted the invitation, much to Maria's chagrin. Maria told her she was opening the way to the Parkers to be much too intimate with them for the summer, a thing she, for one, didn't intend to condone. But Rachel, having her father and mother's consent, went and enjoyed her visit immensely. She returned home with glowing accounts of the fun in store for them, as well as an accurate description of the cottages for rent.

They were rough, she admitted, and unfinished inside except for a high facing of heavy manila paper. The ceilings were high, extending to the peak of the roof. She felt sure that Maria could make the parlor into a perfect summer alcove, and the rooms, though few, were large and spacious for a place so cheap. The cottage was one floor, with a wide porch for hammocks and a view of the sea and the bay. But when Maria—her interest awakened for a moment—selected silk and velour portieres, Rachel laughed and then looked troubled.

"They'll look out of place, 'Ri," she said. "You should have gone in my place, and then you'd know just what to take—you always know how to make things fit. But I think some of that pretty printed burlap we bought for cushions in our bedrooms would be just the thing."

"If I'd gone," said Maria severely, "I'd probably have brought back such a report that the family would have understood it wasn't a fit place for us to live in. But you seem to be getting everything your own way this time, so I suppose we'll take what curtains you say. I wish we didn't have to spend the summer surrounded by burlap. I didn't imagine things would be that rough."

So Maria fought every step of the way, contesting every plan, until everyone who asked her to help was glad when she left them to finish alone.

Poor Maria! A day or two before they left for the shore she discovered that the place selected was only a mile from a fashionable summer resort. She'd heard it was the most refined and aristocratic summer haunt. She also discovered to her dismay that the De Veres, a wealthy, cultured family of the West End of the city, had taken a cottage there.

Now Maria had met the Misses De Vere and their brother some three or four times at various social functions, and she felt that their acquaintance was worth cultivating. But she knew she would be embarrassed if they discovered her whereabouts and came to see the kind of place in which she was summering. She had taken quite a liking to them and didn't like to think of their looking down on her. It was hard to understand why she didn't feel that people who looked down on her because of the house she lived in weren't worth her caring about—unless she knew she would look down on someone in a similar situation and thus judged them by herself.

She listened to George Parker, Marvie's brother, describe to Rachel some of the cottages at Lone Point. He told her the Spray View people laughed at them and called them "Lone Point Barracks" and other funny names. Maria pictured Roland De Vere driving by their cottage someday and laughing with other strangers about their home. Her whole face turned crimson at the thought; she resolved that by no word of hers would the De Veres find out where she was to spend her summer, even though she missed many pleasant invitations by doing so.

One more experience before they left for Lone Point completed Maria's wretchedness. She and her sister were on some last-minute errands prior to departing from civilization for a time. Just before they took the car for home, they stopped at the public library to secure a supply of books for summer reading. While they were waiting at the desk for their cards to be marked, Roland De Vere, with his arms full of books, stepped up to them and touched his hat. Maria introduced her sister, of course, and the three walked out together.

"By the way, where are you spending your summer this year?" asked the young man as they paused at the corner to wait for a car.

Maria's cheeks reddened. She could never keep her face from telling tales she didn't want told, but she had enough presence of mind to answer vaguely, "Papa is talking of the seashore somewhere." Then she looked eagerly to see if the car was coming.

But Rachel didn't notice her sister's vague response and said eagerly, "Why, yes, we're going quite near where you'll be, if I've heard right. Aren't you going to Spray View? Your sister told a friend of ours. I hoped I might meet your sisters this summer. I've heard so much about them, and Maria is quite in love with both of them. Our place is only a mile from there, Lone Point—do you know it?"

Maria's face was crimson now. She motioned frantically to the car that was still half a block away and told her sister the car was ready, never turning her eyes to see what Mr. De Vere was thinking. She had so rehearsed in her mind how his face would show astonishment when he found out, and he would utter an expressive "Oh!" and turn away, that her imagination became reality to her. Therefore, the true scene which followed couldn't erase the impression. So vexed and embarrassed to the point of agony, she stepped out into the street with the other waiting passengers, hoping to prevent further conversation.

Mr. De Vere didn't notice, however, because he was taken up with talking to Rachel. His face lit up, and he said: "Know it? I should think so. It's a wonderful little place. I had a good friend there last year. I hope we'll see each other often. You go tomorrow, you say? That's terrific! We go the first of next week— sooner if Mother can get ready. Good afternoon, Miss Rachel; Miss Hammond, good afternoon. I'm glad we may see each other often this summer."

He touched his hat, and they stepped onto the car and were soon speeding away. The car was crowded, and the two girls had difficulty at first in finding seats. But closer to the suburbs the passengers grew fewer, and Maria took a seat beside her younger sister.

Rachel was blissfully unaware of her sister's state of mind, for she was excited about the possible pleasure in store for them that summer. Maria had been bottled up for nearly twenty minutes, however, and her wrath hadn't cooled in the process.

"Rachel Hammond!" said Maria, trying to lower her excited voice so none of their fellow passengers could hear. "I would think you might learn to keep your mouth shut occasionally. Every time I introduce you to one of my friends, I regret it bitterly. You should be old enough now to know how to behave."

Poor Rachel! She roused herself at once to remember what terrible breach of etiquette she had committed, but could think of nothing. She dreaded Maria's tirades and constantly tried to avoid them; perhaps as a result she received more of them.

"What did I do, 'Ri?" she asked.

If Maria hadn't been so angry she would have been touched by the trembling lips and the grieved look in Rachel's eyes.

"What did you do, indeed! You little tattletale! Don't tell me you don't know. You did it just to annoy me—or from some high and mighty notion that you would rebuke me for not telling everything I knew. You don't have to tell everything you know to avoid telling a falsehood. Why did you need to explain to that elegant Mr. De Vere in what a humiliating state we're to spend our summer? I should think things were uncomfortable enough for me already without adding that. I'll simply die of shame if they come over to that horrid little place and find us rusticating in a cow shed. I think you've fully overstepped the mark this time. You've chosen your friends, and I have a right to mine. I shall ask Papa to let you know that after this you're not to interfere with me and my friends."

Maria became angrier as she talked. During the silent ride she provoked her imagination with scenes of meeting Fannie De Vere at Spray View, until she scarcely could contain herself. Rachel's fair face grew almost white at her sister's words. She tried to explain, but Maria was in no state to be reasonable.

"But, Maria, dear," she pleaded, "I didn't dream I was saying anything unpleasant to you."

"Then you must be blind," snapped Maria. "You certainly must have seen from the way I answered him that I'd have bitten out my tongue sooner than to have him know."

"But I didn't, 'Ri. I didn't dream of such a thing! I was only delighted for your sake, for I thought you'd have some company, and he seemed so pleased about it."

"Oh, yes, he was pleased!" sneered Maria. "He's too polite to show anything else, but he's probably laughing in his sleeve this minute. You needn't worry. We won't see either him or his lovely sisters at all this summer. As soon as he said he was acquainted with Lone Point, I knew what to expect. I heard a man from Spray View talk about Lone Point the other day, and they don't consider the place fit for Spray Viewers to wipe their feet on."

Poor Rachel quivered under her sister's upbraidings. When they reached home she could bear it no more and went to her room to do an unusual thing for her—have it out with her tears. And then she went to her heavenly Father with her bruised heart and found comfort.

Chapter 3

Meanwhile Roland De Vere was walking down Walnut Street. *Strange,* he said to himself. *What could have been her reason? Was she ashamed of going to a quiet, unfashionable resort? She was angry with her sister for telling me. I could see that. The first time I saw her she struck me as being intellectual, and pretty too, but I didn't notice that discontented curl to her lips. I've never seen her in the daytime before, though. Gaslight makes a wonderful difference. It's not so good as I thought at first. But that other face is like a flower. The younger sister must be worth getting to know. I enjoyed her frank eagerness. Fannie would like her. I mean to take her over to call as soon as possible after we get to the shore.*

How Maria's eyes would have opened in surprise had she known his true feelings. It's a pity some inventor couldn't give us a little instrument for divining occasionally what others think of us. It would sometimes save a world of worry. But how careful we should then have to be of our own thoughts of others. Perhaps someone greater than Edison will arise one day and search out the hidden law that governs thoughts and let us look into one another's hearts. Then how much better—or how much worse, alas—we shall be! For surely the kingdom of heaven will be near at hand when men's judgments of one another are kind and loving.

The Hammonds journeyed to Lone Point on a Saturday, so that father and brother could escort them and help unpack and arrange their belongings for the summer. Maria looked sadly about on familiar objects as she walked toward the nearest station in the early morning. She felt as if she were leaving the world; and when she returned, if she ever survived the humiliating summer, everything would be different, and she could never be the same girl again.

Rachel, however, went ahead with Win. He saw how her bright spirits were clouded by her sister's gloomy mood and made a pretext of some errand to get her with him. Somehow he found out from Rachel what her sister said to her on the streetcar the night before and was indignant with Maria for being so hard on the sensitive younger sister. He resolved to talk plainly to her on the first opportunity and save Rachel from further annoyance of that sort. He managed the seats in the cars so that Rachel was with him, his father and mother together, and Maria installed with a fresh magazine and a pile of hand baggage in a third seat. This suited Maria exactly, and since Rachel was in front of the others, she didn't have to think about Maria and her troubles during the journey.

Rachel looked a little pale that morning from her unusual vigil of the night before, and Win set a goal of helping her forget it. Soon her face lit up, and her silvery laugh could be heard from time to time. That made Maria look up and frown, to think that any member of the family could be cheerful on such a journey. She felt as if she were attending her own funeral, and the procession would never cease. The magazine was interesting, though, and she soon forgot herself for a little while.

They traveled through pleasant garden villages and wastelands of sand and scrub. The time seemed short to Rachel until they wound their way out at last upon the lovely bay and ran for several miles with water on either side and the sea breeze blowing fresh in their faces through the open windows of the car. Rachel and her mother drew in long breaths. Even Maria sensed relief from the heat and felt her heart grow lighter, though she didn't stop to explain to herself why it was so.

Finally they came in sight of Spray View in the distance; its cottages and hotels seemed imposing beyond the blue waters of the bay and with the deep green sea as a background. When Maria heard the name of the place, she looked ahead and wished that the tallest dark green cottage with the trumpet vine in full bloom over its lordly porch were to be theirs, instead of—

Suddenly the train halted, and the brakeman called out "Lone Point." They were hustled out onto a bare platform in the sand, and the train raced on toward the towers of Spray View a mile ahead.

"Why did we get out?" Maria demanded. "We aren't there yet. They said that was Spray View on ahead. Isn't the place on the other side of it? This doesn't look like anyplace at all," she said, looking scornfully at the waste of sand with the cluster of small buildings near the beach.

But no one was paying attention to her, so she was obliged to pick up her umbrella and hand satchel and follow the rest.

"Here we are," shouted Rachel, "and there it is! There! That's ours, that green one over there with the white trim. And here comes Marvie to meet us, and her brother, George. Oh, I'm so glad we're here!" she exclaimed and dashed over to greet her friend.

It was just as humiliating as Maria expected. The "Parker boy," as she referred to him—though he was as old as young Mr. De Vere—offered to help and insisted on taking her hand baggage from her. Further, they would be obligated to the Parkers, whose cottage was next door and who had kindly prepared dinner for the Hammonds and had it on the table by the time they had their hats off. To Maria it was unheard of and dreadful, and she had no appetite to choke down the delicate fish and fresh vegetables. She wished her mother had declined any help, and she'd rather have starved until their own servant could prepare some kind of a meal. But the rest of her family didn't share her feelings and did ample justice to the dinner.

Even distressed Maria found enough to do that afternoon, leaving her no time to think. They brought one servant with them and depended on her to make everything move smoothly and bear all the burdens. But she also had her own ideas about watery places. She went outside and looked over the place briefly and, above all, the ocean, which she hadn't seen yet. With one glance over the turbulent blue waves she turned and ran back to the cottage.

In her absence the family was setting up an impromptu partition in the kitchen to make a bedroom for her. She surveyed that quickly, exclaimed in dismay over the roughness of things and said "My land!" several times. Then she walked out on the porch and took in the narrow stretch of land between the ocean and the bay. Finally she went inside and told Mrs. Hammond she must return right away to town on the next train, and she "couldn't stand it" and was "sure that water would meet and flood the place."

Nor could any amount of persuasion on the part of the united, dismayed family change her firm decision. No, indeed, she wouldn't stay overnight! She would never expect to see the morning light. She didn't wish to let the sun go down and darkness settle on her with that awful ocean roaring and surging back and forth so near her. What did it matter to her that the Hammonds had paid her fare down from the city, had in fact bought her a return ticket? What did she care about losing her place? Fear had seized her, and her frenzied soul cared only about fleeing. And flee she did on the two-o'clock train.

Then the family, alarmed, sat down to consider what to do next. Rachel was cheerful. She had gone to the beach and was exhilarated. She was ready for anything and would call it fun, even if it meant washing dishes and peeling potatoes. They looked anxiously at Maria, who had made her misery so evident all day that they dreaded how this last blow would affect her.

Maria stood up with martyr-like resignation. She hadn't gone to the beach and didn't wish to go. One place on this deserted island was the same to her as another. Since she was condemned to stay here, what difference did it make where she stayed or what she did during that time? If someone must have a disagreeable time, why not have it as disagreeable as possible and so get more credit for enduring? (This last she didn't say out loud.) She would do the work. She was perfectly capable of doing as much as that good-for-nothing girl. If she wasn't, she'd learn. She could at least save a few more cents from the girl's wages to add to the family treasury and so increase the vast sum they were to make during this summer of humiliation. Their downfall was complete; why not accept it and go to the bottom gracefully? They had to live in a hovel and, of course, do their own work; it was no more than she expected.

Maria didn't say all this; instead her sentences were short and her words few. But by her tone and manner she conveyed her meaning to the family, and they felt it. A gray look spread over the father's face, and the mother sighed. Rachel's brightness faded. Maria seemed determined to dampen their spirits.

But Win was determined that this first day should not be spoiled. Without hesitating an instant he took up Maria's proposal, not in its spirit, but in its words.

"Yes, of course, why shouldn't we? Mother, we can all help. I can't do much all day, but I can make it up in the evenings. I'll make sure the wood is cut and the coal handy, start the fire in the morning and get the ice in the refrigerator, and run errands. I'll have plenty of time for errands before breakfast and train time if I get up a little earlier. And Sundays I'll wash dishes three times a day to make up for what I can't do on weekdays. I can wash dishes beautifully. It'll seem like old times when I was little and 'Ri was a baby. Mother had no girl then, and I helped wipe dishes. Mother, don't you remember? Then I can run over to Spray View on errands in the evenings after supper. We don't need to live high, anyway, and there can't be much housework to do in such a small house."

"Of course we can do the work," echoed Rachel eagerly. "Maria and I have both had cooking lessons. Besides, here's Mother, who knows how to do everything and can direct us in anything we've forgotten or never learned. It'll be fun. Come on—let's wash the dinner dishes right away, Win, and then we'll have more room to put things in order."

She ran humming out of the room with her brother, and the two were heard clattering the dishes while talking and laughing.

Maria, with her chin tilted slightly upward, followed them and was soon stirring up a mysterious concoction for supper and starting bread for the next day. The closest bakery was in the neighboring town, and everyone was too busy to go there.

A half-hour or so later they were deep in work. The girls with their sleeves rolled up and improvised kitchen clothes were taking things from the open boxes and trunks. Mr. and Mrs. Hammond were unpacking and sorting out the most immediate necessities. And Win in his shirt sleeves with a large apron tied about his waist and a towel over his arm was drying a white soup bowl—and whistling and joking with his sisters in between.

No one saw a light rig pull up in front of the cottage or heard someone get out and walk up the steps.

"I say, 'Ri!" called out the brother cheerfully. "Don't look so cross or that bread'll be too sour to eat. It'll be 'rye' bread. See?"

Just then a distinct knock was heard on the open door. The brother disappeared through the calico portiere that belonged to the house and separated the dining room from the parlor. He went to answer the knock, thinking it might be the butcher or baker and not caring about his appearance. Wasn't he on a lark and on a desert island where he didn't know a soul? Besides, he had a spirit that didn't feel degraded by an apron or a dish towel.

But he wasn't prepared for the immaculate person who stood before the door, politely trying to keep a smile from playing around his mouth.

"I beg your pardon—I hope I'm not intruding," said the young man on the porch, tipping his hat. "But isn't this Mr. Hammond's—"

"Shanty? Certainly," finished Win with a low bow and mock solemnity. "Walk right in. Things aren't quite shipshape yet, but I think we can find you a chair."

Win Hammond was not to be embarrassed by any strange gentleman in fashionable driving attire. He dusted off a chair with a flourish, using the dish towel as a duster.

Then Rachel appeared in the doorway, one cheek dabbed with flour and her arms dripping with soapsuds. Her dark hair, loose about her face, had curled itself into little rings, and her cheeks, under the flour, were flushed with excitement and work. She heard her brother's banter and guessed he was joking for their benefit with a grocer boy or fish man.

The young man at the door stepped into the room laughing good-naturedly, then, catching sight of Rachel in the doorway, he crossed the room to where she stood.

"Good afternoon, Miss Rachel," he said. "Welcome to the shore. Have you just arrived? You didn't expect to find me here ahead of you, did you? Mother sent me on ahead to make some arrangements and get everything ready for them on Monday. Up to your eyes in work, eh? Is this your brother? I thought so. Glad to meet you, Mr. Hammond. Having a good time, aren't you? I envy you. I'd like nothing better than to pitch in and help. Don't you have something for me to do? I have a horse here and can run errands. Do put me to work. I've weeded my own garden and don't have a thing to do till the folks come Monday. I'm by myself and would enjoy it. Is your sister here?"

"She's in the kitchen making bread," laughed Rachel, entering into the spirit of their guest's speech. "Maria!" she called and went to find her sister.

But Maria had listened to the voice at the door in dismay and fled.

Chapter 4

Into the midst of their work and settling in came the calm of the Sabbath. A small church was located nearby, and at the appointed hour they could see the neighbors making their way there in simple clothes.

After completing her morning work and helping all she could to prepare dinner, Rachel said she meant to go to church. The others were too weary, however, and even Mrs. Hammond thought it was better to wait until the next week to get acquainted with the place. But when she came out a few minutes later in a dark serge skirt, clean shirtwaist and sailor hat, Win picked up his hat and followed his sister down the steps.

"For pity's sake! Rachel Hammond! You're surely not going to church in a strange place in that outfit?" called the horrified Maria as she caught sight of her sister going out the door. "You don't have any gloves, either. You might have a little sense of decency left, at least."

But Rachel was out of hearing and went serenely on her way, drinking in the salt air and the Sabbath quiet as she walked.

Watching her, Maria wondered how her sister could be so happy, half-envied her for her sweet, happy nature and then went off alone to shed some discontented tears. She had refused to listen to any account of the previous day's visitor and remained in hiding during his short stay. Then she disappeared as suddenly again when he returned with some packages Rachel had laughingly sent him to get.

Maria didn't approve of taking Mr. De Vere into their family at this stage of events and letting him see all the ins and outs of the crude cottage and their makeshift family life. She wanted to receive her guests in the right way or not at all, and so she removed herself from that day's activities. Her soul was in turmoil at the thought of the laughing account Mr. De Vere would give his stately mother and elegant sisters of his visit to Lone Point. She resolved to stay out of their sight as much as possible and wondered why it was necessary to add this humiliation to her list of troubles for the summer.

After her little cry she went to the kitchen, where her martyr spirit bore her up grimly. She made the rest of the family uncomfortable with the elaborate dishes she prepared and tasted only a little of herself. She didn't intend to make them all unhappy but wasn't averse to their knowing how uncomfortable they'd made her and how well she was bearing up under the circumstances.

She kept it up during the week, even refusing to go to the beach, when she could have gone as well as not. She declared she had no wish to meet the people of the place. They were common, anyway; she could tell that from their appearance on the Sabbath. As for the sea, she never cared much for it. The usual pleasures of seaside life weren't here to make the place endurable, so she'd rather stay at home and let others who could enjoy things go to the beach. So she stayed in the cottage, cooked and arranged the cheap draperies into graceful fashionings.

She didn't take pride in her work as she might have done at another time, but worked at it from fierce necessity. If the De Veres called at any time she would at least make things as presentable as possible so they wouldn't see a barren place. She firmly resolved, however, to be absent and unfindable when they called. Thus she worked, and the room grew beautiful in spite of the rebellious spirit of its artist. She asked for little help from anyone, but her brother and sister were both watching to be of assistance and supplied the needed help without being asked.

In one corner of the parlor a cozy couch took on vast dimensions, composed on one side of the woven-wire cot on which Win slept and on the other of the box in which the curtains and tin dishes had traveled. This was upholstered deftly in dark blue burlap bearing a wreath and crest design, and the whole was united by a deep valance around the sides. In the corner were many cushions, some only filled with straw or excelsior from the packing; others were the pillows used for Winthrop's bed at night and stuffed during the day into calico and chintz covers of bright design. Two or three were genuine eiderdown with embroidered denim covers, and the effect was not only lovely but luxurious.

Maria manipulated pretty screens out of cheap torn paper ones, and one corner was curtained off in a novel way with a heavy bamboo pole Win found on the beach. Curtains of green and brown figured burlap hung in folds from it. No one would have suspected that behind this were Win's washstand and a few hooks on which he hung some of his clothes. Maria thought it was common that someone had to sleep in the parlor. But since it couldn't be helped—the house had only two other sleeping rooms—she disguised the fact as prettily as possible.

Crêpe paper lamp shades and a quaint, oddly shaped bookcase of original workmanship, from a shoebox and an old peach crate, also gave touches to the room. When finished, the entire family pronounced it a perfect gem of beauty, comfort and coziness.

"Isn't this beautiful! What a transformation!" exclaimed Roland De Vere. It was the next week, and he had come to announce that his family would call as soon as the Hammond girls were willing to receive them.

"I never saw such a change. What fairy has waved her wand so effectively?" he asked and looked at Rachel.

She immediately disclaimed any part in the work and gave it all to Maria. Meanwhile, Maria remained invisible to all callers. Mr. De Vere didn't notice this fact so much, however, as he would have if he hadn't enjoyed being with her brother or sister. They began planning excursions and moonlight sails; she was always included in them but not in their preparation. She felt wounded at the way things were going, blamed it all on the others and didn't see that it was her own doing. She wouldn't even go to the beach, though the others begged her and invented various ways of trying to get her there. She had set her stubborn will against all their pleadings and wouldn't be coaxed by anything or anyone; at last they gave up.

As if to emphasize her martyrdom, Maria arranged her hair in an unbecoming way, took on hard lines about her mouth and worked in an old apron most of the time. Rachel grieved over it as much as she had time for amid the delightful activities open to her. She enjoyed wandering over the beautiful beach in search of shells with Marvie and Marvie's brother, George, who proved to be as bright and interesting as she'd prophesied. But he was a busy student and had little time for fun, even during summer vacation. She also enjoyed meeting her father and brother at the train station each evening and then talking later with Win. And she considered visits from Maria's friend, as she called Roland De Vere, some great treat she was permitted to share with the others but one that didn't belong to her. The summer seemed to be unfolding before her with promise.

One evening she was sitting in her room. She looked out on the bay in the distance and saw the softly rippling waters calming into glass before the setting sun. The white sails here and there were speeding homeward. In a few minutes the train would roll along by the water, and she would run down to meet her father and brother.

Supper was nearly ready. The clam bisque was perfect; she had made it and was proud of it. Maria was busy with one of her special concoctions and seemed to want the kitchen to herself. Rachel was glad to slip away for a minute to rest and think and pray. Since they'd been doing their own work, she found little uninterrupted time for her Bible and was glad to find it anywhere. As soon as the morning work was done, Marvie was sure to run in and claim Rachel for some activity. They'd been by the sea only a week, and yet things had already settled into a routine.

Rachel thought sadly of it, for Maria, her dear sister, seemed left out of everything. She wouldn't have anything to do with the Parkers and seemed as loath to be with her own friends, the De Veres.

Rachel wondered what it meant and if she could do anything about it or if she was to blame for suggesting this summer scheme. Then she thought of her mother's face taking on a glow of health from the sea breezes and of her father, whose face had dropped its anxious look and who seemed to be enjoying life again. No, it was clearly not her fault, and she mustn't mourn over it. It was turning out to be the best for all of them.

But what could she do for Maria? She picked up her Bible, from habit perhaps, for she didn't know. She felt it was her responsibility to do something for her sister; but what could it be? Neither coaxing nor sacrifice nor pity would avail; she had tried them all. They merely seemed to irritate her sister.

The Bible opened by itself, as it often did, to the call "Come unto me, all ye that labor and are heavy laden, and I will give you rest. Take my yoke upon you, and learn of me; for I am meek and lowly in heart; and ye shall find rest unto your souls." Rachel had marked those verses with bright red ink when she was a little girl. She had turned to them many times since, at first because they were familiar words and seemed like old friends with the red lines around them, and afterward because they comforted her and grew dear for their own sakes.

She didn't linger over them now. She thought their message seemed more for her sister than for her and sighed as she started to turn the page; she wished Maria could find rest, so that her life would reflect peace and joy. Then suddenly a thought stopped her hand before she finished turning the page. Wasn't that message for her after all? She felt burdened by her sister's dark mood. Couldn't she find rest from that as well as her own burdens? The Lord surely didn't want her to carry that burden. If she came to Him, He would show her what, if anything, she could do to help lift the cloud that hung over Maria. She could come to Jesus and find rest and strength, so that even the burden of her sister's attitude wouldn't disturb her calm—for it would be His calm.

She turned the pages slowly to another verse she had marked and been helped by many times. "Ye have not chosen me, but I have chosen you, and ordained you, that ye should go and bring forth fruit, and that your fruit should remain, that whatsoever ye shall ask of the Father in my name he may give it you."

Then it wasn't her business to look after the fruit. She was to do His work because He chose her. She would do whatever He put into her hands to do. She'd forgotten that whatever she asked the Father He would do for her, and she could trust Him to do it in His own good way and time. She would trust Him with her sister.

Rachel knelt and poured out her heart. It was filling up each day with petty irritations in the kitchen and parlor and all over the house. She tried to bear them patiently, but they wore on her usually gentle spirit until now and then sharp words escaped her. She told her heavenly Father everything and asked for her sister's happiness above all.

Then she smoothed her hair and rushed out into the kitchen with her heart full of love for Maria and trust for the answer to her prayer. She wrapped her arms impetuously around her weary sister's neck and, hugging her, whispered softly, "'Ri, dear, forgive me. I've been awfully cross and teased you a great deal to do what you don't want to do, and I haven't helped you half enough. Will you forgive me? I'm sorry."

Now Maria was frying fish and turning over a large, beautiful piece carefully so that its perfection should remain unmarred. She was also very warm, and the stove had been acting abominably all afternoon; the fish was brown only because of Maria's repeated shaking and coaxing with kindling and bits of paper. Her hair was coming down, so that any movement on her part was precarious. She had also burned her wrist, and the pain was aggravated by the heat of the stove.

Therefore Rachel's eager hug was scarcely pleasant just then. And Rachel's willingness to confess her fault, when she herself, the greater offender, was very unwilling, irritated Maria more than words could tell. Perhaps she wasn't so much to blame because she was having such a difficult time, though it was largely her own fault. She had just received a letter from one of her dear friends describing in detail how much she was enjoying a lovely mountain resort. It was no wonder her tone was ungracious.

"For pity's sake, do get out of my way, Rachel!" she said crossly. "Don't you see what you're doing? You'll make me break this piece of fish. I wish you'd be considerate. I'd much rather you show your sorrow by your actions than your words. Words are cheap."

With that Maria jerked the fish over, knocking the teakettle and two or three pans around on the stove with such a clatter that any words Rachel might have spoken were silenced.

Rachel, with tears filling her eyes, headed for the train, sorry she'd made another mistake. *I never seem to know what to do or say to please her,* she said to herself. *If she spoke crossly to me and asked me to forgive her, I'd have been so happy and forgotten it all. But it only seemed to make her feel angrier with me.*

Then Rachel remembered the results weren't her work and that she'd taken her burden to her heavenly Father and given it to Him to carry. She mustn't pick it up again; it wasn't hers. So she tossed it aside and hurried toward the station with a lighter heart.

Chapter 5

Maria stood on the porch later that evening. The sunset glow was fading over the bay. The supper dishes were washed and put away. There was nothing more to be done in the kitchen that night. She was at liberty to watch the pearl-colored sail that floated lazily on the pink and gray waters.

Win and Rachel had gone over to the pavilion directly after supper with Marvie Parker and her brother. They didn't think it worthwhile to ask Maria to join them tonight. In fact, Rachel hinted to her brother that perhaps it would be better to say nothing of their purpose to Maria since everything like it seemed only to make her feel badly. So for the first time since they'd come to the seaside, they went off without coaxing her to go with them.

Maria had declined these invitations curtly every time, but she nevertheless felt hurt by the omission tonight. Tears filled her eyes and blurred the pearl-colored sail as she thought how easily they could get along without her. Before this she'd been the life of the family, the center of every excursion, the witty talker, the graceful leader in everything. Now Rachel, who was hardly grown up yet, seemed to have taken her place. She wasn't as indispensable as she thought. Even her father and mother had strolled away, arm in arm, like a pair of lovers, pointing out a bright star overhead or calling one another's attention to a sail in the distance. Maria felt very lonely.

Things proved a great deal worse than she feared. She thought that after the family saw how uncomfortable things were going to be they would set about to right them. They would perhaps go over to Spray View and take a respectable cottage where they could live in some decent style, as she phrased it to herself. There would be some enjoyment in that, and perhaps they would try to get another servant. But she was willing to help in the kitchen and get along with a very poor one to save enough to live in what seemed a respectable manner and, what was more important to her, would seem so to her friends. Then she would gladly welcome the De Veres and enjoy whatever they offered her in the way of pleasure.

Now, however, everything was different. The family seemed entirely indifferent to their surroundings. They were actually happy. As she thought over it she couldn't remember seeing her father and mother enjoying themselves so much before. She wondered why they didn't see how unhappy she was.

Oh, if she could only go to that mountain resort where her friend Nellie Mayhew was having such a delightful time! To be sure she couldn't hope to share in everything because she couldn't buy the clothes to wear to many of the social functions with her friend. But if she could only get there and stay in that great hotel, with a few dollars she could construct a wardrobe that would make her look equal to the others. But what was here? Nothing but views and air! And a father, mother, sister and brother too absorbed in their own pleasures to think of her or know she was at home moping alone after a long hard day working in the kitchen.

And at that very minute her father and mother, as they pointed out the stars and the sails, were discussing whether or not they could manage to scrape together enough money to send Maria to the mountains in the style she wished to go. The mother, strange to say, was the one who objected this time.

"No, Richard," she said, "I can't help feeling, even if we might afford it, that it wouldn't be best. Maria is young yet. I think she can be trusted to behave herself and take care of herself, but it might be better for her to have the discipline of this summer. She's already shown character traits I didn't dream she had. It grieves me to see it. She's been very selfish and inconsiderate. You don't see it all day as I do.

"She works like a slave, harder than she ever worked before. I'll put a stop to that overwork pretty soon, for a great part of it is unnecessary. But she's unkind to me and to her sister and as disagreeable as she can be. I've been thinking about how to talk with her but decided to wait a little while and study her present mood. Sometimes I'm afraid she has never understood what it means to be a true Christian; she's so rebellious at her situation."

And then the father, in a tender voice, tried to excuse her and pity her. So they talked and walked much farther and longer than they'd expected to. And the evening wore on while Maria sat alone. Finally, from being weary of herself and her own thoughts, she was forced to go to bed.

The next day was Saturday, and Maria was at last driven to the beach. Win had remained at the shore since his father felt he wouldn't be needed that day at the store. Dinner was over. Maria's dress was too soiled to wear until it was washed, so she retired to her room to change quickly. She felt like putting on something ugly; but fortunately for her nearly all her clothes were tasteful and lovely, and she had already worn the garments she brought along for rainy weather or hard work. So she chose a clear blue and white sheer dimity. The belt and collar were light blue ribbons with fluttering bows. Maria tried to fit on a linen collar and go without a belt, but the effect was so incongruous that she finally gave in to her own innate sense of beauty and put on the blue ribbons.

Then her hair didn't seem to harmonize with the outfit. By this time her sense of fitness was so aroused that she loosened her hair and coiled it in the old, becoming way. Altogether she was like her familiar self when she was ready to leave the room.

She passed the window to pick up a novel she'd been reading, and her eye caught sight of a double surrey, drawn by handsome horses, just turning the corner by their cottage. Three ladies and a young man were in the carriage, and the elder lady was looking through a lorgnette at the unpretentious dwelling. That lorgnette made up Maria's mind.The carriage contained the De Veres— mother, daughters and son. They had come, at the son's insistence, to patron- ize the Hammonds.

Maria, for one, didn't intend to be investigated through a lorgnette. She caught up her book and a white parasol belonging to Rachel, flew out the back door and ran across the sand lot to the next street. She stayed out of sight of the carriage, which was now standing in front. Then she turned and hurried to the most unfrequented portion of the broad beach she could find. There she sat behind her parasol and a mound of sand and concentrated on reading her book, certain no unwelcome visitor could find her there.

Rachel opened the door with a smile and greeted the elegant Mrs. De Vere graciously. At the same time she remembered glimpsing Maria's blue dimity on the bed as she passed the door. She thought Maria must be dressed in it by then, for of course she would be obliged to come out of her shell now.

Mrs. Hammond felt that Maria might need an extra word from her to put aside her current notions and so went in search of her elder daughter. But Maria was nowhere to be found—not even by Rachel, who looked in tucked-away places where she'd found her before.

The De Veres may have thought Maria's absence strange, although the young man had told his mother and sisters she was never present when he called; but they were too well-bred to mention it. They weren't nearly so over- powering in their manner as Maria anticipated.

Mrs. Hammond was charmed with Mrs. De Vere's friendliness, and a mutual liking drew the two ladies to each other at once. Meanwhile the young people were planning countless get-togethers. The time passed quickly, and the visit lasted much longer than fashion dictated.

Then, in a manner that would have shocked Maria if she'd been present, the three De Veres followed Rachel through the sand. Finding George and Marvie Parker, they insisted they join their moonlight sail planned for the com- ing week. The De Veres had discovered she had friends in the Parkers and del- icately suggested the invitation. Then they proposed to go at once and give it.

On the way Rachel wondered if Maria would blame her for it or cause trou- ble about the Parkers going with them. She finally resolved to say nothing about it to her sister and let things come about as they would.

Meanwhile Maria felt more at peace with the world than she had for many days. She was dressed in fine clothes, as was her habit, and had succeeded in getting away from her visitors without being seen or suspected. She settled her- self without her usual scowl to enjoy her book. So much are clothes of value that the subtle awareness of being well-dressed often has the power to lift one for a time at least above fretful circumstances or sordid surroundings.

Now if Rachel Hammond had been consulted as to the answer of her earnest prayers for her sister, she would have suggested something other than what happened. The least promising thing, in Rachel's opinion, was for Maria to run away from the De Veres and spend the entire afternoon in a lonely part of the beach, reading a novel in which the heroine suffered impossible things and was crowned with untold rewards for her pains. She would have said a pleasant afternoon in the company of pleasant people, planning a delightful excursion, forgetting things that might have been, and learning to be interested in things that are and are to be, would have been the best thing for her sister.

But God knew better. He was leading this child of His through a narrow, thorny path, but through the only straight road that would take her home.

Maria hadn't visited the beach before and knew little about the peculiarities of the wind and the tide. So she did as most newcomers and settled herself by the edge of the surf, as near as it seemed safe and pleasant, so she could watch the water.

After a good look she soon forgot to watch the water in favor of her heroine's fortunes. The ocean's tide at that time was going out, but almost at its turn. It receded a little, and Maria read on. Eventually it no longer receded but gained a little, until it crept closer to the seat on the sand and the straying blue ribbon that fluttered out from the white silk parasol. Now a larger wave came and almost stretched its lip of foam to kiss the foam of white lace on the blue dimity ruffles. Then it rolled back again to gather force, and now another came and just touched the dainty ruffle and dampened it.

But still the wearer read on, oblivious to receding or approaching waves. She had turned herself sideways to keep the ocean glare from her page and didn't notice. Moreover, the heroine was at the point of being rescued from a desert island; she'd been cast there with a noble hero who loved her, by an ignoble lover who was searching for her. The situation was thrilling, and Maria had eyes only for the story. She also didn't see a young man who was sauntering down the beach toward her from the lighthouse, a mile or two away.

The Rev. Howard Fairfield, in the most unclerical garb he could find in his very unclerical wardrobe, had been visiting the Point Rock lighthouse and joking with its keeper. He entered with zest into the stories the old man told of his wild life as a young sailor and was, in fact, posing as a young man who understood and enjoyed such escapades.

He was walking slowly along the beach, unaware of any incongruity. In his mind he was weaving the wonders he'd seen and heard of God's providence and man's skill into a fine illustration for the conclusion of an address. He was preparing for the first sermon he would preach after his vacation ended. He was young for the important charge he occupied. He chose this simple resort as a suitable place for him to spend his vacation; he thought the absolute quiet and solitude would be conducive to rest and study both. Thus he would return to his city church thoroughly fortified in health and with a store of material for sermons for the winter.

He wasn't an unspiritual minister, nor was he ashamed of his calling. But in college and seminary he had acquired some "advanced" notions concerning the doffing of clerical clothes and the "clerical manner" which, while they might be good to a degree, he had carried to their extreme. When he went to a place, he delighted in keeping the people from finding out he was a minister. Indeed, he carried this so far that he let others take him for almost anything rather than know his true character or profession. He thought he could do a great deal more good this way, by entering into other people's lives and sympathies and not letting them feel that he did so because it was his business.

Perhaps there was some truth in this. But he spent so much time entering into people's lives that he often forgot or found it awkward to do the good that might have resulted from the influence he gained. Sometimes, too, others felt that he glossed over the line between right and wrong a bit in this "entering in" business. He called it "being all things to all men."

However that may be, he was a student, an eloquent preacher and somewhat conceited because of the extraordinary praise he had received during his short pastorate. He was also opinionated but nevertheless much in earnest. He considered himself quite spiritual indeed and in his heart longed to be all that his Lord would have him be. In person he was handsome, with a scholarly air, gracious in manner, a little distant but attractive to most people, especially when he chose to be so.

Rachel Hammond, if she'd known him, would have considered him the most unlikely person to help her sister, Maria. Yet he was walking toward her on the beach, and the waves were creeping toward her on the sand, and the Lord was ordering it all. For the winds and the waves obey His will, even in such a slight matter as this.

The young man was nearing Maria. He hadn't noticed her especially, except to realize that his favorite combination of light blue and white was lying there on the sand like a picture against the background of sky and sea. As he drew closer he saw it was a young woman with a shapely hand holding a book. He was a student of human nature and wondered what sort of young woman she was, reading alone so close to the sea. And what book absorbed her so much that she didn't mark the hungry waves approaching? He thought he must warn her if she didn't look up before the next wave and lingered a little to see if she stirred.

Then, before he could think further, the largest wave so far rushed and tumbled in unexpectedly. It soaked the crisp ruffles of the dimity, then dashed into the young lady's lap, wetting her feet and book and sending her flying back from the spot in alarm. Then the wave calmly seized the white silk parasol with its solid gold handle, a treasured present from a rich uncle to Rachel, and hurled it out in its retreating arms, a toy upon the billows.

Maria found herself on solid ground but saw her sister's precious parasol tossed on the water. She made a dash to catch it on the crest of the next wave, but the water was too quick for her. It floated out, this time a little farther, where the breakers tossed the delicate thing so rudely that Maria despaired for its frail structure. At this juncture the young man standing by took two strides in the saucy waters and brought the wet, dripping thing to Maria with as much dignity as he could command in his wet, white duck trousers.

Both young people were embarrassed. But the Rev. Howard Fairfield enjoyed carrying off trying situations in a gracious manner, and he did himself justice in this instance, to the young woman's admiration.

"Oh, not at all, let me carry it home for you," he said, as she reached her hand for the parasol. "Your cottage is nearby, isn't it? Nothing is far away from anything else in this place, is it?" Here he stopped to pick up her book, more from curiosity to know its name perhaps than anything else. "No, no, let me carry it. You'll have enough to do to walk in this sand with your wet gown. I'm going this way, and it's no trouble whatever."

So against her will Maria walked the length of the beach to her home with a stranger, a young man. Her dress was wet and bedraggled; he carried her borrowed parasol and book; and his own costume was rather the worse for water. She thought it was too dramatic for her to appear at home in this condition after the lofty way she'd been acting. She knew her brother would never cease teasing her.

She was trying to plan some way to retreat or get rid of the stranger, who was chatting pleasantly while she replied in monosyllables. Then she lifted her eyes to see her sister, accompanied by the Misses De Vere, their brother and Miss Parker, walking toward them. Maria caught her breath and, hearing her sister's exclamation, knew there was no hope but to turn and face the situation.

Chapter 6

Howard Fairfield was an old college friend of Roland De Vere's, and the two young men greeted one another companionably. Introductions followed all around, covering Maria's chagrin. In a moment she recovered herself and, smiling an apologetic retreat, left the minister to explain.

The lively party followed her, however, and Rachel, who had hurried on with her sister, was kind and eager to help. She was concerned that she might catch cold and plied her with questions as to how it happened. The others arrived at the cottage a few minutes later and chatted until Rachel and Maria, who had hastily replaced the dimity skirt with one of black serge, appeared again.

Then the De Veres said they needed to go home and drove away with promises for the next day and a few words about the moonlight excursion. The minister lingered after the carriage departed, saying he hoped the unexpected sea bath hadn't harmed Miss Hammond. He was grateful to have such a pleasant meeting with his old friends and, bowing, turned toward the hotel, leaving a good impression behind him.

As he walked he reflected: *Two pretty girls—I hadn't bargained on friends this summer. It may interfere with my plans for hard study, but, after all, why shouldn't I have a little recreation? I can't enjoy the society of women at home. If I look at one young woman more than another, the gossips of both sexes almost proclaim marriage banns from the housetops for us. But I don't believe it's good for a man to be only with men all the time. One forgets how to treat his sister after a while.*

It was pleasant meeting up with De Vere. I always liked him in college. And it gave me a break from the routine of the place. Well, things are turning out better than I'd expected. I may stay the month out, after all. At any rate, I won't give up my room yet until I decide.

Then he went in to prepare for supper.

The afternoon's experience drew Maria out of her shell at last and obliged her to pledge to go on the moonlight excursion. She reluctantly gave up her role of martyr little by little and by Sabbath evening was sufficiently herself to go to church. She decided it would be more bearable than always staying in the house, which was wearing on her patience. Besides, her brief glimpse of young, lively company the day before had made her restless for more.

Lone Point had no settled minister. The church itself was built by the donations of visitors. They spent their energies one summer raising the money and constructing a pleasant house of worship for the chance sojourner by the sea. Some of those who lived there for a great part of the year took it upon themselves to keep the services going all summer.

Occasionally ministers visiting over Sunday would preach, to the delight of the small audiences. But the rest of the time, earnest workers from city churches, who weren't taking a vacation from their religion as well as their other work, took turns either reading a sermon or giving a short talk to the little group gathered there. The songs of praise swelled forth from worshipping hearts as thankful as if they were feeding on the bread of life dealt by regularly ordained hands. These services were divided among several men, who were always willing to help out.

The Rev. Howard Fairfield, in spite of finding old friends the day before, had succeeded in remaining incognito so thoroughly that no one dreamed of asking him to preach. He was thankful, since he needed the rest. He had perhaps, though, a little of the natural feeling of a man who was fresh from the ecclesiastical atmosphere of the seminary. He wasn't certain of the genuineness of Sabbath services conducted by a man who hadn't gone through a seminary course or even college; for laymen to handle sacred phrases and forms was almost the same as children "playing church." Young theology students are apt to feel more anxious at first for the orthodoxy of worship than for its spirituality, though they might argue it couldn't be spiritual unless it was orthodox.

Mr. Fairfield sat through the morning address, given by a white-haired brother who had served his church for fifty years. The man was competent, by his wide Christian experience, to minister even to the needs of a theological student. The young man's face wore a look of gentle tolerance, which scarcely masked the criticism in his thoughts. He told himself that an hour spent at home with his Bible would have been more profitable. But respecting his Lord's command not to "forsake the assembling of yourselves together," he returned in the evening.

Now in the evening, the service was led by a younger man who spent some time in a training school for Christian workers. Though versed in the Bible, he wasn't thoroughly trained in the English language. He didn't attempt a sermon. Instead, the service was composed mainly of songs. His own part in it was two or three earnest talks interspersed with practical illustrations, which carried home the true meaning of the Bible verses. The people sang between each of these talks. And when the hour passed, the thoughtful soul went out into daily life with something to help in preparing for heaven.

The service was short, and no one complained of being weary. They issued forth into the bright moonlight from the cheerful chapel, some with kind greetings or encouraging words.

The young minister walked beside the two young ladies he met the day before, and they chatted pleasantly along the way. He stopped a moment on their porch to watch the moonlight on the bay, and they began talking about the church and the services, for want of another topic in common.

"I thought we'd hear you preach this evening, Mr. Fairfield," said Maria pleasantly. She was regaining her good humor and liked the young man. She'd never had a ministerial friend and found it new and interesting.

"Oh, no, indeed," said the minister, laughing. "I took care not to let anyone know I was anything other than an idle young man on a pleasure trip. I don't want to preach. It isn't fair when I'm on vacation. It isn't fair to my people, either, you know. They expect me to rest and not use up my strength on some other church when they're sending me away to be refreshed.

"You don't know how a minister feels when he gets away from his work. A clerical friend of mine said last year with a sigh of relief, when he started on his vacation, 'No more preaching, no more praying, no more reading of the Bible for six whole weeks.' I wouldn't go quite so far as that myself," he added. "But at the same time it's a relief to get away from all reminders of work when I go off to rest."

Maria laughed at the story and thought he was clever. Perhaps this desolate place might have something lively, after all.

But Rachel glanced up quickly. "Did he really say that?" she asked with a troubled look in her eyes. "A minister of Jesus Christ?"

Something in the anxious expression of those clear eyes stirred Howard Fairfield. For the first time since he'd told that story, he reflected that it wasn't altogether the feeling for a minister of Jesus Christ to have, even if the thought had been expressed in fun. He was vexed with himself for telling the story, started to excuse his friend and ended up mildly condemning him. But he was uncomfortably aware of something—he didn't know what—which he knew he'd have to face when he was by himself.

"Well," said Maria, hurrying to cover what she considered her sister's rudeness, "I suppose it's all very well for the poor ministers who have to work all the time, but I must say I don't enjoy hearing a man who doesn't know how to conduct a service. Did you ever see such a mess as that meeting tonight? I'm surprised they didn't ask us all to get up and recite some verses or stories."

She laughed merrily. Maria was used to saying bright, daring things that people laughed at. The young minister was no exception. He was tired of being lonely and was refreshed by her laughter.

"Well," he said, "that man did very well for a layman. He probably got some of his thoughts from one of Moody's books or one like it. But that first bit of talk he gave us on what we live for wasn't so bad. I never heard the story about the old sea captain. It did sound odd when he kept repeating, 'When I'm at the North Pole I live sperm whale; when I'm at the South Pole I live sperm whale.' But it was well expressed and a good illustration. I suppose some of those old fishermen would say for them to live was fishing. I know a man in the city whose entire life is for money, just like the man he was speaking about tonight. It really was a good thought to bring before those young people."

"But," said Maria, laughing again, "did you hear him say 'opportoon-ity'?"

She imitated the broad "oo" of the tone as it was uttered earlier. But her laugh was interrupted by Rachel.

"Mr. Fairfield," she said, lifting her clear, thoughtful eyes with the moonlight shining into her face, "do you suppose anyone—that is, young people— well, I—can say with perfect truth, 'For me to live is Christ'?"

The minister felt strangely embarrassed again, this time with a desire to answer the question right and feeling unable to do so. His pastorate had been short, and his experience slight, and not many inquirers had come to him who seemed to be searching so earnestly for the light. The question was easy enough to answer in a theological sense; but he knew by the look on Rachel's face that she meant more than an ordinary question asked out of curiosity. She really wanted to know so she could use the knowledge.

He searched his mind and his catechism for a suitable reply, but none came. At last, in his usual positive tone, which convinced so many who questioned him, he replied: "Why, yes, surely—why not? If you're a Christian, you certainly can say that."

"No," said Rachel, shaking her head in a troubled way, "I can't. I've been thinking about it ever since Mr. Brown told the story about the sperm whale. My life isn't 'sperm whale.' But if I answered truthfully, I'd have to say that for me to live is having my own way and having a good time. I'm afraid I put that above Christ. I certainly must, or I would be happy with whatever He gives me."

Maria was surprised to hear that. During the meeting she thought uncomfortably that for her to live was to have her own way, but she would never have laid that charge at her gentle sister's door. Rachel, who was always willing to give up when others insisted on having their own way! But Maria didn't like for the conversation to drift into such a solemn theme and welcomed her brother's arrival on the porch with relief.

"Mr. Fairfield," she interrupted, "you haven't met my brother yet."

During the introduction Rachel slipped away. She wanted to be quiet and think. Perhaps she could find the minister alone for a few minutes, and he would give her some help. Ministers knew how to help, and he was young; she wouldn't be afraid to ask him—unless he was like the minister who said he didn't want to read the Bible or pray for six whole weeks. She shuddered at the thought of a minister being so much like the rest of the world. But she wanted her Bible to answer her now, and, entering her room, she lit her shaded lamp and went to her Rock for help.

Mr. Fairfield didn't remain long that evening. He didn't as a rule call on Sunday, unless from necessity or mercy. Before he left he looked about for Rachel and was both troubled and relieved to find her gone: troubled, because he felt somehow he hadn't done his duty; relieved, because "what business had duty to follow him around on his vacation?"

After all, the girl's question had been true enough. How many people in the world could say that? Could he himself? Was it for Christ he lived, or was it fine sermons, a good name, a large church roll? When he preached, did he think more of speaking to the hearts of people to lead them to Jesus, or more of gaining their praise? Didn't he look around to see if a committee from that big Chicago church was sitting in the room and wonder what they thought of that rounded sentence? Could it be that for him to live was whether he would receive a call to a better church in a few years, with a larger salary and a greater name?

He wandered down by the sea in the deep moonlight where he could be alone with his conscience and God. "How is it that a man, who is evidently not highly educated, can with his few words stir a heart to ask such questions as that girl asked me tonight?" he wondered out loud. "Did anyone ever go home after one of my sermons and ask such searching questions? But I'm doing it again; I'm concerned about what other people think of me and my words. No, it's not just that. Maybe I'm concerned about what God thinks of me too. I need to find that out."

Chapter 7

D oes Satan also walk sometimes beside the sea? Perhaps he saw the direction of this young man's thoughts and hoped to turn them aside. Perhaps he feared the searching questions that would surely come to this thoughtful heart. Once the heart was awakened to itself and the possibilities, it would be a dangerous enemy to the powers of darkness and this world. Or maybe what happened next was simply another link in God's wonderful chain of influence to draw this disciple nearer to Himself.

"Hello! Wait a minute!" shouted a voice barely heard by the preoccupied man above the roar of the waves.

"Is that you, Mr. Fairfield?" called the man, a fellow boarder at the hotel. He was hurrying along the sand, trying to catch his breath. "I wasn't sure in the moonlight. There's a telegram for you at the hotel. They've been hunting everywhere for you. The boy came over from Spray View with it."

The minister thanked the man, turned and quickly retraced his steps along the beach to the hotel. He hoped nothing had befallen his mother or sister, who were traveling abroad, or that a member of his church wasn't gravely ill or even dead.

Telegrams, whether slight or significant in meaning, set a person's heart beating faster till they are safely read.

It was only a notice of a special business meeting that was important to him and his church. But he was called home to it early the next day to accommodate a member of the church committee; the member was also called away suddenly and wanted some matters attended to before he left.

The minister stood on the moonlit porch a moment after reading the telegram, then crushed the yellow paper irritably between his fingers. It didn't suit him to rush back to the city in the heat now. He'd expected that meeting to be delayed until the first week in September.

It annoyed him, too, to receive such a message on Sunday evening. He didn't analyze why, except to think it might have been sent the night before or the next day. It seemed to disturb the harmony of the day's rest and his evening's thoughts. He was so troubled that he didn't return to his musings by the sea.

It was late, and he had to take an early train in the morning. He had to prepare his mind for the business in town, as well as get ready for his hurried journey. So he went reluctantly up to his room, wondering if he'd ever find time to talk over those matters with himself and resolving to take the first opportunity for it.

He remembered the moonlight sail planned for that week, the new friends he'd made and the old ones he discovered there. He could leave his baggage here in this secluded place beside the sea and return on the evening train or by the next day if possible, rather than pack up and move on to some new place as he had planned to do three days before. The place possessed a new charm now that he had found friends, even though he'd wished to get away from social obligations. The family in the pleasant cottage by the bay interested him. He wanted to talk further with the bright older sister and maybe even hear more of the sweet-faced younger sister's searching, innocent questions. They weren't bad training for him in many ways, he thought.

Mr. Fairfield was scarcely seated in the uptown car the next morning in the city when he noticed two bright eyes waiting to catch his attention. Across the car sat a young lady who was one of his parishioners. Miss Lou Marlow greeted him with her customary good-natured openness. To most people she was Miss Lou, while others called her simply "Lou." She was comfortable with everyone, as intimate on the first day of acquaintance as she might be ten years later, and a pretty girl. In her presence the minister felt as if he'd been splashed with brilliant sunlight, as did most people.

Still, she could point out a person's faults or virtues and laugh over them with a lively, ruthless hand, and for this reason the minister rather dreaded a tête-à-tête with Miss Lou. He particularly shrank from one in a streetcar, since her voice, like her taste in clothes, wasn't altogether subdued.

But she had moved to one side and made room for him beside her on the seat. Further, she was indicating she had something to tell him, and he knew she wouldn't be deterred by a mere car aisle. The minister changed his seat, but he also assumed his most dignified air in order to check her if she appeared too exuberant.

"Oh, Mr. Fairfield, when did you come back? Why, I'm surprised," began Miss Lou. "Really this is quite a coincidence. I had the strangest dream about you last night, and it was so real and vivid. Now to think I should meet you when I thought you were far away! There really must have been something meant by it," she said, laughing.

Mr. Fairfield looked nervously about the car to see if he knew anyone else.

"Oh, it was too funny!" she continued.

"Yes?" said the minister faintly.

He hoped it wasn't connected with selecting a wife for him or anything of that sort. But he feared from her tone it might be a silly dream linking him with someone in his congregation. That it was embarrassing he felt sure. He waited, hoping he would be given the grace not to turn red or look angry if it were, and he was ready with a hearty but insincere laugh if he needed to cover up what she told him.

"Why, I dreamed I was riding in a car down this very street, and it was summer as it is now. You were away on your vacation—at least we all thought you were. Suddenly you came into the car and told me you'd been called home to attend a funeral." Miss Lou laughed again. "I asked you who it was, and you said it was Lillie Hartley—you know, the carpenter's little girl who sings in the children's Sunday school exercises so sweetly. You told me when the funeral was and asked me to come and sing, and I said I would.

"Well, I went to the house at the hour, and we sat there and sat there, and you didn't come. It got awful late, and still you didn't come. They had to go way out to Mt. Laurel for the burial, so they got awfully worried. Finally they sent for you, and the girl where you board said you were in your study—that is, she hadn't seen you come out. So they went up to the study and found the door locked on the inside. The girl said that was the way you always had it when you were studying hard.

"They called and knocked and got no answer. They finally broke in the door and found you sitting there dead by your desk with your book of funeral prayers, or whatever you call it, beside you. The page was open to the children's burial service, and everything looked as if you were just ready to go out, and you dead! There was an awful time just beginning, but I woke up and didn't see the end.

"But isn't it too funny that you came in the car just now? Oh! Here's my street. I must get off. I hope you haven't come home to any funeral. Good-bye. Wasn't it funny?"

The young woman swung herself off the car, after completing her last two or three sentences as she moved hastily toward the door. She ended with a loud giggle in which the minister felt called upon to join, at least with a sickly smile. Then he scowled. Of all things to happen, this seemed the most disagreeable right now. Not that he cared about the dream. He wasn't superstitious or nervous, but it grated on his fine sensibilities to have the solemn and ridiculous mixed in this way. He could scarcely brush it aside and forget his unpleasant return to the city, so he bought a morning paper and tried to bury his thoughts in it. But he felt irritated even when he reached the house he called home and went to his rooms for any letters or papers that hadn't been forwarded during his two weeks' absence.

It was almost time for him to go out again to meet the board of trustees, when the house servant tapped at his door.

"Please, Mr. Fairfield," she said, "there's a man downstairs who was here yesterday to see you. He come back again this morning to get your address. I told him you came back unexpected, and he's awful anxious to see you."

"You don't know who it is, Jane? He didn't send up his card?" said the minister, consulting his watch. "I have an engagement in five minutes. I can't spare much time."

"No, sir," said Jane, "I don't. But he's a plain-lookin' body, and if you're busy I'll tell him to come back again when you can see him."

"Oh, no, I'll go down," he said, picking up his hat and some papers he wanted to carry to the meeting.

A chill pierced the minister's heart when he reached the hall to see Mr. Hartley standing there, sad and heavy-eyed, his shoulders sagging.

"Mr. Fairfield," he said, tears forming in his eyes. "I'm so glad you're here. I didn't have the nerve to trouble you before this. But the wife wanted you and said she couldn't have Lillie buried without the minister she loved so much. It's tomorrow afternoon. And could you get somebody to sing? The wife, she wanted 'Safe in the Arms of Jesus,' same as Lillie sung herself last Children's Day in the church."

There was something strange about it. The minister thought of it after the man left, when he had to hurry to his meeting. The brokenhearted father had said so much about his little girl and how she loved her minister and how ready she was to go to heaven! He laughed an empty laugh as he walked down the street in the hot sunshine; if he were a superstitious man this would be a good chance for him to run away. He held his head high, proud of the fact that he wasn't superstitious.

In spite of it all he couldn't get away from Miss Lou's dream and the strange coincidence of the child's death. He wiped the perspiration from his brow and longed for the cooling sea breeze he'd left behind. He almost wished he'd told the father he couldn't stay and suggested a brother minister for the funeral. Then he remembered how the father's face lit up when he saw him coming down the stairs. He knew in his heart he never could have done such a thing and was glad he was here to offer some comfort to the stricken parents.

It was strange, too, after the day's business was over. He thought about the funeral and remembered the father's request for a singer; the only singer to be found in the city available at the hour of the funeral was Miss Lou Marlow. He knew she would come and that her voice was rich and sweet, though not as highly cultivated as some. With her generous nature she would be willing to do anything in her power for the sorrowful family. She often went to funerals to sing; people liked to hear her because she sang with a great deal of sympathy in her voice.

There were good things about Miss Lou, and her pastor knew it. Nevertheless, he searched far and wide before he decided there was no one else to ask. He told himself he didn't do this in the least for his own sake, but merely because he shrank from what she might say in her blunt, giggling way. At last he sent a message by Jane with the request of the father and mother, leaving himself out entirely. He didn't care for Miss Lou to see any more likeness to her dream than was necessary.

Then he shut himself in his study. As he turned the key, he remembered Miss Lou's words vividly; they came and knocked and called with no answer, and then they broke in the door and found him dead. Nevertheless, he locked the door as usual and sat down in the study chair, as was his custom, beside his desk and tried to think.

A strong feeling of destiny took hold of his mind. He felt as if he were living out something that had been established for him to do. He couldn't help it but must live it out to the end, even to dying. He couldn't shake it off. He'd heard of people dying with less cause than this, just because they thought the time had come.

He wasn't afraid he would die, but he wondered what he'd like to do before that and, if it was true, what a short time he had to prepare! He had to put papers in order and leave messages. And what about his mother and sister and his church? How could he leave his church? His work wasn't completed. He hadn't carried out his plans; he hadn't won the souls he hoped to win. Those young men who sat in the back by the door and whispered instead of listening—something should have been done for them. He had even thought seriously of calling for a policeman at times. Now he realized he might have won them some other way. Was it too late?

Then he thought of all his people, one by one. He might have comforted one and issued a word of warning to another. What was his preaching, now that he faced the thought of its being over forever? It was true he studied his sermons for hours. But even if the sentences were complete and perfect in grammar and rhetoric, and sometimes even eloquent, would that stand before God?

And then he looked at himself. Was his soul ready to meet his Master? Hadn't he lived selfishly, serving the Master second and himself first, gratifying his desire for the intellectual, filling his soul with ambitions for a high calling on earth rather than one in heaven?

Then the souls he was charged to keep—what of them? While he sought to supply them with the flowers of his oratory, had they starved for lack of the plain bread of life? He was searching his own heart and accusing himself as he never had before.

He knew the time was near for the funeral, that he must prepare, and yet he couldn't turn his thoughts to anything else. Once he reached out for the book of forms and funeral services and, opening it, found the little child's funeral service. But he couldn't read the words; he could only think he must set his own heart right.

If someone had stepped to the door just then and asked, "Are you afraid you're going to die in a few minutes? Are you nervous about this dream and the strange coincidence?" he would have answered, "No, certainly not. I'm not afraid to die. I know these strange coincidences cannot hasten or delay the day of my death one second. All is as it was before I heard these things. But in some way I've suddenly realized what it would be to leave this world and my work—my unfinished work—with these few moments' notice. It isn't impossible for me to die at any moment. If not now, it may come, *will* come, at some equally unexpected moment. And I'm not ready—not as ready as I *would* be."

That was the undercurrent of his reasoning as he sat in the study chair, his face buried in his hands, and thought. He heard footsteps below, reminding him it was almost time for the funeral. In a few minutes, if he didn't hurry, someone would actually come to his door to see why he hadn't come, or to say the carriage was waiting and the people were wondering where he was.

He knelt and spent those last few minutes in prayer, as he never prayed before. Out of the depths of his soul rose a mighty cry for forgiveness for his past and a longing for the Savior to come into his heart and cast out self from him. Yet, as he knelt, the room was still as death. Not one audible syllable did he utter. He'd never prepared in such a way for any of his public duties in the ministry.

And a few minutes later when Jane tapped at the door to say the carriage had come, he rose from his knees, his face shining with a holy light of something deeper than he understood. He forgot the curious dream and didn't watch to see if he died; instead he prepared to live.

He took the book of services and went to the funeral, feeling utterly unprepared and yet, strangely enough, not worried about it. He knew that preparation was important; but sometimes God took that out of His messengers' hands and drew them to look at Him for a while and then supplied the words.

And the words were supplied now. He gave verse after verse of comfort from God's holy Word, with now and then a bit of explanation. But surely the Lord Himself guided his selections, which he made as he rode along in the carriage. For broken hearts were comforted and wounded spirits bound up. Many other hearts that were there from sympathy were touched and led to feel how near and sure and grave a thing death is, and the life to come.

Miss Lou's clear, rich voice broke the stillness of the room following the minister's prayer, in the tender refrain of "Safe in the Arms of Jesus." The minister, listening, remembered the dream and bowed his head. He was thankful he was alive with a hope for a better life and better work. Christ lived in him, the hope of glory, and no longer the hope of the glory of his own intellectual powers.

Chapter 8

I t was night, and along the coast the wind raged wildly. The ocean waves pounded against the stolid black sands. The sky was black velvet, slashed here and there with flashes of lightning. Above the roar of the waves and the voice of the wind came the distant roll of thunder as it announced its approach.

In the cottages the dwellers nestled deeper in their beds, barely aware of a storm outside. Mrs. Hammond sighed as she turned over, relieved to have more water in the cistern again; they wouldn't have to carry it from the hotel well. It was a little thing, but she felt that lack of water was one thing that made Maria's life harder the last few days. Now things might be a little easier. Maria was also getting acquainted with pleasant young friends, and perhaps their summer would be a happy one after all. She was glad they could rent this cottage for so little and needn't feel they were extravagant in taking this vacation. Then she slept soundly again, aware that the storm was about to break and grateful for the refreshing sound.

The rain fell at last and pattered on the high roof, and soon it poured. Rachel was awakened by a cold dampness on her cheek. At first she was startled and couldn't make out what it was; before she was fully awake it was followed by another, until they fell at regular intervals.

She lay still for a few minutes, unaware that her pillow was getting quite wet. Then she heard sounds from her parents' room—their voices low, the striking of a match, the moving of furniture. She realized the roof was also leaking in there. She could hear drops falling out in the room on the floor and now a new one on the dressing bureau. Suddenly her sister started up in bed with an angry exclamation that water was falling on her head.

It all struck Rachel as funny, as such things often did, quiet and sober as she usually was. It irritated Maria when Rachel laughed at a trying time. But Rachel always said it was better to laugh than to cry or be cross, and she must do something. Maria said she had an "hysterical nature" and should control her feelings. Then Maria would control hers by being cross. But Rachel always forgot about hysterics and laughed a pure, mirthful laugh.

It bubbled forth now, as she climbed out of bed and got her sun umbrella, raising it over their heads as she crawled back in. She thought it was fun to camp out picnic-style and go to bed under an umbrella.

Maria lay down again angrily. "Rachel Hammond, I do wish you'd grow up and learn not to giggle when anything happens. I'm sure I don't see anything funny in being dripped on when you're asleep."

That was the beginning. In a few minutes Maria could hear furniture being moved in the next room, conversation, and trips back and forth for waterproofing and awning cloths to protect the beds from the steadily increasing drops. She was thoroughly awakened, and her temper was roused to an unbearable level. She found fault with the house and the landlord and said it was what could be expected of the cottage at the ridiculous price they paid for it.

Then when the family had hushed into silence she started in on her sister, in a whisper: "Rachel, you may be grown up in years, but not in your mind. You did something Sunday night that made me so ashamed I didn't know what to do. I haven't had a chance to talk to you about it. You manage to keep yourself so busy away from us except just when you're helping with the work that I never have a chance to see my sister anymore," she said in an injured tone. "I hope the Parkers appreciate your society. Perhaps you manage to be more agreeable there than here. At any rate, please confine yourself to being polite when you're with me and my friends, whatever you do when you're with yours."

"What in the world have I done now, Maria?" asked Rachel in a troubled voice. She wanted to please her sister, though she found it much harder than usual these days.

"Done!" said Maria, growing irritated as she remembered her discomfiture two days before. "Why, you acted like a perfect little prig and almost insulted a minister. What in the world did you think Mr. Fairfield would think of you Sunday night, turning around and as much as contradicting what he said? It wasn't the least bit more polite that you put it in the form of a question. He's bright enough to see through that. Who are you to rebuke a minister, anyway? You might as well try to find fault with the Bible."

"Why, 'Ri, I didn't rebuke him. I only asked him a question that honestly puzzled me. What do you mean? I never intended—"

"Nonsense!" said Maria sharply. "You were rude and you know it. If a man doesn't come up to your standard you immediately tell him so. You'll simply get yourself put down as an insufferable little prig for your trouble if you keep on that way. I was surprised Mr. Fairfield didn't tell you you were a child and didn't know what you were talking about.

"For my part, I hope I won't have to endure another insult like that to my callers. If I do, I'll call Mother to come and take you in. It's the only fitting rebuke for that. You talk religion too much, anyway. It isn't ladylike to stick it in everyone's face. A minister hears enough of it in his profession without having to talk about it in his social life. Religion is much better acted than talked, I think. I hope you'll take that to heart. If you attempt any of that talk with the De Veres you won't be tolerated in their company very long. I'm ashamed of you. Now go to sleep if you can. I don't want to talk anymore." Maria turned over with a twitch and pretended to go to sleep.

But sleep for Rachel was routed. She lay there thinking while the tears chased each other down her cheeks. It hurt her when her sister talked to her like that. She felt as if she should make some protest, but what could she say to help matters? Her protests always seemed to anger her sister more. Was Maria right, and did the minister feel as she said? If so, was she wrong in her way of feeling about things? Of course a minister must be right, for he spent his life in preparing to preach Christ's gospel and gave up everything to that work. He should be consecrated if anyone was. But surely a person should be able to go to him with a question about Christian living.

Then she remembered Roland De Vere and how differently he talked about religion in just the few words he'd spoken on the subject. Somehow she felt that Maria was mistaken about Mr. De Vere at least, and she wished he would talk to Maria and perhaps influence her.

This minister might know how to help Maria eventually. Ministers ought to be able to influence those around them, without any words, as Maria said. She would pray for that. Meanwhile, wasn't there some little thing she could do for her Master? Her life was so full of pleasure this summer that without some definite, special work to do she might grow selfish. She had tried to help Maria, but it only seemed to irritate her. Perhaps it was wrong for her to help an older sister. She would just pray and try to keep from troubling her with her words. Her tongue seemed to be a very unruly member. So she closed her eyes and prayed to be shown what to do; then, like a tired child, she threw off her burden and went to sleep.

In justice to Maria she was feeling chagrined that Mr. Fairfield had neither called nor come on the beach when they were there. Nor had he appeared since to renew his acquaintance with them, which he seemed eager to do on Sunday evening. It puzzled Maria. While she cared nothing about the man in particular, she was still deeply sensitive to the opinion of anyone, either stranger or friend, whose manner and appearance seemed to make his judgment of value in her eyes. She feared that he considered them a family of fanatics and that the fault lay with Rachel's babyish way of talking religion, as if it were an everyday matter.

With nothing else to do, she brooded over the matter until it was magnified. She was sure the minister was intentionally slighting them. Now that he found his friends at Spray View, he wished to show them he was polite to Maria only because of the awkward accident that threw them together on Saturday. Maria's imagination was so vivid that, as the rainy days passed, she thought the pleasant times ended even as they just began. Of course there was no moonlight excursion.

Maria stood on the porch one afternoon, toward the end of the dreary week, gazing discontentedly at the desolate landscape. The mist of fine rain was still falling, when it wasn't varied by heavy showers. A stiff breeze was blowing, first from one direction and then from another, as if uncertain what to do.

Off to her right Maria could see the banks of sand piled high, looking almost like cliffs in places. The low underbrush of huckleberry, wild sage and laurel seemed to be the only growth on the island, for not a tree was in sight. Now and again the waves of the ocean would dash so high that the spray would be carried up in clouds above these sand banks. The banks were broken in one place at the end of their street, where one could gaze far out over the wild, turbulent ocean in its dull gray and brown tones, with a seething touch of vivid green here and there and froth of maddened yellow-white. It all looked so cold and wild and awful to Maria.

She turned from it, shuddering. On her left stretched the steel-colored bay, once bright and reflecting tints like an opal, now an almost interminable stretch of mist and desolation. The long reaches of sand waste and heavy, wet-headed salt marsh grass, bending with the wind, only added to the dismal scene.

The girl walked back and forth on the green porch, wet with the mist, and looked with horror, almost with hatred, at the view. Yes, for one can hate even sky and grass and water in the right mood. The scene embodied to her the desolation in her life. It was like that waste of water and sand and dark-leaden sky. There seemed to be no hope of brightness for the future, just as it seemed impossible now, after these days and days of rain, that the sky could ever be bright again or the waves would ever grow soft and lovely and the bay take on its gem-like look. God seemed nowhere to her. She felt desperate, as if she couldn't endure another hour of this dreadful existence.

It almost frightened her to feel this way. She knew it was wrong. She was brought up too well not to know how wrong and hateful her recent feelings and actions were. She wondered if she had ever loved God or been a Christian and whether there was anything in it. Wild ideas ran through her brain. Where was God, anyway? Why did He want her to be so unhappy? Had He forgotten her?

Over and over a line from an old hymn she learned in childhood ran through her mind: "Has God forgotten to be kind?" She tried to shake it off, but it came again and again. She brushed back the misted hair that clung to her hot temples and went into the cottage.

Anything was better in this vast desolation alone. She went to the kitchen and in desperation looked in her recipe book for the most difficult thing she could make for supper. It would at least occupy her hands and her mind. She could read a book, but none of them interested her. A book was nice and cozy on a rainy day, when all was cheery indoors, but Maria didn't feel cheerful or hopeful for the future.

The trouble went deeper than these few days at the seashore. It went back to the time when her father lost his money. She rebelled against giving up that money and the position it carried. Now that it was gone, there was nothing else in the world worth living for. She was a pretty good Christian, according to her way of thinking, in the days when things were prosperous. Why hadn't God seen that? She could have done much more in the world for Him if He'd left her life as it was. Now she was no Christian at all, and He must see how He caused her to fail in her Christian work by taking away her father's money and her social position. She didn't say these things even to herself, in so many words. She wouldn't have dared, because she was taught to be reverent in her speech, and to a degree this teaching had reached her thoughts; but she felt them deeply, fiercely.

And Rachel sat in the other room, apparently reading her book, but all the while she was watching her sister and praying quietly for her. Oh, why couldn't her heartfelt prayer for her beloved sister be answered? Hadn't she prayed earnestly enough? Or must she pray longer? What was the matter? God promised to give what the believing heart asked for. She laid down her book and went into the bedroom, fastening the curtain behind her to prevent interruptions.

She knelt and prayed fervently for Maria, but she didn't feel the sudden sense of answer she heard other people talk about. She could hear Maria rattle the pans and kettles as fiercely as ever in the kitchen. But she saw no sign of any spiritual change in her.

Rachel's was a sweet nature, struggling for light, and she wasn't being guided by human help perhaps as much as would have been good for her. She believed everything intensely and at once and wanted to see a vindication of her belief, like other eager, impatient ones, but she was willing to be led. Her Bible aided her many times when she was perplexed. She turned to it now from habit and read one of her favorite psalms. "Delight thyself also in the Lord, and he shall give thee the desires of thine heart."

She read the verse over without thinking about it, when a thought caught her attention. Was it possible God sent her that very promise now? Did He want her to delight herself in Him first before He gave her what she was asking for? Perhaps she hadn't made Him her chief delight.

She closed the book slowly and returned to the sitting room and her story. And though she held the book in front of her, she wasn't reading. She was reviewing her life, thinking how she might make the Lord her chief delight and how she hadn't done it. It was a revelation to her of herself; if she'd been asked a little while before reading that verse, she would have said that Christ and His life work were her chief delights. But now she saw she'd made other things chief and Christ's work only a very small part of the pleasures of her life. Here was something needing a radical change in her soul. Then Christ would be in her pleasures, the source and center of everything, instead of an outsider, as she felt she regarded Him before.

Meanwhile, she remembered that peaches needed to be peeled for supper. She disliked this job and didn't always remember promptly that it was hers. But tonight she arose with alacrity, saying to herself, *He wants me to peel those peaches; I'll try to remember I'm doing it for Him, and then perhaps I can take delight in it.* And soon she was singing a happy little song:

> There is sunshine in my soul today,
> More glorious and more bright,
> For Jesus—

"For pity's sake," snapped Maria, "do select something more appropriate, if you *must* sing. It doesn't look as if there'll ever be any sunshine anymore anywhere."

And for once Rachel laughed, replied pleasantly and went on singing, instead of closing her mouth and letting the tears steal up to her eyes at the sharp words, as she usually did. And so supper was prepared in much more peace than usual.

Chapter 9

The sun shone out at last, bright and clear, as though it had never thought of anything else. The bay, blue in the distance, sparkled in the sun's rays like a sapphire set in emeralds. White-winged sailboats, like great birds, floated lazily across the glassy surface, carried hither and thither by the light winds. As one looked westward toward the bay, no sign could be seen of the gloom that had shrouded the landscape for days. Turning toward the sea, radiant with brilliant coloring, bordered by a shining garment of newly washed sand, the late rage of the elements was more apparent. The sea, slower in rousing to terrible wrath, is more reluctant to cease from its anger and, long after nature smiles, pours thunderous billows upon the unresisting shore.

Had Howard Fairfield been there, he would have passed the day at the very edge of the surge, gazing far out to sea over the majestic spectacle, still more striking by the contrast it presented to the calm sky overhead, until his soul was filled with the wonder of the scene. But much to his disappointment, a series of unimportant details still held him in the city.

It was Saturday, and Rachel sat on the porch peeling peaches. Her father had brought some fruit from the city the night before, for such luxuries had to be imported to their island home. In the salty atmosphere they decayed rapidly, so Rachel was preparing them for preserving and canning. She always found this task distasteful, but the morning was so bright and beautiful that she caught its glad spirit.

Moreover, wasn't her life henceforth to have a new motive, to be filled with a joy not of this world? Jesus was now to be a delight, and to her surprise she discovered that that delight shone through the most commonplace tasks. She rejoiced in the brightness of the morning because He made it bright. Thus her mind was filled with pleasant thoughts, and she worked deftly at her task and sang a cheerful song as she did.

Maria felt differently about the change in weather. What good was the sunshine when one didn't care to go out in it? She had no place to go and no one whose companionship she cared for, who was likely, as she told herself, to care enough about hers to seek it. To be sure, there was the beach to visit, mother and sister for company, books and embroidery for occupation, to say nothing of the kaleidoscopic scenery of sea and sky; but these found no place in the catalogue of her desires.

A fierce resentment filled her at the mockery of the day's brightness contrasted with the gloom of her own mood. She saw plainly now that she took a grim, self-pitying satisfaction in the melancholy of the weather. It represented a distinct grievance, and now she was almost angry it was taken from her.

As her mother passed through the room, she sighed at the discontentment so often on her elder daughter's face. Rachel's song floated in through the open doorway and made her wonder why one daughter should find sweetness while the other persisted in drinking only the bitter. It was even more difficult to understand because in her younger days Maria was as sunny as her sister. It was unlike her to cling to her wrongs for so long or to show others only the thorny side of her nature.

Could Maria be on the verge of illness, and here lay the hidden reason for her discontent? With this idea in mind, the mother entered the kitchen again and begged Maria to resign her place at the stove to her and Rachel for the day and lie down in her room. Her entreaty was met with scorn, and Maria decided to cook a more elaborate meal than usual, to prove nothing was the matter with her health.

The mother, rebuffed, returned to her sewing; more than one tear dropped on it, as she asked herself what could be wrong with Maria. She wished that handsome young Mr. De Vere would pay a little less attention to Rachel, who seemed to care nothing about him, and a little more to Maria, who she, with motherly intuition, feared did. Or else that the intellectual-looking minister, who brought her home that day she was drenched, would come again. She wished for anything to take her child out of herself and infuse a new interest into her life; then, perhaps, the girl wouldn't brood over her misfortunes so much and bend her character permanently in the unfortunate direction of melancholy. She had hoped that even the shine would cheer her, but it seemed to have the opposite effect.

Across a strip of neatly mowed marsh grass, not many rods distant, stood a small unpainted cottage surrounded by a well-kept vegetable garden. The wide porch, peculiar to the place, ran across its front. Around this, to cope with the mosquitoes, someone tacked a blue mosquito bar which now hung tattered, waving in the breeze. The Higginses lived in this cottage.

The family was one of many and varied occupations. The father fished a little, gardened a little and drove parties of three in his rickety green spring wagon over to Spray View on errands, at the rate of ten cents per head, or three for a quarter.

When she heard this, Rachel was glad they might take the beach drive often because it was so cheap. But Maria sneered at the idea of driving past the elegant De Vere villa in the old green wagon, so that Rachel didn't mention it again.

Mrs. Higgins washed for a living, besides sewing and cooking for her large family, and carried tomatoes, which she called "tomats," delicious beets, fresh eggs and chickens to the few people who lived near enough to purchase them. She also went into the bay when requested to dig clams, which she sold at a ridiculously low price, and was the delight of everyone who met her, because of her quaint dialect, which was a mixture of Irish, German and Jersey.

Four grown sons lived with their wives and children, some in the same house and some nearby, while others visited often; on those occasions the eggs, "tomats" and fresh fish were scarce for the time being. Two young daughters plodded through the sand every morning at five to perform their daily duties of chambermaid and nurse, respectively, at the Spray View Hotel. A son worked on the railroad when the trains ran (which was only during the summer) and fished between times, and last but not least were Katy and John, the two youngest children. They solemnly and silently appeared at the door from time to time, bringing milk or eggs or other things that were ordered, but fled in dismay if asked any questions.

Rachel had found out about their neighbors during the first few days of their stay at the shore. She was interested in every human being within her sight. The rest of the family knew them only as a convenience for performing odd jobs and supplying cheap vegetables, fish and clams. Maria knew them only to despise, because they never had what she wanted when she ordered it.

But Rachel was interested in watching their movements and realized they were human beings. They possessed emotions like hers, in spite of the fact that they were odd and seemed to exist and be happy under such very different circumstances from her own. And, in contrast to her father's former position, she had unconsciously come to regard those as not the best.

In one of Rachel's intervals of singing, when she was on a trip to the kitchen in search of more peaches and another dish, she heard a burst of song from across the way. It didn't sound like music, though it was evidently meant for that. The singer was one of the young women members of the Higgins family. Rachel could see her sitting on the wide porch behind a tattered remnant of the blue mosquito netting, swinging a much-used hammock. The hammock evidently contained a baby, probably one of the many Higgins grandchildren. The girl's voice was loud and sharp, with a nasal twang, and the song was a lullaby improvised for the occasion. But she sang it in such a high key that it seemed intended to benefit some baby up in the clouds or beyond Spray View.

Rachel broke into soft laughter and called her mother and Maria to listen, as the loud twang of "Sleep, sleep, sleep, baby, sleep. Hush-a-bye, sleep, hush-a-bye" rang out above the sound of the majestic waves. The song continued for a while, and Rachel hushed her own singing, partly to listen and partly because the metallic tones grated on her delicate musical sensibilities. Eventually the singer changed her song, while the hammock still rocked violently. The baby was apparently being brought up to be a sailor, for certainly no other vocation would be more suitable after spending one's infant days in such a turbulent cradle.

"There's a land that is fair-rer than da-ay," rang out the words, *"an' by faith we c'n see it a-fa-ar."*

The girl sang through the verses, her lungs apparently as unweary as when she began. She finished one song and went on to another, a gospel song.

Rachel's eyes grew dreamy as she thought of occasions when she'd sung these very words; they were a little out of date now because of the new jingles that had replaced them. She wondered where this girl became acquainted with the songs so she could sing them from beginning to end. The family, she heard, had lived on the island both summer and winter for several years. They never went to church or Sunday school. In fact, Sunday seemed to be a time of festivities for them, for several sons with their wives were sure to spend the day there. And Rachel noticed a case of beer bottles outside the porch once when she went to get some clams to make clam bisque for supper.

Where, then, did this girl acquire her knowledge of religious songs? She had enough words of the way of salvation in the songs to save a whole family, if words could save. She must have learned them before the family moved to this deserted place. It would be interesting to know where and how. Perhaps she attended Sunday school or a series of Moody meetings and became familiar with the songs there.

Rachel often let her imagination have free rein, and when she thought out the possibilities she grew intensely interested in the Higgins family and wished to know more about them. She would talk with that girl the next time she came over with the milk and hope to find out something.

Meanwhile, how grand it would be if through those very songs someday the whole family became Christians. Rachel dropped her peach and gazed out across the bay. She liked to scribble little stories for her own amusement sometimes. She never showed them to anyone. This would be a splendid start for a plot. But how would this marvelous change come about? The Spirit of God could do it, of course, but He would likely use some earthly instrument. Someone must speak to them or do some helpful thing or influence them, perhaps a young minister on vacation, like Mr. Fairfield, or even a young lady or—

Here Rachel's thoughts ran suddenly from the imaginary to the practical, and a soft blush stole into her cheeks. Why plan a story when there might really be an opening for work? She asked God for some work for Him; maybe He was showing it to her through that singing. The work didn't seem as attractive or interesting as it would be in a story. But she could probably do it—at least she could try.

She picked up her peach and started peeling again—and thinking. Now that it had presented itself, she shrank from the undertaking and wished she hadn't thought of it or listened to the horrible grating singing. How could she do anything? It would only be another trial for Maria if she associated herself with any of those despised Higginses. Her sister would like them even less than the Parkers. Then, too, she'd never been introduced, and perhaps the girl would resent anything she might do or say as patronizing. Rachel had a horror of seeming to patronize any human being. Her gentle, loving smile and winning way would never be mistaken for that, but she didn't know this.

Finally she dismissed the thought with this: *If God wishes me to do anything along those lines, He'll show me. Perhaps I'm as mistaken about this as I was about trying to help Maria.* Lifting up her heart she cast the thought at her Savior's feet. He knew best.

By this time the peaches were finished, and so was the song from across the way. The baby probably had succumbed at last to the boisterous hammock and song. Rachel carried her peaches into the house, washed her hands and came out again with her workbasket of lace she was making for a centerpiece border. She also brought two books, still in the paper wrappings. They arrived in for her by messenger that morning from Spray View. The handwriting of her own name in bold, manly characters told her who the sender was.

Rachel postponed opening the package until her work was done so she might better enjoy what was in it. Perhaps, too, there was a shy, sweet pleasure in opening the package by herself. At any rate, the morning was charming, and it was nice to have a package to open and her pretty work lying beside her, and nothing to do but enjoy it all. She untied the knots of the string slowly, at the same time tracing the strong, open letters of her name, "Rachel Weldon Hammond."

Then she unwrapped the package. She knew they were books, for Roland De Vere told her he had two books he wanted her to read. He felt sure she would enjoy them, and they might lead her to read along new lines.

One, called *A Castaway*, had a dark red paper cover, with attractive print and short paragraphs and chapters. She glanced through it and found it was the one he said would help her pass the long Sabbath afternoon and aid in her Christian life. She smiled as she turned the pages, snatching a sentence here and there that seemed written just for her circumstances and thoughts. Aside from the Bible, Sabbath reading like this didn't often come her way. She would take a few peeps into it and leave the rest for Sunday's treasure.

The other volume was covered in pale green and gold with thick, creamy paper and clear print. Rachel loved its exquisite feel and look. Inside it contained poetry. She opened it at random and read a poem titled "Day's Parlor." That day seemed to be fashioned in just the way described.

The day came slow till five o'clock,
Then sprang before the hills
Like hindered rubies, or the light
A sudden musket spills.

The purple could not keep the east,
The sunrise shook the fold,
Like breadths of topaz, packed a night,
The lady just unrolled.

The happy winds their timbrels took;
The birds, in docile rows
Arranged themselves around their prince
(The wind is prince of those).

The orchard sparkled like a Jewel,
How mighty 'twas, to stay
A guest in this stupendous place,
The parlor of the day!

Rachel caught her breath and looked up at the bay and the blue sky, drinking in their loveliness. How those jeweled words brought out the beauties! She turned a few pages and read again:

She sweeps with many colored brooms,
And leaves the shreds behind;
Oh, housewife in the evening west,
Come back and dust the pond!

You've dropped a purple raveling in,
You dropped an amber thread;
And now you've littered all the east
With dust of emerald!

And still she plies her spotted brooms,
And still the aprons fly,
Till brooms fade softly into stars—
And then I come away.

Ah! Rachel drew her breath again, as if to catch the delicate scent of a new perfume, and feared to lose a single atom of the delightful sensation. This poetry suited her dreamy imagination, which liked to personify nature, and the last poem described that beautiful sunset last week. She was grateful for the book—for the music of the words and their coloring—and dimly felt the fine perceptions of the young man who selected it for her.

And then the answer from heaven appeared in the mist of these thoughts with her work laid out for her. It was a contrast, but a well-tuned nature is ready to turn from the high to the low. And that nature recognizes that what is considered low is in reality the highest of the high, while the high is merely a picture of what pleasure may be after all.

"Did your ma want any clams tonight?" It was the clear metallic voice of the singer, whose coming was so silent that Rachel, lost in her beautiful dreams, started. But the girl didn't seem to notice this. She was gazing at Rachel's basket and the beautiful lace work on its pretty blue cambric background.

"Oh, how pretty!" exclaimed the girl. "Did you do that?"

Rachel brought her basket over for the girl's inspection.

"Ain't it awful hard work? You must be dreadful clever. Does it take a long time? Now I'll just guess that stuff costs an awful lot. I see a woman over to the hotel the other day workin' at a thing like that. You don't say! That's the way you do it. Just sew that braid onto them lines! Why, that looks easy! My, but I suppose it's all in knowin' how!" the girl sighed wistfully. "I'd sure like to know how to do some of them pretty things! I never have no time in summer. But land! In winter, time just drags and drags. Seems like I was fifty years old every winter I go through in this place. I wish I could do something to shorten it."

Thus Rachel's work came to her, and, of all things, it came through a bit of renaissance lace work! She looked at the grayed cottage with its flapping, faded mosquito bar, after the girl left, and then down at her delicate blue and white work. How incongruous the two were, and how little she would have dreamed of influencing a girl from that house through something so fine. God knew best.

When she left it to Him, it was wonderful how He made that to appear. Why hadn't she tried that before? She might not accomplish very much, for after all she'd only promised to teach a girl how to make lace. That might not lead to anything else, but she felt that she'd been given a chance to try, and she thanked her Father for it.

Chapter 10

H oward Fairfield didn't linger in the city heat because he wished to do so. An aged member of his church lay very ill and asked to see him. Then the man who was to supply his prayer meeting sent word he couldn't come, so he stayed for that. Afterward he lingered by the old saint's bedside till he went where spiritual help wasn't needed anymore. So another funeral was held in that one short week, which seemed to stretch out even longer.

Saturday afternoon saw him free at last, for the pulpit was supplied for the next day and the man was there. He had enough time to catch the last train back to the shore. He laid his head wearily against the seat cushion while the train whirled on and thought over the week's experiences.

How he was led! That girl with her dream, and the little girl's funeral, and his own experience in waiting for the hour to arrive! And then those hours by the bedside of the dying saint, where he gained, more than gave, spiritual help. He sensed a new feeling for the old man who just entered heaven, which he'd never felt for anyone who died. It was as if he'd been given an opportunity to know one of the apostles for a few short hours, talk with him and have his eyes opened by him, and love him. Then the heavens opened, and the man was carried to Jesus.

Heaven held new interest for him now. He loved it more than he realized he could. He wondered what sights and scenes that dear servant of God was passing through at that moment, while his friends mourned his absence from earth. The coffin he saw lowered into the earth two hours earlier contained no thought of the grand sweet soul, who wasn't buried there but was high in heaven with the angels. How he wished he'd known the old man better during his time on earth. Oh, those wasted months, when such companionship and help might have been his.

It reminded him of the days when the disciples were with Jesus and didn't know how to value His daily companionship. To know intimately someone like Jesus was, in a sense, like knowing Jesus when He walked in bodily form on earth. Perhaps others in his congregation were like this man. Now that he thought over the list, several families lived simple, trusting Christian lives evidently with strong faith and possessed rich experiences from which he might learn.

There were the Clarks. He considered them good souls but ignorant. In some things they may have been ignorant, but they read and lived their Bibles. Now that he thought about it, they could help him in many ways. How foolish he'd been! How wise in his own conceit! He thought he knew more than everyone else because he was fresh from the seminary. But now he realized he didn't learn true heart-knowledge, which should have gone hand in hand with his head-knowledge.

Had he wasted his preparations so far this summer? He planned a series of sermons on the mystery of the trinity and another series on the lives and works of the prophets. They seemed empty and useless to him now, though they doubtless had good things. They might help certain minds work through perplexing places. But in light of his new experiences they seemed to miss the mark, considering the tremendous truths that needed to be presented, or urged, even thundered from the pulpit day and night.

Howard Fairfield thought a quiet summer by God's sea, with his own intellect and God's good teacher, nature, would assist him as a preacher. But he might have gone somewhere else, to one of the many wonderful spiritual gatherings far and near, beginning with Northfield and Mr. Moody.

He often thought he might like to go to Northfield, but it was in a lofty, condescending way, more out of curiosity than anything else. Now he longed for something he thought he might find there. Perhaps he ought to give up his present plans and go there at once. He closed his eyes and, wondering what his heavenly Father would have him do about it, prayed to be guided. While he wanted to go and thought it would be good, he still longed for the quiet and rest of the seashore and the chance to talk with God alone. He would wait there at least till he was sure what God wanted him to do.

As the train neared his destination he opened his eyes and looked for landmarks. He hadn't realized how tired he was or how eager for a sight of the mighty ocean.

He thought of the few friends he'd met there and wondered if they could be helpful—and, with a strange new feeling, if he could be helpful to them. What about those two girls he met under such peculiar circumstances? He hardly knew where to place them; he saw so little of them. The younger girl asked some strange questions.

Then his last walk and reverie by the sea returned to him vividly. He'd go back, and he felt with a grateful thrill in his heart that his questions would find answers now. Now his eyes were open, and he was beginning to see things differently. He thanked God for this.

Meanwhile, if he could get or do any good, he wanted to be ready. He watched eagerly in the deepening twilight, as the train approached the station, for the few little cottages bathed in the sunset glow of the bay. Out on the platform he breathed in the salt air, glad to be back again. After supper he walked out beside the sea in the dark starry night alone to think and be with God. And he returned from that walk to deep, dreamless sleep and awoke to the restfulness of the Sabbath.

Now the Saturday that brought such brightness to the shore and blew such a life-giving breeze from across the bay also carried the mosquito, on the wings of that breeze, and not alone. The mosquitoes that came were small, sharp and wise. They knew those cottages with their wide cracks and roomy ceilings for hiding. For years they or their ancestors had been blown across the bay on just such breezes and went straight to their haunts. They arrived all at once, swarming through the porches and driving the helpless sitters inside the screen doors. And they rushed in, if not through a door then through other vulnerable points in the cottages. By night, when the lights appeared, they made their presence almost unbearable.

Maria, like many other people of fair skin and highly strung nerves, was particularly susceptible to stings, whether by insects or tongue. She became irritable at once. Perhaps no one would have wondered if one saw the red swellings that appeared in response to the insect's attack. Mosquito bites poisoned Maria, and she suffered intensely. So it was no surprise that her temper was at its highest pitch. She actually sat down in front of the whole family and cried in vexation and despair over the torment of the pests. She declared she couldn't endure it any longer, she'd rather die, and a dozen other extravagant things she didn't mean. Then she went to bed, sick and sore, to fight them there and find little sleep to restore her calmness.

Sabbath morning found her aching in body and mind. The mosquitoes persisted. Maria refused to go to church, though the entire family urged her to do so, hoping it would soothe her troubled spirit. They were glad she refused when they arrived at the church and found thousands of the insects inside on the white plastered walls. The assembled congregation looked more like dancing dervishes than quiet, respectable churchgoers bent on worshipping God. Indeed, the mosquitoes kept up their part of the performance until people were nearly distracted, some going home in desperation.

The morning speaker closed his remarks quickly, and the people hurried home, discussing the unusual visitation of mosquitoes and the wind and weather as causes. Those whose houses were plastered hastened indoors and those whose weren't took refuge in penny royal oil and the smoke of various herbs. Then in despair they went to the beach to find refuge. Even Maria was driven there soon after the noonday meal. She wouldn't have gone if it had been tolerably comfortable at home, for she felt so perverse that she dreaded seeing anyone or having to speak pleasantly. She didn't even want to look neat or pretty for the day. But she finally consented to change her dress and smooth her hair and go to the beach with Rachel.

Rachel hoped the afternoon would be a comfort to Maria and thus loaded herself down with cushions, parasols, fans and a beach chair. Then with her Bible and the new book, which she saved to read this Sabbath afternoon, she walked cheerfully through the sand and swarms of mosquitoes to find the right spot on the beach where the breeze and the view were pleasant. Meanwhile Maria scolded with every step and declared she would go back, but kept going.

Rachel arranged the beach chair comfortably and, stating she preferred them, fixed cushions and sand for herself and insisted her sister use the chair. Rachel opened her Bible first, while Maria sat gloomily looking out on the smooth water and its transparent blue-green sheen. The color of the ocean was worth watching today, and the sky and air seemed perfect. But Maria was in no mood to enjoy it and soon closed her eyes. She felt impatient with the day and the summer and with the emptiness of her life as it stretched out before her.

Rachel felt her sister's gloom. It was apparent, and Rachel was impressionable. She knew she couldn't do anything to lighten her sister's heart, and yet she couldn't enjoy her own reading or the day. She read one of the short chapters in her new book and was charmed with the plain, everyday language and sympathy expressed by the writer. But in spite of her interest in the book, her mind kept wandering to Maria. She was conscious of every movement her sister made, until at last she thought she was asleep and instantly gave thanks. Sleep would be the best thing for her in her present state of mind.

Unconsciously, Rachel relaxed her tense muscles and nestled back among the pillows. She let her mind wander to the Higginses and the promised lesson in lace-making; she wondered how she could get in a lesson on something besides lace. Soon two figures approached. She'd been watching them as they walked from the lighthouse, and now they were close enough for her to identify them as the two younger members of the Higgins household, Katy and John. They wandered along, bareheaded and barefooted, picking up a shell now and then and trotting on again.

How different the sea must seem to them, Rachel thought. They lived there all year and knew it at its wildest. Evidently it was their friend, and they loved it. Rachel could tell that from the way they looked out across it, pointing to a distant sail or a cloud of smoke from some steamer far off against the horizon.

Rachel wondered if the sea ever spoke to them of God and what idea they had of its majesty and its Maker. Did they associate the two? Had they been taught enough for that, or did they have a natural instinct for it without being taught? She framed questions she wanted to ask them and was eager to know their answers.

And then her second opportunity came. The children sat down on a broken spar that had washed ashore sometime ago and been half-buried in the sand. Katy dug her bare feet in the sand, and John sat still, looking out at the water. They evidently meant to sit there for a while.

Rachel decided to go and talk with them. They looked lonely; perhaps they'd like to hear a story. She missed her Sunday school class of young girls at home. She would enjoy teaching the day's lesson, since she studied it all week to keep up with her class during her absence. What if she talked to them and God opened a way for her to tell that beautiful Bible story to them? Would Maria miss her? She glanced at her sister, who seemed to be fast asleep. Then, moving gently, she laid her books by Maria's side and stood up. She would go for a few minutes, anyway, and see how she was received.

So with her heart beating fast, for she was young and this seemed to be a serious mission to her, Rachel went to see what her first opportunity for soul-winning might be.

Katy and John were startled when the young lady sat down beside them on their spar and spoke to them. At first they picked up their shells and started to run away, but with Rachel's smile and her delight over their pretty shells they soon forgot this idea. Before they knew it they were sitting on the sand, listening with round eyes and open mouths to a story.

She decided to ask her questions later, after she won a place in their hearts and loosed their tongues, for they were too shy to say anything but yes and no, and blushed deeply even at these. They evidently weren't used to talking with anyone except their own family and perhaps not much with them. So Rachel's art of storytelling stood her in good stead. She used a shell to lead up to the story and soon had them interested in it.

Then from that story she went on to tell of Jesus making a fire by the seaside and cooking the fish for His disciples' supper. As they grew interested she forgot everything in her joy of teaching. She drew a bit of a diagram in the sand, using a razor fish's shell for a crayon. The children, who hadn't seen anything like it before, bent eager heads over the picture and drank in her words as if they were listening to music. Perhaps it wasn't the best lesson she might have selected for the first in religious instruction. But presently those two young hearts beat with longing to have been in that weary boat load coming in to the supper and the gracious Master.

Then wonder of wonders! They heard from the young lady that they too might be His children—cared for by Him! And they learned that Jesus, who was no more associated with their idea of God than with some of their own family and whose name they heard only in profanity, might be theirs.

If the young teacher could have looked into those darkened little hearts and known what they really thought and felt about God and how little they knew about Him, her own heart would have sunk at the impossible task; her words might have then grown less eloquent in her hopelessness. Mercifully, she didn't know, as none of us knows just what lies before or about us. But the Father in heaven knew they were filled with a great longing for the first time in their young lives to know Jesus Christ.

So Rachel talked on, and the children didn't grow weary. The sun was setting in the west before she realized how long she'd kept her Sabbath school and been away from her sister, who would doubtless blame her for the neglect.

That night when Rachel opened her Bible in her own room she read these words, "Therefore, my beloved brethren, be ye steadfast, unmovable, always abounding in the work of the Lord, forasmuch as ye know that your labor is not in vain in the Lord." And she wondered what those words meant and if she might claim them and think her Father in heaven sent them as a message to cheer her heart in this new work.

Chapter 11

B
ut Maria hadn't been asleep. She closed her eyes because she didn't wish to talk or see her sister bending over her Bible. It made her uncomfortable to think Rachel could enjoy the Bible. *She* could not. She told herself plainly that she never had; that she only read it from a sense of duty, as of course all church members did. She tried to tell herself Rachel pretended to enjoy it. In her heart she knew there was no pretense about Rachel and that she really enjoyed it, but Maria liked saying this to herself. It made her own unhappy, rebellious life seem less bleak in contrast.

When Rachel laid down her books and slipped away, Maria felt relieved. She wanted to be alone. She felt too ugly in her heart to be near anyone. In time she wondered where her sister went and why she didn't return. Raising herself up and peering out from under the parasol, she looked up and down the beach until she saw Rachel with her young students seated nearby. Maria understood what it meant. She frowned. Rachel was always doing such odd things.

What would the De Veres or some of the other hotel people think if they came along and saw her sitting in the sand with those two barefooted heathens beside her? She almost decided to call her back and reprove her. Then she sat back again, asking herself what was the use, and felt a little relieved she would be alone for a while. Growing in her heart, however, was the determination to charge her sister with neglecting her for two little vagrants.

She settled herself a little more comfortably with some of Rachel's pillows and, seeing the red paper-covered book on the Bible beside her, picked it up. It surprised her a little that Rachel brought a paper-covered novel out on Sunday along with her Bible, for Rachel was apt to be a little puritanical about such things. But Maria knew Roland De Vere had sent some books over to Rachel the day before, and doubtless this was one of them. She reflected that Rachel's scruples would be easily overcome by that handsome young man, who was devoting himself to her, even if she were only a little girl.

She read the title, *A Castaway*, which sounded exciting. It was probably a story of the sea. She opened it at the beginning, with a look of satisfaction that here was something to make her forget herself for a while. But the look changed rapidly to disappointment. A Bible verse at the beginning! It was nothing but a sermon after all, or, worse still, one of those devotional books. She flung it down in her lap and leaned back again. How exasperating! Just when she thought she was going to have a little relief from the monotony and enjoy herself.

Then she picked up the book again and read halfway down the first page. But it was as if she were reading Hebrew. She didn't know what type of speech this was, nor did she take in the sense of the words. They meant nothing to her, and she closed it again and continued with her own thoughts, her fingers carelessly between the pages. But the look of discontent remained on her face. It was good that the parasol was placed in such a way as to hide her expression; otherwise she might have missed what was sent her that afternoon.

Howard Fairfield was walking on the beach alone, having gone out right after dinner to get away from the chatter of the hotel guests. He ambled up by the lonely lighthouse, then turned and retraced his steps. He intended to go to his room to rest or read. His walk by the sea refreshed him, and his thoughts were with God. His face wore a softened expression, which on a man makes it more noble and manly, as if he were growing to be more like the man God meant him to be.

He walked on slowly as he neared the beach in front of the hotel and met some of the guests there strolling and chatting in a lazy fashion. He took a path farther away, so he might not be drawn into conversation with any of them and break the solemn quiet which had stolen over him.

Thus he passed just behind Rachel and her little listeners. Catching a word or two of her earnest lesson, he slowed down and listened too. He wondered at the tact and skill with which this mere girl talked to these two unlearned children. He could learn from even a young girl's teaching, he told himself, as he sauntered on, wishing he dared linger and hear more without spoiling the lesson for the other two.

Then he turned his steps down to the sea and stood close to the waves, looking out. His past life seemed to be rolling out there before him, wave after wave of it, rolling carelessly but certainly on to eternity to meet him again on the other shore. He numbered each wave with a year or period of his life and saw its glaring mistakes. He wished he might ride over the waters and bring those farther ones back and live them again that they might be better lived. At last he turned with a sigh. There was no use looking back. He must go forward and make sure that the waves that followed would be stronger and full of endeavor for Christ.

So walking deep in thought up the sandy bank he came face to face with Maria Hammond. She had of course seen him; in fact, she'd been watching him for some minutes. While she was too proud to arrange her dress or alter her position as if she expected him to stop and talk with her, she still rose to more of a sitting posture. And she changed her expression from one of scornful discontent to one of quiet, dignified Sabbath thoughtfulness.

The young man, realizing suddenly that he was about to walk over a lady and a sun umbrella, raised his head and recognized Maria. Of course he had to pause and speak to her, though in his present mood he would have avoided anyone—especially a lively young girl, as he imagined her to be—if he had the choice beforehand.

But while exchanging a word of greeting, his eyes fell on the Bible and the little paper book. He looked up quickly, almost surprised, yet glad, at the girl. He didn't think she would be one to bring her Bible to the shore where others were. He must have been mistaken. She was after all a Christian, an earnest one, perhaps, like her sister over there who was telling the children about Jesus. He was glad he stopped and thought he may have been led to her for help, for he realized just then he needed help. His face lit up.

"May I sit down?" he asked. "Or are you expecting someone else to occupy this luxurious chair in the sand? I'm a little tired from my long walk."

And Maria, smiling and gracious, though with not a shade too much earnestness for maidenly decorum, told him he was welcome; the seat was Rachel's, but she'd gone on a missionary trip to some little heathens, and there was no telling how late it would be before she returned.

If Maria hadn't noticed something different in this new acquaintance of hers, she might have included a shade of scorn for Rachel and her menial service in this sentence. But she saw in the young man's face something that reminded her he was a minister and that ministers were wont to respect and praise such acts as Rachel's present one. Therefore her tone told nothing of the scorn she felt, and she spoke of Rachel's work as a natural, perfectly praiseworthy occurrence. Later she wondered what kept her from saying several things that were on the tip of her tongue.

"She's doing her work there well," said the minister, his face serious again. "I couldn't help hearing a little of her lesson as I passed and wished I were a barefoot heathen too, for what I heard helped me. She must have remarkable talent as a teacher of little ones."

Maria was somewhat astonished but accepted the compliment for her sister with sisterly pride. While they were talking Mr. Fairfield reached over and picked up the little paper volume. Maria's face flushed slightly. She was about to disclaim any connection with the book and tell how miserably disappointed she was a few minutes before over the contents. Again something held her back, and she sat still while Mr. Fairfield turned the pages.

"Ah! Mr. Meyer!" he said, as he opened the title page. "You've been reading this?"

He flashed his bright dark eyes into hers again with that sudden pleasure and surprise that confused her a moment before. "I never read it myself. I was foolish enough to lose my opportunity to hear the man when he was in this country. I listened to some negative criticisms about him, but I've since come to believe they were completely false and unfounded. I wish I could undo that loss and hear this address as he delivered it in my own city. A saint who has just gone to heaven told me about it."

Maria listened in respectful, surprised silence, glad some intuition kept her mouth closed a moment earlier. This certainly wasn't the same young man she knew, or thought she knew, two weeks before. She prided herself on being a quick judge of character and reading faces readily. What made the difference? She watched him while he turned the pages slowly.

"Have you been reading this?" he asked again suddenly. "Have you read it all? Perhaps you wouldn't mind reading it out loud to me, if you haven't. No one reads out loud to me now that my sister's abroad. Do you like to read aloud for other people's pleasure?"

"No, I haven't read it all," Maria admitted, her face flushing slightly. She wondered whether, if he knew the fact, he would call that the strict truth to answer thus. "But I'm very fond of reading out loud and shall be delighted to read it if it will bring any pleasure to you."

Now it happened that Maria was gifted in the art of reading aloud. Her family seldom reaped the benefit of this gift, for there were few occasions when she thought it worthwhile to exercise it, and they seldom asked favors from her. But from time to time, when her audience was appreciative and worthwhile, she could charm a friend or a whole room full of friends, as she read from a story or a poem, and evoke their tears or laughter at her will. Her voice was sweet and clear, and her expressive face helped to interpret whatever she read, by flashes of fun or earnestness. Everybody liked to hear Maria Hammond read; when she was a little child, guided by her family's wishes, the father, mother, brother and sister had been very proud of her abilities.

It was interesting, not to say romantic, for a girl who'd moped at a dull seaside with nothing to do but cook and be cross to find herself sitting by the sea with a handsome, evidently cultured young man. It was further so to be asked to read aloud something he was deeply concerned about, along his personal lines of thought, for his benefit. Even though she'd just scorned the book and the theme chosen was dull to her, what did it matter? Religious writing was always easy to read and lent itself to good expression in an elocutionary sense. She took the book with alacrity, pleased at the turn the afternoon had taken, and wondered why the sea looked more beautiful than a half-hour earlier.

She read the wonderful Bible text that started the address and then continued as naturally as if the writer of the simple, thoughtful sentences were present delivering them. She was constantly aware of the earnest eyes watching her. He listened intently to what she read and took in the slightest turn brought out by her good rendering, appreciating to the full the homey, apt illustrations sprinkled throughout the short sermon.

Unknown to her, she was thinking most about what he thought of her reading. As the reading went on, however, she couldn't fail to be interested too; for a good reader, like a good singer or actor, throws his whole soul into what he is voicing and lives it and believes it with all his heart.

She read to the end without interruption, except for an occasional barely articulate sound issued from the listener as he noted some peculiarly good point. As she finished the splendid prayer closing the address, she raised her eyes to his, and they were full of tears.

Those tears seemed almost dreadful to Maria, as she thought about them afterward, as if she gave an impression she had no right to give; she dropped her eyes quickly.

A strange exalted look crossed his face too, as if he were pleading for forgiveness with his eyes from one unseen and realizing there was something hurtful in his life. He had hardly seemed conscious of the girl by his side. But then he spoke slowly, quietly; he was solemn, with a peculiar light in his eyes, she saw, as she glanced up shyly again.

"Miss Hammond, I can't thank you enough for the help you've been to me in reading that. It fits my life better than anything I ever heard. Do you know, it touches me in a vital spot. I've been afraid in the last few days that I was a castaway, even before I was of any real use. An hour ago I didn't think I could speak of this to anyone; but perhaps it'll do me good to tell someone, and you've been so kind and helpful. In fact, I can see that you know just how to help someone in trouble."

Here he looked up with a pleasant smile, not in the least the smile of the ordinary young man of society who is giving a young woman a compliment. It was more a kind acknowledgment of her womanhood and its natural province of helper, comforter, sympathizer.

"I've had a strange experience since I left the beach so suddenly. I never thought to tell it to anyone, but I believe I'll tell you if you don't mind."

And then he gave the astonished Maria an account of his hasty summons to the city, of his meeting with the dreamer and of the strange fulfillment of the dream. He even told her of his own feelings as he waited for that summons to the funeral and of his full surrender to God and the experiences by the bedside of the dying saint.

When he finished, they rose by tacit consent to walk slowly toward home. He gathered up the cushions and parasol and silently helped her collect her things, and she walked subdued and wondering beside him. Not that she was silent. No, she was naturally too tactful for that. She knew how to sympathize with people in other things than religion, and she knew how to put in the quiet, helpful word and listen with rapt attention.

Moreover, she was intrigued with this young man and his story. She'd never listened to a real heart story like this before, nor had anyone given her his confidence to such an extent. She couldn't help but be sympathetic and feel that something in what he said was true for her as well as for him.

"It's all very wonderful," she said as they neared her home.

Mrs. Hammond, awakened by voices from an uncomfortable nap in the mosquito-netted hammock on the porch, looked up to see a strange new light on her elder daughter's face. She wondered again about Maria.

They paused at the steps, and the minister said earnestly, "You've helped me this afternoon. I'd like to talk with you more about this. May I hope to have some more of that wonderful reading soon?"

Then something was said about attending the evening service in the church. The mother, behind the porch screen, didn't hear or pay attention. She was puzzling over how Maria, whom they'd known since their stay at the seashore, could possibly help anyone in her present state of mind.

Chapter 12

That's a remarkable girl, said Mr. Fairfield to himself as he walked slowly back to his hotel. She'll be a help to me—I can see that at once. And what a fine reader she is! She seems utterly unconscious of the fact. She's as sweet and natural as a flower. She must be an unusual Christian!

It's a good thing people are blind sometimes; otherwise much of the good of this world might be left undone because the workers would think it was hardly worthwhile. God in His mysterious kindness lets us see each other, no worse, no better than we really are, so we may help and be helped.

Had the Hammond family known the young minister's conclusions about Maria, they would doubtless have thought it their duty to warn him how mistaken he was. Yet nothing could have come to Maria that would have done her as much good as this afternoon of being happily misunderstood and the consequent impression she made upon the minister. Otherwise, how could she spend the days afterward in such reading and talk she never dreamed of participating in before? Or how could she enjoy pleasant companionship of a higher character than any she experienced before? God had just as surely sent Mr. Fairfield to be a missionary to Maria Hammond as He intended Maria Hammond to awaken and help the young man. And yet a weak human judgment would have kept these two apart from growing spiritually.

For the first time since arriving at the shore, Maria entered the door of the despised green cottage without thinking of the cottage or its shabbiness or her own hatred of the surroundings. She went thoughtfully to her own room and laid the two books on Rachel's table, then freshened up before getting supper. But her face didn't wear its recent usual expression of distaste and weariness. Instead, she looked bright and happy.

She wasn't thinking of the deep spiritual things she read from the little book or entirely of the young minister's experiences, though they impressed her strongly. She was instead satisfying her own starved love for admiration with thinking that the young man cared to confide in her and thought her worthy of such confidences. She recognized that they were unusual confidences, and her own conscience, a well-educated one, soon began to trouble her that she'd let him suppose her to be better than she was.

She went back over the afternoon talk. While she realized she didn't tell any falsehoods, or say or do anything out of keeping with actual truth, still she acknowledged to her soul with crimson cheeks that she remained silent several times. And at those times, in order to be perfectly honest, she ought to have spoken out and told him she wasn't at all what he thought; he must go to her sister, or others, whom she'd half despised for their eagerness about such things, if he wanted any help.

And yet, if she'd done this, she would have lost the privilege of that talk, and she began to realize it was a privilege to her. Nor was it wholly on account of her desire for companionship and pleasure. Something deeper in her restless heart said to her, *Here, here is something you've longed for. This man may show you a way to get it. He's different from what you thought him to be at first. And perhaps you're a little disappointed he is, for you fear you can't have quite so much of what you call "fun" with him if that's the case. But underneath it all you know you like him better since he's of a higher type than you at first thought.*

What odd conversations people carry on with themselves, and how they analyze their own feelings and think they know themselves. Yet they can read only a little piece of their own hearts and not know its follies or its goodness either. Then straightway they forget what manner of men and women they are and go on committing the same follies again.

But Maria's cheerfulness lasted while she prepared the evening meal. Rachel expected a storm because of her desertion and was astonished, almost uneasy. Finally she felt she needed to explain to her sister why she didn't come back sooner. But Maria answered pleasantly that she'd heard an account of the delightful little lesson she was teaching, and she hoped it wasn't thrown away on those poor ignorant children. It was a pity Rachel didn't have better material to work on down here, but it was good of her to be willing to help those poor children, she supposed. Then Maria went out to the refrigerator actually humming a tune under her breath while she took out the butter for supper.

Rachel walked out to the porch where her mother was sitting and asked, "Mama, is Maria sick, do you think? She's not acting like herself. I wish I hadn't left her alone this afternoon, but I thought she was asleep."

The mother glanced up anxiously, always fearful for her children. Then remembering, she smiled. "No, dear, I think she's had a glimpse of pleasure, and it might be doing her good. She's had a hard time, poor child, though of course we couldn't help it."

"Well, Mama," said Rachel, wrinkling her smooth brow, "I think she's working too hard. I wish you and Papa would make her stop and go out on the beach and let me take my turn awhile. I know I can't do as well as she, but I'll try my best. I don't feel happy with Maria working so hard."

"You dear child!" said the mother, drawing Rachel toward her and smoothing her hand. "I know how much that means for you to say. You don't like kitchen work, and you've been good at it too. But you don't need to do any more than you've been doing. Your father and I have talked over the same thing. We've been worried about your sister's health and decided last night to have that Higgins girl come over every day. She's not skilled and will need help and watching, but she'll learn. And she's willing to come for very little if I teach her our ways, she says; so you needn't think the expense will be too great. That will set both you and Maria free for most of the time, and I'm very relieved."

Maria called her mother just then to ask a question about supper, and Rachel was left standing in the dying twilight. How wonderful everything was! God was actually going to send the girl she'd hoped to help a little, right into their daily lives, giving her endless opportunity. She closed her eyes and lifted her heart in prayer that her life would show forth God's glory and that she might help lead the girl to Jesus.

She liked to remember the eager little faces that listened to her lesson that afternoon and rehearsed in her mind their questions and her answers and the way they were received. Her heart leaped within her at the thought of telling the story of Jesus for the first time to two little human waifs for whom He died.

Maria saw the minister only a few minutes more that night. The mosquitoes were too merciless for them to linger outside the cottage or light it up and invite people in, and the minister wasn't one who would propose a walk. He felt that both their hearts had received a benediction and that the young woman would sympathize with him in wanting to be alone with God a little while after the Sabbath blessing.

But Maria's conscience was pricking her. He thanked her again as he bade her good night for the help she gave him, and she felt guilty as she let him go away thinking of her in this way. Her natural honesty wouldn't allow her to accept quietly this homage to her supposed goodness. She must explain soon and then say good-bye to friendship with him, for he was evidently much in earnest. He would hardly waste time on someone like her.

Well, what did she care? She could go on as she had and endure the summer to the end. The man was a stranger, anyway, and not her kind. Her restless spirit was returning.

She knew nothing of the proposed domestic help. She remembered the next day and the petty miserable cares she had of her own free will taken upon herself. The mosquitoes were again a terrible thorn in the flesh, and she imagined the piles of greasy dishes that would have to be washed in the morning. She thought of the struggle with the grocery boy to get him to send the yeast in time for tomorrow's baking; otherwise they'd have to buy some of the baker's miserable stuff disguised as bread which all the family cordially detested.

Win came in then with his steady stream of fun and, choosing the wrong time, teased Maria with questions about Mr. Fairfield. Her replies were short and sharp; she said with icy dignity that she cared nothing whatever for Mr. Fairfield and wished he would stay away; that she supposed he was some nobody, anyway, since no one else would come to such a place for the summer unless he had to.

Then she went to her room with tears of vexation in her eyes and thought of the same man's earnest "thank you" spoken a few moments before. She recalled her own gentle good night, her acceptance of his words of Christian friendliness and how she evidently deceived him as to her character, and felt herself a hypocrite indeed.

The morning found her as unrested and unhappy as in the days before. She even resented the new arrival in the kitchen instead of being glad and relieved. After repeated attempts to monopolize the work and show that a girl was an extra expense, she went gladly to her room, declaring that if they wouldn't let her work she supposed she could sit down and endure life in some way with folded hands. No, she wouldn't go to the beach, and she wouldn't go bathing, and she wouldn't fix up her muslin dress to wear to Spray View that afternoon; she wasn't going to Spray View to call on those two stuck-up girls. She didn't care to be patronized if Rachel did, and as for Roland De Vere, she thought she was greatly mistaken in him. He didn't seem nearly as intellectual as she at first supposed.

Then when Rachel in despair left her, she barred the door and buried her face in the pillow and cried as hard as her overwrought nerves demanded.

Fortunately for her, she didn't cry long before Rachel's voice called to her again that someone was in the parlor to see her. This stopped the tears suddenly, but not the stubbornness. She wouldn't go to the parlor to see anyone. Rachel might make any excuse she pleased, that she was too busy or sick; but she wouldn't come out, and she wouldn't unfasten the improvised door which the father and brother had contrived for more privacy than the cottage afforded.

Nevertheless, she rose from the bed and went to the small, disfiguring mirror. She knew that the few moments of crying must have left their mark already on her face. Yes, her eyes and nose were red and swollen. She couldn't go out if she wished to, without disgracing herself. She wondered who wanted to see her—maybe some of those De Veres, who had now become hateful, because she imagined they were looking down on her and hers; or maybe the minister. Well, if it was the minister, what did she care? she asked herself fiercely and went nervously to the washbowl and dashed cold water on her swollen eyes.

Then at the door she heard her mother's voice, always low and sweet, but very low now lest the caller in the parlor of this very "open" house should hear. The voice also held a note of command which Mrs. Hammond seldom used toward her children, but which Maria didn't dare disregard.

"Maria, let me in at once. I have something to tell you."

Maria answered her mother's summons then and let her in, mopping her face with a wet towel all the while.

"Are you ill, Maria?" asked the anxious mother as she saw the traces of tears on her elder daughter's face.

"No," answered Maria, choking at her mother's tender voice. She almost wished she were really ill and lying in bed to be taken care of. The tears welled up into her eyes again.

The mother wound her arm about the daughter's waist.

"Well, then, dear, is there any reason why you don't care to see Mr. Fairfield? Tell me about it. I must know the reason, you know, before I can excuse you."

"Is it Mr. Fairfield?" asked Maria, a hint of satisfaction in her voice in spite of herself. "But look at my eyes, Mother. I can't go out. I'm a sight. It'll be hours before I get over looking like a fright. You'll have to tell him something."

The mother noticed the disappointment in Maria's voice. She determined to make an effort to get Maria out of herself and into the fresh air, where her nerves might rest.

"Nonsense! Your eyes will be all right in a few minutes, dear!" she answered quickly. "Bathe them and brush your hair. Here, slip on your pretty beach dress. You haven't worn it since you came, and the air is fresh this morning. I want you to get out and have the air and sunshine. You'll be ill if you don't, and we're not going to allow that. Now hurry, dear. Mr. Fairfield is quite anxious to see you. I'll excuse you for a few minutes, and Rachel will take him down to the new clam beds while you're getting ready. Now hurry."

The mother went out to do what she promised with more confidence in her manner than in her heart that Maria would do her bidding.

But something came over Maria. She desired suddenly above everything else to go out in her pretty beach dress, walk beside Mr. Fairfield, have him think her good for a little while and say she helped him. It wouldn't do any harm just for once, and she was tired of the hateful way things had been going. She washed her face feverishly and hurried to get ready; between times she dashed over to the disfiguring little glass to see if her eyes and nose would soon assume their proper color and shape. And the mother, returning, was relieved to find that Maria was ready.

And so it came about that Maria and the young minister started out on a jaunt to the life-saving station two miles away on that lovely summer morning. A fresh breeze was blowing in their faces, and Maria looked her prettiest in her dark blue and white yachting suit. Her cheeks were a pleasant pink from the recent tears, and her whole face expressed sudden happiness. When Maria gave way after a fit of stubbornness she was often lovely and subdued and humble, and somehow her mother's tone and wistfulness had conquered her that morning.

Moreover, she felt humiliated, and the humility sat well upon her face, where so much haughty pride had been lately. The minister looked at her in the Monday morning light and decided she was fair as well as good. He was glad to walk with her and talk beside the sea, and before the morning was over they found many interests in common.

When Maria came back she didn't feel as much of a hypocrite that she hadn't confessed to him how unworthy she was of his praise; the talk hadn't been on things in which she felt she was lacking. The Lord in His wisdom saw that this child of His needed a little of the brightness and joy of life. He gave it to her, weaving about her the cords of His own love which were to draw her to Himself. Let no skeptical one fancy all this beneath Him. We barter away the whole comfort of life if we so think. For these things, and things like them, are among the "all these" the Master promised would be added to those seeking first the Father's kingdom.

Chapter 13

It was several days since Maria and Mr. Fairfield had walked to the life-saving station together, and since then they had taken several similar expeditions. The afternoon was warm and lovely.

Maria lay in the screened and netted hammock on the porch with a book in front of her, but she wasn't reading. Instead, she was thinking. Her troubled conscience had pursued her day after day through all the pleasant walks and sails and rides and talks. She felt herself to be more and more a hypocrite. She tried feebly, two or three times, to explain to the minister that she wasn't "good" as he seemed to think; that she was, in fact, wicked and worldly and unlovely in her character. But her efforts failed, for it was so pleasant to have someone think well of her and include her in his pleasure as this man had done.

This afternoon her conscience arraigned her strongly. Something needed to be done. She mustn't go on reading religious books and pretending to be devoted to them, though she realized the books were not so wholly without interest as they seemed last Sunday. They held intensely interesting items, and she liked to hear the minister talk about these things. Her own part in these conversations was a meek assent to what he said. She even added a word or two now and then when he seemed to expect her to say something and when something quite original occurred to her which fit the discussion.

He thought her very bright, and so she was; her additions to the religious conversations were apt and striking ones. She knew she was brought up to say such things well and to know when to say them.

But she also knew that her life for sometime ran counter to her words, and she hated hypocrisy above all things. She planned conversation after conversation in which she told her new friend the truth about herself. In some of these imaginary scenes she was humble and begged him to teach her to think as he did. But for that she was too proud. In others she withdrew from his acquaintance entirely, told him she wasn't his kind and he was mistaken about her.

Then it occurred to her: Why not turn about and try to be what he thought she was? She reached that point this afternoon for the seventeenth time, asking herself over and over whether she could do it and how to begin, and if she did, would it be exactly honest for her to do so?

And then, why, after all, should she do it? Mr. Fairfield was a pleasant acquaintance, but in all probability he would go away in a few days and she might never see him again. Why did she care to appear good before him, and not only to appear good, but to be what she appeared? She couldn't understand why he brought out the best and highest longings her soul contained.

Well, if she assigned herself the task of being good, what should she do first? She might refrain from being cross and saying sarcastic things; but that seemed a rather hopeless task, for her tongue was so used to bitter words that she scarcely knew when she spoke them. Then, too, that held nothing interesting in it. Still, that would be a necessary part of any such change in her life. She might take up some philanthropic work. But what could it be? Rachel always seemed to find some work to do for others, now that there was help in the kitchen. Maria felt that her life had been made too easy for her to show her good works by any great sacrifices such as she was seeking.

At this point in her conversation with herself her sister came on the porch with a rocking chair, workbasket, scissors and thimble. And in the distance across the sandy dunes could be seen the lank, awkward form—arrayed in a neat blue calico and white apron—of their new maid, bearing in her arms a bundle of what looked like old hats. Her work was done for the afternoon, and Rachel's first lesson, instead of being in lace work, was to be in millinery. Annie Higgins desired above all worldly goods a nice hat to wear to an entertainment that evening over on the mainland. Her cousin's wife's brother had asked her to accompany him in his sailing vessel, along with other family members.

Rachel, through tact and kindness, discovered Annie's desire and readily offered her assistance. But she sighed as she thought what a much better hat Annie would have if only Maria were to make it instead of her. She kept the matter to herself, though, because she dreaded Maria's scornful looks and words if she knew.

Rachel offered her help to Annie without remembering the cracks in the kitchen wall, however. Maria heard the entire arrangement that morning as she sat in her room mending a tear in her blue dress. She thought about how easy it was for Rachel to find out and do such things for other people. Had Rachel been present and known she heard it, Maria would have felt compelled to show her scorn of the deed. But away from sight Maria could appreciate her sister's kindness, although she disapproved and wished she wouldn't do such odd things.

Now, as she saw Rachel come out on the porch, she almost wished she were gifted with doing things for other people so that she wouldn't feel so unworthy of the friendship of an earnest Christian minister. She languidly watched her sister put on her white work apron and select the needle she expected to use. Maria knew that making a hat was a big task for Rachel, who would rather write a description of a hat or draw a picture of it than go through the intricacies of producing one. It wasn't likely to be artistic when finished, either, as both sisters knew from experience. But Rachel would do her best.

Just at that moment two handsome horses trotted around the corner by the church, pulling an elegant carriage bearing Roland De Vere and his two sisters. The two sisters were seated in back, the young man was driving, and the seat beside him in the front was vacant. The carriage drew up at the little green cottage doorsteps, and its occupants greeted Rachel effusively.

Maria was glad she was screened from their view, for somehow she felt as out of sympathy with them as she did with herself or anybody else. Several months before, however, her heart would have jumped with joy at their appearance, and she would have done anything to be the fourth member of that riding party. She knew they'd come for Rachel and saw by the sudden rush of color to her little sister's cheeks that Rachel knew and was glad. Indeed, she was gladder perhaps than they had any idea of, for she was so quiet about her likes and dislikes; sometimes she was in danger of losing much she cared for in life through other people's supposing she didn't care. Maria's eyes were opened a little by the look on her sister's face as she quietly laid aside her basket and went down the steps to greet her callers and ask them in. Maria was glad they declined, for she couldn't help listening to the conversation.

Roland De Vere, in his gallant way, invited Rachel to put on her hat and join them in the carriage; they were off for a long drive up the beach and must have her company, or else their pleasure would be spoiled. Maria saw, through the cracks in the porch screen, how the soft color stole again into Rachel's cheeks and then how her bright face clouded with disappointment.

"Oh, I'm so sorry I can't go," she answered instantly. "I would love it, and it's such a perfect day for a drive on the beach. How delightful it would be to fly along on the edge of the waves with horses like those! But I really can't."

"Now we won't have any 'can't' at all. What is it in the way?" asked the young man earnestly. "Because whatever stumbling block is there, I'll remove it. Are you mending and can't leave your task till it's finished? If that's it, give me a needle, and I'll help, and we'll finish the work in no time."

Amid the laugh that followed, Rachel's perplexed face grew firm.

"No, it isn't anything like that," she answered, with a troubled laugh. "It's the Higgins girl."

"The Higgins girl! Who is she, and what does she have to do with it? Bring her along! We can stow her in somewhere and make her comfortable. Fannie, can't you and Evelyn make room back there?"

But Rachel hastened to explain, with an irrepressible smile at the idea.

"No, no, it's her hat. I promised to help her make a hat to wear tonight. She's the fisherman's daughter who lives over in that little house, and she wants to go out with a friend tonight. I promised her, and she seems very happy about it; so I mustn't disappoint her."

Mr. De Vere emitted a prolonged whistle, and the Misses Fannie and Evelyn looked curiously at Rachel, making Maria's blood boil within her.

"Dear me!" said Evelyn, shrugging her shoulders. "Can't you put her off?"

"Yes," put in Fannie, seeing her brother's disappointment and Rachel's firmly set red lips. "Tell her it's a great deal smarter to go bareheaded to events this time of year and wear a flower in her hair."

These girls were well-bred and liked Rachel very much. Moreover, they desired to please their brother. But evidently they weren't quite equal to giving up an afternoon's pleasure for the sake of making a hat for a fisherman's daughter. Rachel felt this more than saw it; she also felt she had the brother's sympathy in her confusion.

Maria, listening, saw it all and suddenly resolved. This was her opportunity. Without her usual calm deliberation, she acted impulsively, almost as Rachel might have done.

"Rachel!"

No small part of Rachel's confusion and embarrassment had arisen from the fact that Maria was listening on the porch, unable to get away; she would make all sorts of sneering comments as soon as the visitors were out of sight. But she didn't think Maria would speak at that moment, revealing her presence, for she knew her sister's hair was tousled from lying in the hammock and her dress wasn't one she'd want the De Veres to see her wearing.

With crimson cheeks she excused herself and went to her sister, trembling for fear Maria was about to reprimand her severely in the hearing of these friends. She had once or twice threatened to do so if Rachel persisted in her puritanical notions.

But to her amazement, instead of the proud, scornful look she expected to see on Maria's face, she found one of interest.

"Rachel, go!" she said in a quiet, sisterly voice. "I'll trim Annie's hat. Yes, go on at once; it's all right. You know I can do it as well as you. Get ready right away."

Rachel could hardly believe her ears. Maria offering to trim a servant girl's hat! Maria giving up her ease, without being urged, to do a kind work for one she despised!

But the friends in the carriage were waiting, and Maria was hurrying her. She must go and explain. After a moment's hesitation, she saw her sister meant it and would be displeased if she didn't accept it. So she returned to the carriage with a happy face and explained that Maria would see to the hat. Then she ran in to get ready and soon drove away with a bright face.

As Roland De Vere touched his whip to his horses, he said to himself: *I must have been mistaken about Maria after all. I wouldn't have expected her to do such a kind deed.*

Maria seemed fated to give false impressions of her goodness, in spite of herself and her honest endeavor to right matters with her conscience. As soon as the carriage was out of sight she went in to the kitchen. The Higgins girl had slipped around to the back door with her pile of old hats and soiled ribbons and funny artificial flowers. From there with dismay she watched her expected helper drive away in the beautiful carriage, her anticipation of a pleasurable evening now dimmed by the thought of the old worn-out hat.

She was only a poor girl after all, and of course Miss Rachel wouldn't miss out on her own fun on account of her. Then she sighed and told herself Miss Rachel was no better than other folks after all, even if she did teach the children a whole lot of religion last Sunday. Christian folks were all alike. She was almost tempted to believe Miss Rachel was different, but now she wouldn't believe in anybody who had pretty clothes and lots of friends. Then she sat down at the back door, looked out at the sea and thought of the long, dull winter ahead.

Maria explained why Rachel went, and she said pleasantly she would do the work. She invited Annie to bring her materials so they might look them over. But Annie didn't have such a charming idea of Maria's character and felt a bit afraid of her. So she only sat still and said she needn't bother; it didn't matter anyhow.

Maria knew her services were much better than her sister's along this line and expected them to be accepted with overwhelming joy. But she found she had to urge them upon this poor fisherman's daughter. She became indignant and told herself she wouldn't touch the hat if she hadn't promised Rachel, that the girl deserved no hat at all.

A promise was a promise, however, so she set herself to win Annie out of her glumness and soon had her interested in the hat. While Annie heated irons, according to her direction, for steaming velvet, she hunted among her own ribbons and flowers for something suitable to help out the meager trim. And she wondered why she had done this. Was it for Rachel or the minister or her own conscience' sake?

Chapter 14

The porch was the only comfortable place to work that warm afternoon. So after a brief struggle with her pride, Maria transported Annie and her trimmings to a spot behind the screen. Neighbors might pass or the riding party return, or even the minister might come by before she completed her task. But she cared little about the neighbors, and she would enjoy shocking those De Vere sisters; as for the minister, well, she might have done this for him, and if he didn't understand, her work would have been in vain.

She settled down to make a pretty hat and be friendly with this uninteresting girl if she could. She was determined for once to try her hand at philanthropy. On the whole, after the first half-hour she found it not so boring. Trimming hats was always pleasant work to her. She enjoyed thoroughly making "a whistle out of a pig's tail," figuratively speaking. And to make this old hat into something respectable, even into a work of art, was as good as playing a new game. She really liked it when she got into it.

Annie was kept so busy steaming velvet for the first few minutes that she didn't have time to talk. She was thankful for that, for she nearly resented Maria for touching her hat. She had no reason as yet to like Maria and would almost rather have done without a hat than accept a favor from her. She felt as though she were being patronized.

But she at last emerged from the kitchen with the brushed and steamed velvet and saw the hat that looked like a shapeless mass to her a few moments earlier. Under Maria's skillful hands the hat had assumed the shape she'd seen in stores and on ladies at the hotels. Annie's heart gave a great leap of joy, and her allegiance immediately went out to Maria even more warmly than it had to Rachel. Such is the vanity of all flesh, or shall we say feminine flesh?

To watch the fingers twist the renewed velvet folds about the now gracefully shaped straw was marvelous. Annie sat and gazed in speechless delight and proved herself a sharp helper with foresight. She anticipated the needs of the milliner, handing her a pin or spool of thread at the right moment and restoring the scissors when they slipped to the floor, as scissors often do. Maria noticed and appreciated this and felt an impulse to speak a kind word, but she could think of nothing except about the hat.

"I think it'll look very nice when it's finished," she said at last, holding the hat off to survey it. The admiring silence was becoming oppressive to her.

"It's jes' perfec'ly lovely!" exclaimed Annie effusively, her eyes shining with delight at possessing anything so satisfying. "I jes' don't see how you can do it so good! Don't you feel awful proud to be able to? How did you learn how? Did you ever work at a milliner's store?"

Maria's cheek flushed. She didn't like this question. She felt inclined to be indignant and take the girl's words for an insult. The idea of her working in a milliner's shop! This came from their hiring such a ridiculously cheap cottage and making even the poor fisher folk think they were from the common walks of life.

Then she glanced up and saw the evident admiration in Annie's face; she reflected that the girl had lived on the island much of her life and knew little of the different strata in society. Of course she had no intention of insulting her. Indeed, she perceived from the girl's face when she answered no that she would have stood a trifle higher in her estimation as a skilled artisan if she could have boasted that advantage. So she let the little discomfiture pass, a fact which almost surprised her and would have astounded her family beyond measure. She even smiled at the strange questions which followed, getting a little quiet amusement out of them.

"Your sister Rachel says you know how to do most everything," went on Annie, clasping her hands about one knee and rocking back and forth on the broad low step on which she was seated. "She said you could paint pictures. Say, did you ever do any of them crayon pictures of live folks? What they hang in best parlors, I mean, that look just like the folks, only all dressed up better than they gen'ally are when they're alive? They have two of them over to my friend's on the mainland. They've got red plush and gold frames, awful pretty, and they hang over the organ and the sofa. It's of her ma and pa when they was first married.

"I'd like awful well to get one of my oldest brother that died when he was ten, for Ma. She hasn't never forgot to mourn about him. Jes' seems if none o' us could take his place. Do you s'pose you could do one if I was to tell you how he looked? You see he never had no photograph taken, cause they didn't even have a tintype place here when he come here to live, nor in Spray View either. Could you do one o' them kind o' pictures, do you think? If you could, I'd work all summer jes' fer nothin' to get that picture, fer it would please Ma and Pa so. And I know where I could get a real pretty frame made cheap. A friend of mine is in a store where they make 'em."

Annie's eagerness quite overcame the milliner. She tried to repress the smile that kept trying to come and to explain that no one would be able to make a likeness of a person who was dead, without some kind of photograph to go by, especially one who hadn't known the person in life. Annie looked disappointed. She went from one extreme to the other and felt that a person capable of transforming her old hat could do anything. She was silent a few minutes watching the deft fingers at work, and then she began again.

"Your sister says you made them couches and pretty stuffings and curtains in your parlor. I think you must be awfully smart. You're sort of a 'Jack of all trades,' as the sayin' is, aren't you?"

She laughed heartily over this intended joke, and Maria couldn't refrain from joining in. Coupled with her powers of elocution, Maria possessed a rare ability as a mimic of a person's tones and manners. She began to think she would have rich material in this girl for quite an amusing entertainment for her friends if she chose to give it to them.

"Say! If I was to get some calico," Annie finally asked, "would you kind o' pin it up fer me like that green stuff hangin' in your dinin' room door? I'd like awful well to fix up our front room a little. I hate it the way 'tis. I never knew how to do them kind of things, but I always knew it looked horrid.

"I tried once or twice. I sent all the way to New York for a motto I saw advertised in a paper. It was 'Little Church Around the Corner.' That was just the year they built the chapel there, and I thought it would look kind of nice to have that motto in the parlor. It said it had the directions how to make it, and the stuff an' all for twenty-five cents, so I got it an' it took me a good part of the winter workin' evenin's to finish it.

"I done it in blue with green trimmin's and a brown steeple, them was the colors they sent, and it looked real pretty, and I stuck some shells on pasteboard and made a frame for it, but I ain't never had anything else to go with it. I would jes' give anything if we had a organ. It would look so nice under where it hangs, an' Jim and the girls would all like the music so much. I guess they could play it too after tryin' a little, for Jim can play the accordion real good. He plays 'Swanee River' and 'Home Sweet Home' an' 'Sweet By an' By' every Sunday night when he don't have to go down the bay. Say! How did you get them cushions in that corner to stand out so pretty with them ruffles all around? Do you s'pose I could fix up our house a little like this if I tried real hard?"

Maria couldn't help being interested in the poor, forlorn little house and this girl's helpless, hopeless attempt to "fix it up." She suggested some simple things which seemed too simple to Annie to make any effect. But as Maria continued and grew interested herself in describing the changes she'd make in a bare room if she had limited means, Annie's eyes began to sparkle and her cheeks grew pink with eagerness. She saw a chance their home might have a few bright, cheerful things someday as well as others.

"Why, I could do that," she said, as Maria paused with a pin in her mouth to try the effect of the ribbon she was arranging on the hat.

"Jim, he could saw the boards. I know he wouldn't mind helping. He has lots o' time Sundays."

Maria's strict training concerning the Sabbath as a day of rest made her doubt the good she might be doing if she were starting a family to work on the Lord's day. But Annie went on eagerly, leaving her little time for reflection.

"Say! Would you mind coming over someday soon and jes' lookin' at that room an' tellin' me where you think that shelf you said how to make would look pretty, and how far down the side of the wall the seat ought to reach? It ain't very far over there, you know, an' I could show you some cute little chickens and ducks if you'd come."

Maria began to see that her philanthropy was expected to last beyond this afternoon, and she was doubtful whether she relished the idea. She was willing enough to make a hat. But as for enduring this questioning and being taken on such a friendly social level, she had no such intentions. She already felt herself swelling in her own estimation until she almost came up to the minister's ideal. Surely she must be pretty good, after all, to undergo with a smile such a storm of talk as she'd been sitting under for the last hour.

But worse followed. She didn't like to refuse the girl's eager request, so she said perhaps she would come sometime, in what she meant to be an indefinite time. But the eager Annie accepted it all in good faith and thanked her profusely.

Suddenly she turned upon her. "Say!" she said earnestly. "You're one of them church folks too, ain't you? I didn't think you was at first, because you didn't go so much to the chapel or run around talking Bible like your sister. But I knew quick as I saw you at that hat so nice an' good that you was.

"I never thought much of them church folks till lately. Pa thinks they're all frauds, 'cause some of 'em have treated him mean. But then folks ain't all alike, an' I always used to say that folks that is mean will be mean even if they are church folks, an' the church can't make 'em any worse—only it looks worse, them pretendin' so much.

"But when that there minister come along and was so awful nice about our boat an' all—I s'pose he told you how it was—why I jus' made up my mind it wasn't the church that made 'em all so mean. He bein' a minister an' a kind o' head of it all, he would be meaner than the hull lot of 'em if 'twas the church made 'em so. An' I began to tell Pa he must uv made some mistake. Well, he did allow that if that young feller should run the chapel awhile he would go an' hear him preach himself. He's awful nice, ain't he? Say! Ain't you an' he goin' to marry? Folks say you are. I heard it over to Spray View. It's awful nice you like the church an' are so good if you're a-goin' to marry a minister!"

Before Maria could lift her flaming face or steady her voice to reply to this remarkable series of questions and remarks, she heard a step on the single board which formed a walk over the sand in front of their cottage. Looking up, annoyed beyond measure, to see who was coming and perhaps overheard the last remarks, she saw Howard Fairfield standing before her. His face was a study, to say the least, perhaps a bit too serious. But the seriousness was evidently put on to hide a twinkle Maria felt must be in his eye. It was impossible to tell how much he overheard. He betrayed no sign whatever of overhearing anything, but the irrepressible Annie arose from her step in confusion, adding to Maria's consternation.

"Goodness gracious me! If here he ain't now! 'Talk of angels an' you hears their wings,' as the sayin' is." And she disappeared into the cottage and began rattling the cook stove to hide her embarrassment.

Chapter 15

The minister sat down on the step vacated by Annie. His acquaintance in the Hammond cottage had progressed so far that he felt sufficiently at home to be seated without an invitation from the young hostess, who was too perturbed to think of offering him any seat less lowly.

He looked at her with a curious expression on his face. He never considered her in this light. Her blushes were certainly becoming, and he rather enjoyed her embarrassment. He was quiet for a moment, not caring to interrupt his study of her face.

Meanwhile she was struggling with her thread, which had snarled in the strangest way just as she was taking the final stitch in the completed hat. Instead of cooling down, her cheeks turned fairly purple. She grew more and more indignant over what that impertinent girl had said, as she realized how much the man in front of her must have heard.

"What are you supposed to be doing?" Mr. Fairfield asked at last, with an amused expression on his face.

At the sound of his voice the hold on Maria's tongue was broken. She ignored his question. Indeed, she didn't know a word he said.

"Mr. Fairfield," she burst out impetuously, "I do hope you won't believe from the last words that impertinent girl said that *I* have been discussing *you* and your matters with *her!*" She emphasized each pronoun a little more till the final one expressed fully her scorn.

"And if you had, would my humble self be so far beneath your notice that you'd speak of me in that tone?"

Howard Fairfield's voice was light and cheerful. It was more the way he used to speak to his young associates ten years earlier when he entered college, before the serious things of life reached him. Something in this afternoon's occurrence set him back for a while and made him feel young and full of mischief.

Besides, he possessed wonderful tact and saw that Maria was extremely embarrassed and could only hope to regain her composure through laughing it off. He proved himself correct in this conclusion; his tone, so different from the grave, earnest one he normally used in their conversations, roused Maria from her wrought-up feelings to look up and wonder and even laugh.

She attempted to make him understand once more that she wasn't discussing him. Instead she was treated to a catalogue of his virtues—something connected with a boat. To her relief she suddenly remembered Annie suggested he might have told her the story; so she at once asked for an explanation.

The young man was evidently annoyed that a mere act of kindness on his part was brought out so that he was obliged to tell about it himself. But he saw it would help Maria to regain her composure if he did. So in a few words he told her how he gave the father a bit of advice and loaned him a little money when their fishing boat, their main source of revenue, was in danger of being confiscated for a small debt.

If Maria had been less upset she might have read between the lines. But that was to the young man's credit, for she must have seen how little he made of the matter. Then he described a walk he took that afternoon and a beautiful spot he discovered and thus helped Maria forget her discomfiture entirely.

"And what have you been doing all afternoon?" he asked suddenly. "What's that creation you're holding? It looks as if it might be pretty and certainly is marvelous in its construction. Are you preparing to leave this desert island and fly back to civilization, and is that part of your plumage?"

Maria laughed again. The color mounted in her cheeks as she looked at the hat and wished she'd never seen it, since it had caused her discomfort. At the same time she realized she'd failed utterly at trying to do good and resolved to be honest with herself and him and everybody else and not let people think her better than she was. She would show everybody just how mean and contemptible she was. Then at least she would no longer be tormented by her conscience, whatever other unpleasantness she might have to endure.

"No," she answered half-laughing, half-troubled. "It represents a vain attempt on my part to right myself in the eyes of the world and be honest. I've been trying to be 'good' and do unto others—well—as they would have me do to them, at least, if I didn't do as I would have them do to me. But I think I'll give it up. I'm not made that way, I see, and seem to have failed completely. And, indeed, Mr. Fairfield, I've been rarely punished for my attempt to deceive others and myself."

"I don't understand," said the minister, puzzled, reaching out his hand for the hat. "It seems to be all right as far as I can judge, though I admit I'm not a judge of millinery. But I was told that a hat to be all right must have so much straw, so much ribbon, so much velvet and so many flowers or feathers put together in the right proportions. You seem to have all those things. Isn't it becoming? Is that the matter?"

Now Mr. Fairfield saw at once something deeper, something he wanted to know, behind Maria's half-laughing, troubled face. Their conversations together had been the kind that draw human hearts to sympathize with one another. He saw she needed help, or thought she did; since he felt she helped him, he wished to help her. But he'd find out what she meant from her own lips. He wouldn't ask her questions, for he judged from his own nature that that method might only shut the truth from him forever; so he continued his bantering tone.

Although Maria laughed, her face sobered suddenly.

"The hat isn't mine," she answered him quickly. "I'm supposed to be doing it for the love of doing good to others. It's for Annie Higgins. It's some of my sister's philanthropy. I never originated any, not to carry it out, in my whole life.

"Ray promised to trim this hat so that girl could go to some sort of picnic tonight, and then her friends came to take her for a drive. I acted on a sudden impulse and offered to do it for her. I think the real reason I offered to do it was to see if I could just for once be as good as you've persisted in telling me I am. But I'm not. I want to tell you the truth. I can't be miserable any longer at being thought to be good and helpful and all that, when I don't know or care the first thing about it.

"I let you misunderstand me in the first place, and then it went on. I began to see it was just as bad as if I started out to act a lie. I haven't had the rich reward of doing good that you find in the Sunday school books. I may have succeeded in making a respectable-looking hat, but I've had a most uncomfortable afternoon. Along with that I was almost insulted by questions and a disagreeable intimacy thrust upon me, which I can see will embarrass me endlessly.

"Now you can see just how much of a fraud I've been. Of course it doesn't matter to you. There are other people in the world who are what you thought I was. They can talk with you on the subjects you enjoy and be honest, but I can't rest comfortably to have anyone think I'm something I'm not."

Maria tumbled these words out one on top of another, scarcely realizing what she was saying. She was just anxious to get the horrid explanation over and have the visitor go so she might escape to her room and cry as she never cried before. The tears were already coming to her eyes.

As she raised her face to make her meaning more real, Mr. Fairfield saw them. He also saw at that moment what neither of them noticed before, that the carriage containing the De Veres and her sister, Rachel, was just driving up to the door. His heart went out to the overwrought girl before him with sympathy and something deeper—a longing to help which he couldn't understand.

His ready tact stood him in good stead now. He arose with a bow and walked to the carriage, shaking hands with the young ladies and saying a bright word to his friend Roland De Vere. This gave Maria time to recover before she stepped forward. He spoke of the charming day and said in a loud cheery tone that he just dropped in to see if Miss Hammond wouldn't like to walk to the pavilion and watch the sunset on the bay for a few minutes.

Then he turned toward Maria and said in an aside: "Are you nearly ready to go, Miss Hammond? I'm afraid we'll miss the best of it unless we hurry. Just get your hat and let's go without waiting longer, can't you?" He turned again to the carriage to help Rachel out.

It seemed a doubtful venture to him, for he could scarcely tell what Maria in such a mood might or might not do. But he was relieved to see that she took his words as a cover for a hasty retreat into the cottage, ostensibly to get her hat.

He hoped she would get her equilibrium there as well, at least enough to greet and pass the De Veres. She could go with him then to some secluded spot where they could understand each other; there he might also help this young woman who seemed so strong in faith before and without need of help.

When Maria reached her room and the tears began to fall, she was tempted, even determined, not to leave her room that night but to give herself over to misery. Yet human nature is so odd that, more than anything else, she wanted to go out and walk with the minister to the beach and see what he would say to her, for she knew he intended something in his kind and strangely given invitation. And so without the least delay she dashed the refreshing cold water over her flushed face, smoothed her hair and, seizing her hat, hurried out to the porch. She was relieved to find the ordeal of speaking to the visitors shortened by her companion's haste to get away and see the sunset.

The walk to the beach was brisk. The minister talked incessantly and gave Maria no chance for even a word, pointing out a cloud over the bay, or the etching of a lonely, deserted fisher's hut in the distance, against a sea of pink and gold off at the right. He joked about the shape of some of the cottages and remarked humorously, though not maliciously, about some of the small town's inhabitants, just to keep Maria from thinking of herself or what she said or what she meant to say. He was scarcely aware of what he was saying as he strode along. His one aim was to talk.

And so he guided her to a quiet knoll a little way up the beach, too far to be disturbed by loiterers at this late hour. He talked on while he arranged a seat for her in the sand, with two pillows and a shawl he took from the hammock on the porch. He had her sit down in the purple and golden light that hung between the glittering bay and the opal-tinted sea. Then he stopped a moment and turned to her with a quiet smile, to remind her their friendship was deeper than the afternoon talk had been.

"And now will you explain just what you wanted me to understand a few minutes ago? I think you're troubled in some way, and I couldn't quite get at it. You surely didn't mind my hearing those foolish things that poor girl said. It was something deeper. May I understand?"

Maria had never heard him use such a gentle tone before except once—and that to a little frightened child they passed one day running in terror from the incoming waves. She felt as if she were a little child adrift; and, now that he'd found her, somehow she would be brought ashore. She dropped her eyes to the sand and tried to tell just what was in her heart.

"I mean that I'm not 'good.' I'm not like Rachel or you or anybody that *loves* good things. When I first knew you, I didn't feel I was so different. You seemed to enjoy fun, and I didn't think you cared much about serious things. But when you came back and were changed, I was surprised. I understood the difference after you honored me by telling me of your strange experience. You were good before, I think, only I hadn't seen that side of your nature brought out yet.

"You took me for better than I was because, when we first met after you came back, I had my sister's Bible and a religious book Mr. De Vere had sent her, lying beside me on the sand. I saw you thought more highly of me because they were there, and I always like to please those I'm with.

"You asked me to read, and I like to read. I'm afraid I'm proud of my reading too. It was selfish pride that made me read that book well, for I scoffed at it a few minutes before. I took it for a novel at first and thought I'd enjoy reading it. I let you think I was reading and enjoying it before you came. Then you told me all those wonderful things about yourself, and I felt ashamed I'd let you do so, for I knew I wasn't worthy of such confidence.

"Well, I don't have anything else to say, except I let you go on thinking I was interested in religious things more than in anything else. I was lonely and enjoyed talking with an intellectual person who could make anything, even religion, interesting. I've been ashamed of it every day, but I didn't know how to get out of it. Some sort of spell seemed to be on me when I was with you, preventing me from showing you my real character. I tried once or twice to see how it would seem to act the way you thought I was, but I didn't succeed. I'm just a frivolous creature who loves a good time and her own way.

"I feel very much relieved that I've told you the truth. But I'd like to thank you for the very pleasant hours we've had together before we part. I feel sure they *have* helped me, and you were very good to spend so much time in making it pleasant for me."

Maria said all this in a torrent of words as though it were one long sentence.

She started to rise, as if she were ready to bid him farewell and go, but he detained her.

"Please sit still," he said quietly. "I want to ask you a few things. In the first place, you surely don't suppose that because of what you've said we're going to be any less friends than before? Friendship can't be cut in two by a few words and a farewell. You've come into my life and helped me, in spite of all you say. And if you've felt as you say you have, that's all the more reason I should try to help you if I can. Will you tell me one thing, Miss Hammond? Do you mean by all this that you don't love the Master?"

It's very strange how hard a simple little question is to answer sometimes. Maria had heard and read that question so many times; in her childhood she answered it glibly and carelessly, taking it as a matter of course that she did. Now her voice trembled, and she hesitated a long time at the earnest question.

"I'm afraid I don't," she said at last in a very low voice, almost inaudible above the sound of the waves.

"And do you mean you don't *want* to love Him?" asked the quiet voice.

This time the hesitation was longer than before. Maria was questioning her own heart carefully and shuddering at the thought of answering it in the affirmative.

Very slowly then came the words: "No, I don't mean that."

"Thank God for that!" said the listener under his breath.

Maria looked up to see a light in the minister's face which awed her into silence and caused her to drop her eyes again and wait for him to speak.

One step further the minister dared to go as he breathed a prayer for guidance. He was so much concerned about this young friend, who suddenly seemed in his sight one very precious to his Master.

"Wouldn't you like to belong to Him, to rest in Him, just as we've talked about so many times? I can't think that all we've said together has been of no interest to you. Don't you care in the slightest to be His dear child?"

And Maria answered in an unsteady voice and humbly, "Yes, I care. I believe I care about that more than anything else on earth. I didn't know quite what it was before, but that's what I want. But, oh, I can't get it. It doesn't belong to me." And the cry of her soul reached out to her Father in heaven, as she seemed to be groping in the darkness for His hand.

Chapter 16

The sunset flashed and faded unnoticed. The twilight crept softly over the ocean and stole up the sands. The young moon looked out and climbed the sky. And still they sat and talked.

What they said is recorded above, and it meant a great deal to both. The minister was going through his first real experience of leading an immortal soul to Christ, and the girl was face to face with the Master. Out of the gathering shadows on the waters it seemed to her that He came and spoke peace to her troubled heart. Many days after, she found a poem among others in a book sent to her sister; it fit into her memory of that evening and her experiences, and she copied it on the margin of her Bible.

> Out in the night on the wide, wild sea,
> When the wind was beating drearily
> And the waters were moaning wearily,
> I met with him who had died for me.

For a short while these two conversed concerning the things of the kingdom. The man felt that he was conveying a message of vital importance from his Master, the first like it entrusted to him or, at least, the first whose importance so impressed him. He mustn't think of himself; he must choose only the words the Spirit spoke; he mustn't let his faith waiver; he must pray as he breathed every instant, for at any moment Satan might step in and thwart the work. This joy was wonderful beyond any experience he'd known, as she yielded her will to her Savior's.

To the young woman who thus reviewed her life and her motives, the man beside her carried a heavenly message. She forgot they stood in mutual relations in the world which made it natural she would desire to appear well in his eyes, admire his earnest, well-spoken words and be pleased he spent his effort on her. Her heart-hunger for something better in her life at last spoke, and she recognized its eternal right to be heard. She heard Jesus pleading through those quiet, earnest words.

And yet each knew that in a sense Maria was already a Christian, that is, before the world. She had taken Christ's vows upon her. She was brought up to keep the commandments outwardly at least. She was even active in Christian work, to the extent of being zealous at certain times, when the work was particularly pleasant to her. Yet, she hesitated and knew that if she once gave over her will, her whole life hereafter must be changed.

They sat so long upon the sand that their figures, etched against the fading sky, became blurred by the evening mist. When the great decision was finally made and the minister sealed it with a prayer, in a few words from the deep joy of his heart that God had blessed his message, the quiet night shut out their bowed heads from view.

Supper in the hotel was over when they walked back along the sand and passed the porch, filled with the lively talk of guests who watched the new moon travel its silver pathway over the waves. And the people laughed and made commonplace remarks, as though it were a common night and a common sight.

Supper in the green cottage was over also, although delayed a while for Maria's coming. Rachel went over to the Parkers' with her brother. The father and mother strolled to the bay and could be seen in the distance slowly walking up and down the little platform by the water. The sky was lit by the last memory of the dead sunset, making a clear background for their dark figures.

The Higgins girl was seated on the front steps. She was waiting impatiently to tell Maria that the hot biscuits were in the oven covered with a tin plate, the butter was in the top of the refrigerator, and the rest of the things were on the table for her supper. She was eager to go home to join in the merry evening accompanying the arrival of several brothers-in-law and other relatives. Boisterous laughter issued across the marsh from the little house. Her errand accomplished, the Higgins girl hastened away. She felt embarrassed in front of the minister and Maria after what happened in the afternoon.

Maria was relieved to find the house empty. She wanted to understand herself before she met the others. She paused at the top step to say good night and then suddenly realized the minister had missed his supper.

She invited him in for something to eat, and to her surprise instead of declining he asked, "May I?"

Maria scarcely knew whether she was glad or sorry he accepted her invitation. Eating supper together was rather embarrassing to her, after foraging in the refrigerator and the oven and exposing their crude dwelling to this young man evidently used to luxury; yet it was pleasant too. He entered into it like a boy, held the lamp for her while she got the butter and stirred the fire to make the kettle boil for a cup of tea.

It covered her shyness too. After their long talk, she would scarcely attempt common everyday living again at once lest she mar the wonder of the great peace in her soul. She didn't take her change of heart as Rachel would have, with a bubble of joy that touched everything in her life. It was too new, and her nature didn't so quickly accept and appropriate new situations.

She felt that her experience was too sacred even to think about. Indeed, it could hardly be called an experience. She felt no joy, though she did feel at peace; she didn't think life was now to be rose-colored. She wasn't perfectly sure that tomorrow she might fall from her high resolves.

The only difference in her feelings from two hours ago was this deep peace, a peace that comes of decision and a fixed purpose to surrender her will and to trust. Henceforth, her life was to be different. Not because she could make it so, but because she chose another motive for its center. Now her life was to be ordered for different ends and whatever of joy or sorrow came, they were alike to be brought to Christ, the end to be His glory.

For Maria, getting supper together with the minister so freely was a novel experience. Before this her intimate friends weren't the kind who were admitted to the kitchen; indeed the kitchen in their home was always until lately ruled by a regiment of good servants. Their sitting down together had a certain hominess and comradeship.

Maria felt embarrassed at first at the idea of it, fearing that Rachel or her brother should come in and find what was going on and be surprised at her. She had always looked down on such things as plebeian—more like what the Parkers might do. And yet here she was actually enjoying it. She wondered why and then forgot to wonder.

Mr. Fairfield seemed boyishly happy, and Maria caught the infection of his spirits and was happy too. Each realized there was deep feeling in the heart of the other. The minister fully intended to leave as soon as they put away the rest of their impromptu meal. He thought Maria needed the rest and quiet and a time alone with God after the long struggle of decision.

They were just going to the porch, for the minister to say good night, when they heard steps and cheerful voices. Maria hastily set the lamp on the little shelf back in the kitchen, where its light would only dimly reach the front door and tell no tales of the tête-à-tête supper. Then she quietly and quickly followed her guest to the porch. She didn't wish her brother and sister to tease her about anything that went on tonight. It was Rachel and Win, with the Parkers and some others, coming to sit on the veranda and sing.

While the quartet grouped themselves on the steps and Rachel brought the lamp for them to see the penciled words of a new song, Howard Fairfield stepped closer to Maria and said quietly, "You're tired."

He didn't say it with the rising inflection of a question that demanded answer, nor was there time for an answer before the singing began. But Maria felt he was reading her thoughts and feelings with a fine sympathy, anxious to help her. She smiled gratefully. Then the singing began.

All at once Maria realized these were the people to whom she'd clearly showed her dislike and disdain. With a sudden resolve, which seemed a response to a bidding voice within, she determined to take the first step in a new direction at once. Throwing aside her distant manner since coming to the shore, except with the minister or the De Veres, she joined in the talk and laughter when the song was ended.

The Parkers were delighted with her bright words and ready agreement to plans they proposed. She was indeed a charming girl. Why were they so deceived at first? Rachel and Win sat silent through sheer amazement, and the minister wondered and guessed the reason.

It was strange how well he was beginning to understand this girl who was unknown to him a few short weeks earlier. He watched her in the dim lights and shadows thrown by the flickering lamp and saw a gentle, softened look as she talked. He remembered her face at different times as she pondered his questions by the shore that evening, and the grave sweetness in her eyes when she at last decided. To him she seemed all sweetness. He hadn't yet realized she'd indeed been hateful, as she told him. Isn't it blessed that some people can't and won't see our faults, even though we tell them they are there?

Maria was glad when they rose to leave—not that she wasn't enjoying the talk. It was pleasant, and she was surprised to find herself interested in the Parkers. But she longed for the quiet of her own room.

Mr. Fairfield had been watching her during the last few minutes. Now, as they rose to go, he took her hand to say good night and said in a hushed tone: "Are you any happier, Miss Hammond, than you were this afternoon?"

"I think so," she answered softly. "And, oh, I want to thank you. I never would have found the right way if it hadn't been for you."

The young man bowed his head humbly. "That's the most welcome thanks I ever received. I don't think I was ever the means of leading anyone to Christ. That's a terrible admission for me, a minister of the gospel, to make, and maybe it isn't true. I hope not! But I never knew it at least, and I haven't been the sort of minister I should have been, you remember. You've helped me, you know, in spite of all you've said to the contrary. So I'm very grateful to be allowed to bring a little of the same comfort to you."

Then Maria went in to the quiet moonlit window of her room and sat there amazed at all that had passed since she left that room so hastily a few hours before. She thought about the minister's kindness, his earnest face and tender words, the quiet lovely night about them, the walk home and the pleasant little supper together.

Somehow their eating alone together made them better friends. Something about that supper she didn't want to put into words yet, a strange, pleasant something, into which she dared not look for explanation. She may think it out sometime and see if there was any foundation for real pleasure in it; but now it would simply hover on the horizon of her mind, a pleasant memory connected with this wonderful night.

Then she thought of the arrival of the others and their songs. She must learn to join in their fun. This might be one of the hardest things for her to do—letting down her prejudices and being agreeable when her heart wasn't in what was going on. Could she do it? She trembled at the mountain of difficulties that rose before her untried feet.

She was almost afraid to think about the great event of that day, the decision to make Christ the center of her life, because it seemed so new and sacred. She couldn't get used to it. She must wait till the others were asleep before she let her thoughts dwell on that.

Rachel came in soon and stole softly up behind her, putting her arms around her neck and kissing her. Maria returned the embrace lovingly and rose to prepare for rest. She felt she couldn't sleep soon with so much to think about. When she knelt to pray, as was her habit, the act and the words meant so much more than ever before.

Contrary to her expectations, she fell into a deep, dreamless sleep. Her Father knew she was weary and needed rest more than making resolutions and planning difficult paths. Now that she was willing to walk as He would have her, He would choose her paths and carry her over the hard places without resolutions. Plans and resolutions may sometimes be signposts for Satan to read which way we intend to go, that he may lie in wait there and intercept our progress. If she only put her hand in Christ's, all would be well.

> Trusting the one great Pilot of the deep
> To be for aye my tender, low voiced Guide,
> I look aloft and say—
> Though tossed upon life's ocean wide—
> "All's well! All's well! By day or night, all's well!"

Chapter 17

S he's a great friend of Maria Hammond's," said Fanny De Vere, as she skillfully opened an egg at the breakfast table. "I suppose that's the reason she chooses that place for the remainder of the summer."

"Well, I should imagine she would be just about Maria Hammond's stamp," said Evelyn. "They must have a good many interests in common. Nannette Davenport cares only about herself. She's the most self-centered person I know of. I suppose it's unkind for me to say so, but I don't believe her grief over her mother's death is more than skin deep. She never seemed to care for her in the least when she was alive."

"I'm sorry she's coming," said Fanny. "Of course we won't necessarily have much to do with her, but at the same time we'll have to be civil for decency's sake. It's a great pity she couldn't have gone somewhere else. But I guess she chose Lone Point this summer because she's in mourning and the company she moves in would be scandalized if she were to appear anywhere else. Here she can do as she pleases. If she indulges herself in a little amusement, no one is the wiser. I suppose Maria Hammond couldn't stand it any longer without some of her friends around her. Roland, I wonder why that girl is so different from her sister. You never would dream they were from the same family, would you?"

The young man hesitated a minute before answering.

"I'm not sure," he said. "I've seen several things lately that make me think she might be different from what we thought at first. Something about her must be interesting, or Fairfield would never waste his time on her. He isn't a lady's man, by any means. In college he would never have anything to do with shallow, insipid girls. There had to be some intellect before he would look at them, much less talk with them, unless he was absolutely compelled to do so."

"Oh, I suppose she's bright enough, as far as that goes," said Evelyn. "But I think she's decidedly disagreeable, and she'll be twice as much so when backed up by Nannette Davenport. I can't think how Nannette will endure the simplicity at the Lone Point Hotel. She never washed out her own bathing suit in her life or waded through deep sand to get to the beach. As for the crude cottages there, she'll probably take the next train back home when she sees them. Are you sure, Roland, that Miss Hastings said she was going to Lone Point?"

"Perfectly sure," answered the young man. "Miss Hastings was up there yesterday afternoon to reserve a room for her at her aunt's request. She's coming unchaperoned, since her aunt considers it such a quiet spot and so near Miss Davenport's intimate friends that a chaperone is hardly necessary."

Evelyn laughed.

"If she's the same Nannette who went to Boston a year ago, she'll need a chaperone more in Lone Point than she does in a crowded city. She's kept somewhat in check there by custom and her position, but she'll consider Lone Point good game. If you have the least concern for your minister friend, you'd better warn him to flee. In spite of his intellect and his present devotion to Miss Hammond, he'll soon be caught in the wiles of Miss Nannette. Why, consider, my dear brother. He's about the only eligible young man in Lone Point, unless you count Mr. Hammond and Mr. Parker. But she considers it nothing to have three or four on hand at once."

"Well, if Fairfield can't take care of himself, I'm sure he deserves to suffer—that's all I can say," said the young man with a laugh as he rose from the table and picked up the morning paper.

By the morning mail Maria received a gushing letter from her sometimes friend, Miss Nannette Davenport. She always gushed when she had a point to gain. At present it suited her purpose to spend a few weeks in a quiet place, and Maria would be useful to her in passing the time. The letter expressed great delight over the thought of a quiet summer in which to hide the deeper grief she professed. She wanted to get away from the world and decided to be near her friend. She delayed to send Maria word until the day before her arrival so her coming might be a pleasant surprise. But her room was already reserved at the hotel, and Maria might meet her at the Lone Point Station at three the next afternoon.

This came as a surprise to Maria, but it was anything but a pleasant surprise. Nannette Davenport was never a deeply loved friend. She had a certain prestige because of her mother's wealth and standing in society which Maria thought she couldn't ignore. Through Nannette she gained entrance to several homes in a high social circle where she feared she couldn't have gone otherwise since her father's failure. Indeed, through Nannette she met the De Veres.

The two girls were thrown together at the start of their friendship, if it could be called a friendship where no real love or even strong liking existed, when they were both away at school. Maria knew just how much real friendship Nannette held for her. She knew what a shallow, heartless girl she was. And she didn't rejoice at the thought of her coming to Lone Point.

Had the letter come three or four days earlier, she'd have worried that Nannette would see her in such humble surroundings. But somehow the events of the past few days had made surroundings seem of less importance. Now, as she read the letter with a distressed pucker between her eyes, it wasn't because of the little green cottage or their circumstances that her first objection was raised. She thought first for her new life. How hard it would be to mix thoughts and feelings so at variance! Her utter distaste for Nannette's pleasures was a revelation even to herself. She didn't know how much her own likings were wrapped up in her desire to carry out her new aim in life.

She thought about what to do. It wouldn't do to be rude to Nannette. Christ wouldn't wish that. Was she afraid to stand up to her and say firmly that her motives in life were changed? Or did she fear her own self and dread lest she lose this wonderful calm that came into her life three nights ago? Did she think she'd be tempted back to her old ways, old thoughts, old bondages?

Suddenly she remembered a verse she read that morning in her sister's Bible. Rachel's Bible was always lying open somewhere with verses marked to catch her eye when she was in a hurry. She used to say she kept her Bible nearby so she could snatch a thought now and then as she was going by, to help keep her from temptation. Maria didn't have the courage yet to bring out her Bible in the open as Rachel did. She wanted to read it by herself first and get used to the thought of her new way of living; so she chose a verse from her sister's Bible as she dressed.

"God is faithful, who will not suffer you to be tempted above that ye are able; but will with the temptation also make a way to escape that ye may be able to bear it."

How strange that that verse came in her way that morning! How wonderful to think God was actually answering her thoughts in His own words! Surely, this girl's arrival was nothing she was responsible for, and therefore she wasn't to blame. He had allowed the temptation; couldn't she trust Him to make a way of escape for her? She arose and fastened the door and then knelt down to ask for faith. She knew it would seem very strange to Rachel to come in in the daytime and find her praying. She was still in bondage. Her fetters had been forged tight, and it was hard for her to drop them even now that they were broken.

She didn't feel that she knew how to pray very well, but she knew God would understand. As she stood up she wondered if He would turn Nannette Davenport's decision in some way and send her elsewhere even at the last minute. Or did He have other ways of working? Of course He might mean this was a discipline she was to pass through before she was fit to be His child. If so she'd try to do what was right, but it seemed much harder even than taking in the Parkers. They'd become quite tolerable, even pleasant, and it was only three days since she decided to become acquainted with them.

With remembering the Parkers came the question, *What would Nannette think of the Parkers? Would she make it very unpleasant?* Maria knew that Nannette possessed the uncomfortable quality, among others, of sneering at people and things; she could make a person rather do anything than confess to liking the person or thing she scorned. What was she to do with Nannette?

Maria hadn't become good all in a night. By no means. To all outward appearance she was the same Maria but a little sweeter tempered, a little more willing to give up her wishes for those of others. In one respect that was rather surprising; she freely mingled with the young people and notably with the Parkers, making them feel comfortable and happy in her presence. She lost her temper once or twice. She let slip a scornful remark about the pump on one occasion, which, while she felt no peculiar animosity at the time, had become such a habit that she scolded without realizing it.

She noticed the weary look about her mother's eyes at the time and at once knew the mother was sighing over her. She had an impulse then to throw her arms around her mother and tell her how different she meant things to be. But something within restrained her, and the next instant her mother went out to talk with the grocer's boy.

She reasoned also that she should first show some signs of repentance before announcing to the others what she was going to do. Moreover, her recent experience was too sacred to be talked about yet, and it wasn't a question of witnessing for Christ in this case, since they already knew she professed to follow Him. It would be much wiser for her to let them see she was different.

She forgot her mother and sister would have been relieved she was willing to be different; they would have overlooked many things in her and helped her in countless ways, if she'd taken them into her confidence. If people only understood each other in this world there would be much less friction, less sighing and less worry about one another.

So the mother prayed daily for her daughter and wondered why her prayers were of no avail. Was it because she was unworthy to be answered or because of her lack of faith? But all the time the dear Lord had prepared a loving answer and set it down beside her, and she was too worried to notice it. It would be well, in our praying, to lift the head sometimes and see if the answer isn't shining in the heavens or standing clothed in joy beside us or even lying at our feet waiting to be recognized.

Maria thought deeply about what to tell her new friend the minister about her old friend Nannette and finally decided to let him judge for himself. She had no opportunity to tell him anything, however, for Mr. Fairfield was away all that day and the next attending to some business on the mainland. And he only arrived at Lone Point on the very train that carried Nannette in her black robes.

The three days since Maria's decision were wonderful for her. Her friendship with the minister was becoming very pleasant to think about. The intimacy hadn't as yet grown into its larger possibilities as personal. But in each of their hearts was developing something warmer than a mere interest for the other, and occasionally little glimpses of alluring maybes would flit across their minds.

Beneath Maria's distaste for Nannette Davenport's arrival was perhaps an uneasiness that the pleasant friendship between the minister and her might be interrupted. But if this was so she didn't confess it even to herself. She was never quick to think a man wished to pay her special attention or to appropriate one to herself. She rather erred in the other direction. And while he admired her for this, she kept him, in a sense, at a distance, even though they talked more intimately than most young people do about that most sacred emotion of life, one's personal love for his Savior.

Chapter 18

Maria waited on the little platform the next afternoon for the incoming train. Her emotions weren't pleasant. She saw Nannette's curling lips as she first took in the situation and observed the crude cottage life. She heard her sarcastic comments, and, strange to say, they were much what her own had been on arriving here.

Suddenly the thought flashed across her mind that she'd changed, in this respect at least, for she had in her heart a real love for the place, a desire to protect it from what scornful strangers might say. Why? Was it because she found Christ here? Or was it because of her new friendship with the man?

She looked up at the blue sky and smiled in answer to its heavenly look. She gazed over the yellow-green waves of marsh grass, once bare to her, and lo! they had taken on beauty. She felt gladness in their smooth stretches of level green and discovered that in a night they seemed to have burst into a million stars of meadow pinks dotted all over in the grass as far as eye could reach. She stooped and gathered a handful of them and placed them in her belt, adding a pretty touch to her dress.

Nannette's influence was already felt in her careful arrangement of that afternoon's outfit. She worried more about her dress and took more time to get ready that day than any since arriving on the island. Even now she looked down at herself doubtfully. She hardly cared to come in for sarcasm herself just at the outset.

After scrutinizing her wardrobe, she had chosen a white duck costume that was plain and somewhat inexpensive. Its great beauty in her eyes was its exquisite cut and fit. She had committed her greatest extravagance of the summer by taking that duck dress to a well-known tailor to be cut, and in her eyes and in Nannette's as well, she knew that fact would cover a multitude of sins in other ways. She half-intended Nannette would soon discover that Melton had cut her dress. She would then be sure to admire it.

And yet, she was annoyed to find herself so concerned about her dress and thinking about how she could reveal where it was cut. She sighed and wondered if this were a sign that Nannette was going to win her forever back to worldly things.

Before she went out she knelt and prayed. She had seen Rachel kneel often before going out, when she thought she was by herself, and such a habit might now be a good thing for her. Certainly she needed much help.

Maria looked fresh and pretty and thoroughly in keeping with her surroundings, in white with a black velvet belt and collar and band about her sailor hat. Even the most exacting taste could find no fault with her. The fresh ocean breeze had loosened a few soft strands of a waving lock about her forehead and flushed her cheeks, and the touch of pink blossoms in her belt made her look exquisitely sweet.

At least so thought Mr. Fairfield as he alighted, hot and dusty from his ride in the train, and his face lit up with sudden joy. In spite of herself, the color came into Maria's cheeks as she bowed to him. She was a bit embarrassed too, for just a moment, since it must look to him, until Nannette appeared, as though she came to the train to meet him.

But now the porter handed Nannette with her bag, dress suitcase, bundle of golf sticks and tennis racquet, along with several other accessories for a fashionable girl at a summer resort, down onto the platform. And the train moved on toward Spray View, and Maria found her hands full.

Nannette's greeting was effusive, mingling kisses and adjectives and a few stylish tears that required pushing up the becoming black veil in which her head was swathed in spite of the heat. This over, Miss Davenport turned her dark eyes upon the minister, who stood by Maria as if he belonged there, and an introduction had to follow.

Maria felt annoyed beyond measure that she hadn't told the minister of Nannette's expected arrival before this. Just why she felt so annoyed she didn't look into her heart then to see. As a matter of course the minister rode with them in the surrey which was sent down from the hotel to convey the new guest from the station. Though Maria also went with them and sat in the back seat with her friend, Nannette monopolized the conversation entirely and addressed it all to Mr. Fairfield.

She gushed about her friendship with Maria, dating its origin much further back than Maria had guessed it could be. Then she showed reasons why Maria was her warmest friend and was therefore the one she turned to in her deep trouble. Here she punctuated her remarks with a few tears wiped carefully away with a correct handkerchief, deeply bordered with black.

She was a dashingly handsome girl—tall and slender, with black eyes and reddish brown hair. She wore her hair loose over her ears and coiled low at the nape of her neck, giving her an innocent, childlike appearance. She was an excellent actress when she chose to be.

Mr. Fairfield was nonplussed and disappointed. He felt instinctively that this girl would have little sympathy for the quiet walks and talks he and Maria had indulged in lately. He feared that her presence at the shore would be anything but a good influence for the girl he was becoming so deeply interested in.

Maria, on her part, was greatly distressed. What would Mr. Fairfield think of her friends? What would he think of her past life? She must explain how little real friendship ever existed between them. Yet, how could she, without deliberately making the other girl out a liar?

She was glad when the surrey drew up to the hotel and they got out. She was more glad than she dared say, even to herself, that no conversation came up about the place and the cottages they passed during the short ride. At least she was spared having the truth dawn upon Nannette while the minister was with them.

She went upstairs with Nannette at her request, though she preferred going straight home to have a good cry or wandering off on the sand and telling Mr. Fairfield all about it. She felt a childish desire to tell him her troubles and ask him what to do. But she shut her lips tightly and walked up the stairs like a soldier, so that he thought she was only too happy to be with her own kind again and he would have no more opportunities to see her.

Nannette's several trunks were at last deposited and unstrapped, so she took off her hat and talked with her friend.

"Now, 'Ri, tell me all about this hole," she said familiarly, settling herself in a rocker by the window. "Is there anything going on to keep you alive? Isn't it dreadfully dull? You see, Aunt Lilian is old-fashioned and terribly rigid, and she wouldn't at all consent to my appearing at any interesting place. She wanted me to stay at home with her all summer! Just imagine! She said I shouldn't want to go anywhere when my mother was dead.

"But, dear me!" she said with a shrug of her shoulders. "What good would it do Mother for me to mope? I told Aunt I'd die of grief among Mother's acquaintances, and that seemed to touch the right spot, so she consented to my going away. She would have come with me if she could, but Cousin George is worse this summer and can't be moved, and she couldn't leave him. I think she wanted me to stay and devote myself to him, read to him and make messes for him. But he's too devoted to his dead wife's memory to waste my time on him. Besides I hate sick people and he isn't likely to get well anyway. So I'm here. First of all, who is that handsome Mr. Fairfield? A minister? Dear me! Is he very good? Because that would be dreadfully tiresome."

"I'm sure I don't know," said Maria. "You'll have to find that out for yourself." Her voice showed her disgust plainly, but Nannette was too absorbed to notice.

She rattled on. "Say, 'Ri, is he very devoted? I thought he looked at you as if he was. Are you engaged?"

"No, *indeed,*" answered Maria icily.

It flashed over her then that something about Nannette's face reminded her of Annie Higgins. She thought if the two were compared there would be a balance in favor of the Higgins girl.

"Not engaged? Then I give you fair warning, 'Ri, dear. I shall do my best to have a good time. You don't mind, do you, dear?"

"Certainly not," said Maria again, in a voice the minister never would have recognized.

Nannette seemed to feel that it would be just as well to change the subject.

She leaned out of the open window nearest her, looking toward the cottages.

"And now do tell me where the town is, what there is of it. Of course I know it's small, but I've seen only cow sheds so far. Why in the world do they need so many? Or are they bathhouses? No, they're too far from the ocean."

The Maria of a few weeks ago would have blushed crimson and hesitated, tried to apologize and explain, or even have invented some way out of the truth, perhaps. But the Maria of today was too deeply stung and disgusted. She was shown herself and just how low she had fallen in being ready to bow down to a girl whose thoughts and feelings were as low as this one's. It was such a great contrast with the high and holy thoughts in which she'd been dwelling with the minister lately that she was in danger of going to the other extreme and despising this girl for motives really lower than belonged to her. For Nannette Davenport was only selfish, that was all. But that perhaps is enough.

Maria arose and with dignity walked to the window and pointed out.

"Those are cottages," she said, trying to control her voice steadily. "That white one nearest to you is where our friends the Parkers live. The green one trimmed with white next to it is ours. The others belong to very nice people. You'll meet them all soon. There's no reason why one shouldn't have a pleasant time here if one chooses."

Maria remembered her own actions of two weeks ago and was amazed at herself.

Nannette looked curiously at her and then without further remark turned toward her trunks, saying with a sigh: "You don't say! Well, I suppose I have no choice but to make the best of it this year, with these horrid black things on. But I'll make up for it next year, you may be sure. And I warn you I'm going to be just as wicked as I please, so look out for your own interests. By the way, 'Ri, don't you have a brother? Is he nice looking? How old is he? A person must have friends, you know, in a desert like this. They say Roland De Vere is over at Spray View. We had a terrible quarrel a year ago, but I may be able to patch that up. He's so old-granny particular! Now what shall I put on for dinner, and what hour do they have that meal in this out-of-the-way place?"

"They have dinner at one o'clock. It was over four hours ago. Supper is at six," answered Maria severely.

She took a fierce pleasure in shocking this girl. She was glad this feeling possessed her instead of the fear she was afraid would tempt her to do things out of accord with her new views. She felt so little trust in her own self, and her trust was so recently given to her Savior, that she didn't realize He would hold her and she didn't need to worry that she wouldn't hold onto Him.

She was anxious to get away now, and the many elaborate dresses Nannette took out and spread on the bed and chairs for her admiration wearied her. She felt as if she'd always given an undue amount of time and thought to clothes. No doubt these things were pretty; yes, they certainly were. She couldn't help letting her eye dwell in delight upon an elaborate waist of black taffeta. Nannette certainly had good taste—there was no denying that—and plenty of money with which to exercise it.

When everybody was flaunting bright colors this season, it was hard to get up a beautiful and varied outfit with only black and white, with strict severity and the necessary crêpe, but Nannette had succeeded. And Maria, in spite of dislikes and resolves, began to grow interested in the pretty clothes. Nannette insisted upon her remaining until she arrayed herself in a plain white dress with black ribbons. Maria was obliged to say, at the demand of the newcomer, that she was enchantingly pretty even in the trying dead black and white.

"Now, you may go, dear, for I suppose you're awfully tired of me. But please tell me first," she said, holding Maria off at arm's length, "do you think I'll captivate him? I mean that young minister, of course. I must have something to amuse myself, and I should hate to fail at the very beginning."

"I'm sure I don't know," answered Maria in her most sober tone. She drew back, stung deeper than she realized.

"He must be good and have infected you," laughed Nannette. "Never mind. I won't hurt him much, and I'll let him go in the end. Don't blame me much, dear. It's all I have to live for now, you know." And she put her mourning handkerchief to her laughing eyes in the smart little pat she affected.

Maria coldly promised to come back that evening and walked away. She couldn't stand anymore. All she had to live for! Flirting! How boldly she confessed it.

Could she have ever admired a girl like that? She bowed her head and was ashamed.

The minister, standing at the window of his hotel room, saw her, watched her walk down the street, wondered, sighed and turned away thoughtfully.

Chapter 19

When Maria reached the cottage her mother searched her face, expecting to find it wreathed in smiles because of Nannette's arrival. Instead, she saw a gray look about her eyes and felt the same anxious tugging at her mother-heart she had felt so often the last few weeks. Was Maria plunged again in gloom because of her friend's talk and dress? Was she contrasting her own life with that of Miss Davenport?

When at supper her brother asked a laughing question about Nannette, Maria looked up at him anxiously and answered him more shortly than she had for at least three days. The family couldn't understand it. They expected her to be pleased to have a friend in this lonely place.

She ate very little supper. When Win proposed going with her to the hotel to call on the young lady, she promptly declined, saying Nannette must be tired and wouldn't want to see anyone that evening. Her conscience gave her a sharp twinge as she said that, but she looked after her brother with a sigh as he whistled and left the table. Then she went quickly out to the porch and stood alone in the purple and pink twilight with tears blurring her vision.

A new feeling of love for her brother had suddenly stirred in her heart. She saw a possible danger to him lurking in the future and felt inadequate to ward it off. Oh, if only she had always been such a sister to him that a word from her would have served as a shield to him. But now she felt that if she should point out her fear to him he would walk straight up to it laughing, more perhaps to tease her than anything else.

Things were becoming complicated. There was her brother, and there was the minister, and there was Nannette, and there was she, and where was the Lord? She thought it reverently. She stood looking up into the clear opal tints above and wished she might see Him, if only for one second, that her poor weak faith might have something to bind itself to forever. She felt a great longing for Christ to come and touch her. She wanted Him more than anything else just then.

Her mother slipped quietly out behind her and put her arms about her daughter, pulling her head down to her shoulder.

"What is it, little 'Ri? Tell Mother," she said tenderly, just as she used to speak to Maria when she was a child with a bumped head or bruised knee.

Then Maria hid her face in her mother's neck and cried. And she tried to tell her all her troubles and how she wanted to live a changed life.

Her mother's heart was suddenly full of gladness and light. It seemed too good to be true. She drew her down to a chair beside her on the porch and stroked her hair, talking softly with her as they hadn't talked together for a long time.

She wasn't a mother who often talked with her children about personal religion; therefore it would have been hard for Maria to tell her mother of her changed feelings on the subject if it weren't for this sudden openness of her nature and her mother's opportune coming. It was hard too for the mother to talk on religious subjects, so her words of comfort were few. But to Maria, who knew her mother's nature, they meant much and carried true solace with them. When she said, "Maria, I am glad," Maria knew she meant more than if she'd used a dictionary full of adjectives. When she advised her daughter to "give over worrying and take her trouble to her heavenly Father," Maria sensed that her mother knew what she was talking about.

When her daughter finally kissed her and went to the hotel, Mrs. Hammond carried one load on her heart that she didn't have before. Maria hinted of possible danger for Win in Miss Davenport's arrival. Her heart became anxious as soon as she thought about it, and she needed to take the advice she gave her daughter.

Win, her only son, was very dear to her, and she knew he was fond of bright company and susceptible to its influence.

When Maria reached the hotel, she began to frame an excuse for being so late. Ascending the steps of the long wide porch that ran around the building, however, she saw in the distant corner, standing out against the background of moonlit ocean, the figures of Miss Davenport and Mr. Fairfield. The sudden chill that crept over her made her pause and draw about her shoulders the light shawl she'd carried on her arm. She turned to leave, thinking Nannette was in no need of her presence and she would come again in the morning. But Nannette saw her and waved her handkerchief and called, so she had to go over and sit down in another large rocking chair beside them.

"You dear naughty thing, you deserted me!" said Nannette in her most gushing voice. "Why in the world were you so long in coming? If it hadn't been for Mr. Fairfield I'd have been so lonely I'd have wished to take the morning train back to the city. But he's been so very kind that I actually forgot this place was called Lone Point."

Howard Fairfield had had no intention of having anymore to do with Nannette Davenport than was absolutely necessary. The dislike he experienced for her at first sight only deepened as they rode along to the hotel. But a gentleman can't be actually rude to a lady, especially if that lady is a professed friend of one who has his deep friendship and respect. Thus, when, by some skillful maneuver, the old woman who usually occupied the place at Mr. Fairfield's right in the dining room was seated across the room, and Miss Davenport was found seated beside him, he was obliged, in ordinary courtesy, to talk with her.

He didn't exert himself to make the conversation pleasant for her; indeed, this wasn't necessary. Nannette was vivacity itself. She was adept in small talk and almost made the studious young man feel ill at ease. His replies grew short.

But the young woman perceived her mistake and at once subsided, becoming meek and inquiring. Presently she discovered that books amounted almost to a passion with the gentleman and molded her conversation accordingly. Before the meal was over she professed an overpowering desire to read and have explained to her a certain book being much talked about in the literary world.

To Mr. Fairfield's exceeding disgust he found he'd promised not only to lend her the book, but to give her at no late date an exhaustive explanation of the discussion in current magazines over certain passages in the book. How they came this far he couldn't explain, but he awoke to the fact as Nannette was thanking him most sweetly for being so kind to help her.

As they rose from the table she said innocently enough, "What in the world do you do here in the evenings? Won't you show me where to go? I don't know a soul but you, you know."

She flashed her eyes up at him in a confiding manner, and he felt duty bound to take her to the porch. He went there rather than to the parlor, in a vain hope that Maria might soon come and redeem the situation. But time passed, the sunlight faded from the sky, the moonlight extended over the water, and still the young woman by his side gave him no opportunity to leave, without absolute rudeness on his part. He was growing more and more uneasy, when Maria at last arrived. And if she hadn't been so engrossed with her own feelings at the sight of him and Nannette sitting together in such evident good fellowship, she must surely have noted the joy that broke over his face on seeing her and the warm welcome he gave her.

Be assured Miss Davenport saw it and ground her pretty white teeth; in spite of all the charms she exerted she hadn't once brought to his face the true pleasure that was there now. She resolved that before many days passed this should be different. Thenceforth Lone Point was no longer a desert island to her, for there was a man there who must be conquered and added to the long line of conquered admirers in the past.

Maria, however, in spite of her mother's comforting words, was ill at ease again the moment she entered Nannette's presence. If she replied to Nannette, she was at once thrown back into a past she didn't like to think was ever hers and didn't wish Mr. Fairfield to know she was familiar with. If she spoke to Mr. Fairfield, what should it be about? Not Mr. Meyer's book! Not the Bible verse they talked so freely about yesterday, for what would Nannette think, and how could she drag sacred things into a conversation so filled with the froth of that young woman's remarks?

Mr. Fairfield finally settled back to wait till Maria went home, thinking he'd walk with her and they could have a quiet word together after all. He found his mind wandering out of the talk so that he was often silent. He was thinking of what he'd say to Maria.

Did Nannette read what passed in his thoughts? Certainly she acted as though she did. When Maria rose to say good night, she followed her to the steps.

Then, as if the thought just occurred to her, she put her hand lovingly on Maria's arm and said: "Why, I guess I'll walk over with you, 'Ri, if Mr. Fairfield doesn't mind bringing me home. I should get lost, you know, if you didn't," she said, turning laughingly to him. And she looked him straight in the eyes in the full moonlight and saw that he was disappointed.

When Maria reached her room that night it was late, for Mr. Fairfield determined to take his revenge upon the new arrival and proposed a walk. He knew Maria was used to the sand and could stand it well and that to the young woman from the city streets it would be harder work. He hoped to tire her out and take her back to the hotel before Maria went home, and still have his quiet half-hour with her.

He had reckoned without Nannette, however, who possibly perceived his intention; or perhaps she was stronger than he judged possible. She bravely waded through the sand wherever he led, exclaiming in delight over scenes that barely reached her mental retina at all and still saying she wasn't tired. On he took them, this way and that, nearer the bay, then nearer the ocean. Not to the walks he and Maria had taken together; they were full of pleasant thoughts and shouldn't be marred by the memory of this walk. He grew lively in his effort to gain his point, and Maria wondered at him and became more silent herself.

He perceived that she was becoming very weary, for there was a droop about her mouth he hadn't seen there before, and for her sake he proposed that they go straight home.

There was triumph in Miss Davenport's eyes as she looked in the mirror of her room at a late hour, and her lips had a firm set. It was a hard race, for she was very tired; but she didn't give up, and she gained her point. She would win him yet even if she had to be "good," as she phrased it, to get him.

In her room, with only the moon to light her to her bed, Maria threw herself on her knees beside her sleeping sister. She was tired out, soul and body— too weary to pray and too weary to cry. If only the dear Christ could come to her gently, as her mother did, and tell her what all this meant and why she was so unhappy. She didn't want to think and reason it all out. She guessed she felt an ugly jealousy in her heart; she wanted that young minister to admire her and be with her all the time. She hadn't known she was so selfish.

He had helped her to a better life. Why didn't she want Nannette to have the same opportunity? Had she made that great decision just because she admired the man who asked her to do it? Had she fallen so low that her motive was only self-pleasure, after all, and that she didn't give up to Christ but to a man she admired? Didn't she love Christ?

With this question came a surge of feeling. Yes, she did love Christ. She felt now as if her all depended upon Him. She would give up everything for Him. She only wanted His rest, His peace. He promised it, and she accepted it. It was hers. No one could take it from her. Nannette couldn't touch it. The minister might turn his entire attention to Miss Davenport and forget her. It would be as well if he did, for evidently she was beginning to think too much of him. He might help bring Nannette to Christ and then perhaps have a deeper feeling for her, even marry her. It ought to be nothing to her. She was Christ's. From now on she would do as He bade, go where He sent her, live as He would live in her.

What a glorious, precious thought! Would it last till morning? Could she trust it to be there when she awoke, and could she go to sleep saying, *I am Christ's. I am Christ's. He is mine?*

In some strange, wonderful sense came an answer from her inmost soul, *I can,* and she fell asleep.

The minister couldn't know her thoughts as he stood beside his window, looking out with disappointment on the now-dark night with only a glimmer of light here and there of a belated cottager, for the moon had set. Otherwise he might have prayed for her a prayer whose words he knew and loved, instead of wondering gloomily why everything seemed to have gone wrong.

Rest her, dear Master! . . .draw very near
In all thy tenderness and all thy power.
O speak to her. Thou knowest how to speak
A word in season to thy weary ones,
And she is weary now. Thou lovest her—
Let thy disciple lean upon thy breast,
And, leaning, gain new strength to "rise and shine."

Chapter 20

As Howard Fairfield gazed out over the sparkling waves the next morning, he felt new life and joy enter his soul. Why be downcast when the world was so lovely? He was a child of the living God. He would be given all he needed for his good and happiness in life. Why should he doubt and grow gloomy because he feared the Lord would take some pleasure from him? Surely it wasn't worthwhile to fear anything until he saw it plainly before his eyes? What did he fear anyway? Was his anxiety wholly unselfish?

He recognized clearly a danger menacing Maria's newfound joy in Christ, but couldn't they both trust the One to whose keeping she committed herself? He remembered the words, "He is able to keep you from falling and to present you faultless," and knew he was wrong to fear for her.

No, that wasn't all, though there was a quick recognition of Maria's danger. What was this other feeling that came and went, a warm, rich, new current in his heart? She had become more than a mere acquaintance—more than one to whom he was trying to bring a message from God, though that relationship is precious. A personal tie had formed. He told himself she was the first really intimate friend he had had since his college friend died, and he tried to be satisfied putting it that way.

But somehow he knew there was something not altogether sincere about that statement either. He decided to go for a quiet stroll along the beach in the early morning light and think it out. There he would be quite alone with God. Something serious here ought to be settled at once, he felt sure. Strange he didn't think of it before! Could this girl, an acquaintance of a few weeks, be growing indispensable to him?

Before he walked very far or turned that thought over many times in his mind, he knew it was so and that he loved Maria. He sat down on the sand and looked off at the ocean without seeing a single wave of it, to take in the wonder and beauty of this thought. It fairly overwhelmed him. It was something like the day and experience when he first realized he loved his Savior.

He remembered now that he had heard Henry Drummond once say that an earthly love was the highest and best example of, and the only thing really approaching at all, the soul's relation with Christ.

"Get acquainted with Jesus just as you would with an earthly friend," the great simple man said, and the young theology student was inclined to call him irreverent then.

But now he saw it in all its beauty, the earthly love, so real and warm and dear, a type of the heavenly, just as close and warm and dear and real, only infinitely more in every way than the human heart could comprehend. Was this what God had made earthly love for, that He might show us better what His love for us must be?

As he sat there in the midst of the lovely morning, he felt as if God spoke to him out of His grandeur and beauty and was very gracious to him. Most gracious of all because of this wonderful gift of love which he found in his heart for another of His children. He sensed that he loved his heavenly Father more intensely, more intelligently than ever before, because of the sudden blessed realization of another love.

He arose from his hour's meditation feeling that whatever came after, he would always be a better man for that sacred experience. He could better preach of the love of God now that he could understand a human love, like the love of a man for a woman; yes, he would be a better man for having harbored this love in his heart, even though he might fail to win her—though, please God, he would *not* fail if he could help it.

As he walked back toward the hotel he suddenly remembered Miss Davenport and her proximity to him at the table. He wished he'd remembered sooner. It must be late. He would like to get his breakfast and get away before she came. He didn't care for a tête-à-tête with her just now. He felt that her rattling conversation would be a desecration to his joyous mood. How hard it was to come down from the heights to everyday living and everyday disappointments and perplexities! Yet, that was the discipline of life and must be cheerfully borne. He hastened his steps, hoping she'd be late to breakfast, as indeed she was, and he hurried his breakfast to get out before she came. He did succeed, but little good it did him.

Nannette Davenport slept later than she intended, for she had business at hand that day and mustn't let the enemy get any small advantage at the beginning. To her dismay her watch had run down, and she had no means of telling the hour. Glancing from the window, she saw Mr. Fairfield, watch in hand, hurrying toward the hotel and rightly concluded that breakfast must be ready. With unusual alacrity for a girl of her ordinary lassitude she hurried through her careful preparations intended to deepen the interesting pallor of her supposedly grief-stricken face. Then she hastened to the dining room.

She found to her chagrin that the prize had already escaped her, and the maid was clearing the dishes away from Mr. Fairfield's place at the table. He must have breakfasted hurriedly, or else she was longer than she thought. As she sat biting her red lips in vexation, she saw him through the opposite window at the other end of the long room, walking with determined steps down the sandy path.

One glance at the landscape told her he was heading toward the green cottage. She watched him a moment and saw that her guess was correct; for he ascended the steps, knocked at the door and then sat down in one of the big rockers on the porch. Her decision was made in a moment. Taking a few swallows of coffee from the cup just set down before her, she slipped up to her room for her parasol and hat and followed the path he had just taken.

During his brief breakfast Howard Fairfield felt that the thing he wanted most right then was to look upon the face of the one he just discovered he loved. Not that he intended to tell of his love just now—no, indeed! He saw it was too soon for that. She hadn't known him long enough. She might not love him—how could she?—and he would not startle her by telling her of it abruptly. No, he would wait and see if there was any chance for him before he told her. But whatever came of telling, the precious fact remained that he loved her, and he wished to see her in light of that fact.

He rushed his morning meal to go to her home and ask for a walk, before Miss Davenport could claim her time. Thus, he walked happily down the path, whistling a few notes of a popular song, then humming a line of a hymn.

Rachel answered the door and told him her sister had run next door on an errand for her mother but would be back almost immediately. He sat down to wait while Rachel continued with the work she was doing, which she couldn't leave just then. The acquaintance between the Hammonds and Howard Fairfield had grown intimate enough for Rachel to feel free to go on working and occasionally come to the door to make some pleasant remark or answer something Mr. Fairfield called in to her.

Maria came in the back door with the basket in which she'd just carried some fish to Mrs. Parker, a present from her mother, who had purchased more than she needed. She heard the minister's voice and, responding to Rachel's motion, slipped into her room to change her dark working calico for her beach dress.

Rachel, meanwhile, was buzzing about in the kitchen finishing Maria's morning work so she wouldn't be kept from her friend any longer. She didn't see the tall, black-robed young woman who presently came up the steps onto the veranda and greeted its occupant with such effusiveness, seating herself in the next rocker and entering into a discussion of the morning and its charms.

To Mr. Fairfield a black cloud was suddenly cast across his sky, but he tried to remember that this was Maria's friend. While she wasn't in the least like Maria, she might have a great many delightful qualities if one could only get at them. At least she had a soul, and if he couldn't be interested in her in any other way, he would try to remember that and let his courteous treatment of her reflect his Master's example.

If he had known her heart he might have felt more tempted to take up a scourge of small cords to drive her out from the temple of that day, in which she set tables for her barter in hearts. If good was to reach her soul, at least he wasn't intended to bring it, not in the way he brought it to Maria. This one was not capable of receiving the good Word, not yet at least, for the ground was stony and shallow and barren.

Maria came cheerfully to meet her friend and found the two seated side by side. Nannette was bending over the other's chair to inspect a tiny gold ring he carried on his watch chain which she herself had asked about. That Nannette's action annoyed Mr. Fairfield, Maria couldn't be expected to know. She would never have asked about a gentleman's personal accessories, or reached out and handled them of her own accord; and she naturally judged that no other girl would so far forget herself, especially with an acquaintance of barely one evening. The natural inference was that he was telling her the story of the charm and had invited her to examine it.

Of course it was evident they came together from the hotel to see her—anybody would know that. She half wished they'd gone off together and not brought her in at all; then her life and her troublesome feelings wouldn't confuse her so. Nevertheless they'd come, and her part was to be pleasant and polite. She quickly recalled the memory of the night before, as a frightened child will reach out its hand to its father and remind him of his promise to protect. She understood the swift upward look of her soul to the Savior, asking Him to help her forget all but that she was His, and her heart thrilled with the strength that came in response to her need.

Nannette instantly saw her advantage. Indeed she gave up her breakfast, scarcely hoping she might gain the porch before Maria came out; she wished to give her the impression she'd come with Mr. Fairfield. If Maria would withdraw and leave the minister to her, her task would be more than half done. Maria's presence hindered her own charm from working. It piqued her to think Maria could be considered more charming than she. But Maria was there first, and there was no telling what a man might not take to if he had nothing else at hand. Nannette's idea of a man was that he must always have a woman to amuse him, as her idea of a woman was that she could never be happy without an adoring man or two about.

"You were so long in coming last evening, dear, that we thought we'd run over after breakfast and stir you up," said Nannette lightly.

It occurred to the minister that Nannette must have eaten her breakfast long before he did or else gone without. He gave her a searching look and decided on the latter. Then he wondered what her object was. He wasn't a conceited man, and therefore her real object hadn't dawned on him. He took her merely for a disagreeably bold, worldly girl and decided to keep away from her as much as possible. He didn't know yet how much control this skillful coquette had over the possible when she chose.

Maria sat down clothed in her new strength. She tried to look at Mr. Fairfield merely as a chance acquaintance she wasn't interested in at all and enter into Nannette's talk heartily, at least insofar as she conscientiously could. She didn't talk to Mr. Fairfield this morning. It was easier for her not to do so.

Mr. Fairfield was disappointed at the way things turned out and solaced himself by retiring from the conversation, as he did the evening before, except when absolutely pressed into it by Miss Davenport. He studied the fair lines of Maria's face, thinking how lovely she was, and wondered why he hadn't noticed her beauty as being so unusual before. He thought he saw a new touch of gravity and earnestness about her too, which sat well on her countenance. As he watched her and noted her replies, he decided she was in no present danger from Miss Davenport's influence.

But Nannette perceived that the conversation, which she was monopolizing, was becoming strained. Searching for some way to change it, she discovered in the distance along the Spray View road a carriage containing the De Veres. She immediately began to expand on that family's excellencies. Remembering that quality in man, jealousy, which often served her well, she professed special delight in Roland De Vere's approach.

"We were always such good friends," she said, turning her eyes sweetly upon the minister. "We used to play together by the hour as children, and as we grew older our friendship was really something lovely till he went away to college. Don't you think he has a very remarkable mind, Mr. Fairfield?"

Maria remembered Nannette's account of her quarrel with Roland De Vere and listened in wonder. Nannette neglected to state that her exchanges with Roland De Vere from their earliest childhood were strictly upon a war footing. He was never afraid to tell her of the shams and falsehoods he saw in her, and this made her almost hate him. Nevertheless, it was sometimes expedient to seem to love your enemies, at least for a time. This was one of the unwritten commandments in Miss Davenport's code.

Maria felt greatly relieved at the De Veres' appearance. So did Howard Fairfield, and so did Nannette, but each for a different reason.

A sailing party was the order of the day, and the De Veres drove over to secure their Lone Point friends to join them. The yacht would wait for them at the Lone Point wharf in an hour; they were to send the carriage back by the driver and go out across the bar and fish in the open sea, returning by moonlight.

Maria couldn't help but be happy and forget her troubles. They seemed to melt away in the light of the congenial company. She hurried in to call Rachel and consult with her mother about some additions to the ample lunch which the De Veres brought with them.

"We'll go in and tell the Parkers," said Fannie De Vere, starting off through the sand.

"The Pahkahs! And who are the Pahkahs?" asked Nannette, amid the pleasant stir that prevailed. Nannette always used a Southern drawl when she wished to be interesting.

"They're nobodies, Nannette—just nice, pleasant people, not at all like you and me. You won't care for them in the least," answered Roland De Vere with a touch of the old rudeness which always characterized his conversations with her.

Chapter 21

During preparations for the excursion, Mr. Fairfield diligently studied how he might secure Maria's company on the way to the boat and for as much of the day as possible. But though he offered assistance to Maria and Rachel in countless little ways and gladly bore all the burdens of wraps and lunch baskets he could find belonging to the green cottage, he didn't seem to succeed. Maria was busy and dignified.

If he tried to walk beside her she suddenly discovered an errand with another member of the party or rushed back for her forgotten parasol. Laden as he was he could scarcely follow her. And when he waited behind the rest, Nannette pounced upon him at once, calling him a "poor, lone man" and sweetly insisting upon holding her parasol over him and carrying Maria's blue jacket, which he'd taken special delight in possessing. He could only submit, for he was helpless, and walk grimly on to the wharf as fast as possible and hope for better fortune.

Maria didn't seem to see all this. In fact, she remembered just then that Mr. Fairfield had never told her the story of his gold ring or even spoken of it. He took her for a girl who didn't care for such things. It was as well. He helped her; he was a minister, a—no, it wouldn't do to call him her friend. There must be a more dignified name for their relationship than that. "Spiritual advisor," that's what he was.

As such she could enjoy his conversation and feel that she was right to take pleasure in his company. But not when Nannette was about. Maria, therefore, walked forward and began to talk eagerly with the first unoccupied one of the group. This happened to be Marvie Parker, and Maria silently blessed her for her cheerful, girlish conversation; in spite of her, this cheered her thoughts and turned them in another direction from the one they were tempted to take.

At the last moment George Parker joined the group on the wharf. Nannette had given his sister a sweep of her eyes and ignored her beyond the slightest inclination of her head. When the brother arrived—tall, serious, somewhat diffident in his manner toward strangers and with a rather homely face and figure—by some mischance she wasn't introduced. It was as well, perhaps, for she stood in the shadow of a sail and curled her lip as she looked at him.

Of the party standing about and greeting the newcomers warmly, only Marvie saw that glance. Instantly she resented it for her brother, and her anger flamed up till she almost shot out a well-deserved reproval. Marvie Parker was a girl of tremendous impulses. But fortunately her impulses were under the control of One wiser than herself. A moment more, a hasty prayer, and she was ready to look again at the silly, conceited miss, forgive her and say, "Poor thing." Then she set out to do some kindness for the one who had smitten her so hard upon the one cheek. She knew her brother far too well to carry revenge in her heart for his sake.

Maria placed herself between Fannie De Vere and Marvie Parker when they seated themselves in the boat, and when Mr. Fairfield looked about to get near her he found no opportunity. Miss Davenport wasn't so discreet. She took good care there should be a vacant place beside her, but the disappointed young man for once got the better of her. If he couldn't sit beside Maria, at least he wouldn't subject himself for an entire morning to the chatter of her disagreeable friend. He went to the bow of the boat and seated himself among the coils of rope. Here he could be quiet and think and watch Maria without being observed.

Roland De Vere swung himself aboard at the last minute and took his seat, without noticing, beside Nannette. When he discovered her proximity, he was fully as dissatisfied as she with the arrangement. He wondered what he'd done to deserve such punishment. But since Rachel was at his other side, with George Parker next, he devoted himself as much as possible to them.

Like some beautiful, intelligent creature, the boat spread her white wings and, turning, glided from the bank. Something seemed almost unearthly in the beauty of the day and the flying of the boat along the shimmering bay, swiftly to the place where the soft, benignant blue of the sky came down to meet the water.

Perhaps Mr. Fairfield was the only one who enjoyed it all. He was by himself with pleasant thoughts for company. The others were arranging themselves comfortably and answering one another, as polished shafts of sarcasm and bubbling mirth went from one to another.

Nannette was cross. She had missed her aim. True, she managed to separate Maria and Mr. Fairfield, though she felt pretty sure Maria did this herself, and she couldn't even claim the credit of it. But she didn't gain his company. She felt certain that a whole day by her side amid such lovely surroundings would surely fix her in Mr. Fairfield's good graces by night. Now she had no one but that hateful Roland De Vere, and she saw instantly that he wasn't disposed to be forgetful or friendly.

She decided to show her pique by making fun of those ungainly Parkers. If the young man were just the least bit better looking or glanced at her with admiration, she might have flirted with him. But with such a man as Mr. Fairfield by, unwon, she felt she couldn't stoop so low. She decided, however, that Mr. Fairfield mustn't see her making fun of that solemn-looking Parker boy. Since he was a minister, she supposed he would disapprove. She had a theory that young ministers always disapprove of wrong things because their churches obliged them to do so, and not at all because they felt any strong convictions on the subject.

Her opportunity to practice on young Parker came soon, and for want of better material she set to work at once. As early as possible during the morning

Roland De Vere made an excuse to change seats with George Parker. He felt sorry for George when he did it, but George was one of those people who always have disagreeable people and places thrust upon them and the grace to accept them pleasantly. His sister watched him as he sat down and turned his keen, gray eyes upon Miss Davenport, with a remark about the beauty of the day.

Nannette imagined him shy and was astonished to find he had a fine voice and spoke with ease and unusual grace in his manner. She plunged into a conversation with him, her most disagreeable expression upon her face, determined to embarrass him as soon as possible. From the talk of the others she learned he was something of a musician and guessed him wise in his own conceit as a superficial amateur. She thought this would be as good an opportunity as any to "take a rise out of him." Summoning her slight knowledge of the musical world, which amounted to the names of a few leading performers and titles of several brilliant productions, she began.

"Did you say you lived in the city?" she asked him, turning toward him with one of the cold stares which usually disconcerted its poor victim. "Then I suppose if you're so fond of music you heard Josef Hoffman last month."

She hardly expected him to know whom she referred to, but to her amazement his plain face lit up with joy, thinking he discovered a kindred spirit.

"Yes, I did," he answered at once. "I heard him both times. I wouldn't have missed him for the world. I couldn't get a seat since I had to rush there just at the hour, and there was scarcely standing room left. But I might have been standing on my head for all I knew while he was playing. Wasn't it fine? What did you think of his rendering of Beethoven's E-flat major sonata? Wasn't that first movement perfect? Didn't he bring out the orchestral effects marvelously in Liszt's transcription of the overture to 'Tannhäuser'?"

It was Nannette's turn to be embarrassed. She hadn't heard Josef Hoffman and wouldn't have understood him if she had, for she wasn't a musician. Worse than that, she didn't possess one atom of delicate appreciation of good music; it was a bore to her and nothing more, unless it accompanied dancing. Only then did it find an answering chord in her soul.

She flushed slightly, paused, but rallied and tried again. Her malice was stirred. She never quite forgave anyone who made her feel uncomfortable. She flew to a subject with which she felt more at home.

"Were you at the opera house last month? Did you see 'The Wife's Revenge'?" she asked, a wicked look flashing across her face.

The young man looked at her with instant comprehension of the mistake he made earlier.

"Yes," he said, "I was at the opera house last month, but I didn't go to see a play. I was with Mr. Moody."

Now Miss Davenport was so out of the religious world that she didn't at first know who Moody was.

"Moody," she said, puzzled. "Who is Moody?"

"Moody, the evangelist. Surely you heard of the two weeks' series of meetings held in the opera house."

"What! Moody and Sankey Sunday school songs?" she exclaimed with a disagreeable laugh. "Oh, you're good, are you?" The sneer on her face was decided this time, but to her disappointment it had no effect on her listener.

He turned his serious, gray eyes upon her. "Just what is your definition of goodness, Miss Davenport?" he asked quietly.

Nannette was nonplussed. She hadn't expected to be answered like that. She looked for a wave of color over his face and immediate disclaiming of any right to the adjective she applied; in the midst of it she would laugh scornfully and make him feel that to be "good" was above all else a thing to be laughed at and disclaimed.

"Oh, I never deal in definitions," she answered uneasily. "I leave that to the dictionary."

"The dictionary gives some ten or twelve different meanings to that word, if I'm not mistaken," he said. "But the one I like the best was given years ago by Paul: 'For scarcely for a righteous man will one die; yet peradventure for a good man some would even dare to die.' If I might claim that sort of goodness, Miss Davenport, I would count it the highest honor."

After that, conversation between these two languished. Nannette had nothing to say. She felt she was worsted from the first and with weapons that were new to her. She took refuge in teasing the fish they soon began to catch. Strange to say, she was among the successful catchers that day. The line she held was often taken by some poor unwary fish. She would jerk him out of the water and let him down again, only to give the line a stronger jerk and keep the poor creature in agony. The girls protested once or twice, and at last Roland De Vere turned with sudden vehemence upon her.

"Nannette, stop torturing that poor creature. It'll rise in judgment against you at the last day." He perhaps didn't mean his words literally, but he was angry at her cruel action.

Nannette laughed scornfully and gave the fish another jerk. "Your theology is all wrong. They don't have fish in heaven," she responded saucily.

"Mr. Fairfield," she called laughingly, "set Mr. De Vere straight. He thinks we'll have fish in heaven. Do tell him they haven't any souls."

"I leave it to you, Fairfield," said the young man, turning toward the minister, "if some animals haven't more soul than some human beings."

Thus appealed to, the minister recalled his thoughts from their pleasant wanderings and answered: "Certainly, De Vere, I imagine animals will have some part in the future life. Whether they have souls or not, I can't say. But I do think they'll have their part with all of God's creation in the heaven that's being prepared."

This statement aroused a discussion and exclamations from the rest of the party, and Nannette and her fish were left to themselves while the others con-templated the new thought. Maria was charmed with the idea, a new one to her, and looked at Mr. Fairfield with her old admiration, contemplating what a delightful talker and deep thinker he was. She wished he'd go on and talk more about this, but he wasn't inclined to say much. He seemed to be changed from the congenial friend she knew so well for a few weeks.

She wondered what made the difference and if Nannette had been the cause. How pleasant to have him by herself just for a while, so she might ask him some questions about her new life which were confusing her. But she supposed that mustn't be, for it was better for her not to see too much of him. What if he'd seen how much she enjoyed his company and pulled away from her, to save her from the shame of showing him her heart? Her face burned at the very thought. How dreadful that would be! Surely she couldn't have seemed to care for him! How could she when she didn't know it? Of course she didn't really care for him; she only feared she might. But she wouldn't, now that she saw her danger. That would be terribly unwomanly. It was bad enough to realize her own danger. If she'd been more careful she wouldn't have had to endure that thought.

But then she might have missed the blessed joy of finding Christ. And her heart was happy with the perfect peace she felt with God. She could even stand for him to think humiliatingly of her for the sake of that sweet peace. But she would show him in the future that she had no interest in him apart from the spiritual help he gave her.

What a happy day this would have been if these two could have looked into one another's hearts! But God knew best, and He had some wise end in view through this discipline.

I cannot say, beneath the pressure of life's cares today,
    I joy in these
But I can say that I had rather walk this rugged way,
    if Him it please;
I cannot feel that all is well when darkening clouds
    conceal the sun;
But then I know God lives and loves; and say, since it is so,
    "Thy will be done."
I cannot speak in happy tones;
    the teardrops on my cheek show I am sad;
But I can speak of grace to suffer with submission meek,
    until made glad.
I do not see why God should e'en permit some things to be,
    when he is love;
But I can see, though often dimly, through the mystery,
    his hand above!

Chapter 22

Nannette felt very discontented and dissatisfied with her first week at Lone Point. The weather was perfect, but what is weather when a storm blows within? The party was a lively one, but somehow she felt out of harmony with it. Perhaps they felt this lack of harmony more than she did.

The fishing was abundant and successful. What fishing party could ask for more? The sea was calm. The sunset was one of the most magnificent ever seen at Lone Point, and the moonrise was equally resplendent. They floated slowly home, drawn by zephyrs that seemed willingly to obey the hand that held the helm.

But one thing was lacking in it all for Nannette, the only thing that made fishing parties and moonlight trips home again filled with pleasure. That was an adoring man at her side who would chatter nothings and feed her vanity by likening her eyes to the sparkles on the wave and her complexion to the dazzling whiteness of the moonbeams.

Mr. Fairfield persisted in keeping a dignified distance, at least as far as the length of the boat permitted. Once, during a change of places, she got beside him as they returned from supper at the hotel on the mainland and were reembarking for their homeward ride. But after a few words he abruptly excused himself and went to help one of the sailors, who she felt sure didn't need him at all. It was very humiliating to her pride.

Anyone, even George Parker, would have been better than no one at all. She was tied down to the companionship of the girls, and to her that was as low as she could fall. She never took pains to make any true friends among the girls and felt, what was true, that she was only tolerated out of politeness. This she cared not one straw for when she had plenty of men at hand. She looked over at George Parker and wished she'd been less disagreeable to him in the morning. It would at least have amused her to subjugate him, an easy task to her, and enjoy the dismay of his pious little sister. Nannette was as unhappy and disagreeable as she'd ever been in her life.

All the way home there was singing. She asked for one or two songs, but no one seemed to know the airs she called for, most of them society sentimentalities; or if they did, they didn't care to break the harmony of the evening by bringing them in. The songs they sang were old ballads mostly; soft, sweet strains that seemed to be in tune with the murmuring waters. Eventually someone started a hymn, and they sang on from one to another favorite. How much more the words seemed to mean when sung on the water.

Far, far away like bells at evening pealing,
The voice of Jesus sounds o'er land and sea.

Nannette had an uncomfortable feeling that a supernatural voice might speak to them soon. The songs chosen seemed to follow one thought:

Jesus, Savior, pilot me,
Over life's tempestuous sea. . . .

And as the last words died away Rachel's voice took up the words of another:

Jesus, Jesus, visit me,
How my soul longs after thee.
When, my best, my dearest friend,
Shall our separation end?

Then Roland De Vere started with

My Jesus, as thou wilt.

And his sister took it up at the close with the lovely tune of "Dorrnance" in the words,

Jesus calls us, o'er the tumult
Of our life's wild, restless sea;
Day by day his sweet voice soundeth,
Saying, Christian, follow me.

Maria sang the words, feeling every one in her heart. She was enjoying this song service almost more than she could endure. Tears of deep, unspeakable gladness would mist her eyes now and then, as she said over to herself: *He is my Jesus. I can feel it. I know it. I love Him.* And she realized at that moment that all her Christian life she'd been dissatisfied with herself and longing for just this thing to come to her. But she wasn't willing and didn't know how to take the steps to bring it about.

As they neared the shore and the lights of Lone Point began to shine out over the water, Rachel and Marvie, sitting together, started the sweet strain:

One sweetly solemn thought, comes to me o'er and o'er,
I'm nearer my home in heaven today, than ever I've been before.

Nannette felt the hush that hung over the little company as the boat slipped up to the dock when the last words were ended. She was reminded so strongly of her mother's funeral that she felt tempted to jump overboard in order to create some kind of excitement. Just as the boat touched the wharf, Howard Fairfield repeated in the clear rich voice that had hushed a congregation to attention so often:

And I pray that every venture
The port of peace may enter,
That safe from snag and fall,
And siren haunted islet,
And rock, the unseen Pilot
May guide us one and all.

It seemed like a benediction at the close of a beautiful meeting.

They landed in silence and walked toward their homes with a quiet reverence upon them.

Nannette was seated before her mirror—she always made a practice of sitting before her mirror after going anywhere so she might see how she looked and what impression she made. She curled her lip in intense scorn.

"I feel exactly as if I'd attended a revival meeting and been sitting on the mourner's bench all evening. This is worse than reading to Cousin George. I have half a mind to go home. If it weren't for making that stuck-up minister come down a peg I believe I would, but he must be conquered! If I could only catch Maria at a disadvantage when he's along! I must try to work up something. I see plainly, however, that I'll have to try the pious dodge before I can be very effective. Ah me! What a bore! I'll make up for this next summer!"

Then she went to bed, but not to sleep. She lay there planning a campaign that meant victory and the downfall of the ministry in Lone Point at least.

The days passed with much the same relationship between the three—Maria, Howard Fairfield and Nannette—that there was the first day of Miss Davenport's arrival. Nannette annoyed Mr. Fairfield not a little, asked services of him and accepted them graciously, as if it were a favor to him to be allowed to run her errands. She circumvented his plans to meet Maria in the most ingenious ways, often making it appear perfectly natural that it happened, so he hadn't even begun to suspect how deeply laid her plan was.

Nannette didn't forget her wish to show Maria off to disadvantage before him, and constantly her mind was searching for some means of doing this. She went about her work with an ingenuity worthy of a better cause. One morning at the table she began a conversation to ascertain his views on certain questions.

"Mr. Fairfield, what do you think of cards? Aren't they awfully wicked? Don't you find they do a great amount of harm?"

Mr. Fairfield turned in amazement from contemplating his plate. This wasn't a subject in which he would have thought Miss Davenport interested. As for discussing the right and wrong of card-playing, he didn't deem it profitable. He supposed, of course, she must be a card-player, as indeed she was, though she chose this morning to pose as one who greatly disapproved of it.

"I find that card-playing among Christians, as a rule, leads to worldliness," he answered stiffly.

He judged Miss Davenport's object in asking the question to be to force him into an argument, and he didn't care to discuss worldly amusements with a person who professed to belong wholly to the world. He was a little surprised she didn't pursue the subject further, but thought no more about it. He had more important things to think of.

A fine orchestra was giving a concert on the veranda of one of the Spray View hotels. The Lone Point young people were invited over to attend it that evening with the De Veres. Mr. Fairfield was hoping for at least a few minutes with Maria, so he might ask her to walk with him the next day. He had a new address by Mr. Meyer he was sure she'd like to see, and he wanted the pleasure of reading it with her for the first time. It must—it surely could be planned. It was absurd that he couldn't get a chance to speak to her alone anymore. He would have to resort to writing soon if things continued as they were, though he feared that for him to write would appear strange to her and accelerate matters before the time was ripe. He wondered, with a sigh, how long Maria's friend would stay in Lone Point. Perhaps he could ask her and find out the limit to this, to him, distasteful state of things.

The fact was, if Maria hadn't resolved that Mr. Fairfield shouldn't imagine her anxious for his company, Nannette couldn't have contrived so many separations as she did. But with them both at work to keep him from his object it was even more difficult for him.

During this time Winthrop Hammond remained in town continuously for some days, taking care of a friend who was alone in the city and ill with typhoid fever. The young man's parents had at last arrived, and Win felt at liberty to leave him. So he was staying at the shore for a few days, without going up to the city, since he felt he needed rest after his many nights of nursing and being awake.

The concert at Spray View was the first one of the young people's gatherings at which Win was present and therefore was the first time Nannette met him. Strange to say, they never met in town.

Maria prayed earnestly before going out that evening. She asked Win several times if he wouldn't rather remain at home and rest, saying she'd gladly stay with him. But as he seemed anxious to go, she ceased talking about it.

Perhaps Nannette was so interested in Mr. Fairfield that she wouldn't set any snares for Win. At any rate she put the dear brother into God's keeping, and nothing more could be done. She hovered about him and tried to be as cheerful and interesting as possible. Indeed, he noticed how she'd changed and wondered what it meant. It was pleasant to have her care to be with him, though it was unlike her too, for she always had plenty of admirers of her own.

Nannette's plans weren't thoroughly made, though she knew she meant to make some decisive move that evening. She had a shadow of a plan that would depend upon circumstances, and upon this occasion circumstances favored her. Early in the evening, she met a company of young people she was well acquainted with.

Among them was a particularly fast young fellow, whose face showed plainly what his life must be. Nannette took pains to introduce them to Maria. This young man in particular seemed to be greatly taken with her and whispered in an aside to Nannette: "I say, Nan—she's a 'beaut'! Where'd you pick her up? I like her style. She's not so slow as a 'looker,' is she? Say, give a fellow a chance to talk with her for a while."

"All right, I will," she agreed readily enough, "if you'll do something for me in return. Promise me to get a set for whist or euchre with her in it in the small card room to the left of the office, the one with the wide windows on the porch, you know. I have a special reason. I'm setting up a little joke on someone, that's all. I think she knows how all right, but anyway, if she doesn't, you offer to teach her."

"You're a jewel, Nan," he responded eagerly, glad of the chance to teach such a pretty girl as Maria anything. "Just command me, and I'll obey."

"Well, you be in there with the girls in five minutes, and I'll send her in," she said and went airily on her way.

She was by no means so sure of Maria, as she pretended, but she would do her best. Fortune favored her a second time as she walked back to the end of the porch, where the De Vere party was seated. Win Hammond met her near the parlor door. He stopped and begged her to send the others to him as he'd secured better seats for the music but couldn't leave them lest someone else preempted them. Here was one more aid for her scheme. A few minutes' delay one way or another would make no difference about the seats, and Win Hammond would never find out. Yes, she'd try it.

"Maria, dear," she said in a low tone as she came up to the party, who hadn't noticed her absence, for she only walked away with her old friends for a few moments. "Maria, I just met your brother, and he wished me to ask you to come to him. You'll find him over there in that small room to the right of the office."

Maria rose at once and went in the direction she'd pointed, wondering what in the world her brother wanted. She felt a thrill of joy that he wanted her instead of someone else. As she walked away, Mr. Fairfield broke off in the midst of a sentence to Marvie Parker and rose to go with her.

But Nannette quickly stepped to his side and, in a tone which all could hear, said sweetly: "Oh, Mr. Fairfield, would you help me find my friends again? I've lost them and am very anxious to see them before the music begins."

Of course as a gentleman he could only offer her his arm and march away down the wide porch, inwardly fuming at his trying position—and at its pretty cause.

Now Nannette could not, for her own purposes, have better timed their coming to the part of the porch where the little card room window opened out upon it, if she were gifted with supernatural powers.

"I think I heard them say they'd be near here. Would you just look in that window, please, and see if you catch a glimpse of them?" With her quick eye she'd already seen the groups forming within. A table stood in the center of the room, and the company of young people Nannette recently introduced to the Lone Pointers sat around it. One seat was vacant, and the fast young man was just bowing and holding it ready for Maria to be seated as Mr. Fairfield looked in. From where they stood in the darkness, gazing into the brilliantly lighted room, he could plainly see the cards on the table and in the hands of those about it.

Then a soft little hand stole quickly over his eyes, and Nannette, in a cheerful, shocked laugh, said, "Oh, please come away. I'm so sorry. I wouldn't have done it for the world if I'd known. She wouldn't have you see her in there, I know. But you won't think badly of her for it, will you? She's been having such a hard time keeping up, you know, and one can't be good always. One must have a little fun occasionally. Besides, Maria has done bravely. She isn't used to such a straight-laced life, you must remember. She's been telling me how hard it was for her. But she'd be terribly broken up if you saw her. She told me about your—well, perhaps, I'd better not say anymore, for she might not like it, you know," Nannette broke off hesitatingly.

They were walking toward a secluded end of the porch, entirely deserted now, for the guests were gathering for the music. Nannette determined to strike while the iron was hot, for she thought she saw that Mr. Fairfield was greatly taken aback at what he saw. Here were seats and the loud dashing of the waves. No place could be better for confidences and a pleasant little flirtation. What if the music did go on and pass, no matter if she fought for and won this trophy.

"Let's sit down just a minute, please," she said as if out of breath, putting her hand to her heart. "I feel so upset by this. I'm afraid she'll blame me for it, and I'd feel so sorry. She's been telling me all about it, you know, and, well—excuse me, but I have these little turns with my heart ever since Mother's death. It'll soon pass. There—oh, please sit down just a minute."

She leaned her head back against the wall and let it incline till it almost rested against her escort. Only just an instant did she let it remain, and then she seemed to come to herself and gain strength to sit up and beg his pardon. She hoped he might feel impelled to do as other young men did before when she was attacked in a like manner; but since she saw no sign of any such movement on his part, she withdrew discreetly.

Mr. Fairfield, on his part, was startled almost out of his usual composure. He wouldn't have thought it such a great thing to see Maria playing cards, for she told him herself that she lived a worldly life; she wouldn't be expected to have thought over all these questions and decided them, in so short a space of time. But to be told that she thought about it and deliberately went in there to play, planning he shouldn't know about it—that she was actually trying to deceive him and appear better in his eyes than she was, was another matter. Worst of all was to know that the sacred words which passed between Miss Hammond and him about a better, nobler life were recited in detail to this worldly, unsympathetic listener. This was what cut him to the quick. He sat dumb for a few minutes with the pain of it.

Chapter 23

One might have supposed that Howard Fairfield, a minister of the gospel for three years, had lived long enough in the world and experienced enough of it, not to believe all that a girl like Miss Davenport told him. Indeed, he never put much faith in anything she did or said from the first. But the little he saw with his own eyes tonight suddenly broke down his good common sense, and he began to doubt Maria.

Nannette had hoped for this. She thought that with his first doubts of Maria he might turn to her, and then she would have gained an influence over him which she well knew how to use. But Nannette showed in this that she wasn't a good judge of human nature. She didn't understand the pure, high nobility of such a man's heart or she would never have thought to turn him thus to herself.

When she saw that the minister was sitting by her side and waiting, she pulled out her little black-edged handkerchief and sobbed softly.

"It frightens me terribly when I get one of those heart attacks," she said in a soft, childish voice. She was a very good actress when the occasion demanded private theatricals. "I feel as if I weren't good enough to die."

She paused. She thought if there was a spark of the true minister in him he would turn now and try to preach to her, but instead he sat quite silent beside her.

After a moment in which nothing could be heard but the beating of the waves, he spoke in a stern, controlled voice: "Are you quite able to return to your friends now, Miss Davenport?" It was all he could bring himself to say. He had detected the false note in her voice instantly. He couldn't try to talk to her of spiritual things. He felt instinctively that it would be casting pearls before swine. "If you don't feel able to go back, I'll go in search of assistance for you," he added.

Nannette rose hastily from her chair, stung by anger and defeat. During the long walk down that porch neither of them spoke a word.

It was a pity Mr. Fairfield couldn't have lingered just an instant longer before that brightly lighted window. He would have seen Maria coldly decline the seat at the card table and, after a glance about the room and a dignified word or two of inquiry about her brother, leave the room again. He might have been spared the pain that continually surged back and filled his heart, for then he would have seen that the whole thing was manufactured in Miss Davenport's fertile brain.

Perhaps, too, it might have dawned upon him sooner that the young woman in question had an end of her own to gain, namely himself. But the man's nobleness of character cannot better be described than by saying that such an idea didn't even occur to him. Not until he was in the quiet of his own room and remembered that head almost laid upon his shoulder did he begin to see what sort of girl Miss Davenport really was. A blush of shame mantled his brow for her sake and for the sake of the womanhood which in his thought she, even in that slight act, had dishonored.

Meanwhile Nannette, humiliated and resentful, directed the party to where Win Hammond was waiting for them and disappeared for a time from the room as she saw Maria approaching.

Mr. Fairfield slipped away as the music began. His excuse was that he'd promised to preach the next day and needed the time for preparation. No one thought it strange, though all were sorry to lose his companionship.

As he walked down the long porch, intending to walk home by the beach instead of the road, he spied two people ahead of him. They were some distance away, and he couldn't see them distinctly. In the uncertain light of moon and dashing spray, he scarcely noticed them at first, except to know that the dark figure was a man and the white garments belonged to a woman. But as they turned out into the brighter moonlight to walk on the silver sand close beside the waves, he saw the man's dark arm steal out and encircle the waist of the white dress beside him.

Then in the confiding, unresisting attitude of the woman he suddenly realized a familiar memory and as suddenly became aware of two long, black sash ends, with fluffy little black chiffon ruffles about them. He recalled noticing them on Miss Davenport's dress as she walked before him on the way from the De Vere home over to the hotel. It occurred to him when he first set eyes upon them that he felt morally certain that if her bereavement hadn't positively forbidden it, that sash would have been a bright red.

He was drawing nearer and could see their faces now. Nannette was looking sweetly up into the man's eyes so close above hers, and he saw that the man was the same one who had a few moments before placed Maria's chair at the card table. At least it was a relief to know Maria wasn't playing with that man. He almost wished he'd remained to see what became of Maria, but he wouldn't go back now. Moreover he'd witnessed all the flirtations he cared for in one evening. He turned abruptly off over the sand and struck straight across the country to the carriage drive, regardless of hillocks or wire fences or even quicksands.

It wasn't a pleasant walk, and he felt as if he lost rather than gained strength for his work the next day. He went straight to his knees, and in communion with his heavenly Father he soon lost the heavy strain that the evening's events put on him and could think of what he intended to say tomorrow.

He chose for his text, "For me to live is Christ." That verse had been deeply impressed upon his mind since the first evening when he visited the Hammond cottage, and Rachel asked her innocent, earnest question.

By the time for church service, the rest of the night, the morning's beauty and above all the peace Jesus Christ gave him lifted him above his troubled thoughts of the evening before. He felt "in the Spirit on the Lord's Day" as he went forth to speak in Christ's name.

For just a moment after he was seated in the pulpit, while the congregation was gathering, he felt a disagreeable sensation as Miss Davenport came in and seated herself in front of him in her elegant black robes. Perhaps he was hard upon her, but he was a noble man with high ideals of womanhood. His soul shrank from the thought of what he saw of that young woman the night before.

He caught a glimpse of Maria's face, however, on which unconscious loveliness sat so sweetly, and of Rachel's calm brow; and he remembered there were women in the world who wouldn't stoop to what was beneath them. He wondered, as he looked at the sisters, why he never noticed how much alike they were.

Happily for him he forgot for the moment the trouble about Maria that had come to him the night before, for the sight of her face in its Sabbath peace seemed so foreign to anything deceitful. Not until his work for the morning was over did the event suddenly return to his memory.

God's servants need most earnestly to watch and pray when they've just finished some special work for Him that required attention and alert nerves. The tension over, they don't feel the need to watch and pray immediately. Satan steals up unaware when they're unprepared for attack and takes them in their weakest place, sometimes undoing or rendering useless the good work done.

So at the hour of exaltation, Mr. Fairfield almost stood upon the mount with his Savior and face to face with Him gave the message of life. As he spoke he felt in his heart that though to live for Christ was glorious, to die for Him would be better than all; he would welcome death at once if Christ should send it. After all this Satan stole upon him on his way home and told him his preaching had no effect; that his dearest hopes were vain; that the woman he felt was the one in all the earth for him was vain and deceitful and possessed a number of other qualities he couldn't bear to think of.

Since Satan was busy with the preacher, however, he didn't have time then to pick up the good seeds that had fallen upon the open mellow ground. When he got back to that work, much of the seed had already taken root and was growing. Only what fell on the rocks could he pick up and destroy.

Maria felt encouraged by the morning sermon. It helped her more than anything she'd heard before. It may have been because the preacher wrote his sermon just for her. He had in mind her heart experience and seemed to have anticipated all her doubts and confusion and answered them. He was with God a lot during the days when he couldn't talk with her as he had before, and perhaps the separation was good for them both for this very reason. They were learning to find help first in God and only after that in one another. She thanked God over and over again that day for that sermon.

She wasn't unaware that the preacher's face, in its high intellectual refinement, wore a look of spiritual illumination that to her made it more handsome than any face she ever looked upon. It troubled her that the speaker's personality came so often to her mind. But after several vain attempts to put it away she decided to enjoy the day and the sermon and not trouble herself about this part of it, which apparently couldn't be helped.

Just one speck of trouble appeared on the bright surface of the day to her. Her brother walked beside Miss Davenport back to the hotel from church, and after dinner he declined Rachel's request to accompany her to the Sabbath school and went directly back to the hotel. From the porch of the green cottage she saw him emerge soon after from the hotel carrying Miss Davenport's shawl and parasol, and with her by his side they sauntered down the beach. She had evidently decided that such a spiritual preacher would hardly be good material for a jolly Sunday afternoon and looked about for other prey.

As Maria watched her during the past week or two, she became more convinced of the shallowness and perhaps wickedness of her heart. She felt sure that she was an unprincipled girl, and she couldn't bear to see her brother walk into the net spread for him.

In this fear she was evidently joined by Rachel, although neither said anything to the other. But Rachel stood by her side on the porch, her calm brow clouded and the ready tears gathering as she watched their brother. Maria turned and looked at her. As their eyes met she obeyed the warm impulse of her heart and, kissing Rachel, said, "Come with me."

Almost in amazement Rachel understood, though up to now no word of any change in Maria passed between the two. Rachel followed her sister to their room, and together, hand in hand, they knelt down beside their bed. They spoke no word out loud then or after they rose, but Rachel kissed Maria this time and then slipped away to the Sabbath school.

Because of this incident, Maria felt that the day was wonderful, and so did Rachel. It touched Rachel's heart beyond anything that ever happened between them, to have Maria tell her in this way of her new deep feelings. She was a remarkable little sister or she might not have understood.

Some little seed of the morning's word may have dropped on Miss Davenport's heart. She felt troubled. She was reminded unpleasantly again of her mother's death. She always avoided solemn things if she could, but that was the one solemn incident of her life so far that she couldn't avoid. She didn't wish to think about it, because while in her life her mother wasn't as strong and faithful as she should have been. Yet in her death she awakened to her responsibility and spoke a few dreadful words to her daughter; by night and by day those words pursued her, unless she occupied her mind with worldly things. But her mind was shallow, and she easily turned her thoughts to light things.

She recognized the illumination of the minister's face as he preached that morning, though in her words he was judged "decidedly handsome and distingué." She remembered his severity the evening before, and a blush of shame crept over her face, unused to such blushes as it was.

Then to drive out this unusual feeling she wondered if after all there wasn't still hope that she might conquer this man. He'd held out so long it would be quite interesting if she could bring him to her feet now. She might even fall in love with him. She really felt nearer to falling in love than she had for four or five years. And if he had a good church and a large salary it might not be such a bad "catch" after all.

She speculated upon what the position of a minister's wife was and how much would be required of her for propriety's sake. The only drawback she could think of would be that she might be occasionally called upon to attend funerals, and *that* she *would not* do. She would never do it to please anyone! Horrid places! She shuddered involuntarily and took up her fan, deciding she would put her foot down at once on that and declare she wouldn't go. After all, since she had plenty of money and probably would have more than he, she might have her own way about everything.

At that she looked up to the minister's face to see how it would be to look at him as a possible husband and perceived he'd hushed the audience into tears by a simple story of pain and loss and love and loyalty to Christ. She took up her handkerchief and tried to listen with the others as he recited the words:

When his steps
Were on the mighty waters—
When we went with trembling hearts through nights of pain and loss,
His smile was sweeter and his love more dear;
And only heaven is better than to walk
With Christ at midnight over moonless seas.

During the prayer that followed the sermon she formulated the plan she carried out that evening, her final plan for his capture. Then with the benediction, she rose, satisfied with her morning's worship, and turned to Win Hammond with her sweetest smile. If the plan should fail, this one was left; he was handsome, of a good family and not very hard to subdue as she could easily see.

As Mr. Fairfield passed down the aisle, his exaltation yet upon his face, she stretched out her daintily gloved hand and just touched his coat sleeve with the tips of her fingers.

"Oh, Mr. Fairfield," she said with a reminding quiver in her voice, "thank you for that sweet sermon. It was just perfectly lovely. I did enjoy it so much."

And the minister suddenly remembered that he still lived on the earth.

Chapter 24

Mr. Fairfield received two letters of note in Monday morning's mail. One had no postmark. The other was from his city home, telling of the severe illness of a woman who belonged to his church. He read this first, naturally anxious to know the home news, and sat with it in his hand pondering whether his duty didn't call him home, at least for a day or two. Then he suddenly remembered the other letter. It was written in high, angular strokes on a thick cream, violet-scented paper. And since the handwriting was very "high" indeed and the letter long, it was bulky. It read as follows:

> *My dear Mr. Fairfield:*
> *My heart is filled with conflicting emotions as I write you this note. I feel as if I've come to a crisis in my life. The moment I met you I realized you were one who was to wield a great influence over me and have something unusual to do with my life. This morning when I listened, entranced, to your eloquent words I realized this even more. More than anyone I've ever met, I believe you've influenced me. I was deeply affected. I've been thinking the matter over and have decided to ask your help and spiritual advice. My dear mother used to tell me that someday I would meet with someone who would have the power to reach my stony heart religiously, and I now see she was right. Oh, I'm very wretched and miserable! If you can bring me any consolation from the religion you preach so beautifully, I shall be forever grateful to you. I know you won't leave a poor girl comfortless when she has no one else to turn to. You'll come to me and let me tell you the story of my life, and you'll teach me how to be good like you. I can't endure yet to have my friends know I've taken this step. It's too new and sacred. So I ask you to meet me by the inlet, up toward the lighthouse, where the old mast is buried in the sand. There we can sit and talk to our heart's content without being observed. I'll be there at half-past ten in the morning, and I know you won't fail me. Until then, farewell. Yours penitently,*
>
> *Nannette M. Davenport.*

The minister felt a cold chill creeping over him as he read this letter. He was more convinced of the writer's insincerity as he thought over the matter and read and reread the letter. In his heart was not one particle of response to that summons for help. He examined himself to see whether his prejudice made him feel so. But, no, he couldn't think of anyone else, no matter how humble, whom he wouldn't have gladly gone to meet and help. He couldn't feel that the Spirit of God was sending him to this one.

Saturday night's experience stood out too plainly in his mind, and the horror he felt grew as he thought about it. If there were no one to talk with her, the case would have been different. He would have risked all on the mere chance that she was in earnest. Or if she hadn't worded her letter so strangely and chosen such a secluded spot for their talk, he wouldn't have been half so suspicious. What should he do?

He felt strongly that this letter was written in much the same spirit as one a tramp brought to him some months before, poorly spelled and ungrammatical in wording, purporting to be from a scholarly member of his church. If he, the minister, would give the man some help from the church funds, this church member felt sure they might win the man to Christ. He was disposed to beware of this letter as he was of that one, for in the former case his suspicion that the man was an arrant fraud and the letter a forgery had proven correct.

He felt now that for the sake of the love he bore Maria he shouldn't meet this strange young woman. What if Maria should be walking upon the sand and come upon them? Perhaps Miss Davenport meant to plan just such a *renconter*. Now that his eyes were open he felt she might descend to any depths to gain her end, whatever it was.

Then the letter had no genuine ring. There was too much talk about him and his influence on her. There was no confession of having sinned. Why did she see it necessary to write at all? Why didn't she boldly ask him to talk with her on the porch or anywhere? There were plenty of opportunities. Why, if she wanted religious help, didn't she go to Maria who, according to her own statement, had talked with her on these topics?

He went to his room and asked his heavenly Father's advice. This matter was too important for his own inclination to decide. He couldn't easily refuse a call for help, even though he doubted it. He prayed, trusting that an answer would come, and it did.

As he rose from his knees the other letter, the one about the sick woman, fluttered from his hand to the floor. On the back of the sheet where he hadn't noticed it before he saw a short postscript, asking him to come home. The woman seemed to have something on her mind to tell him and wished to see him.

Quick as a flash he felt this was his heaven-sent answer, and he must obey. A glance at his watch told him the next train was due at the station in one hour, just ten minutes before the time Miss Davenport set in her letter for him to meet her at the inlet. He would go home. His church was his first duty, and this woman was dying.

Hastily he gathered together his belongings and settled a few matters before he left, thinking all the while what to do about Miss Davenport's request. He might ask someone else to meet her. He thought of a dear old Christian woman at home and wished she were here, but she wasn't. He thought of Maria but disliked asking her to go on such an errand to her own friend, lest she suppose he'd formed an intimate friendship with Miss Davenport. Of course, the circumstances of the past week well bore out such a supposition. Nevertheless, he at last made up his mind that Maria was the only one he could turn to now. He went at once to the green cottage, leaving his orders about baggage at the hotel, so that he wouldn't have to return.

Nannette was far up the beach practicing pretty little maneuvers with her deepest bordered handkerchief and failed to see him go. But when Mr. Fairfield reached the green cottage he found to his dismay that Maria, with her mother, had been driven over to Spray View in Mr. Higgins's green wagon to do some Monday morning shopping. They wouldn't likely return before the city train left. His heart was filled with such regret when he thought of leaving her so abruptly that for a few minutes he forgot about Nannette in her self-appointed trysting place.

Rachel was at home and gave him writing materials, and he was trying to construct a farewell note to Maria. Perhaps he should write a note to Miss Davenport. It was only courteous to do so, but in his soul he shrank from addressing a word to her. He glanced up at Rachel as she sat shelling peas on the upper step of the porch. Her far-away, dreamy expression told him her thoughts were on high and lovely things.

Suddenly a new idea came to him. It would be late when Maria returned, too late for her to reach Miss Davenport at the inlet before she left. Here was Rachel. She would know how to help that girl. He thought of the verse about how the Lord kept some things from the wise and prudent and revealed them unto babes. While Rachel was no babe, she was still a child at heart. He remembered how well she taught the children on the sand. She had the root of the matter in her and could surely bring the message of salvation to another soul. He would send her.

In a few words he explained the situation to Rachel, telling her only what was absolutely necessary: Miss Davenport was affected by yesterday's services and wrote him a note, in his capacity as a minister, asking for his help spiritually. He was called suddenly to the city by sickness in his congregation and didn't know how long he'd be detained. Would she go and meet Miss Davenport and help her find Christ?

Rachel's face beamed with a holy light to think she was being sent on an errand of mercy. She was genuinely glad Nannette wanted to be a Christian. She had been secretly praying for her ever since her arrival, for to Rachel, Nannette seemed much in need of a Savior. She promised eagerly to go at the appointed time and immediately went away to get ready.

Such joy was on her face at the thought of the work before her that the minister felt ashamed and that he shouldn't have shrunk from it. He reflected, however, that since Rachel didn't share his doubts about the would-be inquirer, she might be able to do more good. She was trusting that her mission would be blest, and perhaps it would. He pledged to pray for this.

Then to his dismay he had little time left and could only write a line to tell Maria he was sorry to leave without seeing her. He left the Meyer book for her, asking that she read it with him on his return, if he was able to return that summer. Then he heard the train whistling at Spray View and, hastily bidding Rachel good-bye, went to the station. He felt that he was leaving all that was precious in this world. It was very hard for him to go. If only he could have had a little word with Maria and one of her lovely smiles to light him on his way!

Rachel, with an exalted expression and her little Bible in her pocket, walked swiftly up the beach. She was praying as she went that she might be led to say the right words.

Nannette was seated on the sunken mast, her back turned toward the entrance of the secluded amphitheatre-shaped place she selected for her morning's confessional. Her idea was to be deep in meditation, though affected, when the young man arrived and thus make a good impression. She reasoned that if anyone else came by and saw her sitting thus they would think she wished to be alone and pass on.

Rachel stepped eagerly almost up to Nannette before she realized anyone was near. Then hearing the rustle of a dress, Nannette turned quickly to see who was there.

"Oh, Nannette! I'm so glad!" exclaimed Rachel, stooping down and kissing the astonished girl on her forehead. "I'm so glad for you, but I wish there was someone better to help you."

"What do you mean?" said Nannette coldly, pushing her back and looking at her strangely. It had been so long since any girl had cared to kiss her that it made her feel odd.

"There! I've done as I always do and plunged into the middle of things without any beginning," said Rachel, distressed. "Why, Mr. Fairfield had to go to the city this morning. He was called suddenly to a woman who's sick. He stopped at the cottage and told me you were troubled, and you wanted to know how to be a Christian. He asked me if I'd come and tell you the best I could about it. I'm sorry it's only I. If Maria or Mama had been at home one of them would have come. But he was anxious someone should come at the hour to explain why he wasn't here, so I've come and I'll do my best, dear. I do love Jesus, and I think I can tell you a little about Him," she said sweetly. "And, oh, I'm so glad you're going to belong to Him too."

Nannette looked at Rachel blankly.

"And so he's gone!" she exclaimed and broke into a harsh laugh. "Well, I've taken a lot of pains for nothing. It was awfully good of you, Ray, to travel way out here in the sand and sun. And you're no doubt just as good a talker as anyone else, so don't worry your righteous little soul about that. But you don't need to trouble yourself to talk religion to me. I'm not in the mood for it, and it really wouldn't pay you. You'd better keep it for the fisherman's children. I hear you're quite converting them."

Nannette arose to go back, a disagreeable look on her face. She was foiled again, and this time badly. She no longer had any hope of reducing the minister to admire her charms; he was gone. He evidently ran away. She laughed out loud again.

"Rachel, I drove him from the ground. He didn't dare stay and fight. It's a sort of victory, after all."

Rachel, who had been watching her in puzzled silence, was now completely mystified and wondered if Nannette was losing her mind.

"What do you mean, Nannette?" she asked.

"Oh, you dear little goose," laughed Nannette. She didn't have the energy to keep up her "pious dodge," as she called it, for the benefit of a girl. What was the use? It would make no end of trouble for her, so she frankly admitted the part she'd been playing.

"Did you really suppose I was anxious about my soul? Well, you must have known very little, indeed, about me. Don't look so worried. I wasn't doing any harm. The nice little words you fixed up will come in handy for someone else. If you weren't such a blessed little goose, I'd be very angry that he sent someone else in his place."

"But, Nannette, he couldn't come, and I was the only one at hand he could send," said Rachel, with her troubled eyes looking earnestly at the other girl. "Perhaps he didn't have time to explain it all out to me. What was it you wanted of him? I don't understand."

Nannette was very amused. She laughed and laughed, using the black-bordered handkerchief to wipe away tears, genuine for once, even if they were born of mirth instead of grief.

"Well, I'd have been a fool indeed if I lured the minister out here just for the sake of talking religion at me, my little innocent," she said when she could control her laughter enough to speak. "My dear, I wanted to bring him out here for a nice, little, harmless flirtation—that's all. Don't be shocked. I wouldn't have hurt the poor man for anything."

"Oh, Nannette!" exclaimed Rachel in a horrified voice. "Don't say that. You surely don't mean it, that you would plan such a flirtation with a minister?"

Nannette fairly shrieked with laughter now. "And did you suppose, my dear, that because he was a minister he had no heart?" she said between her pearls of laughter.

Rachel was silent for a moment, taking in the meaning of what was told her.

"But, Nannette," she hesitated as a new thought came to her, "aren't you engaged to that other man? The one we met last night? Excuse me, but I couldn't help seeing. I stood on the porch with Fannie De Vere as you walked down the beach, and I saw—him—put—his—arm—"

She stopped. She couldn't bring herself to say more, and the tears were coming to the surface now with the effort she was making to do her duty.

A blush of as much shame as this girl could feel stole suddenly upon her cheek as she saw her own act, which seemed to her an everyday affair, standing out in the light of this sweet, pure soul's ideals. It was perhaps the first time Nannette ever felt any real shame in allowing such familiarity with comparative strangers.

"Oh, little Ray! You are good fun!" she tried to say carelessly. "Why, that was nothing. Any nice man would do that and think nothing of it. Just wait till Roland De Vere tries it with you, and you'll understand."

And then Miss Davenport was treated to such righteous wrath as showed her that the gentle-hearted Rachel Hammond had more spirit in her than she thought.

"Mr. De Vere would never do such a thing!" said Rachel, her bosom heaving and her face flaming. Then, her eyes flashing, she added, "But if he *did,* he would never try it again."

She turned and walked a few steps with dignity. But Nannette, rebuked and not wishing to show it, sprang up.

"Oh, come now, Ray. Don't be too hard on people who haven't risen to your heights. We can't all think alike, you know. I guess you're right about Roland. He's too much of an old granny to do anything of that sort. Come, let's be friends and go home. This sun is broiling. Don't tell your good mama about my escapade, I beg of you, or else she might write to my prim old auntie and have me sent home in disgrace."

Rachel walked along in silence. About her in her everyday life it might be said: "Other hope had she none, nor wish in life, but to follow meekly, with reverent steps, the sacred feet of her Savior."

It wasn't often that anything stirred her soul to the depths as this morning's experience had done. Yet, as she grew calmer, she realized that the girl beside her didn't know Jesus and that she'd started out on a mission to help her find Him. She remembered how she committed her cause to her Master before starting and trusted in Him to bless what she should do. And now she was going home without saying one word that could make this other girl think more of Jesus Christ. Was the fault in her? Would it be casting pearls away to speak now, after what had passed between them? And yet could she in conscience leave her without having at least tried to fulfill her trust?

All the way along the beach she was silent, letting Nannette talk as rapidly and vapidly as she would. Suddenly, as they came in sight of the hotel, Rachel paused beside a side path that turned off from the beach and headed down toward the green cottage, a shorter cut than going around by the hotel.

"Nannette," she said, putting out her hand gently to detain her companion, "I came out this morning to bring you a message from Jesus. I thought you were waiting for it and would be glad to get it. I found you weren't. I'm very sorry. But I believe Jesus sent that message to you all the same, even if you didn't want it, and I must give it to you. Nannette, Jesus loves you, and He wants you to love Him."

The tears were in Rachel's eyes, and she felt that she couldn't trust herself to say another word. So she turned and sped swiftly down the sandy path toward home, and Nannette stood still looking after her, a strange smile upon her face, half of wistfulness and half of ridicule. As Rachel disappeared from sight behind the sand dunes she turned toward the hotel again, murmuring to herself, "She's a good little thing."

And who shall say that Rachel's words were not the seed that often lies long in the cold, black earth before it gives sign of life? But at last it bursts and grows and brings forth fruit.

Chapter 25

After that Nannette plunged into a mad flirtation with Win Hammond. She kept him by her side morning, noon and evening. He was certainly devoted enough to make up for all the chagrin she felt in Howard Fairfield's lack of admiration. He bought her candy and flowers whenever they could be procured in Spray View, regardless of the fact that up till now he had kept before him that money was not to be carelessly spent by any member of the Hammond household now.

Nannette discovered a company of friends at Spray View who were lively enough to suit her and had small private gatherings for card playing and dancing. Nannette, unrestrained by onlookers, took her part now and again and began to feel that the summer wasn't such a bitter failure after all.

After reducing Win Hammond to subjection, she set out to make him drink wine. The young people she went with always drank it at their gatherings. She took him among them on all possible occasions where it was present. She ridiculed him when he declined it, and when he allowed his glass to be filled she dared him to drink with her. He was brought up with a strong feeling against the use of wine, and he didn't readily overcome it. Once or twice he drank to please her, because she made such a point of it.

He was out late at night these times, and his mother was troubled about him. His father went so far as to suggest it might be as well for him to return to his business, if he was going to use his rest time to such a poor advantage. But he answered them all laughingly and went on.

It was evident to the family that he had fallen in love with Nannette Davenport, and each wondered at it. They didn't know how charming she could be when she chose, and they couldn't know she was choosing now to very good purpose. Having been foiled in her first attempt she was angry and determined to take her revenge out on the next victim. She appeared to think a great deal of her admirer. But in truth Mr. Fairfield's intellectual face and severe eyes turned full upon her, often rankled in her soul, and she felt deeply ashamed of herself and her whole life.

Things had been going on this way for about two weeks. No word had come from Mr. Fairfield except an occasional paper or book addressed to Maria and once a large box of beautiful flowers, which came by express and contained no card. Maria treasured all these things, but of course said nothing to Nannette about them.

Maria's life just now was a little hard. She worried daily about her brother and prayed often. She tried to make friends with Nannette so she might, if possible, prevent the intimacy between her and her brother.

Nannette apparently had grown quite discreet. She asked one day as they were walking together, "Say, 'Ri, you wouldn't write to that minister, would you, if you were I? I'd hate to hurt his feelings, but really I don't like letter writing. And when a man's gone, why, he's out of it, you know. If he should come back, of course I'd be nice to him, I suppose, but I hardly like to go so far as to correspond. It seems to mean so much, you know. A man always means a good deal by asking for the privilege, especially a man like that. I haven't written him but once, and I don't believe I shall again, would you?"

Maria answered, "I'd do as I thought best," and turned the conversation to other topics. But she couldn't help thinking that Mr. Fairfield had never asked her to correspond with him. She never knew that Nannette was prompted to these remarks by a chance sight of the box of flowers at the express office addressed to Maria in a handwriting she recognized.

Win Hammond was to return to the city to his business the next morning. He was out, and it was very late. Both his sisters silently kept watch, as did the uneasy mother in the next room, for his footsteps. Rachel lay quiet, lest she should rouse her sister from what she supposed was a happy sleep, and wondered if her brother could ever fall so low as to treat Nannette in the way other young men had. She shuddered at the possibility. Yet she saw enough in that daring girl's face on the day she met her at the inlet to feel that her influence over any man would be tremendous if she chose to exercise it.

She and Maria had both prayed a great deal during the past few days for their brother. Rachel felt that an answer would surely come soon.

Win came at last, but his steps were slow and lagging and didn't sound like him. He entered the sitting room and, instead of going directly to bed, sat down heavily in a chair. Once Rachel thought she heard a groan, and then, since all was still, she waited. Presently her brother threw himself upon the couch and groaned again, this time quite audibly.

Rachel sprang to her feet and, throwing a shawl about her, hurried out to the sitting room. But she found that her mother was there before, and Maria not far behind her. Their brother was ill. He was suffering too much pain to talk or give them any idea of what was the matter. But they could tell he had a high fever. The father started almost immediately for the doctor, while the mother and sisters got him to bed, heated water and gave various simple home remedies. Then they waited anxiously for the coming of the physician.

It was as they feared—typhoid fever. The evenings of pleasure after the nights of nursing had told upon him. The doctor warned them that it was likely to be severe. Then the household settled down into that forced quiet and anxiety of critical illness. Maria insisted upon staying with her brother night and day. Strange to say, though Rachel had always been his favorite, he seemed more satisfied with Maria in the room. During the nights and days of waiting and watching and breathless anxiety, Maria had no time to think of herself.

Whenever she had a moment to herself she spent it in prayer. Her life now was one long prayer.

She sometimes looked back on the happy days when she had been unhappy and unreasonable and wondered at herself.

Then she thought gratefully of Mr. Fairfield and the change he was the instrument, in God's hands, of bringing about in her. She wondered how she could have gone through this long, tedious trial without Jesus as her friend. She seemed literally to be living in His presence now; to be bearing all she bore with His strength, not her own; to be watching His face to see if her brother was to live more years with them or be taken away. She felt an assurance that if God took him He would at least first give him time to take Jesus as his Savior.

He was delirious now for days, didn't know any of them and lay in a stupor. The crisis had come. Maria was sitting by his side, while her mother rested near at hand, to be called should there be a change. She scarcely dared to breathe lest she should disturb the one so dear, who hovered between life and death. Her every breath was a prayer for him. Suddenly he opened his eyes and in a feeble voice that was scarcely audible whispered, " 'Ri, can you pray?"

Maria thought he must by dying. Without waiting, so momentous that instant seemed, she dropped on her knees. In soft, controlled tones she prayed that Jesus might stand by her brother and, loving him, might take his hand and hold him in that moment, for life or death, for time or for eternity. She scarcely knew what she said, as with upturned face and eyes that seemed as though they saw the Lord, she prayed on.

The burning, unnaturally bright eyes upon the pillow watched her, drinking in every word eagerly, as though thirsty, while Maria, praying, pleaded promise after promise from God's Word. Soon the restless look faded from his eyes, and a calm, like a shadow of peace, came. At last the eyelids fell, and Maria knew by the soft, natural breathing that he was asleep. Eventually she rose and called the others, and the doctor coming in told them the crisis was past and the young man would live. Then the sister went away and thanked God.

But her work wasn't yet done. As the invalid grew able to talk he wanted Maria and held long conversations with her about the things of life. Maria felt that she was having her reward for the days and nights of watching, and her soul rejoiced in God her Savior.

All this had been so hard that it seemed to put the summer, with its pleasure and brightness and disappointments, too, far behind her. She looked back to those days when she and Mr. Fairfield had walked and talked together beside the sea, wistfully sometimes, but with the sting gone from her heart.

As soon as Nannette learned the nature of the malady that had befallen her devoted admirer, in dire dread and haste she packed her belongings into her trunks and fled. She had a horror of sickness at all times and a superstitious fear that she would take typhoid fever if she were exposed to it. Besides, her conscience troubled her. She knew it was her fault the young man spent so many evenings out late and was drinking wine, a thing to which he was unaccustomed; and she began to fear this was partly the cause of his illness.

Rachel was grateful she was gone. Yet she was indignant to think that the girl to whom her brother devoted his entire attention for three weeks would depart at once without so much as a good-bye or an inquiry about him when she heard of his serious illness. The rest of the family felt only relief.

The De Veres came daily to inquire and offer aid and in many ways showed their true friendship. Rachel often wondered that no word came from Mr. Fairfield and felt sorry on Maria's account. She recognized he was the means of the change in Maria and was disappointed he left so suddenly, for she had liked him. She laid it all at Nannette's door, however, and tried to forget it.

One day in September, when Lone Point was almost deserted and only one guest remained at the hotel, Maria was sitting on the porch reading out loud to Win, who was convalescing. The city train stole softly up the length of the island, its line of smoke, black against the sky, the only warning of its coming till the whistle blew nearby, for the sand seemed to dull all sound of rushing engine and whirling wheels. The two on the porch were so deep in their reading that they didn't stop to glance at the train, though they could easily have seen from the porch who arrived or departed. It was the morning train too, and few ever came at that hour so late in the season.

Presently a step was heard upon the walk, and, looking up, they saw Howard Fairfield standing before them. The pink rose to Maria's cheek, and the instant flutter of her heart told her she hadn't forgotten, as she'd hoped. Her embarrassment was heightened by his steady, earnest gaze, which seemed to be searching her face for some answer to an unspoken question. He took his eyes from her long enough to shake hands with her brother, who welcomed him heartily. Then he looked back at Maria once more with a glad, hungry look. Something, her downcast eyelids and the color in her cheeks perhaps, brought a half-satisfied expression to his face.

Explanations followed. Mr. Fairfield suddenly went to Europe, as much to his own surprise as theirs. When he reached the city he received word by cable that his sister was to be married at once in Berlin and was earnestly beseeching him to come over, if only for a few days. It was a sudden change of plans, for she wasn't to have married for another year. But her intended husband was about to start on a trip through Palestine, Egypt and the Mediterranean, and she and her mother were to accompany him.

Mr. Fairfield decided hastily, having little time to choose since the only steamer that could bring him in time for the ceremony sailed the next day. Therefore he'd had no time to send them a message telling them where and why he was going and for how long.

It occurred to Win that it would have been unnecessary to send them word, and he didn't understand why Mr. Fairfield thought he should have done so. Then, as he looked at the young man and beyond him at his sister's pink cheeks, a new idea dawned upon him. He whistled softly under his breath and drew his brows together. He didn't want to lose this sister now that he'd just found out what a sister she could be, but then—he looked up at the minister—if she must marry, Fairfield was a fine fellow.

He remembered some things in that sermon he preached just before he left. They had come to his mind during those awful days of fever, and he wished then that he'd taken heed to them before. Mr. Fairfield would help him that way now, and he was glad in his heart he'd come, whether he meant to take Maria away or not.

Then it was Maria's turn to explain how things had gone in Lone Point. She told in a few words the story of her brother's illness. And Win, with a tender voice, praised her, adding still richer color to her cheeks. Howard Fairfield looked steadily at her once more, till she invented an excuse to slip into the house and bathe her burning face.

In time Mr. Fairfield went to the hotel, and when he returned he asked Maria to walk with him. All afternoon Win was left to the tender mercies of his mother and Rachel, who did their best to fill her place.

Maria took with her the much-read and treasured copy of Meyer which Mr. Fairfield left with her when he went away. She thought she would grant his request and read it to him. But though they walked or sat upon the sand the whole afternoon, they didn't read Meyer. They had something even better and brighter and more delightful than that to read—and they read it in each other's eyes.

As once before, they lingered long upon the sands, till the sun went down and the moon came up. And when they arose and started toward the green cottage, they understood one another.

There comes a day when Love, that lies asleep,
The fairest island in the mighty deep,
Wakes on our sight;
There do we stay awhile; but so on again
We trim our sails to seek the open main;
And now, whatever winds and waves betide,
Two friendly ships are sailing side by side.
In port of Love 'twas happy to abide,
But, oh! Love's sea is very deep and wide.

Maria thought something like this as she stood that night, somewhat later, out on the porch alone and looked up into the quiet starlit night. She didn't put it into these words, but her heart felt it all and more. She was very happy. Her whole soul went out to God in thanksgiving for the wonderful beauty He suddenly put into her life. It occurred to her, as it had before, only more force-fully, to thank God that He didn't permit her to have her way and go somewhere else for the summer but had set her just here. How otherwise could she have been brought to know Jesus Christ as a dear personal friend? And, oh, suppose she had never met the minister—her minister!

Chapter 26

Rachel Hammond sat in her room by the open window with her Bible on her knee once more. It was summer again, and they were in their own home. Maria's door was open, and a light breeze stirred the muslin curtain just a little and blew the breath of honeysuckles in. But Maria wasn't seated in the other room, for Maria was gone. Just yesterday she stood in that open doorway in her white robes and bridal veil and kissed Rachel.

On her bed lay the identical white sailor, whose wings and ribbons had been such a trouble a year ago. By some mischance in the packing it was left lying there, for Maria didn't want to take it with her. Rachel looked up, saw it and remembered their talk of a year ago.

Perhaps it was because she was used to opening her Bible at that place that the pages that morning fell open of themselves to the very verse she was reading when Maria grumbled about the summer arrangements and she had left her reading to try to brighten her up: "For me to live is Christ."

How strange it seemed to Rachel as she mused. She remembered just how she had longed, as she laid down her Bible with a sigh that morning, that Maria might feel that verse in all the depth and beauty of its meaning. Now, it seemed to Rachel, that in all her list of acquaintances, not one could so nearly truthfully say that verse as her sister, Maria, unless it might be her brother-in-law, Howard.

How strange it seemed to call him Howard! A real minister in the family! She remembered how she wished she might know one well enough sometime to ask him some questions, and now she had not only a minister but a minister's wife to whom she could go with all her little perplexities and doubts.

A tear stole out and down her cheek as she remembered that Maria's room was empty and Maria wouldn't occupy it anymore or be nearby as her companion. But she laughed and brushed it away.

God was very good. She mustn't weep. She tried to claim that promise, "Delight thyself also in the Lord and he shall give thee the desires of thine heart," and surely He had kept it and given her more even than she asked or desired. She was glad and thankful, even though Maria was gone.

Then, too, there was something in the fact that Maria lived downtown, only a half-hour's ride away. And wasn't she going down in a few minutes with Roland De Vere behind his beautiful team of horses to the new parsonage that the church built for their pastor, to put in place several articles and hang a wonderful picture, the gift of Roland De Vere to the bride? And wasn't there something about this even more personal and more wonderful still for her? Oh, life wasn't shadowed much after all!

Rachel rose and went about her room singing, not knowing how appropriate to her life the words were, and were yet to be:

> Judge not the Lord by feeble sense,
> But trust him for his grace;
> Behind a frowning providence
> He hides a smiling face.
>
> Blind unbelief is sure to err,
> And scan his work in vain;
> God is his own interpreter,
> And he will make it plain.

The Story
of a Whim

Chapter 1

Five Girls, an Organ and the Whim

How cold it is! Let's walk up and down the platform, girls. Why doesn't that train come?"

"I'm going in to see if the agent knows anything about it," said the one with a determined mouth and big brown eyes.

They waited shivering in a group until she returned, five girls just entering womanhood. They were part of a small house party, spending Thanksgiving week at the old stone house on the hill above the station, and they had come down to meet another girl who was expected on the train.

"He says the train is half an hour late," said Hazel Winship, the hostess, coming down the stone steps of the station.

"What shall we do? There isn't time to make it worthwhile to go back to the house. Shall we go inside or walk?"

"Oh, walk, by all means," said Victoria Landis. "It's so stuffy and hot in there that I feel like a turkey half-roasted from the little time we stayed."

"Let's walk up this long platform to that freight house and watch the men unload that car," proposed Esther Wakefield. And so it was agreed.

Victoria was humming. "Oh, girls, why didn't we stay and finish singing that short number? It was so pretty! Listen. Is this right?" And she hummed it over again.

"Yes, it was too bad we had to tear ourselves away from that dear piano," said Ruth Summers. "Say, Hazel, what are you going to do with your poor organ? Send it to a home missionary?"

"I'll send it somewhere, I suppose. I don't know anyone around here to give it to. I wish I could send it where it would give pleasure to someone."

"Plenty of people would probably be delighted with it if you only knew them. The owner of this forlorn furniture, for instance," said Victoria as they threaded their way between boxes and chairs that had been shoved out on the platform from a half-emptied freight car. "Girls, just look at that funny old stove and those uncomfortable chairs! How would you like to set up housekeeping with that?"

"The couch isn't so bad if it were covered," said Hazel, poking it in a gingerly way with her gloved finger. "It looks as though it might have been comfortable once."

"That's Hazel all over!" said Esther. "If it were possible, she'd like to have that couch stay over a train or two while she recovered it with some bright denim and made a pillow for it." Clear girlish laughter rang out, while Hazel's cheeks grew pink as she joined in.

"Well, girls, wouldn't that be interesting? Just think how pleased the dear old lady who owns it would be when she found the new cover, and how entirely mystified."

"You might send her your organ," suggested Ruth Summers. "Perhaps she would like that just as well."

"What a lovely idea!" said Hazel, her eyes shining with enthusiasm. "I'll just do it. Come, let's look for the address."

"You romantic little goose!" exclaimed her friends. "Take her away! The perfect idea! I just believe she would!"

"Of course I would," said Hazel. "Why shouldn't I? Papa said I might do as I please with it. Here—this is a card behind here. Read it. 'Christie W. Bailey, Pine Ridge, Fla.' Girls, I shall *do* it. Who has a pencil? I want to write it down. Do all these things belong to the same person? Look on their cards. She must be very poor."

"Poor as a church mouse," said Victoria, "if this is all she has."

"I'd like to know how you're so sure it's a she," said Emily Whitten. "'Christie' sounds as though it might belong to a man or a boy. Don't you think so, Victoria?"

"It's an old mammy—I'm positive," said Victoria.

"If they're black people," said Hazel, "they'll enjoy it all the more. Black people are fond of music, and it will be a real help for the little children. But I don't believe Christie is an old mammy at all. She's a girl about our own age. She's had to go to Florida on account of her health, and she's poor, too poor to board. So she'll keep house in a room or two"—waving her hand toward the unpretentious huddling of furniture about them—"and perhaps she teaches school. She'll put the organ in the schoolroom or have a Sunday school in her own home, and I'll write her a note and send some music for the children to learn. She can do lots of nice things with that organ."

"Now, Hazel," protested four voices. But just then the shriek of a whistle brought them all about-face and flying down the platform to reach the station before the train drew up. In the bustle of welcoming the newcomer, Hazel's scheme was forgotten. Not until the evening when they were seated about the great open fire did it enter the conversation again.

Victoria Landis told the newcomer about it. "Oh, Marion, you can't think what Hazel's latest wild scheme of philanthropy is."

But Marion, a girl after Hazel's own heart, listened with glowing eyes.

"Really, Hazel?" she said when the tale was finished, looking at her hostess with sympathy. "Won't that be lovely! You must send it in time for Christmas. And why not pack a box to go with it? We could all help. It would be great fun and give us something not entirely selfish to do while we're enjoying ourselves here."

"Do you mean it?" said Victoria. "Well, I won't be outdone. I'll give a covering for that old couch, and Ruth shall make a fantastic sofa pillow for it, like no other pillow seen in any house in Florida. What color—blue or red? And will denim be fine enough, or do you prefer tapestry or brocatelle? Speak up, Hazel. We're with you hand and heart, no matter how wildly you soar this time."

And so amid laughter and jokes the plan grew.

"I have a lot of songbooks, if you think there's really a chance of a Sunday school," said Esther.

"There must be something pretty for the house, a good picture perhaps," mused Ruth Summers.

Hazel's eyes grew bright with joy as she looked from one face to another and saw they really meant what they said.

Six pairs of hands can do much in four days. When the guests left for their various homes or schools, standing on the back porch of the old stone house on the hill were a well-packed box marked and labeled, an organ securely boxed and a large roll, all bearing the magic words "Christie W. Bailey, Pine Ridge, Fla."

There was a great deal of discussion and argument between Mrs. Winship and her husband. They were inclined to think Hazel outdid herself in romance this time, though they were used to such unprecedented escapades from her babyhood. But she finally won them all over; she explained how the goods were put off at that particular freight station from up the branch road, to be put on the through freight at the junction, and enlarged upon the desolation of the life of that young girl who was moving to Florida alone. Finally, every member of the party became infected with pity for her and vied with the others to make that Christmas box the nicest ever sent to a girl.

They began to believe in "Christie" and to wonder whether her name was Christine or Christiana, or simply Christie after some family name. And gradually all thought of her being other than a young girl faded from their minds.

Mother Winship had so far forgotten her doubts as to contribute a good Smyrna rug no more in use in the stone house. She did so after the party went down to the freight house, watched the goods repacked in another freight car for the junction and reported that there wasn't a sign of a carpet in the lot. They also told how they peeked through the crack of a box of books and distinctly saw the worn cover of an arithmetic, which proved the "school-ma'am theory," while an old blue-checked apron, visible through another crack, settled the sex of Christie irrevocably.

Hazel Winship had written a long letter in her delicate handwriting on her finest paper, sealed it with a prayer and gone back to her college duties a hundred miles away. Christmas was fast approaching as the three freight pieces started on their way.

On the edge of a clearing, where the tall pines thinned against the sky and tossed their garlands of gray moss from bough to bough, stood a little cabin built of logs. It was set up on stilts out of the hot white sand, and, underneath, a few chickens wandered aimlessly, as unaware of the home over their heads as mortals are of the heaven above them. Some sickly orange trees, apparently just set out, gave the excuse for the clearing, and beyond the distance stretched away into desolation and blackjack oaks.

A touch of whitewash here and there and a bit of grass—which in that part of the world was so scarce that it was usually used for a path instead of being a setting for that path—would have done wonders for the place. But only the white, neglected, "mushy" sand was there, discouraging alike to wheel and foot.

Inside the cabin were a rusty cookstove, a sulky teakettle at the back and the remains of a meal in a greasy frying pan still over the dead fire. An old table was drawn out with one leaf up and piled with unwashed dishes, boxes of crackers and papers of various foods. The couch in the corner was evidently the old bed, and the red and gray blankets still lay in the heap where they were tossed when the occupant arose that morning. From some nails in the corner hung several articles of clothing and a hat. The corner by the door was given over to tools and a few garden implements considered too good to leave outside. Every chair but one was occupied by books or papers or clothing.

Outside the back door a dry goods box by the pump with a tin basin and a cake of soap did duty as a washstand. On the whole, it was not an attractive home, even though sky and air were more than perfect.

The occupant of this residence was driving dully along the sand road at the will of a stubborn little Florida pony. The pony wriggled his whole body with a motion intended to convey to his driver that he was trotting as fast as any reasonable being could expect a horse to go. In reality, the monotonous sand and scrub oaks were moving past as slowly as possible.

It was the day before Christmas, but the driver didn't care. What was Christmas to one whose friends were all gone and who never gave or received a Christmas gift?

The pony, like all slow things, got there at last and trotted up to the post office in good style. The driver climbed out of the shackly wagon and went into the post office, which served also as a general store.

"Hollo, Chris!" called a sickly looking man from the group at the counter. "Bin a-wonderin' when you was comin.' Got some moh freight fer yoh oveh to the station."

The newcomer turned his broad shoulders about and faced the speaker.

"I haven't any more freight coming," he said. "It's all come three weeks ago."

"Well, but it's oveh theh," insisted the other, "three pieces. Your name mahked plain same's the otheh."

"Somebody sent you a Christmas gift, Chris," said a tall young fellow, slapping him on the shoulder. "Better go and get it."

Chapter 2

A Christmas Box That Didn't Match

T he young man, still insisting that the freight wasn't his, followed the agent reluctantly over to the station, accompanied by several of his companions, who had nothing better to do than see the joke out.

There they were—a box, a bundle and a packing case—all labeled plainly and mysteriously, "Christie W. Bailey, Pine Ridge, Fla."

The man who owned the name could scarcely believe his eyes. He knew of no one who would send him anything. An old neighbor had forwarded the few things he had saved from the sale of the old farm after his father and mother died, and the neighbor had since died himself; so this could not be something forgotten.

He felt annoyed at the arrival of the mystery and didn't know what to do with the things. At last he brought over the wagon and reluctant pony, and with the help of the other men he loaded them.

Christie Bailey didn't wait at the store that night as long as he usually did. He had intended to go home by moonlight but decided to try to make it before the sun set. He wanted to understand about the freight at once. When he went back to the post office he couldn't sit with the same pleasure on a nail keg and talk as usual. His mind was on the wagon load. So he bought a few things and started home.

The sun had brought the short winter day to a sudden close, as it has a habit of doing in Florida, by dropping out of sight and leaving utter darkness with no twilight.

Christie lighted an old lantern and got the things into the cabin at once. Then he took his hatchet and screwdriver and set to work.

First the packing case, for he instinctively felt that herein lay the heart of the matter. But not until he pulled the entire front off the case and took out the handsome organ did he fully realize what had come to him.

More puzzled than ever, he stood back with his arms folded and whistled. He saw the key attached to a card and, unlocking the organ, touched one of the ivory keys gently with his rough finger, as one might touch a being from another world.

Then he glanced about to see where to put it. Suddenly, even in the dull, smoky lamplight, the utter gloom and neglect of the place burst upon him. Without more ado he selected the freest side of the room and shoved everything out of the way.

Then he brought a broom and swept it clean. After that he set the organ against the wall and stood back to survey the effect. The disorderly table and the rusty stove were behind him, and the organ gave the spot a strange, cleared-up appearance.

He didn't feel at home. Something must be done about the confusion behind him before he opened anything more. He felt somehow as if the organ were a visitor and mustn't see his poor housekeeping.

He seized the frying pan, scraped the contents into the yard and called the dog. The dishes he put into a wooden tub outside the door and pumped water over them. Then the mass of papers and boxes on the table and chairs he piled into the darkest corner on the floor and straightened the row of boots and shoes. Having done all he could, he returned to the roll and box still unopened.

The roll came first. He undid the strings with awkward fingers and stood back in admiration once more when he brought to light a thick, bright rug and a Japanese screen.

He spread the rug down and puzzled some time over the use of the screen. Finally he stood it up in front of the worst end of the room and began on his box.

There, at last, on top was a letter in a fine, unknown hand. He opened it slowly, with the blood mounting into his face—he didn't know why—and read:

> Dear Christie:
>
> You see, I'm so sure you're a girl my age that I'm beginning my letter informally and wishing you a very merry Christmas and a glad, bright New Year. Of course you may be an old lady or a nice, comfortable, middle-aged one. Then perhaps you will think we're silly. But we hope and believe you're a girl like us, and so our hearts have opened to you, and we're sending you some things for Christmas.

An account of the afternoon at the freight station followed, written in Hazel's most winning way, conveying the words and ways and almost the voices and faces of Victoria Landis and Ruth and Esther and Marion and the rest.

The color on the young man's face deepened as he read, and he glanced up uneasily at his few poor chairs and miserable couch. Before he read further he went and pulled the screen along to hide more of the confusion.

He read the letter through, and his heart woke up to the world and to longings he never knew he possessed before—to the world in which Christmas has a place and young, bright life gives joy. He read it to the end, where Hazel inscribed her bit of sermon full of good wishes and a prayer that the spirit of

Christmas might reign in that home and the organ might be a help and a blessing to all around.

A look of almost helpless misery crossed the young man's face when he finished. The good old times when God was a reality were suddenly brought into his reckless, isolated life; he knew that God was God, even though he'd neglected Him so long, and that tomorrow was Christmas Day.

Seeking refuge from his own thoughts, he turned back to the brimming box.

The first article he took out was a pair of dainty knit lavender bedroom slippers with black and white ermine edges and delicate satin bows. Emily Whitten's aunt had knit them for her to take to college with her. Since Emily's feet were many sizes smaller than her aunt supposed, she never wore them and tucked them in at the last minute to make a safe place for a delicate glass vase; she said the vase would be lovely to hold flowers on the organ, on Sundays.

The girls wrote their nonsense thoughts on bits of labels all over the things. And the young man read and smiled and finally laughed out loud. He felt like a little boy opening his first Christmas stocking.

Christie unpinned the paper on the couch cover and read in Victoria's large, stylish, angular hand full directions for putting it on the couch. He glanced with a twinge of shame at the old lounge and realized the girls had seen his shabby belongings and pitied him. He resented the whole thing, until the delight of being pitied and cared for overcame his bitterness, and he laughed again.

A soft, restful green was chosen for the couch cover. It couldn't have fit better if Victoria Landis had secretly had a tape measure in her pocket and measured the couch, which perhaps she did on her second trip to the freight house.

Ruth Summers made the two pillows—large, comfortable and sensible, of harmonizing greens and browns and a gleam of gold here and there.

With careful attention to the directions, the new owner dressed his old lounge and placed the pillows as directed, "with a throw and a pat, not *laid* stiffly," from a postscript in Ruth's clear feminine hand. Then he stood back in awe that a thing so familiar and ugly could suddenly assume such an air of ease and elegance. Could he ever bring the rest of the room up to the same standard?

But the box invited further investigation. A bureau set of dainty blue and white, a cover for the top and pincushion to match, were packed inside, with a few yards of material and a rough sketch with directions for a possible dressing table, to be made of a wooden box in case Christie had no bureau.

It was from Emily Whitten, who said she couldn't remember seeing a bureau among the things. But she was sure any girl would know how to fix one up and perhaps be glad of some new things for it.

The young man looked helplessly at these things. He finally walked out into the moonlight and hunted up an old box which he brushed off with the broom and brought inside. He clumsily spread the blue and white frills over its splintery top, then fumbled in the lapel of his coat for a pin and solemnly tried to stick it into the cushion.

He was growing more bewildered with his new possessions. As each one came to light he wondered how he could entertain and keep up to such luxuries.

Mother Winship included a bright knit afghan which looked perfect over the couch. Next came a layer of Sunday school songbooks, a Bible and some lesson leaflets. A card said that Esther Wakefield sent these and hoped they would help in the new Sunday school.

A roll of chalkboard cloth, a large cloth map of Palestine and a box of chalk followed. The young man grew more helpless. This was worse than the bureau set and the slippers. What was he to do with them? *He* start a Sunday school! He would more likely start children in the opposite way from heaven if he continued as he had the last two years.

His face hardened. He was almost ready to sweep the whole lot back into the box, nail them up and send them back where they came from. What did he want with a lot of trash with such burdensome obligations attached?

But curiosity made him return to see what was left in the box, and a glance around his room made him unwilling to give up this luxury.

He looked curiously at the box of fluffy lace things with Marion Halston's card on top. He could only guess that they were some girl's things and wondered vaguely what he should do with them. Then he unwrapped a photograph of the six girls which was hurriedly taken and inscribed, "Guess which is which," with a list of their names written on a circle of paper like the spokes of a wheel.

He studied each face with interest; somehow it was for the letter writer he sought, Hazel Winship. And he thought he should know her at once.

This would be very interesting and pass some of the long hours when there was nothing worthwhile to do. It would keep him from thinking how long it took orange groves to pay and what hard luck he'd always had.

He decided at first glance that the one in the center with the clear eyes and firm mouth was the instigator of all this bounty. As his eyes traveled from one face to another and came back to hers each time, he felt more sure of it. Her gaze held something frank and pleasant in it. Somehow it would not do to send that girl back her things and tell her he didn't need her charity. He liked to think she'd thought of him, even though she did think of him as a poor discouraged girl or an old woman.

He stood the picture up against the pincushion lace and forever gave up the idea of trying to send those things back.

One thing more was in the bottom of the box, fastened inside another protecting board. He took it at last from its wrappings—a large picture, Hofmann's head of Christ, framed in broad, dark Flemish oak to match the tint of the etching.

Dimly he understood who the subject of the picture was, although he'd never seen it before. Silently he found a nail and drove it deep into the log of the wall. Just over the organ he hung it, without the slightest hesitation. He recognized at once where this picture belonged and knew that it, not the bright rug or the restful couch or the gilded screen or even the organ itself, was to set the standard henceforth for his home and his life.

He knew this without its quite coming to the surface of his consciousness. He was weary by this time, with the unusual excitement of the occasion, and perplexed. He felt like a person suddenly lifted up a little way from the earth and obliged against his will to walk along unsupported in the air.

His mind was in a whirl. He looked from one new thing to another, wondering more and more what they expected of him. The ribbons and lace for the bureau worried him, and the lace collars and pincushion. What did he have to do with such things? Those foolish little slippers mocked him with something that wasn't in his life, a something for which he wasn't even trying to fit himself. The organ and the books and, above all, the picture seemed to dominate him and demanded of him things he could never give. A Sunday school! What an absurdity! He!

And the eyes in the picture seemed to look into his soul and to say, quietly enough, that He had come here now to live, to take command of his home and its occupant.

He rebelled against it and turned away from the picture. He hated all the things, and yet the comfort of them drew him irresistibly.

In sheer weariness at last he put out his light and, wrapping his old blankets about him, lay down upon the rug; for he would not disturb the couch lest the morning should dawn and his new dream of comfort look as if it had fled away. Besides, how was he ever to get it together again? And when the morning broke and Christie awoke to the splendor of his things by daylight, the wonder of it dawned, too, and he went about his work with the same spell still upon him.

Now and again he raised his eyes to the pictured Christ and dropped them again reverently. It seemed to him this morning as if that Presence were living and had come to him in spite of all his railings at fate, his bitterness and scoffing, and his feckless life. It seemed to say with that steady gaze: *What will you do with Me? I am here, and you cannot get away from My drawing.*

It wasn't as if his life had been filled in the past with tradition and teaching, for his mother died when he was a little fellow. And the thin-lipped, hard-working maiden aunt who had cared for him in her place, whatever religion she might have had in her heart, never thought it necessary to speak it out beyond requiring a certain amount of decorum on Sunday and regular attendance at Sunday school.

In Sunday school it was his lot to sit under a good elder who read the questions from a lesson leaflet and looked helplessly at the boys who were employing their time in more pleasurable things. The very small amount of holy things he absorbed from his days at Sunday schools failed to leave him with a strong idea of God's love or any adequate knowledge of the way to be saved.

In later years, of course, he listened indifferently to preaching. When he went to college—a small, insignificant one—he came in contact with religious people; but here, too, he heard as one hears a thing in which one hasn't the slightest interest.

He had gathered and held this much, that the God in whom the Christian world believed was holy and powerful and that most of the world's inhabitants were culprits. Up to this time God's love had passed him by unaware.

Now the pictured eyes of the Son of God seemed to breathe out tenderness and yearning. For the first time in his life the possibility of love between his soul and God came to him.

His work that morning was much more complicated than usual. He wasted little time in getting breakfast. He had to clean house. He couldn't bear the idea that the old regime and the new should touch shoulders as they did behind that screen. So with broom and scrub brush he set to work.

He had things in pretty good shape at last and was just coming in from giving the horse a belated breakfast when a strange impulse seized him.

At his feet, creeping all over the white sand in delicate patterns, were wild pea blossoms of crimson, white and pink. He never noticed them before. Weren't they just weeds? But with a new insight into possibilities in art, he stooped and gathered a few of them. Holding them awkwardly, he went into the house to put them into his new vase. He felt ashamed of them and held them behind him as he entered. But with the shame was mingled an eagerness to see how they would look in the vase on the "blue bureau thing."

" 'Will you walk into my parlor?'
Said the spider to the fly,
'Tis the prettiest little parlor
That ever you did spy,"
sang out a rich tenor voice in greeting.

"I say, Chris! What are you setting up for? What does it mean? Ain't going to get married or nothing, are you, man? Because I'll be obliged to go to town and get my best coat out of pawn if you are."

"Aw, now that's great!" drawled another voice, in an English accent. "Got anything good to drink? Trot it out, and we'll be better able to appreciate all this luxury!"

Chapter 3

"And What Are You Going to Say to Her?"

The young man felt a rising tendency to swear. He'd forgotten all about the fellows and their agreement to meet and spend a festive day out. So great was the spell on him that he forgot to put the feminine things away from curious eyes.

There he stood foolishly in the middle of his own floor, with a bunch of "weeds" in his hand which he hadn't the sense to drop. Far off the sound of a cracked church bell gave a soft reminder, which the distant popping of firecrackers at a cabin down the road confirmed, that this was Christmas Day. Christmas Day, and the face of the Christ looking down at him tenderly from his own wall.

The oath that rose to his lips at his foolish plight was stayed. He couldn't take that name in vain with those eyes upon him. The spell wasn't broken even yet.

With a quick settling of his lips and daring in his eyes, he threw back his head and walked over to the glass vase to fill it with water. It was like him to brave it out and tell the whole story now that he was caught.

He was a broad-shouldered young man, firmly built, with a head well set on his shoulders. Except for a certain careless slouch in his gait he might have been fine to look upon. His face wasn't handsome, but he had good brown eyes with deep hazel lights in them that kindled when he looked at you.

His hair was red, deep and rich, and decidedly curly. His gestures were strong and regular. If his face didn't have a certain hardness about it he would have been interesting, but that look made one turn away disappointed.

His companions were both big men like him. The Englishman was loose-jointed and awkward, with pale blue eyes, hay-colored hair and a large jaw with loose lips; he belonged to that large class of second or third sons with a good education, a poor fortune and very little practical knowledge how to better it, so many of whom came to Florida to try growing oranges. The other was handsome and dark, with a weak mouth and daring black eyes which continually warred with one another.

Both were dressed in rough clothes, trousers tucked into boots with spurs, dark flannel shirts and soft riding hats. The Englishman wore gloves and affected a certain loud style in dress. They carried their riding whips and walked undismayed upon the bright colors of the rug.

"Oh, I say now, get off there with those great clods of boots, can't you?"

exclaimed Christie, with sudden housewifely carefulness. "Anybody'd think you were brought up in a barn, Armstrong."

Armstrong put on his eyeglasses—he always wore them as if they were a monocle—and examined the rug carefully.

"Aw, I beg pardon! Awfully nice, ain't it? Sorry I didn't bring my patent leathers along. Remind me next time, please, Mortimer."

Christie told the story of his Christmas gifts in as few words as possible. Somehow he didn't feel like elaborating it.

The guests seized upon the photograph of the girls and laughed hilariously over it.

"Takes you for a girl, does she?" said Mortimer. "That's great! Which one is she? I choose that fine one with snapping black eyes and handsome teeth. She knew her best point, or she wouldn't have laughed when her picture was taken."

Victoria Landis's eyes would have snapped indeed if she'd heard the comments about her and the others. But she was safe out of hearing, far up in the North.

The comments continued most freely. Christie found himself disgusted with his friends. Only yesterday he would have laughed at all they said. What made the difference now? Was it that letter? Would the other fellows feel the same if he read it to them?

But he never would! The red blood stole up in his face. He could hear their shouts of laughter now over the tender girlish phrases. It shouldn't be desecrated. He was glad indeed that he'd put it in his coat pocket the night before.

The letter, the pictures and the things seemed to have a sacredness about them, and it went against the grain to hear the coarse laughter of his friends.

At last they spoke about the girl in the center of the group, the clear-eyed, firm-mouthed one he'd selected for Hazel. His blood boiled. He could stand it no longer. With one sweep of his long strong arm he struck the picture from them with "Aw, shut up! You make me tired!" and, picking it up, tucked it in his pocket.

At this point his companions' fun took a new turn. They examined the table decked out in blue and lace. The man named Mortimer knew the lace collars and handkerchiefs for woman's attire, and they turned upon their most unwilling host and decked him in fine array.

He sat helpless and mad, with a large lace collar over his shoulders. Another hung down in front arranged over the bureau cover, which was spread across him as a background, while a couple of lace-bordered handkerchiefs adorned his head.

"And what are you going to say to her for all these pretty presents, Christie, my girl?" laughed Mortimer.

"Say to her!" gasped Christie.

It hadn't occurred to him before that he would need to say anything. A horrible oppression was settling down upon his chest. He wished that all the things were back in their boxes and on their way to their ridiculous owners. He got up, kicked at the rug and tore the lace finery from his neck, stumbling on the lavender bedroom slippers which his tormentors had stuck on the toes of his shoes.

"Why, certainly, man—I beg your pardon—*my dear girl*," continued Mortimer. "You don't intend to be so rude as not to reply, or say, 'I thank you very kindly'!"

Christie's thick auburn brows settled into a scowl, and the attention of the others was drawn to the side of the room where the organ stood.

"That's awfully fine, don't you know?" remarked Armstrong, leveling his eyeglasses at the picture. "It's by somebody great—I don't just remember who."

"Fine frame," said Mortimer tersely as he opened the organ and sat down in front of it.

And the new owner of the picture felt for the first time in his acquaintance with those two men that they were somehow out of harmony with him.

He glanced up at the picture with the color mounting in his face, half pained for the friendly gaze that was treated so lightly. He didn't in the least understand himself.

But the fingers touching the keys now were not altogether unaccustomed. A soft, sweet strain broke through the room and swelled louder and fuller until it seemed to fill the little log house and be wafted through the open windows to the world outside.

Christie stopped in his walk across the room, held by the music. It seemed to express all he had thought and felt during the last few hours.

A few chords, and the player abruptly reached up to the pile of songbooks above him. Dashing the book open at random, he began playing and in a moment, in a rich, sweet tenor, sang. The others drew near, and each took a book and joined in.

> He holds the key of all unknown,
>   And I am glad;
> If other hands should hold the key,
> Or if He trusted it to me,
>   I might be sad.

The song was a new creed spoken to Christie's soul by a voice that seemed to fit the eyes in the picture. What was the matter with him? He didn't at all know. His whole life was suddenly shaken.

It may be that the fact of his long residence alone in that desolate land, with but a few acquaintances, had made him more ready to be swayed by this sudden stirring of new thoughts and feelings. Certain it was that Christie Bailey was not acting like himself.

But the others were interested in the singing. It had been a long time since they'd had an instrument to accompany them, and they enjoyed the sound of their own voices. They would have preferred, perhaps, a book of college songs or, better still, the latest street songs. But since they weren't at hand and "gospel hymns" were, they found pleasure even in these.

On and on they sang, through hymn after hymn, their voices growing stronger as they found pieces which had some hint of familiarity.

The music filled the house and floated out into the bright summer Christmas world outside. Presently Christie felt rather than saw movement at the window and, looking up, beheld it dark with little, eager faces of the black children. Their supply of firecrackers had given out and, seeking further celebration, were drawn with delight by the unusual sounds. Christie dropped into a chair and gazed at them, his eyes growing troubled and the frown deepening. He couldn't make it out. Here he'd been for sometime, and these little children had never ventured to his premises. Now here they were in full force, their faces fairly shining with delight, their eyes rolling with wonder and joy over the music.

It seemed a fulfillment of the prophecy of the letter that came with the organ. He trembled at the possibilities that might be required of him with his newly acquired and unsought-for property. And yet he couldn't help a feeling of pride that all these things were his and that a girl of such evident refinement and cultivation had taken the trouble to send them. To be sure, she wouldn't have done it at all if she had any idea who or what he was, but that didn't matter. She didn't know, and she never would.

He saw the children's curious eyes wander over the room and rest here and there delighted, and his own eyes followed theirs. How altogether nice it was! What a desolate hole it was before! Why hadn't he noticed?

Amid all these thoughts the concert suddenly closed. The organist turned upon his stool and, addressing the audience in the window, remarked, with a good many flourishes: "That finishes the program for today, dear friends. Allow me to announce that a Sunday school will be held in this place on next Sunday afternoon at half past two o'clock, and you are all invited to be present. Do you understand? Half past two. And bring your friends. Now will you all come?"

Amid many a giggle and a bobbing of round black heads they answered as one boy and one girl, "Yes, sah!" and went rollicking down the road to spread the news, their bare feet flying through the sand, and vanished as they had come.

Chapter 4

A Letter That Wrote Itself

W hat did you do that for?" thundered Christie, suddenly realizing what the outcome of this performance would be.

"Don't speak so loud, Christie, dear. It isn't ladylike, you know. I was merely saving you the trouble of announcing the services. You'll have a good attendance, I'm sure, and we'll come and help you out with the music," said Mortimer in a sweetly unconscious tone.

Christie came at him with clenched fist, which he laughingly dodged and then went on bantering. But the two young men soon left, for Christie was angry and wasn't good company. They tried to coax him off to meet some of their other companions; but he answered shortly, "No," and they left him to himself.

Left alone, he was in no happy frame of mind. He'd intended to go with them. There'd be something good to eat and, of course, something to drink, and cards and a jolly good time all around. He could forget for a little while his hard luck, the slowness of the oranges and his own wasted life, and feel some of the joy of living. But he had the temper that went with his hair, and now nothing would induce him to go.

Could something else be holding him back too? A subtle something which he didn't understand, somehow connected with the letter and the picture and the organ?

Well, if there was, he didn't stop to puzzle it out. Instead, he threw himself down on the newly covered couch, let his head sink down on one of those soft pillows and tried to think.

He took out the letter and read it over again.

When he read the sentences about praying for him, a choking sensation came in his throat such as he hadn't felt since he nearly drowned and realized he had no mother to go to anymore. This girl wrote as a mother might talk, if one had a mother.

He folded the letter and slipped it back in his pocket. Then, closing and locking the door, he sat down at the organ and tried to play it.

Since he knew nothing whatever about music, he didn't succeed very well. He turned from it with a sigh to look up at those pictured eyes once more and find them following his every movement. Some pictures have that power of seeming to follow one around the room.

Christie got up and walked away, still looking at the picture, and turned and came back again. The eyes still seemed to remain upon his face with that strong, compelling gaze. He wondered what it meant, and yet he was glad it had come. It seemed like a new friend.

Finally he sat down and faced the question that was troubling him. He must write a letter to that girl—to those girls—and he might as well have done with it at once and get it out of the way. After that he could feel he paid the required amount and could enjoy his things. It simply wasn't decent not to acknowledge their receipt. But the tug of war was how to do it.

Should he confess that he was a young man and not the Christie they thought, and offer to send back the things for them to confer upon a more worthy subject?

He glanced around on his new belongings with sudden dismay. Could he give up all this? No. He would not.

His eyes caught the pictured eyes once more. He'd found a friend and a little comfort. It had come to him unbidden. He would not bid it depart.

Besides, it would only make those kind people uncomfortable. They would think they'd done something dreadful to send a young man presents, especially one they'd never seen. He knew the ways of the world a little. And that Hazel Winship who wrote the letter—she was a charming person. He wouldn't like to spoil her dream of his being a friendless girl. Let her keep her ideas; they could do no harm.

He would write and thank her as if he were the girl they supposed him. He was always good at playing a part or imitating anyone; he'd write the letter in a girlish hand—it wouldn't be hard to do—and thank them as they expected to be thanked by another girl. That would be the end of it. Then when his oranges came into bearing—if they ever did—he would send them each a box of oranges anonymously, and all would be right.

As for that miserable business Mortimer got him into, he'd fix that up by shutting up the house and riding away early Sunday morning. The children might come to Sunday school to their hearts' content. He wouldn't be there to be bothered or bantered.

In something like a good humor he settled to his task.

He wrote one or two formal notes and tore them up. As he looked about on the glories of his room, he began to feel that such thanks were inadequate to express his feelings. Then he settled to work once more and began to be interested.

My dear unknown friend, he wrote, *I scarcely know how to thank you for the kindness you have showered upon me.*

He read the sentence over and decided it sounded right and not at all as if a man wrote it. The spirit of fun took possession of him; and he made up his mind to write those girls a good long letter and tell them all about his life, only tell it just as if he were a girl. It would while away this long, unoccupied day. He wrote on:

You wanted to know all about me, so I'm going to tell you. I don't, as you suppose, teach school. I had a little money from the sale of Father's farm after he died, and I put it into some land down here planted to young orange trees. I'd heard a great deal about how much money was to be made in orange growing and thought I would like to try it. I'm alone in the world—not a soul who cares in the least about me, and so there was no one to advise me against it.

I came down here and boarded at first but found it would be a good thing for me to live among my trees so I could look after things better. So I had a little cabin built of logs right in the grove and sent for all the old furniture that was saved from the old home, which wasn't much, as most things were sold with the house. You saw how few and poor they were.

It seems so strange to think that you, who evidently have all the good things of the world to make you happy, should have stopped to think and take notice of poor, insignificant me. It is wonderful, more wonderful than anything that ever happened to me in all my life. I look about on my beautified room and can't believe it is I.

I live all alone in my log cabin, surrounded by a lot of young trees which seem to me very slow in doing anything to make me rich. If I'd known all I know now, I never would have come here. But one has to learn by experience, and I'll just have to stick now until something comes of it.

I'm not exactly a girl just like you as you say, for I'm twenty-eight years old, and, judging by your pictures, not one of you is as old as that. You're none of you over twenty-two, if you're that.

Besides, you're all beautiful girls, while I most certainly am not. To begin with, my hair is red, and I'm brown and freckled from the sun and wind and rain. In fact, I'm what is called homely. So, you see, it isn't as serious a matter for me to live all alone down here in an orange grove as it would be for one of you. I have a strong pony who carries me on his back or in my old buckboard and does the ploughing. What work I can't do myself about the grove, I hire to have done, of course. I also have a few chickens and a dog.

If you could have seen my little house the night your boxes arrived and were unpacked, you'd appreciate the difference the things you sent make in my surroundings. But you can never know what a difference they will make in my life.

Here the rapid pen halted, and the writer wondered whether that might be a prophecy. So far, he reflected, he had written nothing that wasn't strictly true, and yet he hadn't revealed his identity.

This last sentence seemed to be writing itself, for he had no idea that the change in his room would make much difference in his life, except to add a little comfort. He raised his eyes; as they met those in the picture, it seemed to be impressed upon him that there was to be a difference, and somehow he wasn't sorry. The old life wasn't attractive, but he wondered what it would be. He felt as if he were standing off watching the developments in his own life as one might watch the life of the hero in a story.

There was one more theme in Hazel Winship's letter which he didn't touch upon, he found, after he went over each article by name and said nice things about them all and what a lot of comfort he would have from them.

He was especially pleased with his sentence about the bedroom slippers and lace collars.

> *They are much too fine and pretty to be worn, especially by such a large, awkward person as I am. But I think they would look nice on some of the girls who sent them to me.*

But all the time he was reading his letter over he felt that something would have to be said on that other subject. At last he started it again:

> *There's a cabin down the road a little way, and this morning a friend of mine came in and played a while on the organ—I can't play myself, but I'm going to learn*—he hadn't thought about learning before, but now he knew he should—*and we all got to singing out of the books you sent. Eventually I looked up and saw the doorway full of little children listening for all they were worth. I presume I can give a good deal of pleasure listening to that organ sometimes, though I'm afraid I wouldn't be much of a hand at starting a Sunday school*—that sentence sounded rather mannish for a girl of twenty-eight; but he had to let it stand, as he could think of nothing better to say—*as I never knew much about such things. Though I'm obliged for your praying, I'm sure. It will give me a pleasant feeling at night when I'm alone to know someone in the world is thinking about me, and I'm sure if prayers can do any good yours ought to.*
>
> *But about the Sunday school—I don't want to disappoint you after you've been so kind to send all the papers and books. Maybe I could give the children some of the papers and let them study the lessons out for themselves. I used to be quite a hand at drawing. I might practice up and draw them some pictures to amuse them some-time when they come around again. I'll do my best.*
>
> *I like to think of you all at college having a good time. My school days were the best of my life. I wish I could go over them again. I have a lot of books. But when I come in tired at night, it seems so lonely here, and I'm so tired I just go to sleep. It doesn't seem to make much differ-ence about my reading anymore, anyway. The oranges won't know it.*

They grow just as soon for me as if I kept up with the procession.

I appreciate your kindness, though I don't know how to tell you how deeply it touched me. I've picked out the one in the middle, the girl with the laughing eyes and the loveliest expression I ever saw on any face to be Miss Hazel Winship, the one who thought of this whole beautiful plan. Am I right? I'll study the others up later.

Yours very truly—

Here he paused and, carefully erasing the last word, wrote: *lovingly, Christie W. Bailey.*

He sat back and covered his face with his hands. A strange, warm feeling came over him while he was writing those things about Hazel Winship. He wondered what it was. He actually enjoyed saying those things to her and knowing she'd be pleased to read them and not think him impertinent.

He wrote a good many promises, after all. What led him to that? Did he mean to keep them? Yes, he believed he did. Only those fellows, Armstrong and Mortimer, shouldn't know anything about it. He would carry out his plan of going away Sundays until those ridiculous fellows forgot their nonsense. And, so thinking, he folded and addressed his letter.

A little more than a week later six girls gathered in a cozy college room—Hazel's—to hear the letter read.

"You see," said Hazel, with a triumphant light in her eyes, "I was right. She's a girl like us. It doesn't matter in the least bit that she's twenty-eight. That isn't old. And for once I'm glad you see that my impulses are not always crazy. I'm going to send this letter home at once to Father and Mother. They were really quite troublesome about this. They thought it was the wildest thing I ever did, and I've been hearing about it all vacation. Now listen!"

And Hazel read the letter amid many interruptions.

"I'll tell you what it is, girls," she said, as she finished the letter. "We must keep track of her now we've found her. I'm so glad we did it. She isn't a Christian, that's evident. And we must try to help her into one and work through her a Sunday school. That would be a work worthwhile. Then maybe sometime we can have her up here for a winter and give her a change. Wouldn't she enjoy it? It can't be this winter, because we'll have to work so hard here in college we'd have no time for anything else. But after we've all graduated, wouldn't it be nice? I'll tell you what I'd like to do. I'd like the pleasure of taking Christie Bailey to Europe. I know she'd enjoy it. Just think what fun it would be to watch her eyes shine over new things. I don't mind her red hair one bit. Red-haired people are lovely if they know how to dress to harmonize with their complexions."

"How fortunate we used green for that couch cover! Christie's hair will be lovely against it," murmured Victoria, in a seriocomic tone, while all the girls set up a shout at Hazel's wild flights of imagination.

"Take Christie Bailey to Europe! Oh, Hazel! I'm afraid you'll be simply dreadful, now that you've succeeded in one wild scheme. You'll make us do all sorts of things and never stop at reason."

Hazel's cheeks flushed. It always hurt her a little that these girls didn't go quite as far in her philanthropic ideas as she did. She'd taken this Christie girl into her heart, and she wanted them all to do the same.

"Well, girls, you must all write to her, anyway, and encourage her. Think what it would be to be down there, a girl, all alone, and raising oranges. I think she's a hero!"

"Oh, we'll write, of course," said Victoria, with mischief in her eye. "But call her a heroine, do, Hazel."

And they all wrote, letters full of nonsense and sweet, tender, chatty letters and letters full of girlish pity, attempts to make life more bearable to the poor girl all alone down in Florida. But a girl who confesses to being homely and red-haired and twenty-eight cannot hold for long a prominent place in the life of any but an enthusiast such as Hazel. Very soon the other five letters dropped off, and Christie Bailey was favored with only one correspondent from that Northern college.

But to return to Florida. That first Sunday morning after Christmas, everything didn't go just as Christie planned.

In the first place he overslept. He had discovered some miserable scales on some of his most cherished trees. He had to trudge to town Saturday morning—the man was using the pony ploughing—and get some whale-oil soap and then spend the rest of the day until dark spraying his trees. It was no wonder he was too tired to wake up early the next day.

Then, when he finally went out to the pony, he discovered that he was suffering from a badly cut foot, probably the result of the careless hired man and a barbed-wire fence. The swollen foot needed attention.

Once the pony was made comfortable, he reflected on what he would do next. To ride on that pony anywhere was impossible. To walk he wasn't inclined. The sun was warm for that time of year, and he still felt stiff from his exertions the day before. He concluded he would shut up the house, lie down and keep still when anyone came to call, and they would think him gone.

With this purpose in view he gave the pony and the chickens a liberal supply of food, so he needn't come out again till evening, and went into the house. But he had no sooner reached there when he heard a loud knocking at the front door, evidently with the butt end of a whip. Before he could decide what to do it was thrown open, and Mortimer and Armstrong entered, with another young Englishman following close behind. Armstrong wore shiny patent-leather shoes and seemed anxious to make them apparent.

"Good morning, Miss Bailey," he said affably. "Glad to see you looking so fresh and sweet. We just called round to help you prepare for your little Sunday school."

Chapter 5

A Sunday School in Spite of Itself

Christie was angry. He stood still, looking from one to another of his three guests like a wild animal at bay. They knew he was angry, and that fact contributed not a little to their enjoyment. They meant to carry out the joke to the end.

The third man, Rushforth by name, stood grinning behind the other two. The joke was so thoroughly explained to him that he fully appreciated it. He was noted for being quick at a joke. Armstong, however, seemed to have a complete sense of the ridiculous.

Firmly and cheerfully they had their way. Christie, knowing resistance was futile, sat down on his couch in glum silence and let them do as they wished.

"I stopped on the way over and reminded our friends in the cabin below that the hour was two-thirty," remarked Mortimer. He pulled a large dinner bell from his side pocket and rang a note or two. "That's to let them know when we're ready to start."

Christie scowled, and the others laughed uproariously.

"Now, Armstrong, you and I will go out and reconnoiter for seats, while Rushforth stays here and helps this dear girl dust her parlor ornaments and brickbats. We'll need plenty of seats, for we'll have quite a congregation if everyone I've asked turns out."

They came back in a few minutes laden with boxes and boards which they arranged in three rows across the end of the cabin facing the organ.

Christie sat and glared at them.

He was very angry and was trying to think whether to bear it out and see what they would do next or run away to the woods. He had little doubt that if he attempted the latter they would all three follow him and perhaps bind him to a seat to witness the performances they'd planned. They were evidently "taking it out of him" for having all this luxury and not taking them into the innermost confidences of his heart about it.

He clenched his teeth and wondered what Hazel would say if she knew how outrageously her idea of a Sunday school was going to be burlesqued.

Armstrong tacked up the chalkboard and got out the chalk. Then, discovering the folded cloth map of the Holy Land, he tacked that up at the end wall where all could see it. Mortimer mapped out the program.

"Now, Rushforth, you pass the books and the lesson leaflets, and I'll stay at the organ and preside. Miss Christie's a little shy about speaking out today, you see, and we'll have to help her along before we put her in the superintendent's place. Christie, you can make some pictures on the chalkboard. Anything'll do. This is near Christmas—you can make Santa Claus coming down the chimney if you like. I'll run the music, and we'll have quite a time of it. We can tell the fellows all about it down at the lake next week, and I wouldn't be surprised if we have a delegation from Mulberry Creek next Sunday to hear Elder Bailey speak—I beg pardon; I mean Miss Bailey. You must excuse me, dear; on account of your freckles I sometimes take you for a man."

Mortimer spread open a Bible that came with the songbooks and actually found the place in the lesson leaflet. He made them listen while he read and declared that Christie ought to give a talk on the lesson. Thus they carried on their banter the whole morning long.

Christie sat glowering in the corner.

He couldn't make up his mind what to do. For some strange reason he didn't want a Sunday school caricatured in his house, especially with that picture looking down upon it all, and yet he didn't know why he didn't want it. He was never squeamish before about such things. The fellows wouldn't understand it, and he didn't understand it himself. But it went against the grain.

Now as dinner time approached he thought they might go if he offered no refreshments. But, no, they had no such idea. Instead, they sent Armstrong outside to the light wagon they'd tied at the tree by the roadside, and he came back laden with a large basket they unpacked.

The basket contained canned meats and jellies and pickles and baked beans and all sorts of canned goods that had to be substituted for the genuine article in Florida, where fresh meat and vegetables were not always to be had.

Armstrong went out again and this time came back with a large case of bottles.

He set it down with a thump on the floor just opposite the picture, while he shut the door. The clink of bottles signified a hilarious hour and carried memories of many times of feasting in which Christie had participated before.

His face crimsoned as if some honored friend had been brought to look upon the worst of his hard, careless life. He suddenly rose with determination. Here was something he couldn't stand.

He drank sometimes, it's true. The fellows knew it. But both he and they knew that the worst things they ever did in their lives were done and said under the influence of liquor. They all had memories of wild debauches of several days' duration, when they had gone off together and not restrained themselves. Each one knew his own heart's shame after such a spree as this. Each knew the other's shame. They never spoke about it; but it was one of the bonds that tied them together, these drunken riots of theirs, when they put their senses at the service of cards and wine and never stopped until the liquor gave out. At such times each knew he would have sold his soul for one more penny to stake at the game, or one more drink, had the devil been about in human form to bid for it.

Not one of them was a drunkard, and few even constant drinkers, partly because they had little money to spend in such a habit. They all had strong bodies able to endure much, and their life out-of-doors didn't create unnatural cravings of appetite. Rather, they forced themselves into these revelries to amuse themselves in a land where there was little but work to fill up the long months and years of waiting.

This case of liquor was not the first in Christie's cabin. He'd never felt before that it was out of place in entering there. But now the picture hung there, and the case of liquor, representing the denial of God, seemed to Christie a direct insult to the One whose presence had in a mysterious way crept into the cabin with the picture.

Also he saw in a flash what the fellows planned. They knew his weakness. They remembered how skilled his tongue was in turning phrases when loosened by intoxicants. They planned to get him drunk—perhaps had even drugged some of the bottles slightly—and then to make him talk or even pray!

At another time this might have seemed funny to him. He hadn't realized before how far he'd gone in the way from truth and righteousness. But now his whole soul rose up to loathe him, his ways and his companions.

A sentence of his mother's prayer for him when he was a little child that hadn't been in his mind for years now came as clear as if a voice had spoken in his ear, "God make my little Chris a good man!"

And this was how it was answered. Poor mother!

What Hazel Winship would think of the scene also flashed into his mind. He strode across that room in his angry strength before his astonished companions could stop him. Taking that case of liquor in his muscular arms, he hurled it far out the open door across the road and into the woods. Then he turned back to the three amazed men.

"You won't have any of that stuff in here!" he said firmly. "If you're bound to have a Sunday school, a Sunday school we'll have. But we won't have any drunken men at it. Perhaps you enjoy mixing things up that way, but I'm not quite a devil yet."

They hadn't known he possessed such strength. He looked fairly splendid as he stood there in the might of right, his deep eyes glowing darker brown and every bright curl trembling with determination.

"Aw! Certainly! Beg pardon!" said Armstrong, settling his eyeglasses that he might observe his former friend more closely. "I meant no harm, I'm sure." Armstrong was always polite. If an earthquake had thrown him to the ground, he would have arisen and said, "Aw! I beg pardon!"

But Christie was master in his own house. The others exclaimed a little and tried to joke with him about his newly acquired temperance principles. But he refused to open his lips further on the subject, and they ate their canned meats and jellies and bread moistened only by water from Christie's pump in the yard.

They had scarcely finished when the first installment of the Sunday school arrived in faded but freshly starched calicoes laundered especially for the occasion. They pattered to the door barefooted, clean and shining. Some of their elders followed, lingering shy and smiling at the gateway, uncertain whether to acknowledge the invitation to "Mr. Christie's" cabin. Mr. Christie had never been so hospitable before. But the children, spying the rudely improvised benches, crept in, and the others followed.

Christie stood scowling in the back end of the cabin. Sunday school was on his hands. He couldn't help it anymore than he could help the coming of the organ and the picture. It was part of his new possessions.

He felt determined that it shouldn't be a farce. How he would prevent it he didn't know, but he meant to do it.

He looked up at the picture again. It seemed to give him strength. Of course, it was only his imagination that it smiled approval after he flung that liquor out the door. But in spite of his own reason, he felt that the Man of the picture was enduring insult here in his house and that he must fight for His sake.

Added to that was Hazel Winship's faith in him and her desire for a Sunday school. His honor was at stake. He would never have gone out and gathered up a Sunday school to nurse to life, even for Hazel Winship. Neither would he have consented to help in one if his permission had been asked. But now, when it was, as it were, thrust upon him, like a little foundling child all smiling and innocent of possible danger to it, what could he do but help it out?

They were all seated now, and a hush of expectancy pervaded the room.

The three conspirators over by the organ were consulting and laughing in low tones.

Christie knew that the time had come for action. He raised his eyes to the picture once more. To his imagination the eyes seemed to smile assurance to him as he went forward to the organ.

Christie quietly took up a songbook and, opening at random, said, "Let's sing number 134." When they began to sing he was surprised to find it was the same song Mortimer had sung first on Christmas morning.

His friends turned in astonishment toward him. They began to think he was entering into the joke like his old self, but instead on his face was a serious look they'd never seen there before.

Mortimer put his fingers on the keys and began at once. Christie had taken the play out of their hands and turned the tables on them. They wondered what he'd do next. This was fine acting on his part, they felt, for him to take the predicament they put him in and work it out in earnest.

The song was almost finished, and still Christie didn't know what to do next.

He announced another hymn at random and watched old Aunt Tildy settle her steel-bowed spectacles over her nose and fumble among the numbers. The Sunday school was entering into the music with zest. The male trio who led was singing with might and main, but with an amused smile on their faces as if they expected developments soon.

Just then an aged black man came hobbling in. His hair and whiskers were white, and his worn Prince Albert coat didn't fit his bent figure; but there was a clerical manner which clung to the old coat and gave Christie hope. When the song was finished, he raised his eyes without any hesitation and spoke clearly.

"Uncle Moses," he said, "we want to begin right, and you know all about Sunday schools. Can't you give us a start?"

Uncle Moses slowly took off his spectacles and put them carefully away in his pocket while he cleared his throat.

"I ain't much on speechifyin', Mistah Bailey," he said, "but I kin pray. 'cause you see when I's talkin' to God den I ain't thinkin' of my own sinful, stumblin' speech."

The choir didn't attempt to restrain their risibles, but Christie was all seriousness.

"That's it, Uncle. That's what we need. You pray." He wondered for an instant whether Hazel Winship was praying for her Sunday school then too.

All during the prayer Christie marveled at himself. He conducting a religious service in his own house and asking somebody to pray! And yet, as the trembling, pathetic sentences rolled out, he felt glad that homage was being rendered to the Presence that seemed to have been in the room ever since the picture came.

"Oh, our Father in heaven, we is all poh sinnahs!" said Uncle Moses earnestly. And Christie felt it was true, himself among the number. It was the first prayer the young man ever remembered feeling all the way through. "We is all sick and miserable with the disease of sin. We's got it *bad*, Lord"—here Christie felt the seat behind him shake. Mortimer was behaving very badly. "But, Lord," went on the quavering old voice, "we know dere's a remedy. Away down in Palestine, in de Holy Land, in an Irish shanty, was where de fust medicine shop of de world was set up, an' we been gettin' de good ob it eber sence. Oh, Lord, we praise Thee today for de little chile dat lay in dat manger a long time ago, dat brung de fust chance of healing to us poh sinners—"

Mortimer could scarcely contain himself, and the two Englishmen were laughing on general principles. Christie raised his bowed head and gave Mortimer a warning shove, and they subsided somewhat. But the remarkable prayer went on to its close, and to Christie it seemed to speak a new gospel, familiar, and yet never comprehended before. Could it be that these poor, ignorant people were to teach him a new way?

By the time the prayer was over, he'd lost his trepidation. The spirit of it put a determination into him to make this gathering a success, not merely for the sake of foiling his tormentors, but for the sake of the trusting children who had come there in good faith.

He felt an exultant thrill as he thought of Hazel Winship and her commission. He would try to do his best for her sake today at least, whatever came of it in future. Neither should those idiots behind him have a grand tale of his breaking down in embarrassment to take to the fellows over at the lake.

Summoning all his daring, he gave out another hymn, which happened fortunately to be familiar to the audience and to have many verses. And he reached for a lesson leaflet.

Oh, if his curiosity had only led him to examine the lesson for today, or any lesson, in fact! He must say something to carry things off, and he must have a moment to consider. The words swam before his eyes. He could make nothing out of it all.

Did he dare ask one of the fellows to read the Scripture lesson while he prepared his next line of action?

He looked at them. They were an uncertain quantity, but he must have time to think a minute. Armstrong was the safest. His politeness would hold him within bounds.

When the song finished, he handed the leaflet to Armstrong, saying briefly, "You read the verses, Armstrong."

Armstrong in surprise answered, "Aw, certainly." Adjusting his eyeglasses, he began, "Now when Jesus was born in Bethlehem—"

"Hallelujah!" interjected Uncle Moses, with his head thrown back and his eyes closed. He was so happy to be in a meeting again.

"Aw! I beg pardon, sir! What did you say?" said Armstrong, looking up innocently.

This came near to breaking up the meeting, at least one portion of it. But Christie, with a gleam of determination in his eye because he'd caught a thread of a thought, said gruffly: "Go on, Armstrong. Don't mind Uncle Moses."

When the reading was over, Christie, annoyed by the actions of his supposed helpers, seized a riding whip from the corner of the room and came forward to where the map of Palestine hung. As he passed his three friends, he gave them such a glare that they instinctively crouched away from the whip, wondering whether he were going to inflict instant punishment upon them. But Christie was only bent on teaching the lesson.

"This is a map," he said. "How many of you have ever seen a map of Florida?"

Several children raised their hands.

"Well, this isn't a map of Florida. It's a map of Palestine, that place Uncle Moses spoke about when he prayed. And Bethlehem is on it somewhere. See if you can find it anywhere. Because that's the place told about in the verses that were just read."

Rushforth suddenly roused to help. He recognized Bethlehem, and at the risk of a cut with the whip from the angry Sunday school superintendent he stepped forward and put his finger on Bethlehem.

Christie's face cleared. He felt that the waters were not quite so deep, after all. With Bethlehem in sight and Aunt Tildy putting on her spectacles, he felt he had his audience. He turned to the chalkboard.

"Now," he said, taking up a piece of yellow chalk, "I'm going to draw a star. That was one of the first Christmas things that happened about that time. While I'm drawing it, I want you to think of some of the other things the lesson tells about. And if I can, I'll draw them."

The little heads bobbed eagerly this side and that to see the wonder of a star appear on the smooth surface with those few quick strokes.

"I reckon you bettah put a rainbow up 'bove de stah, fer a promise," put in old Uncle Moses, " 'cause de Scripture say somewhere, 'Where is de promise of His comin'?' An' de rainbow is His promise in de heavens."

"All right," said Christie, breathing more freely, though he didn't quite see the connection. And soon a rainbow arch glowed at the top over the star. Then desire grew to see this and that thing drawn, and the scholars, interested beyond their leader's wildest expectations, called out: "Manger! Wise men! King!"

Christie stopped at nothing from a sheep to an angel. He made some attempt to draw everything they asked for.

And his audience didn't laugh. They were hushed into silence. Part of them were held in thrall by overwhelming admiration for his genius, and the other part by sheer astonishment. The young men, his companions, looked at Christie with a new respect; they gazed from him to a shackly cow, which was intended to represent the oxen that usually fed from the Bethlehem manger, and wondered. A new Christie Bailey was before them, and they didn't know what to make of him.

For Christie was getting interested in his work. The board was almost full, and the perspiration stood out on his brow and made little damp, dark rings of the curls about his forehead.

"There's room for one more thing. What shall it be, Uncle Moses?" he said as he paused. His face was eager, and his voice was interested.

"Better write a cross down, sah, 'cause dat's de reason for dat baby's comin' into dis world. He came to die to save us all."

"Amen!" said Aunt Tildy, wiping her eyes and settling her spectacles for the last picture.

Christie turned with relief back to his almost finished task. A cross was an easy thing to make.

He built it of stone, massive and strong. And as its arm grew, stretched out to save, something of its grandeur and purpose entered his mind and stayed.

"Now let's sing 'Rock of Ages,'" said Uncle Moses, closing his eyes in a happy smile.

The choir hastily found it and began.

As the Sunday school rose to depart and shuffled out with many a scrape and bow and admiring glance backward at the glowing chalkboard, Christie felt a hand touch his arm. Glancing down, he saw a small girl with great, dark eyes set in black fringes gazing up at the picture above the organ, her little hand on his sleeve.

"Is dat man yoh all's fathah?" she asked him, timidly.

A great wave of color stole up into Christie's face.

"No," he answered. "That is a picture of Jesus when He grew up to be a man."

"Oh!" gasped the little girl in admiration. "Did you draw dat? Did yo all evah see Jesus?"

The color deepened.

"No, I didn't draw that picture," said Christie. "It was sent as a present to me."

"Oh," said the child, disappointed. "I thought you'd maybe seed Him sometime. But He look like you, He do. I thought He was you all's fathah."

The little girl turned away, but her words lingered in Christie's heart. His Father! How that stirred some memory! His Father in heaven! Had he perhaps spoken wrong when he claimed no relationship with Jesus, the Christ?

Chapter 6

"My Father!"

The three young men who came to play a practical joke stayed to clear up. Gravely and courteously they went about the work, piled the hymnbooks neatly on top of the organ, and placed the boards and boxes under the house for further use if needed. The entire Sunday school had declared, upon leaving the house with a bow and a smile, "I'll come again next Sunday, Mistah Christie. I'll come *every* Sunday." And Christie hadn't told them not to.

The young men bid good evening to their host, not once calling him "Miss Christie," voted the afternoon a genuine success and were actually gone.

Christie sank to the couch and looked into the eyes looking down upon him. He was tired. Oh, he was more tired than he'd ever been in his life! He was so tired he'd like to cry. And the pictured eyes seemed yearning to comfort him.

He thought of the words of the little black girl. "Is dat man yoh's fathah?"

"My Father!" he said aloud. "My Father!" The words echoed with a pleasant ring in the silent, lonely room. He didn't know why he said it, but he repeated it again.

And if the traditions of his childhood had been filled with the Bible, a host of verses would have flocked around him. But since his mind hadn't been filled with holy things, he had to learn it all, and his ideas of the Man, Christ Jesus, were vague and crude. Perhaps, as to the children of old, God was speaking directly to his heart.

Christie lay still and thought. Went over his useless life and hated it; went over the past week with its surprises, and then over the strange afternoon. His own conduct surprised him the most, after all. Now why, just *why*, did he throw that case of liquor out the door, and why did he go ahead with that Sunday school? A mysterious power was at work within him. Was the secret the presence of the Man of the picture?

The sun dropped over the rim of the flat, low horizon and left the pines looming dark against a starry sky. All the earth went dark with night. And Christie lay there in the quiet darkness, yet not alone. He kept thinking over what the little girl had said to him, and once again he said it out loud in the hush of the room, "My Father!"

But, as the darkness grew deeper, a luminous halo seemed to be up where he knew the picture hung, and while he rested there with closed eyes he felt that Presence growing brighter. Those kind eyes were looking down upon him out of the dark of the room.

This time he called, "My Father!" with recognition in his voice, and out from the shadows of his life the Christ stepped nearer till He stood beside the couch. Stooping, He blessed him, breathed His love upon him, while he looked up in wonder and joy. And perhaps because he was not familiar with the words of Christ, the young man couldn't recall in what form those precious words of blessing fell on his ear during the dream, or trance, or whatever it might be, that came upon him.

When the morning broke about him, Christie, waking, sat up and remembered, and decided it must have been a dream induced by the unusual excitement of the day before. Yet a wondrous joy lingered with him for which he could not account.

Again and again he looked at the picture reverently and said under his breath, "My Father."

He wondered whether he was growing daft. Perhaps his long loneliness was enfeebling his mind so that he was susceptible to what he always considered superstition. Nevertheless, it gave him joy, and he finally decided to humor himself in this notion. This was the permission of his old self toward the new self that was being born within him.

He went about his work singing.

He holds the key of all unknown,
    And I am glad—

"Well, I *am* glad!" he announced out loud, as if someone had disputed the fact he'd just stated. "About the safest person to hold the key, after all, I guess." And even as a maiden might steal a glance to the eyes of her lover, so the soul in him glanced up to the eyes of the picture.

The dog and the pony rejoiced as they heard their master's cheery whistle, and Christie felt happier that day than he had since he was a little boy.

Toward night he grew quieter. He was developing a scheme. It would be rather interesting to write out an account of the Sunday school, not, of course, the part the fellows had in it, for that mustn't be known, but just the pleasant part, about Uncle Moses and Aunt Tildy. He would write it to Hazel Winship—not that he'd ever send it, but it would be pleasant to pretend he was writing her another letter. He hadn't enjoyed anything for a long time as much as he enjoyed writing that letter to her the other day.

Perhaps after a long time, if she ever answered his letter—and here he suddenly realized he was cherishing a faint hope in his heart that she would answer it—he might revise this letter and send it to her. It would please her to know he was trying to do his best with a Sunday school for her, and she would likely appreciate some of the things that had happened. He would do it this very evening.

He hurried through his day's work with a zest. He had something to look forward to in the evening. It was foolish, perhaps, but surely no more foolish than his amusements the last four years had been. It was innocent, at least, and could do no one any harm.

Then, as he sat down to write, he glanced instinctively to the picture. It still wove its spell of the eyes about him, and he hadn't lost the feeling that Christ had come to him, though he'd never made the slightest attempt or desired to come to Christ. And under the new influence he wrote his thoughts, as one might wing a prayer, scarce believing it would ever reach a listening ear, yet taking comfort in the sending. And so he wrote:

My dear new friend:

I didn't expect to write to you again—at least, not so soon. It seems impossible that one so blessed with this world's good things should have time to think twice of one like me. I don't even know now whether I'll ever send this when it's written, but it will while away my lonely evening to write and give me the pleasure of a little talk with a companion I appreciate very much. And if I never send it, that will be all right.

It's about the Sunday school. You know I told you I could never do anything like that; I didn't know how, and I never dreamed that I could—or would, perhaps I ought to say—more than to give the children the papers you sent and let them hear the organ sometimes. But a very strange thing has happened. A Sunday school has come to me in spite of myself.

The friend who was playing the organ this Christmas morning, when the black children stood at the door listening, as a joke invited them to a Sunday school, and they came. I was vexed because I didn't know what to do with them. Then, too, the friend came, bringing two others, and they all thought it was a huge joke. I saw they were going to act out a farce. While I never had much conscience about these things before, I sensed that it wouldn't be what you would like. Then, too, that wonderful picture you sent disturbed me. I didn't like to laugh at religion with that picture looking on.

You may perhaps wonder at me. I don't understand myself, but that picture has had a strange effect on me. It helped me do a lot of things Sunday that I didn't want to do. It helped me take charge and do something to get that Sunday school to go right. I didn't know how in the least. Of course I've been to Sunday school; I didn't mean that. But I never took much notice of things and how they were done. And I

wasn't one to do it, anyway. I felt unfit, and even more because my
friends were here, and I knew they were making fun. I had them sing a
lot, and then I asked old Uncle Moses to help us out. I wish I could
show you Uncle Moses.

Here the writer paused and seemed to debate a point for a moment, and
then he wrote: *I'll try to sketch him roughly.*

There followed a spirited sketch of Uncle Moses with both hands crossed
on top of his heavy cane, his benign chin leaning forward with interest. One
could fairly see how yellow with age were his whitened locks, how green
with age his ancient coat. Christie had his talents, though there were few out-
lets for them.

It is of interest to note here that, when this letter reached the Northern college, as it did one day, those six girls gathered together and laughed and cried
over the pictures. Finally, after due counsel, Christie Bailey was offered a full
course in a famous woman's college of art. This he smiled over and quietly
declined, saying he was much too old to begin anything like that, which
required that one should begin at babyhood to accomplish anything by it. This
the girls sighed over and argued over, but finally gave up, as they found
Christie wouldn't.

But to return to the letter. Christie gave a full account of the prayer, which
had touched his own heart deeply. Then he described and sketched Aunt Tildy
with her spectacles. He had a secret longing to put in Armstrong with his glasses
and the incident of his interruption with the Bible reading. But, since that
would reflect somewhat upon his character as an elderly maiden, to be found
consorting with three such young men, he restrained himself. But he put an
extra vigor into the front row of little black heads, bobbing this way and that,
singing with might and main.

I knew they ought to have a lesson next, but I didn't know how to
teach it any better than I know how to make an orange tree bear in a
hurry. I determined to do my best, however. I happened to remember
something said in what was read about a star; so I made one and told
them each to think of something they heard in that lesson that they
wanted me to draw. That worked first-rate. They tried nearly every-
thing in the encyclopedia, and I did my best at each till the whole big
chalkboard was full. I wish you could see it. It looks like a Noah's ark
hanging up there on the wall now, for I haven't cleaned it off yet. I
keep it there to remind me that I really did teach a Sunday school
class once.

When they went away, they all said they were coming again, and
I don't doubt they'll do it. I'm sure I don't know what to do with them

*if they do, for I've drawn all there is to draw. As for teaching them
anything, they can teach me more in a minute than I could teach them
in a century. Why, one little child looked up at me with her big, round,
soft eyes, so wistful and pretty, and asked me if that picture on the
wall was my father.*

*I wish I knew more about that picture. I know it must be meant
for Jesus Christ. I'm not quite so ignorant of all religion as not to see
that. There is the halo with the shadow of the cross above His head.
And when the sun has almost set, it touches there, and the halo seems
to glow and glow almost with phosphorescent light until the sun is
gone and leaves us all in darkness. Then I imagine I can see it still
glow out between the three arms of the cross.*

*And now I don't know why I'm writing this. I didn't mean to
when I began, but I feel as if I must tell about the strange experience
I had last night.*

And then Christie told his dream. Told it till someone reading could only
feel as he felt, see the vision with him, yearn for the blessing, and be glad and
wonder always after.

Tell me what it means, he wrote.

*It seems as if there was something in this presence for me. I
can't believe it's all imagination, for it would leave me when day
comes. It has set me longing for something, but I don't know what.
I never longed before, except for my oranges to bring me money.
When I wanted something I couldn't have, before this, I went and
did something I knew I shouldn't, just for the pleasure of doing
wrong, a sort of defiant pleasure. Now I feel as if I want to do
right, to be good, like a little child coming to its father. I feel as if I
want to ask you, as that little soul asked me yesterday, "Do you
all's know that Man?"*

Christie folded his letter and flung it down on the table with his head upon
his hands. With the writing of that experience his strength left him. He felt
abashed in its presence. He seemed to have avowed something, to have made
a declaration of desire and intention for which he was hardly ready yet, and
still he didn't want to go back. He was like a man groping in the dark, not
knowing where he was, or whether there was light, or whether indeed he wanted
the light if there was any to be had.

But before he retired that night he dropped on his knees beside his couch,
with bowed and reverent head. After waiting silently awhile he said out loud,
"My Father!" as if he were testing a call. He repeated it again, more eagerly,

and a third time, with a ring in his voice, "My Father!"

That was all. He didn't know how to pray. His soul had grown no further than just to know how to call to his Father, but it was enough. A kind of peace settled down on him, a feeling that he was heard.

Once more he sensed that he was acting out of all reason, and he wondered whether he could be losing his mind. He, a red-haired, hard-featured orange grower, who only yesterday carried curses so easily upon his lips, and might again tomorrow, to be allowing his emotions thus to carry him away! It was simply childish!

But so deep was the feeling that a Friend was near, that he might really say, "My Father," if only to the dark, that he determined to keep up the hallucination, if indeed it was hallucination, as long as it would last. So he fell asleep again to dream of benediction.

The next day a sudden desire took him to mail that letter he wrote the night before. What harm, since he would never see the girl and since she thought him a poor, forlorn creature—this letter might prove him half daft. But even so she might write him again, which he found he wanted very much when he thought about it. So without giving himself a chance to repent by rereading it he drove the limping pony to town and mailed it.

Now, as the middle of the week approached, a conviction seized superintendent Christie Bailey that another Sunday was about to dawn and another time of trial would perhaps be his. He virtually bound himself to that Sunday school by the mailing of that foolish letter. He could have run away if not for that, and those girls up North would never have bothered their heads anymore about their old Sunday school. What if Mortimer should bring the fellows over from the lake? What if! His blood froze in his veins.

Chapter 7

"I Love You"

After his supper that night he doggedly seized the lesson leaflet and began to study. He read the whole thing through, hints and elucidations and illustrations and all, and then began again.

At last it struck him that the hints for the infant class would about suit his needs, and without further ado he set himself to master them. Before long he was as interested as a child in his plans, and the next evening was spent in cutting out paper crosses as suggested in the lesson, one for every scholar he expected to be present, and lettering them with the golden text.

He spent another evening still in making an elaborate picture on the reverse side of the chalkboard, to be used at the close of his lesson after he led up to it by more simple work on the other side.

He even went so far as to take the hymnbook, select the hymns and write out a regular program. No one should catch him napping this time. Neither should the prayer be forgotten. Uncle Moses would be there, and they could trust him to pray.

Christie was a little anxious about his music, for upon that he depended principally for success. He felt surprised over himself that he so much wished to succeed, when a week ago he hadn't cared. What would he do, though, if Mortimer didn't turn up, or, worse still, if he'd planned more mischief?

But the three friends appeared promptly on the hour, dignity on their faces and helpfulness in the atmosphere that surrounded them. They had no more practical jokes to play. They had recognized that for some hidden reason Christie meant to play this thing out in earnest, and their liking and respect for him were such that they wanted to assist in the same spirit.

They liked him none the less for his prompt handling of the case of liquors. They carried a code of honor in that colony that respected moral courage when they saw it. Besides, everybody liked Christie.

They listened closely to Christie's lesson, even with interest. They took their little prayer crosses, studied them curiously and folded them away in their breast pockets—Armstrong had passed them about, being careful to reserve three for himself, Mortimer and Rushforth—and they sang with a right good will.

And when the time came to leave, they shook hands with Christie like the rest and, without the least mocking in their voices, said they had a pleasant time and would come again. Then each man took up a box and a board and stowed them away as he passed out of the room.

And thus Christie was set up above the rest to a position of honor and respect. This work he had taken up—that they partly forced him to take up—separated him from them somewhat. Perhaps it was this fact that Christie had to thank afterward for his freedom from temptation during those first few weeks of his acquaintance with his heavenly Father.

For how could he have grown into the life of Christ if he had constantly met and drunk liquor with these boon companions?

The new life could not have grown with the old.

Christie's action that first Sunday afternoon made a difference between him and the rest. They recognized it, admired it in him and, therefore, lifted him up. What was there for Christie but to try to act his part?

Before the end of another week a package of books and papers and Sunday school cards and helps arrived from the North, such as would have delighted the heart of the most advanced Sunday school teacher of the day. What those girls could not think of, the head of the large religious bookstore they went to thought of for them. And Christie had food for thought and action during many long, lonely evenings.

And always these evenings ended in his kneeling in the dark, where he imagined the light of Christ's halo in the picture could send its glow upon him, and saying out loud in a clear voice, "My Father." Outside in the summer-winter night was heard only the wailing of the tall pines as they waved weird fingers dripping with gray moss, or the plaintive call of the tit-willow.

With the package a letter for Christie came too. He put it in his breast pocket with eager anticipation and hustled that pony home at a most unmerciful trot; at least, so thought the pony.

When Hazel Winship read that second letter out loud to the other girls, she didn't read all of it. The pages containing the sketches she passed about freely, and they read and laughed over the Sunday school and talked enthusiastically of its future. But the pages which told of the Sabbath evening vision and of Christie's feeling toward the picture Hazel kept to herself.

She felt instinctively that Christie would rather not have it shown. It seemed so sacred to her and so wonderful. Her heart went out to the other soul seeking its Father.

When they left her room that night, she locked the door and knelt a long time praying, praying for the soul of Christie Bailey. Something in the longing of that letter from the South reproached her, that she, with all her enlightenment, was not appreciating to its full the love and care of her heavenly Father. And so Christie unknowingly helped Hazel Winship nearer to her Master.

And then Hazel wrote the letter, in spite of a Greek thesis, "the" thesis in fact, that was waiting and calling to her with urgency—the letter that Christie carried home in his breast pocket.

He didn't wait to eat his supper, though he gave the pony his. Indeed, it wasn't a very attractive function at its best.

Christie was really handsome that night, with the lamplight bringing out all the copper tints and garnet shadows in his hair. His finely cut lips curved in a pleasant smile of anticipation. He didn't realize before how much he wanted to hear from Hazel Winship again.

His heart was thumping as he tore open the delicately perfumed envelope and took out the many closely written pages of the letter—and his heart rejoiced that it was long and closely written. He resolved to read it slowly and make it last a good while.

My dear, dear Christie, it began, *your second letter has come, and first I want to tell you that I* love *you.*

Christie gasped and dropped the sheets upon the table, his arms and face on them. His heart was throbbing painfully, and his breath felt like great sobs.

When he raised his eyes eventually, as he was acquiring a habit of doing, to the picture, they were full of tears. They fell and blurred the delicate writing of the pages on the table, and the Christ knew and pitied him and seemed almost to smile.

No one had ever told Christie Bailey of loving him, not since his mother those long years ago held him to her breast and whispered to God to make her little Chris a good man.

He grew up without expecting love. He scarcely thought he knew the meaning of the word. He scorned it in the only sense he ever heard it spoken of. And now, in all his loneliness, when he had almost ceased to care what the world gave him, to have this free, sweet love of a pure-hearted girl rushed upon him without stint and without cause overpowered him.

Of course he knew it wasn't his, this love she gave so freely and so frankly. It was meant for a person who never existed, a nice, homely old maid, whose throne in Hazel's imagination was located in his cabin for some strange wonderful reason. Yet it was his, too, his to enjoy, for it certainly belonged to no one else. He was robbing no one else to let his hungry heart be filled a little while with the fullness of it.

One resolve he made instantly, without hesitation, and that was that he would be worthy of such love if so be it lay in him to be. He would cherish it as a tender flower that was meant for another but fell instead into his rough keeping; and no thought or word or action of his should ever stain it.

Then with true knighthood in his heart to help him onward he raised his head and read on, a great joy upon him which almost engulfed him.

And I believe you love me a little too.

Christie caught his breath again. He saw it was true, although he hadn't known it before.

Shall I tell you why I think so? Because you've written me this little piece out of your heart-life, this story of your vision of Jesus Christ, for I believe it was such.

I haven't read that part of your letter to the other girls. I couldn't. It seemed sacred. While I know they would have sympathized and understood, I felt perhaps you wrote it just to me, and I would keep it sacred for you.

And so I'm sending you this letter just to speak of that to you. I'll write in my other letter with the rest of the girls, about the Sunday school and how glad we are, and about the pictures and how fine they are—and you'll understand. But this letter is about your own self.

I've stopped most urgent work upon my thesis to write this, too, so you may know how important I consider you, Christie. I couldn't sleep last night, for praying about you.

It was a wonderful revelation to Christie, the longing of another soul that his might be saved. To the lonely young fellow, accustomed to thinking that not another one in the world cared for him, it seemed almost unbelievable.

He forgot for the time that she considered him another girl like her. He forgot everything except her pleading that he would give himself to Jesus. She wrote of Jesus Christ as one would write of a much-loved friend, met often face to face, consulted about everything in life and trusted beyond all others.

A few weeks ago this would indeed have been wonderful to the young man, but that it could have any relation to him—impossible! Now, with the remembrance of his dream and the joy his heart had felt from the presence of a picture in his room, it seemed it might be true that Christ would love even him, and with so great a love.

The pleading took hold upon him. Jesus was real to this one girl; He might become real to him.

The thought of that girlish figure kneeling beside her bed in the solemn night hours praying for him was almost more than he could bear. It filled him with awe and a great joy. He drew his breath and didn't try to keep the tears from flowing. It seemed that the fountains of the years were broken up in him, and he was weeping out his cry for the lonely, unloved childhood he had lost and the bitter years of mistakes that followed.

It appeared that the Bible had a great part to play in this new life put before him. Verses he recognized from the Scripture abounded in the letter; he didn't recall hearing them before, but they came to him with a rich sweetness as though spoken just for him.

Did the Bible contain all that? And why hadn't he known it before? He went to other books for respite from his loneliness. Why had he never known that here was deeper comfort than all else could give?

"Think of it, Christie," the letter said. "Jesus Christ would have come to this earth and lived and died to save you if you were the only one out of the whole earth that was going to accept Him."

He turned his longing eyes to the picture. Was that true? And the eyes seemed to answer, "Yes, Christie, I would."

Before he turned out his light that night he took the Bible from the organ and, opening at random, read, "For I have loved thee with an everlasting love; therefore with loving-kindness have I drawn thee." And a light of belief spread over his face. He couldn't sleep for many hours, for thinking of it all.

There was no question in his mind of whether he would or not. He felt he was the Lord's in spite of everything else. The loving-kindness that had drawn him was too great for any human resistance.

Then with the realization of the loving-kindness came self-reproach for his so long denial and worse than indifference. He didn't understand the meaning of repentance and faith, but he was learning them in his life.

Christie was never the same after that night. Something changed in him. It may have been growing all those days since the things first came, but that letter from Hazel Winship marked a decided epoch in his life. All his manhood rose to meet the sweetness of the girl's unasked prayer for him.

It didn't matter that she didn't think of him as a man. She prayed, and the prayer reached up to heaven and back to him again.

The only touch of sadness about it was that he could never see her and thank her face to face for the good she did for him. He thought of her as some far-away angel who stopped on earth for a little while, and in some of his reveries he dreamed that perhaps in heaven, where all things were made right, he should know her. For the present it was enough that he had her kind friendship and her companionship in writing.

Not for words now would he reveal his identity. And the thought that this might be wrong did not enter his mind. What harm could it possibly do? And what infinite good to him! And perhaps through him to a few of those little black children. He let this thought come timidly to the front.

This was the beginning of the friendship that made life a new thing to Christie Bailey. He wrote long letters, telling the thoughts of his inmost heart as he had never told them to anyone on earth, as he could never have told them to one he hoped to meet sometime, as he would have told them to God.

And the college student found time amid her essays and her activities to answer them promptly.

Her companions wondered why she wasted so much valuable time on that poor "cracker" girl, as they sometimes spoke of Christie, and how she could have patience to write such long letters. But their curiosity didn't go so far as to wonder what she found to say; otherwise they might have noticed that Hazel offered less often to read out loud her letters from the South. But they were busy and only occasionally inquired about Christie now or sent a message.

Hazel herself sometimes wondered why this stranger girl had taken so deep a hold upon her. But the days went by and the letters came frequently, and she never found herself willing to put one by unanswered. Some question always needed answering, some point on which her young convert to Jesus Christ needed enlightenment.

Then, too, she found herself growing nearer to Jesus because of this friendship with one who was just learning to trust Him in such a childlike and earnest way.

"Do you know," she confided to Ruth Summers one day, "I can't make myself see Christie Bailey as homely? It doesn't seem possible to me. I think she's mistaken. I know I'll find something handsome about her when I see her, which I shall someday."

And Ruth smiled mockingly. "Oh, Hazel, Hazel, it will be better then for you never to see poor Christie, I'm sure; for you'll surely find your ideal different from the reality."

But Hazel's eyes grew dreamy, and she shook her head.

"No, Ruth, I'm sure. A girl couldn't have all the beautiful thoughts Christie has and not be fine in expression. There'll be some beauty in her, I'm sure. Her eyes, now, I know are magnificent. I wish she'd send me a picture. But she won't have one taken, though I've coaxed and coaxed."

Chapter 8

Sad News From the North

I n his own heart-life Christie was changing day by day. The picture of Christ was his constant companion. At first shyly and then openly he made a confidant of it. He studied the lines of the face and fitted them to the lines of the life depicted in the New Testament, and without his knowing it his own face was changing. The lines of recklessness and hardness about his mouth were gone. The dullness of discontent was gone from his eyes. They could light now from within in a flash with a joy that no discouragement could quench.

By common consent Christie's companions respected his new way of life. And perhaps after the first few weeks if he'd shown a disposition to return to the old way of doing they might have even attempted to keep him to his new course.

They knew their way was a bad way. Each man was glad at heart when Christie made an innovation. They came to the Sunday school and helped, controlling their laughter admirably whenever Uncle Moses gave occasion. And they listened to Christie's lessons, which, to say the least, were original, with a courteous deference, mingled with a kind of pride that one of their number could do this.

They also refrained from urging him to go with them on any more flings. Always he was asked, but in a tone he came to feel meant they didn't expect him to accept and would perhaps have been disappointed if he had.

Once, when Christie, not thinking, almost assented to go on an all-day ride with some of them, Mortimer put his hand kindly on Christie's shoulder and said in a tone Christie had never heard him use before: "I wouldn't, Chris. It might be a bore."

Christie turned and looked earnestly into his eyes for a minute, then said, "Thank you, Mort!"

As he stood watching them ride away, a sudden instinct made him reach his hand to Mortimer and say, "Stay with me this time, old fellow." But the other shook his head, smiling somewhat sadly, Christie thought, and said as he rode off after the others, "Too late, Chris. It isn't any use."

Christie thought about it a good deal that day as he went about his grove without his customary whistle. And at night, before he began his evening's reading and writing, he knelt and breathed his first prayer for the soul of another.

The winter blossomed into spring, and the soft wind blew the breath of yellow jessamine and bay blossoms from the swamps. Christie's wire fence bloomed out into a mass of Cherokee roses, and among the glossy orange leaves many a white, starry blossom gleamed, earnest of the golden fruit to come.

With his heart throbbing and eyes shining Christie picked his first orange blossoms, a good handful, and, packing them according to the most approved methods for long journeys, sent them to Hazel Winship.

Never any oranges, be they numbered by thousands of boxes, could give him the pleasure that those first white waxen blossoms gave as he laid his face gently among them and breathed a blessing on the one to whom they went, before he packed them tenderly in their box.

Christie was deriving daily joy now from Hazel Winship's friendship. Sometimes when he remembered the tender sentences in her letters his heart fairly stood still with longing that she might know who he was and yet say them to him. Then he would crush this wish down, grind his heel upon it and tell his better self that only on condition of never thinking such a thought again would he allow another letter written to her, another thought sent her way.

Then he remembered the joy she'd already brought into his life and go smiling about his work, singing,

> He holds the key of all unknown,
>   And I am glad.

Hazel Winship spent most of that first summer after her graduation visiting among her college friends at various summer resorts at the seaside or on a mountaintop. But she didn't forget to cheer Christie's lonely summer days— more lonely now because some of his friends had gone North for a while— with bits of letters written from shady nooks on a porch or a lawn, or sitting in a hammock.

Christie, you're my safety valve, she wrote once. *I think you take the place of a diary for me. Most girls use a diary for that. If I was at home with Mother, I might use her sometimes. But there are a good many things that if I wrote her she'd worry, and there isn't any need, but I couldn't assure her. So you see I have to bother you. For instance, there's a young man here—* Christie drew his brows together fiercely. This was a new aspect. There were other young men, then. Of course—and he drew a deep sigh.

During the reading of that letter Christie began to wish there were some way for him to make his real self known to Hazel Winship. He began to see some reasons why what he'd done wasn't just all right.

But there was a satisfaction in being the safety valve, and there was delight in their trysting hour when they met before the throne of God. Hazel suggested this when she first tried to help Christie Christward. They kept it up, praying for this one and that one and for the Sunday school.

Once Christie thought what joy it would be to kneel beside her and hear her voice praying for him. Would he ever hear her voice? The thought almost took his breath away. He hadn't dared think of it again.

The summer deepened into autumn. The oranges, a generous number for the first crop, green disks unseen amid their background of green leaves, blushed golden day by day. And then, just as Christie was becoming hopeful about how much he would get for his fruit, a sadness came into his life that shadowed all the sunshine and made the price of oranges a very small affair. For Hazel Winship fell ill.

At first it didn't seem to be much—a little indisposition, a headache and loss of appetite. She wrote Christie she didn't feel well and couldn't write a long letter.

Then a silence of unusual length came, followed by a letter from Ruth Summers, at whose home Hazel was staying when taken ill. It was brief and hurried and carried with it a hint of anxiety, which, as the days of silence grew into weeks, made Christie's heart heavy.

Hazel is very ill indeed, she wrote, *but she has worried so that I promised to write and tell you why she didn't answer your letter.*

The poor fellow comforted himself day after day with the thought that she had thought of him in all her pain and suffering.

He wrote to Ruth Summers, asking for news of his dear friend. But whether from anxiety over the sick one or being busy about other things, or perhaps from indifference—he couldn't tell—no answer came for weeks.

During this sad time he ceased to whistle. A sadness deepened in his eyes that told of hidden pain, and his cheery ways with the Sunday school were gone.

One day when his heart was especially heavy, and he found the Sabbath school lesson almost an impossibility, the little dusky girl who had spoken to him before touched him gently on the arm.

"Mistah Christie feel bad? Is somebody you all love sick?"

The tears almost filled Christie's eyes as he looked at her in surprise and nodded his head.

"Youm 'fraid they die?"

Again Christie nodded. He couldn't speak; something was choking him. The sympathetic voice of the little girl was breaking down his self-control.

The little black fingers touched his hand sorrowfully. In her eyes was a longing to comfort, as she lifted them first to her beloved superintendent's face and then to the picture above them.

"But you all's fathah's not dead," she pleaded shyly.

Christie caught her meaning in a flash and marveled afterward that a child went so directly to the point, where he, so many years beyond her, missed it. He hadn't learned yet how God has revealed the wise things of this world unto the babes.

"No, Sylvie," he said quickly, grasping the timid little fingers. "My Father isn't dead. I'll take my trouble to Him. Thank you."

The smile that broke over the little girl's face as she said good night was the first ray of the light that began to shine over Christie Bailey's soul as he realized that God was not dead and God was his Father.

When they were gone, he locked his doors and knelt before his heavenly Father, pouring out his anguish, praying for his friend and for himself, yielding up his will, and feeling the return of peace and assurance that God does all things well. Again as he slept he saw the vision of the Christ bending over him in benediction, and when he awoke he found himself singing softly,

> "He holds the key to all unknown,
>   And I am glad."

He wondered whether it was coincidence—and then knew it wasn't—that Ruth Summer's second letter reached him that day, saying that Hazel was at last past all danger and had spoken about Christie Bailey. So she, Ruth, hastened to send the message on, hoping the far-away friend would forgive her for the delay in answering.

After that Christie believed with his whole soul in prayer.

He set himself the pleasant task of writing to Hazel all he felt and experienced during her illness and long silence. When she grew well enough to write him again, he might send it. He wasn't sure.

One paragraph he allowed himself, in which to pour out the pent-up feelings of his heart. But even in this he weighed every word. He began to long to be perfectly true before her and to wish there were a way to tell her all the truth about himself without losing her friendship. This was the paragraph.

"I didn't know until you were silent how much of my life was bound up with yours. I can never tell you how much I love you, but I can tell God about it, the God you taught me to love."

The very next day a note arrived from Ruth Summers saying that Hazel was longing to hear from Florida again and was now permitted to read her own letters. Then with joy he took his letter to the office and not long after received a little note in Hazel's own familiar hand, closing with the words: *Who knows? Perhaps you'll be able to tell me all about it someday, after all.* And Christie, when he read it, held his hand on his heart to quiet the pain and the joy.

"Have you written to Christie Bailey that you're coming?" said Victoria Landis, turning from the window of the drawing room car, where she was studying the changing landscape, so new and strange to her Northern eyes.

"No," said Hazel, leaning back among her pillows. "I thought it would be more fun to surprise her. Besides, I want to see things just exactly as they are, as she has described them to me. I don't want her to go and get fussed up to meet me. She wouldn't be natural at all if she did. I'm positive she's shy, and I must take her unawares. After I've put my arms around her neck in regular girl fashion and kissed her she'll realize that it's just I, the one she has written to for a year, and everything will be all right. But if she has a long time to think about it and conjure up all sorts of nonsense about her dress and mine and the differences in our stations, she wouldn't be at all the same Christie. I love her just as she is, and that's the way I mean to see her first."

"I'm afraid, Hazel, you'll be dreadfully disappointed," said Ruth Summers. "Things on paper are never exactly like the real things. Now look out that window. Is this the land of flowers? Look at all that blackened ground where it's been burnt over, and see those ridiculous green tufts sticking up every little way, with an occasional stiff green palm leaf, as if children had stuck crazy old fans in a play garden. You know the real is never as good as the ideal, Hazel."

"It's a great deal better," said Hazel positively. "Those green tufts, as you call them, are young pines. Someday they'll be magnificent. Those little fans are miniature palms. That's the way they grow down here. Christie has told me all about it. It looks exactly to a dot as I expected, and I'm sure Christie will be even better."

The two traveling companions looked lovingly at her and remembered how near they came to losing their friend only a little while before; they said no more to dampen her high spirits. This trip was for Hazel, to bring back the roses to her cheeks. And father, mother, brother and friends were determined to do all they could to make it a success.

The morning after they arrived at the hotel, Hazel asked to be taken at once to see Christie. She wanted to go alone. But since that wasn't to be considered in her convalescent state, she consented to take Ruth and Victoria with her.

"You'll go out in the orange grove and visit with the chickens while I have a little heart-to-heart talk with Christie, won't you, dears?" she said, as she gracefully gave up her idea of going alone.

The old man who drove the carriage that took them there was exceedingly talkative. Yes, he knew Christie Bailey; most everybody did. They imparted to him the fact that this visit was to be a surprise party and arranged with him to leave them for an hour while he went on another errand and returned for them. These matters planned, they settled down to cheerful talk.

Victoria Landis on the front seat with the interested driver—who felt exceedingly curious about this party of pretty girls going to visit Christie Bailey thus secretly—began to question him.

"Is Christie Bailey a very large person?" she asked mischievously. "Is she as large as I am? You see, we've never seen her."

The old man looked at her quizzically. "Never seen her? Aw! *Oh*," he said dryly. "Wall, yas, fer a *girl,* I should say she *was* ruther *big.* Yas, I should say she was fully as big as you be—if not bigger."

"Has she very red hair?" went on Victoria. She had a purpose in her mischief. She didn't want Hazel to be disappointed too much.

"Ruther," responded the driver. Then he chuckled unduly, it seemed to Hazel, and added, "Ruther red."

"Isn't she at all pretty?" asked Ruth Summers, leaning forward with a troubled air, as if to snatch one ray of hope.

"Purty!" chuckled the driver. "Wall, no, I shouldn't eggzactly call her purty. She's got nice eyes," he added, as an afterthought.

"There!" said Hazel, sitting up triumphantly. "I knew her eyes were magnificent. Now *please* don't say any more."

The driver turned his twinkly eyes around, stared at Hazel and then clucked the horse over the deep sandy road.

He set them down at Christie's gateway, telling them to knock at the cabin door; they would be sure to be answered by the owner, and he would return within the hour. Then he drove his horse reluctantly away, turning his head back as far as he could see, hoping Christie would come to the door. He wanted to see what happened. For half a mile down the road he laughed to the blackjacks and occasionally exclaimed: "No, she ain't just to say *purty!* But she's *good.* I might 'a' told 'em she was good."

This was the driver's tribute to Christie.

Chapter 9

The Discovery

Hazel walked up to the door of the cabin in a dream of anticipation realized. The periwinkles nodded their bright eyes along the border of the path, and the chickens stood there on one kid foot of yellow, just as Christie had described.

She could almost have found the way here alone, from the letters. She drank in the air and felt it give new life to her. And she thought of the pleasant hours she would spend with Christie during the weeks that were to follow and of her secret plan to take Christie back home with her for the winter.

They knocked at the door, which was open, and, stepping in, stood surrounded by the familiar things. All three felt the delight of giving these few simple gifts, which were so little to them when they were given.

Then a merry whistle sounded from the backyard and heavy steps on the board path at the back door, and Christie walked in from the barn with the frying pan in one hand and a dishpan in the other. He had gone out to scrape some scraps from his table to the chickens in the yard.

The blood rushed to his cheeks at the sight of his three elegant visitors. He put the cooking utensils down on the stove with a thud and pulled off his old straw hat, revealing his garnet-tinted hair in all its glory against the sunshine of a Florida sky in the doorway behind him.

"Is Christie Bailey at home?" questioned Victoria Landis, who seemed the natural spokesperson for the three.

"*I* am Christie Bailey," said the young man seriously, looking from one to another. "Won't you sit down?"

There was a moment's pause before the tension broke, and then a pained, sweet voice, the voice of Christie's dreams, spoke.

"But Christie Bailey is a young woman."

Christie looked at Hazel and knew his hour had come.

"No, *I* am Christie Bailey," he said once more, his great, honest eyes pleading for forgiveness.

"Do you really mean it?" said Victoria, with amusement growing in her eyes as she noted his every fine point, noted the broad shoulders and the way he had of carrying his head up, noted the flash of his eyes and the toss of rich waves from his forehead.

"And you're not a girl, after all?" questioned Ruth Summers in a frightened tone, looking with troubled eyes from Christie to Hazel, who had turned quite white.

But Christie was looking straight at Hazel, his soul come to judgment before her, his mouth closed, unable to plead his own cause.

"Evidently not!" remarked Victoria dryly. "What extremely self-evident facts you find to remark upon, Ruth!"

But the others didn't hear them. They were facing one another, these two who held communion of soul for so many months and who, now that they were face to face, were suddenly cut asunder by an insurmountable wall of a composition known as truth.

Hazel's dark eyes burned wide and deep from her white face. The enthusiasm that could make her love an unseen, unlovely woman could also glow with scorn for one she despised. The firm little mouth he had admired was set and stern. Her lips were pallid as her cheeks, while the light of truth fairly scintillated from her countenance.

"Then you have been deceiving me all this time!" Her voice was high and clear, tempered by her late illness, and sharp with pain. Her whole alert, graceful body expressed the utmost scorn. She could have posed as a model of the figure of Retribution.

And in that awful minute Christie met her eye for eye and saw the judgment of "Guilty" pronounced upon him, could only acknowledge it as just and saw before him the blankness of the punishment that was to be his. Yet, he had time to think with a thrill of delight that Hazel was all and more than he dreamed of her as being. He had time to be glad she was as she was. He would not have her changed one whit, retribution and all.

It was over in a minute; with the sentence issued, the girl turned and marched with stately step out of the door down the white path to the road. But the little ripples of air she swept by in passing rolled back upon the culprit a knowledge of her disappointment, chagrin and humiliation.

Christie bowed his head in acceptance of his sentence and looked at his other two visitors, his eyes beseeching them to go and leave him to endure what had come upon him. Ruth was clinging to Victoria's arm, frightened. She had seen the delicate white of Hazel's cheek as she went out the door. But Victoria's eyes were dancing with fun.

"Why didn't you *say* something?" she demanded of Christie. "Go out and stop her before she gets away! See, she's out there by the hedge. You can make it all right with her." Pity was in her voice. She liked the honest eyes and fine bearing of the young man. Besides, she loved fun and didn't like to see this most enticing situation spoiled at the climax.

A light of hope sprang into Christie's eyes as he turned to follow her suggestion. It didn't take him long to overtake Hazel's slow step on the soft, sandy ground.

"I must tell you how sorry I am—" he began before he quite caught up to her.

But she turned and faced him with her hand lifted in protest.

"If you're sorry, then please don't say another word. I will forgive you, of course, because I'm a Christian. But don't speak to me again. I HATE deceit!" Then she turned and sped down the road like a flash, in spite of her weakness.

Christie stood in the road where she left him, his head bared to the winter's sunshine, looking as if he'd been struck in the face by a loved hand, his whole strong body trembling.

Victoria meanwhile was taking in the situation. She noticed Hazel's photograph framed in a delicate tracery of Florida moss. Then she frowned. Hazel would never permit that to stay here now, and her instinct told her it would be missed by its present owner and that he had the kind of honor that would not keep it if it were demanded.

"This mustn't be in sight when Hazel comes back," she whispered softly, disengaging herself from Ruth's clinging hand and going vigorously to work. She took down the photograph, slipped off the moss and, looking about for a place of concealment, hid it in the breast pocket of an old coat lying on a chair nearby. Then, going to the door, she watched for developments. But, as she perceived that Hazel had fled and Christie was dazed, she decided she was needed elsewhere and, calling Ruth, hurried down the road.

"If you miss anything, look in your coat pocket for it," she said as she passed Christie in the road. But Christie was too much overcome to take in what she meant.

He went back to his cabin. The light of the world seemed crushed out for him. Even the organ and the couch and the various pleasing touches that entered his home through these Northern friends a year ago seemed to withdraw themselves from him. It was as if they had discovered the mistake in his identity and were frowning their disapproval and letting him know he was holding property under false pretenses. Only the loving eyes of the pictured Christ looked tenderly at him, and with a leap of his heart Christie realized that Hazel gave him one thing she could never take away.

With something almost like a sob he threw himself on his knees before the picture and cried out in anguish, "My Father!"

Christie didn't get supper that night. He forgot there was any need for anything but comfort and forgiveness in the world. He knelt there, praying, sometimes, but most of the time just letting his heart lie bleeding and open before his Father's eyes.

The night fell, and still he knelt.

Eventually he felt a kind of comfort in remembering the little black girl's words, "You all's fathah's not dead." He was not cut off from his Father. Something like peace settled upon him, a resignation and a strength to bear.

To think the situation over clearly and see whether he could do anything was beyond him. His rebuke had come. He could not justify himself. He had done wrong, though without intention. Besides, it was too late to do anything now. He had been turned out of Eden. The angel with the flaming sword had bidden him think no more to enter. He must go forth and labor, but God was not dead.

The days after that passed slowly and dully. Christie hardly took account of time. He was like one laden with a heavy burden and made to pull it on a long road. He had started and was plodding his best every day, knowing an end would come sometime; but it would be hard and long.

Gradually he came out of the daze Hazel's words had put upon him. Gradually he felt himself forgiven by God for his deceit. But he wouldn't discuss even with his own heart the possibility of forgiveness from Hazel. She was right, of course. He knew from the first that her friendship did not belong to him. He would keep the memory of it safe; and in time, when he could bear to think it over, it would be a precious treasure. At least, he could prove himself worthy of the year of her friendship he had enjoyed.

But thinking his sad thoughts and going about the hardest work he could find, he avoided the public road as much as possible, taking to the little by-paths when he went out from his own grove. Thus one morning Christie emerged from a tangle of hummock land where the live oaks arched high above him, the wild grape and jessamine snarled themselves from magnolia to bay tree in exquisite patterns, and rare orchids defied the world of fashion to find their hidden lofty homes. There he heard voices near and the soft footfalls of well-shod horses on the rich, rooty earth of the bridle path.

He stepped to one side to let the riders pass, for the way was narrow. Just where a ray of sunlight came through a clearing he stood. And the light fell about him, on his bared head, for he held his hat in his hand, making his head look like one from a painting of an old master, all the copper tints shining above the clear depths of his eyes.

He knew who was coming. It was for this he had removed his hat. His forehead shone white in the shadowed road, where the hat had kept off the sunburn, and about his face had come a sadness and a dignity that glorified his plainness.

Hazel rode the forward horse. She looked weary, and the flush in her cheeks was not altogether one of health. She was controlling herself wonderfully, but her strength was not what they had hoped it would be when they brought her to the South. The long walk she took under pressure of excitement almost wore her out. She'd been unable to go out since, until this afternoon, when with the sudden willfulness of the convalescent she insisted on a horseback ride. She'd gone much farther than her two faithful friends thought wise and then suddenly turned toward home, too weary to ride rapidly.

And now she came, at this quick turn, upon Christie standing, sun-glorified, his head inclined in deference, his eyes pleading, his whole bearing one of reverence.

She looked at him, started, and knew him. That was plain. Then, her face a deadly white, her eyes straight ahead, she rode by majestically, with a steady, unknowing gaze that cut him like a knife just glinting by from her in passing.

He bowed his head, acknowledging her right to do thus with him. But all the blood in his body surged into his face and then, receding, left him as white as the girl who just passed by him.

Victoria and Ruth, behind, saw and grieved. They bowed graciously to him as if to try to make up for Hazel's act. But he scarcely seemed to see them, for he was gazing down the narrow shadowed way after the straight little figure sitting her horse so resolutely and riding now so fast.

"I didn't know you could be so cruel, Hazel," said Victoria, riding forward beside her. "That fellow was just magnificent, and you have stabbed him to the heart."

But Hazel had stopped her horse, dropped her bridle, and was slipping white and limp from her saddle to the ground. She had not heard.

It was Sunday morning before they had time to think or talk more about it. Hazel had made them very anxious. But Sunday morning she felt a little better, and they were able to slip into her darkened room, one at a time, and say a few words to her.

"Something must be done," said Victoria decidedly, scowling out the window at the ripples of the blue lake below the hotel lawn. "I can't understand how this thing has taken such a great hold on her. But I feel sure it's that and nothing else that's making her so ill. Don't you think so, Ruth?"

"It's the disappointment," said Ruth with troubled eyes. "She told me this morning that it almost shook her faith in prayer and God to think she prayed so for the conversion of that girl's soul—"

"And then found out it was a creature, after all, without a soul?" laughed Victoria. She never could refrain from saying something funny whenever she happened to think of it.

But Ruth went on.

"It wasn't his being a man, at all, instead of a girl. She wouldn't have minded who he or she was, if it hadn't been for the deceit. She says he went through the whole thing with her, professed to be converted and a very earnest Christian and to pray for other people, and talked about Christ in a wonderful way. And now to think he did it all for a joke, it just crushes her. She thinks he deceived her of course in those things too. She says a man who would deceive in one thing would do so in another. She doesn't believe now even in his Sunday school. And then you know she's so enthusiastic that she must have said a lot of loving things to him. She's just horrified to think she's been carrying on a first-class low-down flirtation with an unknown stranger. I think the sooner she gets away from this part of the country, the better. She ought to forget all about it."

"But she wouldn't forget. You know Hazel. And, besides, the doctor says it might be death to her to go back into the cold now with her present health. No, Ruth, something else has to be done."

"What can be done, Victoria? You always talk as if *you* could do *anything* if you only set about it."

"I'm not sure but I could," said Victoria, laughing. "Wait and see. This thing has to be reduced to plain, ordinary terms and have all the heroics and tragedy taken out of it. I may need your help, so be ready."

After that Victoria went to her room, from which she emerged about an hour later and made her way by back halls and bypaths and finally, unseen, down the road.

She wasn't quite sure of the way, but by retracing her steps occasionally she arrived in front of Christie's cabin just as Aunt Tildy was settling her spectacles for the opening hymn.

She looked about for a few minutes till the singing was well along and then slipped noiselessly through the sand to the side of the house. After a few experiments she discovered a crevice through which she could get a limited view of the Sunday school.

A smile of satisfaction hovered about her lips. At least the Sunday school was a fact. So much she learned from her trip. Then she settled herself to listen.

Christie was praying.

It was the first time Christie's voice had been heard by anyone but his Master in prayer. It happened simply enough. Uncle Moses had been sent away to the village for a doctor for a sick child, and there was no one else to pray. To Christie it wasn't such a trial as it would have been a year ago. He had talked with his heavenly Father many times since that first cry in the night. But he was not an orator. His words were simple.

"Jesus Christ, we make so many mistakes, and we sin so often. Forgive us. We're not worth saving, but we thank You that You love us, even though all the world turn against us, and though we hate our own selves."

Victoria found her eyes filling with tears. If Hazel could only hear that prayer!

Chapter 10

Victoria Has a Finger in the Pie

During the singing of the next hymn the organist came within range of the watcher's eye, and she noted with surprise the young man, Mr. Mortimer, to whom she'd been introduced in the hotel parlor a few evenings before. He was a cousin of those Mortimers from Boston who roomed next to Ruth. He would be at the hotel again. He would be another link in the evidence. For Victoria had set out to sift the character of Christie Bailey through and through.

She was chained to the spot by her interest during the chalkboard lesson, which by shifting her position a trifle she could see as well as hear. But during the singing of the closing hymn she left in a panic. And when the dusky crowd flowed out into the road she was well on her way toward home, and no one save the yellow-footed chickens that clucked about her feet were the wiser.

Victoria didn't immediately make known to Ruth the afternoon's events. She had other evidence to gather before she presented it before the court. She wanted to be sure of Christie before she put her finger in the pie at all. Therefore she was on the lookout for young Mr. Mortimer.

She hoped he'd visit his aunt Sunday evening, but if he did he wasn't in evidence. All day Monday she haunted the piazzas and entrances, but he didn't come until Tuesday evening.

Victoria in the meanwhile made herself agreeable to Mrs. Mortimer, and it didn't take her long to monopolize the young man when he finally came. Indeed, he was attracted to her from the first.

They were soon seated comfortably in two large piazza chairs, watching the moon rise out of the little lake and frame itself in wreaths of long gray moss which reached out lace-like fingers and seemed to try to snare it. But always it slipped through until it sailed high above, serene. Such a great moon and so different from a Northern moon!

Victoria did justice to the scene with a fine supply of adjectives and then addressed herself to her self-appointed task.

"Mr. Mortimer, I wonder if you know a man down here by the name of Bailey, Christie Bailey. Tell me about him, please. Who is he, and how did he come by such a strange name? Is it short for Christopher?"

She settled her fluffy dress about her in the moonlight and fastened her eyes on Mortimer with interest. He felt he had a pleasant task before him to speak of his friend to this charming girl.

"Certainly, I know Chris well. He's one of the best fellows in the world. Yes, his name is an odd one, a family name, I believe—his mother's family name, I think he told me once. No, no Christopher about it, just plain Christie. But how in the world do you happen to know anything about him? He told me once he hadn't a friend left in the North."

Victoria was prepared for this.

"Oh, I heard someone talking about a Sunday school he had started, and I'm interested in Sunday schools myself. Did he come down here as a sort of missionary, do you know?"

She asked the question innocently enough, and Mortimer waxed earnest in his story.

"No, indeed! No missionary about Christie. Why, Miss Landis, a year ago Christie was one of the toughest fellows in Florida. He could play a fine hand at cards and drink as much whiskey as the next one. And there wasn't one of us with a readier tongue when it was loosened up with plenty of drinks—"

"I hope you're not one of that kind?" said Victoria, sincerely, looking at the fine, restless eyes and handsome profile outlined in the moonlight.

A shade of sadness crossed his face. No one had spoken to him like that in a long time. He turned and looked into her eyes.

"It's kind of you to care, Miss Landis. Perhaps if I'd met someone like you a few years ago, I'd have been a better fellow." Then he sighed and continued: "A strange change came over Christie about a year ago. Someone sent him an organ and some things for his room, supposing he was a girl—from his name, I believe. They got hold of his name at the freight station where his goods were shipped. They must have been uncommon people to send so much to a stranger. There was a fine picture, too, which he keeps on his wall, some religious work of a great artist. He treasures it above his orange grove, I believe.

"Well, those things made the most marvelous change in that man. You wouldn't have known him. Some of us fellows went to see him soon after it happened. We thought it would be a joke to carry out the suggestion that came with the organ that Christie start a Sunday school. So we invited neighbors from all around, went up there Sunday and fixed seats all over his cabin.

"He was as mad as could be, but he couldn't help himself. So, instead of knocking us all out and sending the audience home, he just pitched in and had a Sunday school. He wouldn't allow any laughing, either. We fellows had taken lunch and a case of bottles over to make the day a success. When Armstrong—he's the second son of an earl—came in with the case of liquor, Chris rose up mightily. Perhaps you don't know Christie has red hair. Well, he has a temper just like it—and he suddenly rose up and fairly blazed at us, eyes and hair and face. He looked like a strong avenging angel. I declare, he was magnificent. We never knew he had it in him.

"Well, from that day forward he took hold of that Sunday school, and he changed all his ways. He didn't go to any more 'gatherings of the clan,' as we called them. We were so proud of him we wouldn't have let him if he'd tried.

"Some of the fellows come to the Sunday school and help every Sunday —sing, you know, and play. We all stand by him. He's good as gold. Not many could live alone in a Florida orange grove from one year's end to another and keep themselves from evil the way Christie Bailey has. Wouldn't you like to see the Sunday school sometime? I'll get Chris to let me bring you if you say so."

Victoria smilingly said she would enjoy it. Then, her interest in Christie Bailey satisfied, she turned her attention to the young man before her.

"You didn't answer my question a while ago, about yourself." There was pleading in Victoria's voice, and the young man before her was visibly embarrassed. The tones grew more earnest. The moon looked down upon the two sitting there quietly. The voices of the night surrounded them, but they didn't hear. Victoria had found a mission of her own while trying to straighten out another's.

But the next morning early Victoria laid out her campaign. She took Ruth out for a walk, and on the way she told her what she intended to do.

"And you propose to go to Christie Bailey's house this morning, Victoria, without telling Hazel anything of it? Indeed, Vic, I'm not going to do any such thing. What would Mrs. Winship say?"

"Mrs. Winship will say nothing about it, for she will never know anything about it. Besides, I don't care what she says so long as we straighten things out for Hazel. Don't you see that Hazel must understand that she hasn't failed, after all—that the young man was sincere and really meant to be a Christian, and that the only thing he failed in was in not having courage to speak out and tell her she'd made a mistake? He didn't intend any harm, and after it went on for a while, of course, it was harder to tell. Now, Ruth, there's no use in your saying you won't go, for I've *got* to have a chaperone, you know. I couldn't go alone, and I *shall* go with or without you; so you may as well come."

Reluctantly Ruth went, half fearful of the result of this daring girl's plan and only half understanding what she meant to do.

Christie came to the door when they knocked. He looked eagerly beyond them into the sunshine, hunting for another face, but none appeared. Victoria's eyes were dancing.

"She isn't here," she said mockingly, rightly interpreting his searching gaze. "So you'd better ask us in, or you won't find out what we came for. It's very warm out here in the sun."

Christie smiled a sad smile and asked them in. He couldn't guess what they'd come for and waited solemnly for them to speak.

"Now, sir," said Victoria with decision, "I want you to understand that you've been the cause of a great deal of suffering and disappointment."

Christie took on at once a look of haggard misery as he listened anxiously, not taking his eyes from the speaker's face. Victoria was enjoying her task immensely. The young man looked more handsome wearing that abject expression. It would do him no harm to suffer a little longer. Anyway, he deserved it, she thought.

"You were aware, I think, from a letter Miss Summers wrote you, that Miss Winship was very ill before she came down here—that she almost died."

Here Ruth nodded her head severely. She felt like meting out judgment to this false-hearted young man.

"Perhaps you don't know that the long walk she took from your house last week, after the startling revelation she received here, was enough to kill her in her weak condition."

Christie's white, anxious face gave Victoria a flitting twinge of conscience. Possibly the young man had suffered enough already without her adding anything to it, but she went on with her prepared program.

"You also probably don't know that the other day when she was riding horseback she controlled herself until she passed you—and then was utterly overcome by the humiliation of seeing you and slipped from her horse onto the road, unconscious. Since that time she has been hovering between life and death—"

Victoria had carefully weighed that sentence and decided that, while it might be a trifle overdrawn, the circumstances nevertheless justified the statement; for truly they had feared for Hazel's life several times during the last two or three days.

But a groan escaped the young man's white lips, and Victoria, springing to her feet, realized that his punishment had been enough. She walked toward him involuntarily, with pity on her face.

"Don't look like that!" she said. "I think she'll get well. But I also think, since you're to blame for a good deal of the trouble, it's time you offered to do something."

"What could I do?" said Christie in hoarse eagerness.

"Well, I think if you were to explain to her how it all happened it might change the situation somewhat."

"She has forbidden me to say a word," answered Christie in clear misery.

"Oh, she has, has she?" said Victoria, surveying him with dissatisfaction. "Well, you ought to have done it anyway! You should have *insisted!* That's a man's part. She has to know the truth somehow and get some of the tragedy taken out of this, or she'll suffer for it, that's all. And there's no one to explain but you. You see, it isn't the pleasantest thing to find one has written all sorts of confidences to a strange young man. Hazel is blaming herself as any common flirt might do if she had a conscience. But that, of course, though extremely humiliating to her pride, isn't the worst. She feels terrible about your deceiving her and pretending you were a Christian, and she was all the time praying out her life for you, while you were having a joke out of it. It's hurt her self-respect a good deal, but it has hurt her religion more."

Christie raised his head in protest, but Victoria went on.

"Wait a minute, please. I want to tell you I believe she's mistaken. I don't believe you were playing a part in telling her you'd become a Christian, were you? Or that you were making fun of her enthusiasm and trying to see how far she would go, just for fun?"

"I've never written anything in joke to Miss Winship. I honor and respect her beyond anyone else on earth. I have never deceived her in anything except that I didn't tell her who I was. I thought there was no harm in it when I did it, but now I see it was a terrible mistake. And I feel that I owe my salvation to Miss Winship. She introduced me to Jesus Christ. I'm trying to make Him my guide."

The young man raised his head and turned his eyes with acknowledgment toward the pictured Christ as he declared his faith. Victoria and Ruth were awed into admiration.

"I almost expected to see a halo spring up behind his copper hair," said Victoria to Ruth on the way home.

Victoria had arranged to send him word when he could see Hazel, and the two girls went away, leaving Christie in a state of conflicting emotions. He could do nothing. He sat and thought and thought, going over all his acquaintance with Hazel, singling out what he'd told her of his own feelings toward Christ. And she thought he did it all in joke! He began to see how hideous his action was in her eyes. Knowing her pure, lovely soul as he did through her letters, he felt keenly for her. How could he blame her for her condemning him? And that day he found in the breast pocket of his old working coat the photograph of Hazel so prized and so sadly missed since the day of her visit. He had supposed Victoria took it, but now he recalled her words about it as she ran after Hazel. Smiling into the sweet, girlish face, he wondered whether she would ever forgive him.

The next day a note came from Victoria, saying he might call at seven o'clock on Saturday evening, and Hazel could likely see him a few minutes. A postscript in the writer's original style added: *And I hope you'll have sense enough to know what to say! If you don't, I'm sure I can't do anything more for you.*

And Christie echoed the cry too deeply to be able to smile over it.

Victoria had laid her plans carefully. She arranged to spend more time with Hazel than she had, pleading a headache as an excuse from going out for a ride in the hot sun and sending Mrs. Winship in her place more than once. She found that Hazel had no intention of opening her heart to her, so she determined to make a move herself.

Hazel had been very quiet for a long time. Victoria thought she was asleep until at last she noticed a little quiver of her lip and the tiniest glisten of a tear rolling down the thin white cheek.

As though she didn't see she got up and moved around the room a moment and then in a cheery tone began to tell her story.

"Hazel, dear, I'm going to tell you where I went last Sunday. It was so interesting! I wandered off alone out into the country and eventually heard some singing in a little log cabin by the road. I slipped into the yard behind some crape myrtle bushes all in lovely bloom, where I was hidden.

"Through a crack between the logs I could see three rows of black children, and some older people too. And at the organ—there was a nice organ standing against the wall—sat Mr. Mortimer, that young man we met in the parlor the other evening, Mrs. Boston Mortimer's nephew, you know. Some other young men were there, too, and they were all singing.

"After the singing there was a prayer. One of the young men prayed. It was all about being forgiven for mistakes and sins and not being worth Christ's saving. It was a beautiful prayer! And, Hazel, it was Christie Bailey who prayed!"

Chapter 11

A Daring Maneuver

Hazel caught her breath when she heard of Christie's prayer, and a bright flush glowed on her cheek.

"Then he taught the lesson," Victoria continued, "and he did it well. Those little children never stirred—they were so interested. Just as they were singing the closing hymn I left in a hurry so they wouldn't see me."

Victoria had timed her story from the window. She knew the carriage had returned and that Mother Winship would soon appear at the doorway. Hazel would have no chance to speak until she thought about the Sunday school a little while. The footsteps were coming along the hall now, and she could hear Ruth calling to Hazel's brother.

She had one more thing to say. Stepping over close to the couch, she whispered in Hazel's ear: "Hazel, I don't believe he's deceived you about everything. I believe you've done him a great deal of good. Don't fret about it, dear."

Hazel was brighter that evening, and Victoria often caught her looking thoughtfully at her. The next day when they were left alone she said, "Tell me what sort of lesson they had at the Sunday school, Vic, dear."

Victoria launched into a full account of the chalkboard lesson and the odd-shaped little cards, which she couldn't quite see through the crack, that were passed around at the close, and treasured, she could see. Then cautiously she told of the interview with Mr. Mortimer and his account of Christie's throwing the bottles out the door. The story lost none of its color from Victoria's repetition of it. When she finished, Hazel's eyes were bright, and she was sitting up and smiling.

"Wasn't that splendid, Vic?" she said and then, remembering, sank back thoughtfully upon the couch.

Victoria was glad the others came in just then and she could slip away. She had said all she wished to say at present and would let things rest now until Saturday evening when Christie came.

Victoria had arranged with Mrs. Winship to stay upstairs and have dinner with Hazel on Saturday evening while the family with Ruth Summers went down to the dining room. She also arranged with the head waiter to send up Hazel's dinner early. And so with much maneuvering the coast was clear at seven, Hazel's dinner and her own disposed of, and the family just gone down to the dining room, where they would be safe for at least an hour.

It was no part of Victoria's plan that Mother Winship or Tom or the judge should come in at an inopportune moment and complicate matters until Hazel had had everything fully explained to her. After that Victoria felt that she would wash her hands of the whole thing.

Mother Winship had just rustled down the hall, and Victoria, who was standing by the hall door waiting until she was gone, walked over to where Hazel sat in a great soft chair by an open fire of pine knots.

"Hazel," she said in her matter-of-fact, everyday tone, "Christie Bailey has come to find out if he may see you for a few minutes. He wants to say a few words of explanation to you. He's really suffered very much, and perhaps you'll feel less humiliated by this whole thing if you let him explain. Do you feel able to see him now?"

Hazel looked up, a bright flush on her cheeks.

Victoria did not betray by so much as the flicker of an eyelash that she was anxious about the outcome of this simple proposal. Hazel's clear eyes searched her face, and she bore the scrutiny well.

Then Hazel sighed a troubled little breath and said: "Yes, I'll see him, Vic. I feel quite strong tonight, and—I guess it will be better, after all, for me to see him."

Then Victoria felt sure it was a relief for him to come and that Hazel had been longing for it for several days.

Christie walked in solemnly with the tread of one who entered a sacred place and yet with the quiet dignity of a "gentleman unafraid." Indeed, so far had the object of his visit dominated him that he forgot to shrink from contact with the fashionable world from which he had been so entirely shut away for so long.

He was going to see Hazel. It was the opportunity of his life. As to what came after, it didn't matter, now that the great privilege of entering her presence had been accorded him. He hadn't permitted himself to believe she would see him even after he sent up his card, as directed, to Miss Landis.

Victoria shut the door gently behind him and left them together. She had prepared a chair not far away, where she might sit and guard the door against intrusion. So she sat and listened to the faraway hum of voices in the dining room, the tinkle of silver and glass, and the occasional burst from the orchestra in the balcony above the dining room. But her heart stood still outside the closed door and wondered whether she had done well or ill, and she feared—now that she had done it—all evil things that can pass in review at such a time for judgment on one's own deeds.

Christie stood still before Hazel. The sight of her so thin and white, changed even from a week ago, startled him—condemned him again, took away his power of speech for the moment.

She was dressed in soft white cashmere, with delicate lace that fell over the little white wrists like petals of a flower. Her silken brown hair made a halo for her face and was drawn simply and carelessly together at the back. Christie had never seen anyone half so lovely. He caught his breath in admiration of her.

For one long minute they looked at each other. Then Hazel, who felt it hers to speak first, since she had silenced him before, said, as a young queen might have said, with just the shadow of a smile flickering over her face, "You may sit down."

The gracious permission, with a slight indication of the chair facing her own by the fire, broke the spell that bound Christie's tongue. With a heart beating high over what he came to say he began.

The words he spoke were not the carefully planned words he had arranged to set before her. They had fled and left his soul bare before her gaze. He had nothing to tell but the story of himself.

"You think I've deceived you," he said, speaking rapidly because his heart was beating in great, quick bounds. "Because I owe to you all the good I have in life I've come to tell you the whole truth about myself. I thank you for giving me a few minutes to speak to you, and I'll try not to weary you. I've been too much trouble to you already.

"I was a little boy when my mother died—" Christie lowered his head as he talked now, and the firelight played fanciful lights and shades with the richness of his hair.

"Nobody loved me that I know of, unless it was my father. If he did, he never showed it. He was a silent man and grieved about my mother's death. I was a homely little fellow, and they've always said I had the temper of my hair. My aunt used to say I was hard to manage. I think that was true. I must have had some love in my heart, but nothing but my mother ever brought it out. I went through school at war with all my teachers. I got through because I naturally liked books.

"Father wanted me to be a farmer, but I wanted to go to college. So he gave me a certain sum of money and sent me. I used the money as I pleased, sometimes wisely and sometimes unwisely. When I ran out of money, I earned some more or went without it. Father was not the kind of man to be asked for more. I had a good time in college, though I can't say I ranked as well as I might have. I studied what I pleased and left other things alone. Father died before I graduated, and the aunt who kept house for him soon followed. When I was through college, I had no one to go to and no one to care where I went.

"Father signed a note for a man a little while before he died, with the usual result of such things, and there was very little remaining for him to leave to me. What there was I took and came to Florida—I had a reckless longing to see a new part of the world and make a spot for myself. I'd never known what home was since I was a little fellow, and I believe I was homesick for a home and something to call my own. Land was cheap, and it was easy to work, I thought, and my head was filled with dreams of my future. But I soon saw that oranges didn't grow in a day and produce fortunes.

"Life was an awfully empty thing. Sometimes I used to lie awake at night and wonder what death would be, and if it wouldn't be as well to try it. But something in my mother's prayer for me when I was almost a baby always kept me from it. She used to pray, 'God make my little Chris a good man.'

"After a while I got acquainted with a lot of other fellows in the same fix with me. They were sick of life—at least, the life down here, and hard work and interminable waiting. But they'd found something more pleasant than death to make them forget.

"I went with them and tried their way. They played cards. I played too. I could play well. We would drink and drink, and play and drink again—"

A little moan escaped from the listener, and Christie looked up to find her eyes filled with tears and her fingers clutching the arms of the chair till the nails were pink against the fingertips with the pressure.

"Oh, I'm doing you more harm!" exclaimed Christie. "I'll stop!"

"No, no," said Hazel. "Go on, please." She turned her face aside to brush away the tears that had gathered.

"I was always ashamed when it was over. It made me hate myself and life all the more. I often used to acknowledge to myself that I was doing about as much as I could to see that my mother's prayer didn't get answered. But still I went on just the same way every so often. There didn't seem to be anything else to do.

"Then the night before Christmas came. It wasn't anything to me more than any other day. It hadn't been since I was a baby. Mother used to fill my stocking with little things. I remember it just once.

"But this Christmas I felt particularly down. The orange trees weren't doing as well as I'd hoped. I was depressed by the horror of the monotony of my life, behind and before. Then your things came, and a new world opened before me.

"I wasn't very glad of it at first. I'm afraid I resented your kindness a little. Then I began to see they'd brought something homelike with them, and I couldn't help liking it. But your letter gave me a strange feeling. There seemed to be obligations I couldn't fulfill. I didn't like to keep the things, because you wanted a Sunday school. I was much more likely to conduct a saloon or a pool room at that time than a Sunday school.

"Then I hung that picture up. You know what effect it had on me. I've told you about my strange dream or vision or whatever it was. Yes, it was all true. I never deceived you about that or anything else except that I didn't tell you I wasn't what you supposed. I thought it might embarrass you if I did so at first, and then it seemed only a joke to answer you as if I were a girl. I never dreamed it would go beyond that first letter when I wrote thanking you."

His honest eyes were on her face, and Hazel couldn't doubt him.

"And then, when the writing went on, and the time came when I should have told you, something else held me back. Forgive me for speaking of it, but I'm trying to be perfectly true tonight. You remember in that second letter that you wrote me, where you told me that you were praying for me, and—you—" Christie caught his breath and murmured the words low and reverently, "You said you loved me—"

"Oh!" gasped Hazel, clasping her hands over her face, while the blood rushed up to her temples.

Chapter 12

The Whim Completes Its Justification

Forgive me!" he pleaded. "It doesn't need to hurt you. I knew that love wasn't really mine. You gave it to the girl you thought I was. I knew without ever seeing you that you would sooner have cut out your tongue than write anything like that to a strange man. I should have seen at once that I was stealing something that didn't belong to me in taking that love.

"Maybe I wouldn't have put it from me even if I'd seen it. For that love was very dear to me. Remember I was never loved in my whole life by anyone but a mother who had been gone for so many years! Remember there was no one else to claim that love from you.

"And remember I thought you'd never need to know. I never dreamed you'd try to search me out. Your friendship was too dear for me to try. And, too, I knew you would consider me far beneath you. I could never hope to have you for the most distant friend, even if you knew all about me from childhood.

"My hope for your help and comfort and friendship was in letting you imagine me as a lonely old maid. Remember you said it yourself. I simply didn't tell you what I was.

"But I don't take one bit of blame from myself. I see now that I ought to have been a good enough man to tell you at once. I should have missed a great deal, perhaps, as human vision sees it, have missed even heaven itself, unless the very giving up of heaven for right had gained heaven for me.

"I can see it was all wrong. The Father even then spoke to my heart. He would have found me in some other way, perhaps. It would have been your doing all the same, and I'd have had the joy of thanking you even so for my salvation. But I didn't, and now my punishment is that I have brought this suffering and disappointment and chagrin upon you. And if I could I'd wipe out of my life the joy that has come to me through companionship with you by letters, if by so doing I might save you from this problem.

"I have one more thing to tell you. Remember that only once, in so many words, have I dared to tell you this in writing, and then only in a hidden way, because I thought if you knew all about me you wouldn't want me to say it. But now I must say it. My punishment is very great, not only that you suffer, but that I've deserved your scorn—for I love you! I love you with every bit of unused love from my childhood days, along with all the love a man's heart has to give. I've loved you ever since the night I read from your letter that you loved me—a poor, forlorn, homely girl as you thought—and that you thought I loved you too. I knew at once that it was so.

"I want you to know that ever since that night I determined to be a person worthy of loving you. I never dared put it 'worthy of your love,' because I knew that could never be for me. But I've tried to make myself a man you wouldn't be ashamed to have love you, even though you could never think of loving in return. And I've fallen short in your eyes, I know. But in what you didn't know of my life I've been true.

"Can you, knowing all this, forgive me? Then I'll go out and try to live my life as you and God would have me do, and remember the joy that wasn't mine. But you gave me one joy that you can't take away. Jesus Christ is my Friend.

"Now I've said all there is to say, and I must go away and let you rest. Can you find it in your heart to say you forgive me?"

Christie rested his elbow on the arm of her chair and dropped his head on his hand, while the firelight flickered and glowed among the waves of ruddy hair again. He had said all there was to say, and he felt he had no hope. Now he must go out. The strength seemed suddenly to have left him.

It was very still in the room for a moment. They could hear each other breathe. At last Hazel's hand reached timidly out toward him and rested like a rose leaf among the dark curls.

It was his benediction, he thought, his dream come true. It was her forgiveness. He held his breath and didn't stir.

And then, more timidly still, Hazel herself slipped softly from her chair to her knees before him. The other hand shyly stole to his shoulder, and she whispered: "Christie, forgive ME. I—love *you*."

Then Hazel's courage gave way, and she hid her blushing face against his sleeve.

Christie's heart leaped up in all its manhood. He arose and drew her to her feet tenderly and folded his arms about her as one might enfold an angel come for shelter. Then he bent his tall head over till his face touched her lily face, and he felt that all his desolation was healed.

At that instant, steps were heard along the hall, lingering noisily about the door. A hand rattled the doorknob, while Victoria's voice, unnecessarily loud from Ruth's point of view, called: "Is that you, Ruth? Are the others through dinner yet? Would you mind stepping back to the office and getting the evening paper for me? I want to look at something."

Then the door opened, and Victoria came smiling in. "Time's up," she said playfully. "The invalid mustn't talk another word tonight."

Indeed, Victoria was most relieved that the time was up. She looked anxiously from Hazel to Christie to see whether she had done more harm than good. But Hazel leaned back smiling and flushed in her chair, and Christie, standing tall and serious, with an inspired look on his face, reassured her.

She led him out by another hall than the one the family would come up by. She was in such a hurry to get him away without being seen that she scarcely said a word to him. But he didn't know it.

"Well, is it all right?" she laughed nervously as they reached the side doorway.

"It is all right," he said with a joyous ring in his voice.

Through the hall, out the door and down the steps Christie Bailey went, his hat in his hand, his face exalted, the moonlight "laying on his head a kingly crown." He felt that he had been crowned that night, crowned with a woman's love.

"He looks as if he'd seen a vision," thought Victoria as she sped back to "view the ruins," as she expressed it to herself.

But Christie went on, his hat in his hand, down the long white road, looking up to the stars among the pines, wondering at the greatness of the world and the graciousness of God, on to his little cabin no longer filled with loneliness. There he knelt before the pictured Christ and cried, "Oh, my Father, I thank You."

Quite early in the morning Hazel requested a private interview with her father.

Now it was a well-acknowledged fact that Judge Winship was completely under his daughter's thumb. Since the interview was a prolonged one, it was regarded as quite possible by the rest of the family party that there might be almost anything, from the endowment of a college settlement to a trip to Africa, in process. And all awaited the result with some restlessness.

But after dinner there were no developments. Hazel seemed bright and ready to sit on the piazza and be read to. Judge Winship took his umbrella and sauntered out for a walk, having declined the company of the various members of his family. Mother Winship calmed her anxieties and decided to take a nap.

Christie went about his morning tasks joyously. Now and again his heart questioned what he had to hope for in the future, poor as he was. But he put this resolutely down. He would rejoice in knowing Hazel's forgiveness and her love, even though it never brought him anything else other than that joy of knowing.

In this frame of mind he looked forward exultantly to the Sunday school hour. When the young men entered, they wondered what had come over him, and the scholars greeted their superintendent with furtive nods and smiles.

During the opening of the Sunday school an elderly gentleman of fine presence came in, with iron-gray hair and keen blue eyes that looked piercingly out from under black brows. Christie had been praying when he came in. Christie's prayers were an index to his life.

During the singing of the next hymn the superintendent walked back to the door to give a book to the stranger and, hesitating a moment, asked half shyly, "Will you say a few words to us, or pray?"

"Go on with your regular lesson, young man. I'm not prepared to speak. I'll pray at the close if you wish me to," said the stranger.

Christie returned to his place, somewhat puzzled and embarrassed by the unexpected guest.

He lingered after all were gone, having asked that he might have a few words with Christie alone. Christie noticed that Mortimer had bowed to him in going out and that he looked back curiously once or twice.

"My name is Winship," said the judge brusquely. "I understand, young man, that you have told my daughter you love her."

The color rose softly in Christie's temples till it flooded his whole face. But a light of love and of daring came into his eyes as he answered the unexpected challenge seriously, "I do, sir."

"Am I to understand, sir, by that, that you wish to marry her?"

Christie caught his breath. Hope and pain came quickly to defy one another. He stood still, not knowing what to say. He realized his helplessness, his unfitness for the love of Hazel Winship.

"Because," went on the relentless judge, "in my day it was considered a very dishonorable thing to tell a young woman you loved her unless you wished to marry her. And, if you do not, I wish to know at once."

Christie was white now and humiliated.

"Sir," he said sternly, "I mean nothing dishonorable. I honor and reverence your daughter, yes, and love her, next to Jesus Christ," and involuntarily his eyes met those of the picture on the wall, "whom she has taught me to love. But since your daughter has told you about my love, she must have also told you about the circumstances under which I told it to her. If I hadn't been trying to clear myself from a charge of deceit in her eyes, I would never have let her know the deep love I have for her. I have nothing to offer her but my love. Judge Winship, is this the kind of home to offer your daughter? It's all I have."

There was something pathetic, almost tragic, in the wave of Christie's hand as he looked around the cabin.

"Well, young man, it's more comfortable than the place my daughter's father was born in. There were worse homes than this. But perhaps you're not aware that my daughter will have enough of her own for two."

Christie threw his head back, with his eyes flashing, though his voice was sad: "Sir, I will never be supported by my wife. If she comes to me, she comes to the home I can offer her. And it would have to be here, now, until I can do better."

"As you please, young man," answered the judge shortly. But a grim smile was upon his lips, and his eyes twinkled as if he were pleased. "I like your spirit. From all I hear of you, you are quite worthy of her. She thinks so, anyway, which is more to the point. Have you enough to keep her from starving if she did come?"

"Oh, yes," Christie almost laughed in his eagerness. "Do you think—oh, it *can*not be—that she would come?"

"She'll have to settle that question," said her father, rising. "You have my permission to talk with her about it. As far as I can judge, she seems to have a fondness for logs with the bark on them. Good afternoon, Mr. Bailey. I'm glad to have met you. You had a good Sunday school, and I respect you."

Christie gripped his hand until the old man almost cried out with the pain. But he bore it, smiling grimly, and went on his way.

And Christie, left alone in his little, glorified room, knelt once more and called joyously: "My Father! My Father!"

⁓

"This is perfectly ridiculous," said Ruth Summers, looking dismally out of the swiftly moving train window at the vanishing oaks and pines. "The wedding guests going off on the bridal tour, and the bride and bridegroom staying behind. I can't think whatever has possessed Hazel. Married in white cashmere under a tree and not a single thing belonging to a wedding, not even a wedding breakfast—"

"You forget the wedding march," said Victoria, a vision of the organist's fine head coming to her, "and the strawberries for breakfast."

"A wedding march on that old organ," sneered Ruth, "with a row of children for an audience and sand for a background. Well, Hazel was original, to say the least. I hope she'll settle down now and do as other people do."

"She won't," said Victoria positively. "She'll keep on having a perfectly lovely time all her life. Do you remember how she once said she was going to take Christie Bailey to Europe? Well, I reminded her of it this morning. She laughed and said she hadn't forgotten it; it was one thing she married him for. He looked down at her wonderingly and asked what was that. How he does worship her!"

"Yes, and she's perfectly infatuated with him. I'm sure one would have to be, to live in a shanty. I don't believe I could love any man enough for that," she said reflectively, studying the back of Tom Winship's well-trimmed head in the next seat.

"Then you'd better not get married," said Victoria. She looked dreamily out of the window at the hurrying palmettos and added: "One might—if one loved enough." Then she was silent, thinking of a promise that was made to her, a promise of better things, signed by a true look from a pair of handsome, courageous eyes.

Christie and Hazel watched the train as it vanished from their sight and then turned slowly toward their home.

"It's a palace to me now that you are in it, my wife!" Christie pronounced the words with wonder and awe.

"You dear old organ, it was you that did it all," said Hazel, touching the keys tenderly. And turning to Christie with tears of joy standing in her eyes, she put her hands in his and said, "My husband."

Then as if by common consent they knelt together, hand in hand, beneath the picture of the Christ, and Christie prayed. And now his prayer began, "Our Father."

An Interrupted Night

by Isabella Alden

Foreword

As long ago as I can remember there was always a radiant being who was next to my mother and father in my heart and who seemed to me to be a combination of fairy godmother, heroine and saint. I thought her the most beautiful, wise and wonderful person in my world, outside of my home. I treasured her smiles, copied her ways and listened breathlessly to all she had to say, sitting at her feet worshipfully whenever she was near; ready to run any errand for her, no matter how far.

I measured other people by her principles and opinions, and always felt that her word was final. I am afraid I even corrected my beloved parents sometimes when they failed to state some principle or opinion as she had done.

When she came on a visit the house seemed glorified because of her presence. While she remained, life was one long holiday; when she went away it seemed as if a blight had fallen.

Her dark eyes had interesting twinkles in them that children loved. Her hair was long and dark and very heavy, dressed in two wide braids that were wound round her lovely head in smooth coils, fitting close like a cap; but when it was unbraided and brushed out, it fell far below her knees and was like a garment enfolding her. How I adored that hair and longed to have hair just like it! In secret I even used to tie an old brown veil about my head and let it fall down my back, to see how it would feel to have hair like that.

She had delicate features and a wonderful smile. Nobody else in the world looked as lovely as she did. But once I found a picture of Longfellow's Evangeline in a photograph album, in exquisite classic profile, and thought it was her likeness. She was like that—if you have that old faded photograph somewhere in an old album with quaint clasps. She was wonderful!

And she was young, gracious and very good to be with.

This radiant creature was known to me by the name "Auntie Belle," though my mother and my grandmother called her "Isabella." Even sharply sometimes when they disagreed with her—"Isabella!" I wondered that they dared. I sometimes resented it.

Later I found that other people had still other names for her. To the congregation of which her husband was pastor she was known as "Mrs. Alden." It seemed to me too grown-up a name for her and made her appear more stately and sedate than she really was. I remember resenting it that these strange people should seem to have rights on her. She was mine. What were they?

But when a little later my world grew larger and knowledge increased, I found that this precious aunt of mine did not belong entirely to us as I had supposed. She had another world in which she moved and had her being when she went from us from time to time; or when at certain hours in the day she shut herself within a room that was sacredly known as a "study" and wrote for a long time, while we all tried to keep still; and in this other world of hers she was known as "Pansy." It was a world that loved and honored her, a world that gave her homage and flowers and wrote her letters by the hundreds each week.

It was not long, too, before I had learned to preen myself like a young peacock because I "belonged" to her. I am afraid I felt a superior pity and contempt for the thousands of other children who read her paper called *The Pansy* which she edited, but who did not "belong" to her. They could only write letters to her, while I could often be with her every day, sometimes for weeks, and could talk with her all I pleased.

As I grew still older and learned to read I devoured her stories chapter by chapter. Even sometimes page by page as they came hot from the typewriter—occasionally stealing in for an instant when she left the study, to snatch the latest page and see what happened next, or to accost her as her morning's work was done, with: "Oh, have you finished another chapter?"

And often the whole family would crowd around, leaving their work when the word went around that the last chapter was finished and was going to be read aloud. Now we listened, breathless, as she read and made her characters live before us. They were real people to us, as real as if they lived and breathed before us.

She was at the height of her popularity just then, and the letters that poured in at every mail were overwhelming—asking for her autograph and her photograph; begging for pieces of her best dress to sew into patchwork; begging for advice on how to become a great author; begging for advice on every possible subject, from how to get the right kind of a husband to how to stop biting one's nails.

And she answered them all!

It was a Herculean task. Sometimes she let us help her when she was very much rushed, but usually she kept her touch on every letter that went out—and there were *thousands*.

Then there was the editorship of *The Pansy,* a young people's paper that was responsible for more thousands of letters from the children who had joined the Pansy Society. They wrote to her about their faults and how to give them up, "For Jesus' Sake," which was their motto.

Sometimes I look back on her long and busy life and marvel what she has accomplished.

She was a marvelous housekeeper, knowing every dainty detail of her home to perfection; able to cook anything in the world just a little better than anybody else—except my mother; able to set fine stitches in patches and darning that were works of art; able to make even dishwashing fun!

Sometimes when we were all together for a season, visiting, or during the winters we spent in Florida and lived together, it fell to her part and mine to do the dinner dishes together every night. We raced—she washing, I wiping and putting away, making a record each night and trying to beat it the next. And such good, good times we had together, my beloved aunt and I, as we worked with a will and left the kitchen immaculate for the next morning. Oh, she was a wonderful housekeeper!

Yes, and a marvelous pastor's wife! She took the whole parish into her life and gave herself to the work. She was not a modern minister's wife, who only goes to teas and receptions and plays bridge and attends to the social end of life, never bothering about the church. She was the real old-fashioned kind, who made calls on all the parishioners with her husband, knew every member intimately and cared for the sick. She gathered the young people into her home, making both a social and religious center for them with herself as leader and adviser. She grew intimate with each one personally and led them to Christ, became their confidante, and loved them all as if they had been her brothers and sisters. She taught the primary class—and the *mothers* of the primary class. She quietly and unobtrusively managed the missionary society and the ladies' aid, not always as its executive officer, often keeping quiet in the background. She became the dear friend of every woman in the church without making any of them jealous. She was beloved, almost adored, by them all.

She was a tender, vigilant, wonderful mother, such a mother as few are privileged to have, giving without stint of her time, strength, love and companionship.

Even while she was quite young, when I was a small child, she began to go out into the world, to speak in public, to read her stories, to lead primary Sunday school conferences. As I grew older and developed a delight in drawing, she sometimes took me along to do her blackboard work for her, at which privilege I swelled with pride. She was much in demand in those days. I remember the awe with which I regarded her as one of the great ones of the earth, who was paid large sums to tell other people the best ways of teaching and to read her fascinating stories. How I loved her and hung upon her every word and smile. How proud I was to belong to her! And am still.

All these things she did and *yet wrote books!* Stories out of real life that struck home and showed us to ourselves as God saw us, that sent us to our knees to talk with Him.

With marvelous skill she searched hearts, especially of the easygoing Christian, whether minister or layperson, young or old, and brought them awake and alive to their inconsistencies. She wove her stories around their common, everyday life, till all her characters became alive and real to those who read. They still live within our memories like people we have known intimately and dwelt among. Ester Ried and Julia Ried, the four girls at Chautauqua, Mrs. Solomon Smith. I almost expect to meet some of them in heaven.

Perhaps she wrote more and better because she was *doing* so eagerly in every direction. Her public, her church, her family, her home.

I wish I might paint you a picture of that home as I knew it; of my home, its counterpart; of the years the two families spent much time together as one family. The days were one long dream. Hard work? Yes, but good fellowship. Everybody working together with a common aim, and joy in the work and the fellowship!

And the evenings! Oh, those evenings, the crown of the days, the time to which we all looked forward as a goal when our work was done! Those evenings are bright spots in my youth. Especially the evenings of the years we all spent together in Florida, when the sun went down sharply and the light went velvet black at evening, until the great tropical moon came out. On those long evenings the soft dense darkness shut us in to a cheerful supper table.

After we had hustled through the dishes, we all gathered in the big sitting-room around the open fire for family worship. Yes, we were as old-fashioned as that! We had family worship both morning and evening. And I am not of those modern ones who tell such things to scoff at them and say how sick they got of religion because of it and attribute to that their present indifference to God and the Bible. I look back to those times as the most precious, the most beautiful, the most powerful influence that came into my life. I thank God for a family that worshipped Him morning and evening and gave me an early knowledge and love for the Bible and the things of the kingdom. Either my uncle or my father would conduct the little service, and often the one or the other would say to my dear aunt: "You read the chapter tonight, Belle," just because she was such a beautiful reader and we all loved to listen to her. At other times, we would recite verses, all around, a verse apiece, and then kneel in a circle for the prayer.

Oh, those prayers of the years that made my life inevitably acquainted with God and the Lord Jesus, so that I never could be troubled by the doubts of today, because I *know* Him, "whom to know is life eternal." I cannot be thankful enough for those prayers and that sacred time of worship every day that brought me into His very presence.

And then the evening that followed!

We would all get our work, sewing or drawing, painting or knitting, or embroidery. My father and my uncle would each take his particular chair in a shaded corner, and a book would be brought out. It was always a book that had been selected with great care, usually a story, now and again a great mis-sionary book but more often a good novel. And this aunt would usually do the reading. Sometimes my aunt and my mother took turns reading. They both were remarkable readers and knit close in spirit since early childhood. For two, sometimes three, beautiful hours we reveled in the book. Reluctantly, when the word went forth that it was time to stop, we folded up our work and went to bed—sometimes pleading for just another chapter—now and then actually staying up breathless till all hours to finish some great climax. We always went off to rest with a bright eagerness for the morrow and the evening, and the story again—or a new one if we had finished one.

So we read the works of George MacDonald—we loved the Scotch, and our readers knew how to put the burr of the dialect upon their tongues—Ian Maclaren, Barrie; much of Dickens; some of Scott, Bjornson, William Dean Howells; Jean Ingelow's few matchless novels; Frank Stockton, with his charming absurdities; and a host of other writers whose stories seem to have become submerged and forgotten in this day of modern literature. But I look back to those stories as my meeting time with the great of the earth. How real the Bonnie Brier Bush and all its quaint true people were! How tender and strong were the Marquis of Lossie and Sir Gibbie! How I thrilled over the *Men of the Moss Hags*, *Ben Hur*, *The Virginian*, *Jane Eyre*. I mention them at random. It is my ambition someday to possess in a special set of shelves every one of those wonderful stories that thrilled me so when I was young. Oh, don't try to tell me I would not care for them now! I do. They were real books, books that do not change because they told of human life as it is really lived in hearts. They may need to be furnished with a few electric lights and radios and airplanes and automobiles to bring them up to date; but otherwise you will not find them out of tune with life as it is today, except that they are perhaps too clean and wholesome to be natural today.

At frequent times this beloved aunt, around whom we all seemed in those days to center, was called away to deliver an address or conduct a conference or furnish an evening's entertainment in some distant place. But when she returned from one of these trips we all gathered around to hear her tell her experiences, for we were always sure of stories. She saw everything, and she knew how to tell with glowing words about the days she had been away so that she lived them over again for us. It was almost better than if we had been along because she knew how to bring out the touch of pathos or beauty or fun, and her characters were all portraits. It listened like a book.

It was on one of these occasions that she told the story of this book. I remember it as if it were but yesterday, though the whole thing happened many years ago. For modern as this story is, the main part of it happened, *really happened*, to her personal knowledge, over thirty-five years ago.

It was told to her by a woman who was so well known all over our country at that time that if I were to name her you could not help but remember how active she was in women's suffrage and Women's Christian Temperance Union work, besides several other notable reforms and organizations. She was a brilliant public speaker, much in demand, and a great worker for young girls. She recounted this story to my aunt as a recent personal experience and gave her permission to use it in a story (after a suitable interval of time, of course, and without the original names).

The story was written in brief form and appeared several years after its happening in a periodical as a short serial; but it is now appearing in book form for the first time. The dear author, after an interval of several years, during which on account of ill health and a feeling that her work was done, has taken up her pen once more. But at what odds! She is now eighty-seven years old and confined to her bed, the result of a fall and a broken hip. In the intervals of pain she has been elaborating and preparing this story for book form.

And now, because the manuscript was to have been in the hands of the publisher long ago, and because pain has held her in its grip for an unusually long period of weeks lately, leaving her unfit for work for the present, she has trusted me with the task of putting it into final shape. This story seems to me peculiarly fitting as a message for this present time.

I approach the work with a kind of awe upon me that I should be working on *her* story!

If, long ago in my childhood, it had been told me I should ever be counted worthy to do this, I would not have believed it. Before her I shall always feel like the little worshipful child I used to be.

I recall a Christmas long ago when I was just beginning to write scraps of stories myself, with no thought of ever amounting to anything as a writer. Her gift to me that year was a thousand sheets of typewriter paper; and in a sweet little note that accompanied it she wished me success and bade me turn those thousand sheets of paper into as many dollars.

It was my first real encouragement. The first hint that anybody thought I ever could write, and I laughed aloud at the utter impossibility of its ever coming true. But I feel that my first inspiration for storytelling came from her and from reading her books in which as a child I fairly steeped myself.

So I beg the leniency of her readers today as I approach the task that is set before me. I know I shall have hers. My one hope is that I shall not in any way mar the message of this true and thrilling tale that certainly is needed in this day and generation. I trust that she may soon be well enough to write once more another tale as good if not better.

Let me tell you a secret. I happen to know that this wonderful little brave aunt of mine is at work on the story of her younger years. She calls it "Yesterdays." I have had the pleasure of reading a few of the earlier chapters where she tells of her childhood and her young womanhood; the quaint things that happened to her; the dear home in which she lived; the great people of other days whom she knew intimately and with whom she grew up.

I pray she may be spared with strength to finish her story of her "Yesterdays" and many more beside.

—Grace Livingston Hill

Chapter 1

The train had limped along all afternoon with engine trouble, and now at evening the passengers learned they were two hours behind schedule and still losing time.

Mrs. Dunlap put away her writing materials and sat up with a sigh to look about her. It appeared as if she might miss her connections unless relief came soon.

She had just corrected the last galley of her new book, which was coming out that fall, reviewed the notes for the new speeches she was on her way to give at several appointed places, and read her magazine from cover to cover. She had even written a couple of letters to friends. And here she was with time on her hands! An almost unheard of thing for this busy woman. Not many hours of leisure came her way, and when one did she was dismayed at the waste of time.

Off in the west a thread of crimson lingered on the horizon, but it soon faded into a line of pale amber and then disappeared. The lights of the train blared out and shut the travelers into the narrow confines of the car. Mary Dunlap leaned back in her seat and studied her fellow passengers.

The usual mother with children who had been a noisy nuisance all afternoon were quieted for now. The mother and the littlest baby slept, while the rest were occupied with a picture book some thoughtful traveler donated.

The passengers in the car had changed during the afternoon. Several people disembarked at the stations along the way, and others came on board. Among the latter were the two people who occupied the seat directly in front of Mary. Before she realized it she was absorbed in studying them, her interest caught by the pure and lovely profile of the young woman's face.

They were apparently a young married couple, though the man was not so young as the girl, who looked entirely too young to be married. As she studied them she couldn't help wondering over the girl's choice of a husband. They didn't seem at all suited for one another. The girl was the more attractive of the two.

Mary decided they were newly wed. The man had an air of proprietorship which she thought could only be explained by that relationship. The girl looked about her as if everything were strange and new, but no happiness shone on her face.

Poor child! thought the watcher. *She has just said good-bye to her mother, I suppose.*

Then, for a moment, memory carried her back to the day when *she* had bid one dear girl the long good-bye.

Still, she reflected, this girl's face showed unrest. At some moments she thought she even saw fear! What could be the explanation?

The husband was attentive, almost oppressively so. Could he be urging her to some course she did not approve?

The man looks like a gentleman tyrant! she told herself. *He'll certainly have his own way in the end. That poor child might as well yield first as last.*

The call for dinner in the dining car took her away. But before she returned, they had also found a table in the diner. Later in the evening when they came back to their seats she noticed they were having a heated argument. The girl was deeply distressed, almost on the verge of tears, and the man alternately vexed and cajoled.

Mary Dunlap was a woman of broad interests and keen insight into character. She couldn't help siding with the young wife and feeling that the man was in the wrong. He appeared to be a man who would have his own way at all costs.

In vain she told herself she was probably wrong. The girl might be a spoiled darling who was insisting on some extravagance which the man, older and wiser, was trying to reason her out of. But try as she would she couldn't make it seem that way. The man had a selfish sophistication about him that made her distrust him.

Both the young people were well dressed, with a quiet elegance that showed they had money and belonged to the higher social class. The trouble could not be about money.

At last Mrs. Dunlap turned her eyes away from them, resolved to wonder no more about these strangers who'd caught her interest. It was none of her business anyway; they'd have to settle their own affairs. She obviously couldn't help them; and perhaps even this kindly observation was eavesdropping. She'd think no more about them.

With her eyes on the dark landscape outside the window, she thought about the two hours the train had lost and wondered what she could do in case she missed her connection at the junction. Being a methodical woman and a careful planner, she was not used to missing her appointments, and it was annoying for the train to crawl along and then stop for unexplainable periods. Nevertheless, there was a certain resignation about her annoyance. She believed that design, not mere chance or fate, determines our ways and reorders our plannings sometimes, in accordance with all-seeing wisdom; so she couldn't help wondering why her plans were jeopardized.

For a long time she watched the lights of the villages fly by; for now the train seemed to have taken up a steady, dogged trot and rolled along without stopping as if it had made up its mind to get home. But when she finally turned her gaze back to the car she saw that the two in front of her hadn't settled their argument yet. They weren't talking much now, but each face spoke eloquently of disagreement. The girl's eyes held unshed tears. Now and then she cast a pleading look at her companion and uttered a wistful word, ending in a sigh. The man was still stubbornly positive, his lips curving in a superior smile of amusement at the girl's repeated objections.

Again Mary realized that her interest in the affair was too intent. She must stop thinking about these two people or they'd soon turn around and catch her staring at them.

But just then her thoughts were interrupted. The brakeman entered the car shouting the name of the junction, like one bearing welcome news.

Mary looked at her watch. Ten minutes past midnight! She quickly straightened her hat, put on her gloves and buttoned her coat. Then she picked up her handbag, briefcase and suitcase, and stepped to the door when the train halted.

But the track on the other side of the station was empty. The connecting train had not waited! The station looked deserted and dirty in the darkness, and Mary's heart sank.

She paused for a moment in the doorway of the station as the crowds surged from the belated train; she sympathized with the frustrated murmurs she heard. It was a new experience to her to be stranded at midnight in a strange place. Her delay would disappoint many people, but it wasn't her fault. She'd planned carefully and must send telegrams to explain her absence; after years of service this was her first disappointment as a platform speaker. She couldn't reach her first meeting in time, throwing off the whole schedule. Too bad, but she must make the best of it.

On her way to the telegraph office the man from the seat in front of her brushed past her. He too had probably missed connections and must telegraph. She wondered where he'd left his young wife and wished she might have had a chance to show her some little kindness. She felt strangely drawn to the girl.

I wonder if they're as frustrated as I am and if they're disappointing someone, she asked herself. *Why was this allowed to happen? I certainly thought I was needed at that meeting tomorrow morning. They've been planning for it so long! It's embarrassing to disappoint them.*

Soon, however, she had to give undivided attention to where she would spend the rest of the night. The Kennard House, recommended by the ticket agent, proved to be crowded, and the sympathetic hotel clerk could give her no encouragement.

"The Albemarle? No," he shook his head in response to her question. "They're as bad off as we are. A car just left here with people who had tried the Albemarle first. It's an unfortunate night for that express train to be late. The city is overcrowded because of the convention. You're alone, madam? I hardly know what to suggest. We rented our last room about three minutes before you came in to a couple who were your fellow passengers."

Was he hinting gently that if she hadn't been so slow she might have had their room?

Then came another hotel official to exchange a few words in undertone with the clerk. A moment, then her sympathetic friend turned to her again.

"Madam, the man who engaged number 38 for the night changed his mind and is staying with friends in town. If you care to wait in the lobby a few minutes we could have it ready for you."

Grateful thanks were, of course, the only reply she could make to this.

Mary took up the pen to register and remarked, "It seems almost foolish to register for the few hours left in the night." But she said it with a congenial smile and the friendly air that made clerks and porters and all who served her glad to help.

The name on the line above hers held her attention: "R. H. Keller and wife." She guessed it must belong to the couple who had interested her so much that evening. They were booked for number 537, four floors above hers. She wished they were nearer, so she might comfort the frightened little bride; if she could only *mother* her a little, she would be glad.

The lobby appeared vast and gloomy in its midnight dimness and solitude. No—not quite solitude. Other occupants, a man and a woman, were present, probably waiting, as she was, for a room.

Her first impulse was to choose a corner as far from them as space would permit. Instead she took a seat on a couch near where they were standing, for she suddenly recognized them as her traveling companions; her interest in the girl rekindled as she caught sight of her face.

What *could* be troubling that girl! The more she saw of the man, the more she distrusted him. Perhaps she imagined it, but it seemed as if he frowned when he saw how close she was! Nevertheless, she determined not to retreat. What if there *should* be a chance to speak a cheery word to the girl? She tucked herself among the cushions and drew her coat about her, seeming to sleep, though she'd never felt wider awake. Her nervousness was becoming a premonition.

The man turned toward his wife. "We may as well be comfortable while we wait," he said. "It's beastly luck to have to wait at all. These second-class towns never have proper hotel accommodations. Let's go over to that couch at the other end of the room where the pillows look plusher."

The girl glanced at the distant couch then back to the one where Mrs. Dunlap rested.

"Oh, no," she said, moving nearer to the fireplace, "I'm chilly. I'd rather stay here. Suppose you push a couple of those large rocking chairs up this way?"

"I can make you much more comfortable on the couch," he said, with a sharp tone. "That fire won't keep you warm. There's nothing left of it but charred old stumps. Do let me snug you up among the cushions."

He tried to put his arm around her as he spoke, but she drew away from him with a wan smile.

"I'd rather stay here. It seems less—lonely to be near a woman. Why did we bother about rooms? I'd just as soon stay where I am."

"Standing?" he asked sullenly.

"No," answered the girl, attempting to smile, "I'd be willing to sit—if you would bring up some chairs. We can't have much longer to wait. What time did you say we could get a train?"

His answer brought forth a wail. "Oh, Rufus! That wasn't what you said before. Why, that isn't until another *day!*"

The woman on the couch kept still with great effort. This was not the tone of a happy wife! She was certain now that something was wrong besides a few hours of delay. This sounded more like a woman half afraid of the man who was supposed to be caring for her.

"It's beastly luck," the man repeated. "Something's always the matter on this confounded branch road! If you hadn't been staying in such an out-of-the-way place, we'd have been saved from this. Still, I don't understand why we should make it any more uncomfortable than it is. You ought to be resting quietly, instead—"

"I cannot rest," she interrupted him loudly. "I *cannot!* I can think only of my mother's utter dismay and—and terror when she hears—"

"H-sh!" The man's sibilant whisper was sudden and fierce, like that of a snake.

No wonder the girl cried out: "Oh, what is it?"

He bent over her and spoke lower. "It is nothing at all, my dear, except that you're tired out and your nerves are on edge. But you must be careful what you say. That confounded eavesdropper has planted herself as close to us as she *can* and may get the idea from your words that I'm a fiend of some kind. Thank goodness, though, she has gone to sleep, at last! I must say they're taking an unreasonable time to get that room ready."

"*That* room!" repeated the still frightened voice. "There are two rooms, of course?"

"Of course," he replied hastily, "but I could wait for mine, you know."

"I don't *like* it," the girl said, quite as if she hadn't heard him. "I don't like anything about it! I wish—oh, Rufus, *can't* we go on tonight? Or go somewhere and talk things over—and make other plans. I don't want *any* room!"

"That's impossible, dear," he said firmly but kindly, "as you'll realize when you think a moment. All the arrangements are made, and—my friend is waiting and will be there for the next train. There's no other train until morning that will do us any good. Why can't you be the sensible girl you've been all afternoon and let me do the extra planning this delay has caused? I assure you I can take care of you."

As he spoke he tried to draw her nearer. But she took deliberate steps away from him. "Oh, I *cannot* make you understand! I know how strange it seems to you, but if you could think for a moment of my side! Can't you realize how different it will be to me when I have the *right* to be with you anywhere and always? As it is, I can't help feeling strangely alone and—and almost *disgraced!* I do, Rufus. I can't help it. Mother has always been so particular about me, and she'd think what we're doing is terrible! I know *now* that she would. Can't we go *somewhere* on the cars and talk it all over? I don't feel so strange when we're moving. Wait! Was that one o'clock? And we were to have been there long before twelve! And you were to telegraph Mother early in the morning! Oh, this is *dreadful!*"

He bent toward her and spoke gently. "Daisy, listen. You're making yourself ill over troubles that don't exist. Everything is all right; we'll be in by noon, and my friend will meet the train. Meantime, in the *early* morning I'll wire your mother, as we planned, and—"

"But we don't *get in* until noon! And what you were going to say won't be *true!*"

"Oh, nonsense! Why, my dear, if you weren't so tired, I'd convince you in a few minutes of the foolishness of that! I'll only be anticipating the truth by a few hours in order to relieve her anxiety."

"Rufus, I *cannot* have our life together begin with falsehood! It's bad enough as it is. I wish we'd waited until Mother had a chance to know you better. She's not a hard or unreasonable woman."

"I see plainly that you don't trust me."

He spoke with such bitterness that the listener on the couch, who caught only portions of the girl's words, felt like springing up that minute and defending her. But the voice rose clearer then.

"Rufus! How *can* you say that to me? If I hadn't trusted you *utterly,* would I be here tonight? If you had a mother you'd understand how perfectly dreadful it is to—"

As she hesitated for words, a hotel official approached them.

"Are you Mr. R. H. Keller, sir? If so, you are wanted at the office telephone."

"Confound the fellow!" muttered Keller.

Then, in a gentler tone, "Don't let that frighten you, Daisy. It's a business call I've been expecting. But it comes at an inopportune time. I'll be right back."

Left to herself, the girl paced back and forth in front of the fire, catching her breath in little sobs. She was so near the couch that Mrs. Dunlap could have put out her hand and touched her. When that woman saw the girl's small hands clenched and heard a low moan, she sat up suddenly and spoke in a low tone.

"Will you forgive me, dear? I'm the mother of a precious girl who was about your age when God called her home. And I miss her *so!* I can't help seeing that you're in trouble. May I be like a mother to you and comfort you?"

But the girl's face expressed such abject terror that she added: "There is nothing to be frightened about, dear. This is a quiet, respectable house, and your husband will be back in a few moments." It was the probing word that this student of human nature had resolved should open her way, and it succeeded.

"He is *not* my husband!" the girl exclaimed. "Not yet," she added quickly. "We were to have been married as soon as the train reached our destination. But—the train was delayed. We couldn't go on, and we couldn't get any rooms without this awful waiting! I wish now that we hadn't—" She stopped abruptly, then began again.

"I must appear very silly to a stranger. But—I can't seem to help it. And I can't explain, either, why it suddenly seems so dreadful to me. But it does! I'm so used to traveling with my mother, and I can't stop thinking it would seem perfectly *awful* to her if she knew that I—"

The unsteady voice stopped again. Right then Mrs. Dunlap felt that she would almost enjoy shooting the man who'd planned such a state of things for this frightened child. She put a protective arm about the girl and spoke tenderly.

"Will you trust me and tell me all about it? You remind me of my own dear daughter. I'm sure you have a precious mother. Does she know you expected to be married tonight?"

"No, oh, no! She hasn't dreamed of such a thing! We *couldn't* tell her because she—she is prejudiced against Mr. Keller. He has enemies, we think, who are trying to injure him because he's a more successful man than they are, and she—why, she wasn't even willing for me to walk out with him, *alone!* But I thought—I mean, I think that when we're married and everything is settled forever, we can make her understand. It really isn't as though I were a *child;* I am of age."

At this, the child-woman drew herself up with an attempt at womanhood. Mrs. Dunlap, under happier circumstances, felt sure she would have asked how many hours had passed since the child attained that dignity!

The uncertain voice continued: "Still, I couldn't live without my mother, and I don't need to, of course. As soon as she discovers how truly good and noble Mr. Keller is, and what a devoted son he's ready to be to her, it will be all right. Mother has always wanted a son."

A note of appeal crept into her voice as though she longed to hear from even this stranger some assurance that all would be well. Mrs. Dunlap's mother-heart bled for her, and thankfulness for the absolute safety of her own daughter swept over her. With it came the determination to do what she could to help this girl, even at the cost of a possible mistake.

"My child," she said, "I feel that I must tell you something. You are registered at this hotel as 'R. H. Keller *and wife*'! And *one* room—not *two*—is being prepared for you."

Chapter 2

For a moment Mary Dunlap regretted her words. The girl's eyes opened wide with terror, and the cry she uttered was like that of a wounded animal.

But she rallied rapidly. "Oh, you're mistaken! It's some other person whose name you've mistaken for his. He wouldn't—why, Rufus couldn't do such a thing!"

"My dear child, I'm not mistaken." The quietness of the woman's voice carried conviction. "The name is R. H. Keller, and the man who is with you tonight is the one who sat in front of me with you yesterday afternoon and wrote his name as I have told you, *just* before I did on the register."

Suddenly the poor girl broke into bitter weeping. "What shall I *do!* Oh, Mother, if only I'd never left you! I've *killed her! I have killed my mother!"*

"No, you haven't!" Mrs. Dunlap's voice had never been quieter or firmer. "You're going home to her this morning, as soon as the train leaves. In a few hours she'll have her arms around you. And when you're really being married she'll stand near you and be the first to kiss you and call you her darling. You wouldn't disappoint her for anything! Come to my room and wait for the train. There ought to be one very early in the morning, and I'll see you safely to it."

The girl seized the little handbag she'd dropped. "Where's the room? Oh, quick! Take me to it. That's what I wanted—a place to be alone and think. I don't know what I can do, but I must decide—and I must do it before Mr. Keller comes back, because—oh, *will* you let me go into your room and lock the door?"

They both turned at once at the sound of footsteps.

It was a porter to say that number 37 was ready, and never were fleeter steps than those that followed his lead.

"Oh, *hurry!"* the girl said breathlessly as they reached the room, and it was she who turned the key in the lock after the retreating porter. Then she dropped into the nearest chair and cried. Mrs. Dunlap left her alone and thanked God for the tears.

"What shall I do if he comes and demands to be let in?" the girl asked suddenly, looking up at her deliverer. "He is so—so masterful, and he doesn't see things as I do. He thinks a few hours won't make any difference. He argued it out with himself that he couldn't leave me alone and that he would shield my name by giving me his in advance, but I won't do it. And if he comes and insists upon talking to me I don't know what will become of me. I don't seem to be able to make him understand."

"You'll go back to your mother, of course, dear. You can't do what *he* wants. This is *my* room; he'll hardly come to it without my permission. If you think it's necessary to explain your absence, *I* will go down to him, if you'll let me, and do so."

"Oh, if you *will!* I mean if you *can!* He's very determined and used to having his own way. I can't think that he'll let me—"

By that time the girl was trembling so that she could scarcely speak.

"Don't think about that anymore," Mrs. Dunlap said, putting her arm around her. "I'm not in the least afraid of him. And I'll take care of you! Have you a kimono in this bag? Why don't you slip into it for a while? I've been studying the train schedule. You can have almost three hours of quiet, then I'll take you to the station. We can plan all the details afterward."

"Oh, you're so kind!" murmured the girl.

"I'm going downstairs now," the woman said when the girl had followed her advice. She resisted the suggestion about the bed but allowed herself to be propped among pillows in an easy chair. "I'll come back soon. Or would you rather have this room to yourself? I can be comfortable down on one of the couches, and I'll come for you in enough time for the train."

"No! Oh, *no!*" the girl cried. "Please don't leave me! And yet—you must! Would you mind locking the door and taking the key with you? I can't help feeling that—"

She's afraid of him! was Mrs. Dunlap's mental comment as she hurried down the hall with the key in her pocket. On the whole she was rather glad of an opportunity to tell that man what she thought of him.

She had little time to collect her thoughts, for the subject of them hurried in soon after she entered the lobby.

An ugly frown had crossed his face. Evidently the telephone call irritated him.

He strode to the corner where he had left his companion and stared about him with confusion. He then turned an angry questioning gaze upon Mrs. Dunlap.

"Are you looking for the lady who was here when you left the room?" she asked pleasantly, determined to be courteous if possible. "She's gone to my room to get some rest. She asked me to tell you she's all right and quite comfortable for the night."

He stepped over to her with a glare in his eyes that would have frightened a less courageous spirit. "Who are you to interfere in the lady's affairs?" he said haughtily. "I have a room for her to rest in, and you'll oblige me by telling her I'm waiting for her—and then by minding your own business."

Mrs. Dunlap had the advantage over this angry man, for she was cool and calm.

"You're mistaken," she said. "I have the right to interfere because the lady has claimed my protection, and I'm abundantly able and willing to give it."

"Protection from what?" he thundered.

"From Mr. Keller, I imagine. I supposed, of course, that the lady was your wife because I'd seen you together during the day and noticed how you registered. Since she told me she isn't—and that she doesn't wish to see you again tonight—I've helped carry out her wishes and must insist that she isn't disturbed."

"Must you indeed! How do you expect to keep me away from the lady who is under my protection and for whom I alone am responsible?"

Both his tone and his eyes were menacing. Mrs. Dunlap lifted her eyebrows with a gesture of contempt, but she spoke quietly.

"This is absurd, Mr. Keller. I have no wish to make matters more uncomfortable than necessary. But of course you know this is a respectable house. You're here with a young woman you registered as your wife, and you ordered a room for yourself *and her.* But she says she is *not* your wife and does not wish to see you again tonight. I don't need to remind you how promptly the proprietor of this house, as well as its guests, would come to her aid if necessary—nor that policemen and lockups are conveniences within call. If you compel me to resort to such measures you'll have *yourself* to thank."

Something about Mary Dunlap when she chose to assert herself commanded respect. Keller looked into the clear stern eyes of this woman and realized he mustn't go too far. He stared at her, baffled for an instant; when she continued to gaze steadily at him, he wheeled and took a few steps away from her. Then, after a moment, with a sneer he turned and approached her again, trying to speak lightly.

"You women are too much for me! I may as well take you into my confidence, as the lady has evidently done. It's true that the formal ceremony which was to have made us man and wife in the eyes of a curious world hasn't taken place yet, but the *mere formality* is all that's lacking. I registered as I'd planned to do after I reached the station where the clergyman was waiting for us. I didn't wish to leave the lady *alone* in her weary state. I hoped to make her comfortable and would have, had it not been for a wrecked engine and this infernal delay. I didn't think I had to explain to the lady that I was ahead of the ceremony by a few hours, in writing her name as mine and thus securing a quiet room for her to rest in.

"Furthermore, business complications involving a good deal of money require me to move with caution in this entire matter. That's why I brought her away with me quietly, before we complied with the outward forms. But she came without any coercion as she'll tell you—if you explain that you suspect me of kidnapping! She'll also tell you she's of age and that nobody has a right to object to her taking a journey at any hour of the day or night with her chosen husband.

"Now that I've satisfied your curiosity, if you'll tell me where to find the lady, I'll escort her to her private sitting room. You don't need to delay your own sleep any longer. I assure you that three minutes of conversation with her will allay any fears you may have succeeded in working up."

The man concluded this biting sarcasm, veiled at times by mock courtesy, with what he intended to be a bow of dismissal. But Mrs. Dunlap was never more quietly determined in her course of action. Every word he uttered increased her distrust of him.

"We don't need to argue," she said. "You've told me nothing I didn't know before. The 'mere formality,' as you call it, which gives you the legal right to take care of this woman, is one that decent people still carefully adhere to. Without it you have acted tonight contrary to law and respectability. So, no matter what your motive is or how many private sitting rooms you've secured in this overcrowded house, I can and will protect the young woman from occupying one of them. And if you make the slightest attempt to see her tonight or interfere with her wishes in any way, I won't hesitate to take the hotel officials and the police into my confidence. If you force me to action you'll find that I'm a woman who is very well known."

During these words the man's face was a study. Fierce indignation, doubt, perplexity, intense disgust—each struggled for the ascendancy. But Mrs. Dunlap was about to leave the room. He felt compelled to appease her in some way.

"Wait!" he ordered. "You don't understand. Please—sit down and let me explain what has happened and what I'm trying to do."

His manner became instantly courteous. In more minute detail than called for, he justified the devious ways by which he'd reached this point; he enlarged upon his deep affection for the lady and his desire to free her from her narrow, cramped life. Her mother was a narrow-minded, prejudiced person who dominated her daughter's life, so that she was in danger of having no individuality, he said. Among other proofs of this she disliked him immensely and forbid the girl to receive a call from him unless the mother was present! He was at an utter loss how to further the daughter's interests when his good angel, as he put it, came to his rescue. The girl traveled to a town a hundred miles from home to spend a month with an intimate friend who recently married. Then, quite unexpectedly, business connected with his firm sent him to that town. He discovered that the young lady's affections were as involved as his own and that she despaired, as he did, of winning her mother to their view. As Mrs. Dunlap would agree, common people were apt to have violent prejudices they couldn't account for and were the hardest persons on earth to move. Still, he would admit he acted on sudden impulse rather than premeditated plans.

When the time came for the lady to return home, Providence seemed to make a way for them to be happy. He'd used no coercion in the matter; the lady realized her mother stood in the way of her happiness and that if she had her way, the daughter would be separated forever from him. She felt she couldn't endure this, and they both believed that, when the irrevocable step was taken, the mother would return to common sense. So in a moment it was all arranged; indeed, it almost arranged itself. He had a friend in the ministry at a town which was an important junction of the railroad; he sent a message to him planning all the necessary details. Everything would have been complete if it hadn't been for the horrible delay caused by that disabled engine.

But the delay and confusion and the need for stopping overnight at a strange hotel had bewildered the girl, since she wasn't used to being alone or planning for herself. Knowing that had led him to register as he did, and he could now see it was a mistake. He knew there was only one room to be had, and his only thought was to secure privacy for her and the right to comfort her. At the moment there seemed no other way; but he would admit it looked bad to others, who didn't understand the situation. These outward conventions never seemed important to him so long as one understood oneself. He hadn't meant to tell the girl about it because, with such a mother, she was trammeled by conventions of all sorts and therefore wouldn't understand that what was true *in spirit* was the same as truth.

But he admitted he'd been foolish. He was even grateful for her interference, when he thought about it, although he'd confess it seemed unpardonable at first. He'd been a law to himself for so many years that he didn't attach the same importance to convention that others did, but he must learn to do so now for the girl's sake. Of course everything should be as she wished. He wouldn't for the world go against her real desires, but he must see her and rearrange their plans. After he learned what she wanted him to do, he would spend the rest of the night in long-distance communications; certain explanations must be made, of course. Would she be so kind as to tell her he was waiting for her and must confer with her at once in order to send his dispatches? He would detain her only a very short time, and then she could return to the room that had been so kindly placed at her disposal.

Throughout this elaborate explanation Mrs. Dunlap had sat silent, with her eyes fixed upon the speaker and her thoughts busy with this new specimen of human nature.

Not for a moment did he deceive her into thinking he was true or that he was led headlong into a foolish and dangerous experiment. Not for an instant did she waver in her determination to keep those two apart until the girl's mother could make a third in their deliberations.

Yet she made no attempt to interrupt the words and grew interested in his skill for explaining the unexplainable.

When he paused, with an air of having mastered a difficult situation, she said, "You're very kind to give me details, but they don't alter the present situation. It's a relief to know you consider your course wrong, but I can't agree with your way of trying to right it. I've given my word to the lady that she won't be disturbed tonight and will take the homebound train in the morning. After she's safe at home with her mother and has rallied from the shock of this, you may be able to make plans that neither of you will be ashamed to look back upon. But she's in no condition to be consulted tonight. I feel quite sure she's learned her lesson and that any future plans must take her mother into full consideration. You must have had many more years than she, in which to learn wisdom; she is only eighteen, I think, while you—"

She paused significantly, but the man she judged to be not less than thirty-five was speechless. He'd staked much and expected to win. She turned and left him before he could think of any excuse to detain her longer.

Chapter 3

The remainder of the night was as unique as its earlier hours. On Mary Dunlap's return to her room she found the girl more composed and able to talk quietly.

"I've had time to think it out," she said, when Mrs. Dunlap had told what she meant to tell. "Mr. Keller doesn't understand; his mother died when he was a child and he brought himself up in a way. He's been a law to himself for so long that he just goes ahead and does what seems best to him. I'm sure he meant right. Even that strange part about registering," her face flushed as she spoke, "was done for my sake. I was so nervous all day and rely so little on myself that he felt he couldn't trust me alone and took that way of caring for me. But it's no wonder I'm nervous, for I've been doing *wrong* all day! I thought because I was of age, I had a right to decide for myself; but I realize there is a higher law than just a legal one, and I'm going home to Mother! I'm afraid she'll feel that she can never trust me out of her sight again—and I don't deserve to be trusted.

"I'll write to Mr. Keller and tell him we must give my mother time to know him and learn what a truly noble man he is. Then we must try by all honorable means to win her consent to our marriage. I will not—cannot—be married till my mother feels right about it."

"That sounds wise," said Mary Dunlap with relief in her voice. "That's what mothers were given for, to help in serious decisions. They seem to have a God-given intuition about the critical things of life. Remember that if you don't succeed in winning her over, she must surely have wise reasons for objecting—"

"Oh, I'm sure we'll succeed," interrupted the girl's voice anxiously. "More than anything else in this world my mother wants my happiness. But if we can't, after a reasonable time, convince her he is worthy of her trust, why then we must just be married without her consent. I have my own life to live"—she drew herself up proudly—"I can't afford to spoil my life and his because of prejudice."

This last was so much an echo from Mr. Keller's philosophy that the listener didn't say a word in response, and the eager voice continued.

"But we must do it honestly; there shall be no slipping away as though we were ashamed! I can't understand how I could have done such a thing! Doesn't it seem strange that I'd know *now* just what to do, when this morning I didn't at all? And so, dear friend—you'll be my friend always, won't you?—Mother will never know how to thank you enough for what you've done for me tonight! If you will put me on the train in the morning, as you said, I'll go directly home—no matter how many broken engines hinder."

Mary Dunlap tried by every means to convince the girl to get some sleep. She rang for a porter and made arrangements for the early train; she planned the smallest details to convince the girl she might be trusted. But there was no sleep for either of them. Her charge was docile enough; she lay down obediently and closed her eyes. But she started at every sound and imagined sounds that were not. Frequently, after a few minutes of silence, she would break into an excited explanation of Mr. Keller's movements, to place him in the best possible light.

"What is his business?" Mrs. Dunlap asked, deciding, after fruitless effort, that to humor the child's restlessness was perhaps better.

"He is—I—don't know—!"

The sentence began eagerly, then a pause, then a half-bewildered conclusion.

"He has to travel a great deal," she added. "He belongs to a firm, but I don't know what the firm is. It's strange I never thought to ask him!"

"Is his home in the West?"

"Yes—no, he's there *winters;* summers he's in the East somewhere. I don't remember which city he calls 'home'; he's in New York a great deal. He really hasn't much *home,* I presume—an unmarried man, whose parents are dead. It must be very dreary."

Poor innocent child! was Mrs. Dunlap's mental comment. *She really knows no more about the man than I do; I'm afraid not as much! For all she knows, he might be an adventurer who is careful not to have a settled home.*

But all she put into words was an earnest admonition to the girl to rest. For herself, she didn't mean to sleep; every nerve was alert for a possible invasion. Who could be sure of what that defeated plotter might attempt?

But the night passed without further incident, and early morning found the two at the telegraph office, from which presently two messages sped on their way.

One read: "Delayed by disabled engine. Coming on No. 2. All safe. Daisy." It had taken nearly half an hour to compose this message satisfactorily.

The other read: "Must fail you for Wednesday. Will give you Thursday instead, if desired. Wire me at Winfield. Mary Dunlap."

Mary had decided that the personal deposit of this young girl at her mother's door was more important than any other "woman's work" she could do that day. What she didn't know was that the man she had foiled was already seated in the smoker of the early train, waiting for her to disappear. She utterly distrusted him and felt instinctively that he would watch for his opportunity.

The girl was astonished when Mary seated herself in the opposite chair, after she'd established her charge in comfort.

"Oh, are you really going this way?" said the unsuspecting girl. "What made me think you were going farther west? How far do you go? To Winfield? Why, that's just beyond my station! How lovely! You'll stop and see Mother and let her thank you herself, won't you?"

But Mary had decided she would not. If the man were only a fool and not a confirmed villain, and the child's heart was bound up in him, it would be better that her prejudices, as well as her knowledge of that tragic night, never reach the mother's ears.

When the journey was over and they drove to the girl's home she waited only to clasp hands with the soft-spoken, grateful woman, into whose arms Daisy flung herself. She declined the invitation to stay, so they could shower kindnesses upon her, and sped on to Winfield.

Arriving in Winfield, Mary Dunlap's sole errand was to read a telegram she found awaiting her, send another and take the first train headed west.

On the fourth morning after these events she opened her eyes in a beautiful room of an elegant home in a New York City suburb. It was still early, and she lay quiet for a few minutes. She loved beauty and thus feasted her eyes on the evidences of abundant means and highly cultured taste spread lavishly about her. She had been too weary the night before to take in any details except a bed. Mary Dunlap was accustomed to being an honored guest in all sorts of homes. She could accommodate herself to the plainest home with a grace that was one of her charms; but she confessed to her most intimate friends that when "the lines fell to her in pleasant places" it stirred an extra note of thanksgiving in her heart. Certainly nothing was lacking here—nothing to offend the most fastidious taste or for the most exacting to desire.

The days and nights since leaving the girl with the mother had been strenuous ones to this ever-industrious woman: first, the rapid journey involving another failure to make an appointment, for this woman who prided herself on never failing; an equally rapid return to the East, reaching her next engagement just in time; then two hours by rail to her evening appointment; and here she was catching her breath in a lovely room with a whole day of rest before she had to start again!

She was in no haste to move. Her thoughtful hostess had urged her not to hurry down in the morning. "We don't eat breakfast until nine, and not always then if the head of the house is absent—as he is now, I'm sorry to say. I've always wanted him to meet you. Dear Mrs. Dunlap, I may as well confess that I'm awfully proud of my husband!" She ended her sentence with an apologetic laugh.

What a transparent lady her hostess was! She ought to be very happy, with a husband of whom she was "awfully" proud, a beautiful home crowded with all the luxuries wealth could produce and probably not a care in the world! Mary couldn't resist a little sigh of pity for herself; she was a lonely woman. Her husband and home and child all gone from her. She, too, had been "proud" of her husband with abundant reason and of her beautiful girl. But her girl was safe. The terrors of this awful world could not touch her. She thought of Daisy and shuddered for the narrowness of her escape. Had she escaped? Would that wretch try to find her again? Perhaps she hadn't done her whole duty. She ought to have warned the mother. What were mothers doing, to be so careless? But for that disabled engine, the child would have gone straight on her dangerous way!

She dressed at a leisurely pace, enjoying luxuries not found ordinarily in hotels or boarding houses. Even in the halls she came upon art treasures to study over. As she lingered in front of them, she told herself with a half-wistful smile that she must take care lest she become envious of Mrs. Oliver.

Then she fell to moralizing. Did her hostess place her heart's desire in things? It seemed so.

There were two daughters, she'd heard, who were their mother's joy and pride also. Certainly the outward appearance of the home left nothing to wish for. In such an atmosphere one could hardly avoid thinking of sharply contrasted lives. Not her own, though the contrast was marked enough. Still, she lived a busy life and, she hoped, a useful life and was happy in her work. But she knew many women to whom the word *happy* could not be applied—women with warped, stunted, even wrecked lives.

Instantly her thoughts flew again to Daisy, the acquaintance of a day, who had been so close to wreckage and made a permanent place for herself in this mother-heart. That awful man! Would she ever meet him again? If so, what would happen? What if she met him under circumstances that would compel her to acknowledge him as an acquaintance? For instance, what if he, after all, became Daisy's husband? She recoiled from the thought. Yet one couldn't be sure; the child had given herself unreservedly to him, unworthy of her as he seemed. Perhaps her love would redeem his life. Shouldn't she hope so? Yet her very soul revolted from it!

She reached the lower hall and glanced over the morning mail, gathering from it letters and telegrams for herself. Then her hostess crossed the hallway to greet her, in a charming house dress with a face as bright as the morning. She hoped the night had been restful and that her guest could give them the entire day.

"I'm so thrilled Mr. Oliver is at home to enjoy you. I had no hope of it. He came home unexpectedly on a later train than yours. He'd started on a long business trip, expecting to be gone for several months. Then one of those unaccountable business changes came up—I never pretend to understand business—and he came back. The children and I held a jubilee over his arrival. You can't think what a trial it is to have him away so much! Fully half his time is spent in the West or the South or somewhere!"

At that moment the dining-room door opened, and the expressive voice flowed on. "Oh, Ralph, are you down already? Mrs. Dunlap, let me present my husband, Mr. Oliver."

And Mary Dunlap stood face-to-face with the man she knew as R. H. Keller!

How they got through that awful breakfast hour Mary was afterward never certain. Of one thing she was certain, though; she must not wreck that poor woman's home—not yet, at least. She must take time and think about what to do. She must keep up appearances; she must seem to receive the man as her host; she mustn't say anything about the Kennard House or the interrupted journey or the disabled engine. What could she say? She didn't address him directly, and his wife did more than her share of the talking, for which Mary mentally blessed her.

Once the wife said: "Why, Ralph, what on earth is the matter? You are white as a ghost! Don't you feel well? I don't think you ought to start again tonight."

He put her off with a pleasantry of some sort, asked if the girls had gone to school already and gave careful attention to serving the guest.

Somehow the ordeal was lived through.

As they arose from the table Mrs. Oliver issued her instructions. "Now, Ralph, I want you to take Mrs. Dunlap to the library and entertain her for the next half-hour. I have a tiresome committee meeting that demands my personal attention; but I'm going to dismiss it in half an hour, and then we'll make plans for the day. It's delightful to have you both all day!"

Neither one attempted to reply. Silently the host threw open the door of his well-equipped library, which under other circumstances Mrs. Dunlap would have enjoyed exploring, and silently motioned her to a seat. While she sank among the cushions of a luxurious chair he closed the door; then, crossing to the doors leading to the music room, he closed them also. He seated himself a few feet from her and spoke in the same tone he used when he'd asked her why she presumed to interfere with him.

"Well, I am at your mercy! What do you propose to do?"

She looked steadily at him but said nothing.

After waiting a moment he added, "I didn't interfere with what you saw fit to do, although I could have. Why you've been silent thus far and have chosen to accept my wife's hospitality, I'm at a loss to understand—unless you're hoping to bring about an even greater sensation. Do you intend to tell me how you mean to blast my home, or do you still prefer to work in the dark?"

The man was actually arraigning her! Or was he merely bluffing? What kind of woman did he take her to be? The blood surged in her veins. She rose from the comfortable chair and took an uncompromising straight-backed one directly opposite his.

"Are you so accustomed to 'working in the dark' that you imagine others are doing it also?" she said, fixing him with her clear gaze. "Did you suppose I had the slightest idea of meeting *you* when I came to this house and accepted its hospitality?"

His face changed suddenly, and he bent forward as if to lessen the distance between them.

"Have I been mistaken in you? Mrs. Dunlap, on your honor as a woman, didn't you find out my name and follow me to this house to thwart me?"

"I certainly did not!" she replied. "Do you think I would have knowingly slept under your roof? I haven't awakened yet from the horror of seeing you."

"Then I beg your pardon," he said with evident relief. "I've wronged you. Now I will literally and gratefully throw myself on your mercy. You see what my home is, and my family—I have children. You have some idea now of what they think of me and what I am in the main—an attentive husband and father, doing his utmost for the comfort of his home. You happen to have seen me under damning conditions and without understanding the—the temptations. And now you have the power to ruin this home and the future of young and trusting lives, as well as break a woman's heart! Or you have the power to save us all! You are a merciful woman, a philanthropist, my wife tells me. I believe you will save us. You see, I'm not asking for justice but pleading for mercy."

He had not moved her by a hair's breadth unless it were to increase her indignation. Her voice was steady and cold.

"Didn't you have it in your power to ruin two homes, one of them widowed and fatherless, and did you spare them? *You* dare to talk to me of 'mercy' and 'philanthropy' when you were not willing to shelter even your own fireside!"

He dropped his eyes from her face and studied the paper cutter he held, turning it over and over.

"You don't understand," he said. "You make no allowances for a man's temptations."

Not seeing the look of scorn she gave him, he continued more quickly. "I don't know what devil possessed me to do as I did that night. I didn't plan it; it just happened. A fellow, whom we called 'the parson' in college because he always took those parts in the plays, had just written me about a mock wedding he'd officiated at, and he was within easy reach. The truth is, the girl tempted me!"

He caught the flash in her eyes just then and heard—and understood—her words: "Oh, *of course:* 'The woman beguiled me'!"

He pulled himself together. "I simply mean that she was—was—very bewildering, and I—" He was finding it hard to explain. He wished the woman would look at the floor, anything, instead of him!

"I'm going to be entirely frank with you," he said at last, with a sudden assumption of friendliness. "My wife is—we are—not congenial, not well mated. Our marriage was a mockery from the first, one of convenience on my part. I thought I ought to marry her because she cared for me, and because—well, for family reasons. I never really loved with my whole soul any woman until I met Daisy. After I knew her, what seemed wrong was to continue the travesty of home life when I knew that home, to me, meant her. I fully intended to set myself free as soon as I could, in order to possess her. But I didn't plan to injure her reputation in any way, nor indeed anyone's reputation. Divorces are common enough, I'm sure. The idea of running away with Daisy for a few weeks came to me, as I said, suddenly. I was going west, and she was returning home, when I met her on the train. I thought we could enjoy a delightful season together at some pleasant resort where neither of us was known—merely as good friends, you understand. The marriage ceremony was to be a temporary convenience to quiet her nervousness, to be explained afterward as a good joke. On my honor I meant nothing else."

He paused suddenly, for Mary Dunlap had risen, her face white with anger.

"I must interrupt you," she said. "I fail to see why you should disgrace yourself and me by exposing such details or attempting to gloss over your sin. If you think to win sympathy, you must have a strange idea of women! You to defile that sacred word *love* in such connection! Why even a wild beast knows that love means protection and sacrifice of self for the sake of the object loved! But you loved this child only enough to practice upon her the most cruel deception a man can offer to a woman, to blight her future and bring despair to her family—simply to gratify your passion for her company for a few weeks! It is foolish to suppose you didn't know what you were doing! You are neither a fool nor a lunatic. Why do you want to grovel before me by exposing that whole vile plot? How have you forgotten so soon what you said to me that night at the hotel? How awfully your words and your position contradict those statements! Before I saw you in this house this morning, as the husband of another woman, I supposed you were a halfway decent villain, who had tried to run away with and marry the girl he fancied he loved."

He too had risen. He trembled visibly and was white to his lips, but he tried to speak with dignity.

"I've made a mistake," he said. "I can't make you understand. But I'm ready to grovel still and beg your mercy. I haven't ruined her; she is free from me forever. I am asking you to take pity on my wife and children and, since no harm can come to anyone by your silence, to spare my family. I'm ready to give you my word of honor I will never see the girl again and never attempt to communicate with her in any way."

Mrs. Dunlap's immediate response to this brought a scarlet flush over his face and set the blood humming in his ears.

"*Your* word of honor!"

He was in real terror now; he had neither cowed nor deceived this woman.

No sentimental twaddle about uncongenial marriages and soul-love had done anything other than deepen her disgust.

He was also realizing something of the power that such a woman would have once she exerted it against him—and she was his wife's friend! Yet he had an instinct that he could trust her. He must beg.

"I deserve that," he said, after a breathless moment. "Well, then, I will swear by all that you hold sacred never to see or try to hear from that girl again. Will you keep my secret?"

For a full minute, which must have seemed an hour to the waiting man, silence hung over that room like a dark cloud. Then Mary Dunlap spoke.

"With conditions, yes—but you must do more than that. There are other girls in the world. I don't ask you to give me your pledged word because—" A single gesture of her hand consigned any "pledged" word of his to the lowest level of contempt. She left it to complete the sentence.

"But you've chosen to speak of me as a philanthropist. Perhaps you're aware that I've given my life to protect young innocent girls who are in danger because of such men as you. And you may understand what forces I can call to my aid anywhere in the civilized world, if need be. Therefore, for the sake of your wife and daughters, as long as you remain steadily within the law that governs respectable men and keep from insulting, by your attentions, not only the girl you tried to ruin, but every other girl and woman on God's earth, I will agree to keep silence to all but the one whose affections you have stolen and her mother! These two shall know all that I do: the girl, that she may learn to turn from the thought of you with loathing, and the mother, that she may guard her child with jealous care from men like you. Then I must remind you that the same forces for righteousness that stand ready to help me are as able to keep me informed as to how closely you adhere to the terms I've made. On these grounds do you wish mercy from me?"

The man's eyes were fixed on her now. Man of the world that he was, hypocrite that he had learned to be, accustomed to sneering at women, to flirting with women, to boasting within himself that he could lead them captive at his will—he looked at this woman whose hair was silvering and felt that she could, and would, keep her word! For a long minute he gazed at her, then bowed silently and looked at the floor.

They heard quick steps in the hall, a hand on the doorknob, and Mrs. Oliver fluttered in.

"It was a long half-hour, wasn't it?" she began. "Those women would talk! I thought I would never get away from them. Goodness! What is the matter with you two? You look as though you were posing for high tragedy. You haven't quarreled, have you?"

Mary Dunlap arose to the occasion.

"My dear Mrs. Oliver, I've decided I'll have to change my plans and start for Albany by the noon train today. I've concluded there's a certain matter that must have my immediate attention."

Mrs. Oliver was voluble with regrets. Such a disappointment! She'd been planning for this one day for so long! And Mr. Oliver was unexpectedly here to enjoy it with them. So sorry especially for her to miss seeing their new YW building that had been planned "in exact accordance with your own ideas, dear Mrs. Dunlap, and it is simply perfect. Do, Ralph, tell her how sorry you are not to be able to show her through it."

Thus urged, Mr. Oliver succeeded in finding voice to say: "Mrs. Dunlap understands, I'm sure, better than I could tell her, how ready I am to do her bidding."

Mary Dunlap got away by the noon train and took the westbound night express, canceling all her engagements for the week; she had more important work to look after. No telegrams or long-distance telephones or even carefully written letters could serve her now. She must go in person to explain, as best she might, to that dear girl who was waiting at home to hear from one to whom she had given her trust, to prove him to her mother as "good and noble"!

As she sped westward that afternoon, Mary Dunlap prayed that she might be able to help save that sweet, periled life.

Chapter 4

Mrs. Sheldon and her daughter, Daisy, were occupying easy chairs in their pleasant living room, surrounded by comfort and luxury. But even a passing glance at the two faces would have suggested unrest. The mother's face looked worn and her eyes anxious, while the daughter's countenance was tense with excitement.

"Daisy, dear—" began Mrs. Sheldon.

"Please, Mother, won't you call me Marguerite?"

The mother's face flushed, but she spoke quietly. "Why, daughter, you know I nearly always say Daisy."

"I know you do. But I—I don't like it tonight. I—Mother, I just *can't* bear the sound of it! That's the only explanation I can give."

Tears formed in the mother's eyes. "I will try to remember," she said, her voice low. "But you are *my* Daisy, you know—all I have left in this world—and your father loved that name."

Suddenly Daisy flung herself on the arm of the great easy chair and, weeping, hid her face in her mother's neck. "Oh, Mother, please try to understand. You know what Father was to me, and you surely know that I love *you* with all my *soul*. If I hadn't I—"

She hid her face once more, weeping again, while the mother's arms clasped her tenderly. A few minutes passed, then the girl sat erect and tried again.

"Mother, dear, forgive me." She slipped to the footstool beside her mother's chair. "I didn't mean to worry you. I don't often go to pieces in this way, do I? But—you can't understand what I'm going through. It seems so strange not to hear a word after almost five days! I thought I would at least get a telegram. Mama, I didn't mean that—about my name, at least not in the way it sounded. I'll get over that feeling, of course. But—you see he didn't know me by any other name. And when you used it, for a second I could almost hear his voice, and—oh, Mother, I couldn't bear it! I spoke right out before I thought. Mother, it seems as though you *must* understand what I mean. Don't you know you told me how you loved Father so very much even right at the first? That's the way I feel about Rufus. Mother, I love him with all my soul, and I always shall! I never knew what love meant, that kind of love, I mean—and I can't tell you how it almost kills me to think that you don't believe in him!

"But you've hardly seen him. You've let yourself be prejudiced by those horrid women who gossiped about him—just because he was polite and helpful to those little flappers who were traveling alone. He showed them the same attention any gentleman would. But I don't blame you, Mother, dear. I suppose it's natural for mothers to feel so—when you've never found out for yourself what a wonderful man he is.

"Besides, think how I helped it along! Why, Mother, when I think of the way I let that awful Mrs. Dunlap, a perfect stranger, manage me so that I almost insulted him, I feel as if I were going insane! Oh, I hope I never see or hear of her again! How could I let her make me treat him so! I don't see how he can ever forgive me. Oh, Mother! How can I live any longer? I wish I could die tonight!"

Just then the doorbell pealed throughout the quiet house. The sound had an instant effect on the nerves of the half-insane girl. She sprang up, evidently making a supreme effort at self-control, and spoke more naturally.

"I'm afraid that's Nelson. I forgot he was coming over tonight to tell me how the vote went—as if I cared how they voted!"

With these last words her voice had returned to bitter sarcasm, but after a moment she continued more quietly. "Will you see him, Mother, and tell him—tell him anything you like? I simply cannot talk with him tonight, nor with anybody else. Oh, Mother, kiss me and let me run away!"

By this time the poor mother had no words to offer about anything. She put her arms around her daughter, kissed her tenderly and opened the door for her to escape by way of the back hall, just as the maid appeared at the sitting-room doorway, card tray in hand.

"For Miss Daisy, ma'am. Has she gone upstairs? Shall I take it up to her room?"

"No," said the weary, faithful mother. "Daisy doesn't feel up to seeing callers tonight. I'll attend to it."

She held out her hand for the card and read: "Mrs. J. C. Dunlap, Albany."

"Dunlap!" The mother flushed, then paled. That was the name of the woman who had watched over her darling with such wise and patient care and brought her safely home! Could it be the same woman who was waiting in the parlor? If so, how could she talk with her now? She felt completely exhausted. Still, Daisy certainly mustn't be called. The name *Dunlap* was common enough, even though she didn't recall it among her acquaintances. A woman who lived hundreds of miles away would most likely not appear suddenly late in the evening to make a call. At last she crossed the hall and opened the living-room door. One glance sufficed; the woman who arose at her entrance was the same one who had kissed Daisy good-bye with unmistakable tenderness only a few days before.

"I'm afraid I've startled you," said Mary Dunlap moving forward.

Daisy's mother had paused the moment she caught sight of her caller, and her pale face expressed pain.

"Of course you didn't expect to see me so soon again, but I—it became my duty to return West sooner than I'd planned. I hope I may see your daughter for a few minutes? There is a—I've heard of—something connected with our journey together that she, perhaps, ought to be told." The faltering words suggested her uncertainty as to what she should do next.

The mother decided at once. Whatever that woman thought she ought to tell Daisy ought to be told! She believed in her. She might be mistaken in judgment, of course—unduly alarmed about a small matter; all people were liable to occasional mistakes. But she was sincere! Of that, Mrs. Sheldon felt absolutely sure, and what she had to say might help to clear away some anxieties.

She held out her hand. "I'm glad to see you again, Mrs. Dunlap. But I'm afraid my daughter won't be able to do so this evening. She's had a somewhat trying day and doesn't feel like talking with anyone tonight. She seems undone by her recent experiences. She has retired, I think, but perhaps you'll trust me with a message?"

"Perhaps I'd better tell you all about it," she said, deciding quickly and speaking as an intimate friend might have. "I've taken a room at the Delport House and probably won't leave until tomorrow afternoon. If Daisy is feeling better I could see her in the morning. I hope you'll pardon my interest in your daughter and my familiar use of her name. She and I grew quite intimate during that one day."

The mother wondered, *What would she think if she knew I'd just been told to say Marguerite!*

Noting the troubled glance of the mother, Mary hurried on: "I had a precious little girl of my own, about your daughter's age, Mrs. Sheldon. She was my only child. That night when your daughter stayed with me in my room was the first time I'd ever been able to say with my whole heart, 'Thank God my dear girl is forever safe in the everlasting arms!' That is my apology for intruding on you again. And now perhaps it would be wiser for me to talk with you, leaving you to repeat as much or as little as you see fit, to your daughter."

Mrs. Sheldon answered quickly. "Oh, I wish you would! I've so longed to see you and ask you questions. Won't you sit down? Please tell me first about that night at the hotel. I know so very little about it, and I want to understand exactly what happened. Daisy has been very vague in her story and is so excitable that I dare not question her. All I know for sure is that because of crowded conditions at the hotel you kindly permitted her to share your room for the night."

"You haven't been told the whole story!" exclaimed Mary Dunlap. It seemed incredible that such a girl as the one she'd protected had kept her mother in ignorance of that night's events.

"Oh, tell me!" said the mother, dropping down on the edge of the couch where the caller had seated herself. "Tell me *all*, please. I've been at an utter loss to understand Daisy's unstrung state of mind."

Mary wondered where she should begin and then plunged into her subject.

"First, may I ask, please, about this Mr. Keller whom I met that night with your daughter? Of course I knew nothing of him whatever. Is he a personal acquaintance of yours? A—*friend?*"

"Certainly not!" she replied. "I've met him once and have never liked anything I've heard about him. He's a traveling agent of sorts, I believe, for some New York firm, and business seems to call him to this particular town more frequently than I could wish. My daughter thinks I'm prejudiced against him because of certain stories we've heard about him, which she thinks are founded only in malicious gossip. But, frankly, he is a source of great anxiety to me. For the past few months he's been quite attentive to Daisy, that is, as attentive as circumstances would allow, and I—do not trust him. I don't know why. But I don't! I'm at a loss to account for the influence he's acquired over her in their few brief meetings. She thinks me hard and cruel because I—well, I can scarcely bear the sound of his name! And yet I have to confess that I have no good reason to offer for such a feeling. It appears that he really asked her to marry him. The idea is so obnoxious to me that I can scarcely bear to utter the words!"

"And this trip they were taking together," ventured the troubled questioner, "you knew about it, of course?"

"Trip!" exclaimed the mother. "They weren't traveling together! Why, I sent her away on a visit to get her out of his vicinity. I'd heard he intended to stay in this town several weeks. They simply met on the train. Daisy thinks it was a coincidence, I suppose, from what he says, but of course he followed her. I'm positive of that. To put it plainly, he seems to be infatuated with her. And she, poor child, has admitted to me this very afternoon that she loves him with all her heart! Oh, it seems so terrible for me to be telling this to you, a stranger, burdening you with my anxiety."

Mrs. Sheldon struggled to keep the tears from falling. "But you've been so kind to Daisy and me, and there's no one else I can go to for advice."

Mary Dunlap slipped an arm around the shoulders of the mother.

"My dear!" she said in a strong, comforting voice. "Just cry if you want to, and don't worry about telling me. I'm used to helping mothers and girls. It's my job in life. And don't worry. I'm going to help you, and I thank God I can. I'm glad too that you've told me this, for now I can speak frankly. It's going to make things a lot easier to set right. And now I must tell you the whole story."

Chapter 5

Her voice was low and tender as she began her story of the afternoon on the train. She had been so busy with her writing that she scarcely noticed who got on the train. Barely conscious of the two who took the seat in front of her, she'd given them only a swift glance and decided they were bride and groom. Once she finished her work and had leisure to look around, she was fascinated almost at once by the lovely face of the girl in front of her.

The mother's troubled face relaxed as Mary Dunlap said this, and she nodded in sympathy as Mary gave her own first impression of the man who was sitting beside the girl.

The tale progressed, with the lateness of the train and the missed connections.

"Oh!" Mrs. Sheldon interrupted. "I'm *so* glad you were there! What *would* Daisy have done if you hadn't been. She's so unused to traveling alone!"

Mary told of the apparent argument between the two, the discomfort on the girl's face and her own continued wonder that such a girl would be married to the type of man he appeared to be.

The mother gasped as she realized that this woman had actually thought her daughter was married to that man!

Not until the story reached the point where Mrs. Dunlap wrote her name in the hotel registry and noted the names on the line just above hers, "R.H. Keller and wife," did the mother grasp the full meaning of it all. Then she leaned forward and took hold of the firm hands of her visitor.

"Oh, Mrs. Dunlap! You don't mean it! You *can't* mean that he *dared* do a thing like that! The wretch! The—the—*beast!*"

Her eyes were full of tears again. She couldn't seem to find words strong enough to express her horror and disgust.

"Of course, my Daisy didn't know that!" she said, lifting her head.

"Not until I told her, sometime afterward," Mary said.

"You told her! She *knows!* And yet she could tell me today that she loves him! Oh, what shall I do?"

"Wait, Mrs. Sheldon," Mary said, reaching out her hand to the distraught mother. "Love is a strange thing. It throws illusions over the object and turns it into something entirely different. Don't blame Daisy too much. She explained that, of course, he must have done that to protect her reputation, since they'd been delayed and all their plans upset. She said they'd expected to reach San Fergus at midnight and that a minister friend of Mr. Keller's was to have met the train and performed the marriage ceremony. She said that Mr.

Keller had telegraphed ahead for the bridal suite to be reserved for them in the San Fergus hotel."

"My Daisy told you that!"

It was years before Mrs. Dunlap forgot the tone in the mother's voice and the look on her face when she said those words. It was as if someone had stolen from her everything in life that was worthwhile, as if all the years of tender rearing and precious love and companionship between her and her child were suddenly wiped out in one great awful act of disloyalty and broken faith with her mother. Oh, by and by the mother would excuse and forgive and bleed over her darling; but this first blow was like the severing of the life bond between them, and it was terrible to witness. Mary felt that it was a pity the girl had not had to suffer that look herself with full understanding of all that it meant to her wonderful little mother.

"My dear! I feel like a surgeon performing an operation, but you must know it all," said Mary tenderly.

"Oh, yes, yes," sighed the mother. "If there is more, go on. Nothing matters if my Daisy would go to such lengths. Actually running away to get married!"

"My dear friend, you must remember she thinks she is very much in love and feels that you've been deceived about her loved one. They were planning to send you a telegram as soon as the ceremony was performed and were counting on your change of feeling as soon as the inevitable step was taken. Your daughter was greatly troubled even then at the momentary deception. As the time drew near and their plans delayed, she began to see the whole thing in more nearly its true light, and it caused her deep distress. So much so that when Mr. Keller left her for a few moments in the hotel lobby, she forgot my presence and began pacing up and down the room and even moaning a little out of her distress. It was then that I dared to interfere and offer my sympathy and any help I could give."

"Oh, how can I ever thank you! How can I thank God enough for sending you there!" cried the stricken mother.

"I think He did plan that I should be there," Mary said. "I was scheduled to be far from there at that time, had important speaking engagements to fill and couldn't understand why my plans were frustrated. But it seems that the Father had need of a servant right there, and perhaps this was more important than any meeting I could have addressed. I felt that as soon as your Daisy turned to me so readily, like the flower-faced child that she is. I had no difficulty in getting her to tell me her trouble. She trusted me at once, and when I offered my room as a refuge for the night she accepted eagerly. Even when I told her how she was booked in the registry, she didn't turn from me, as I feared she might. Instead, she seemed aghast for a moment; then out of loyalty to her lover she attempted to excuse him. But that didn't prevent her from begging me to take her to the room immediately, before he returned from his telegraphing. She seemed to fear his influence upon her and to know that her only safe course was to go while he was gone."

"Oh, my poor child!" exclaimed the mother.

"She made it very plain that Mr. Keller had persuaded her to this marriage," Mary continued, "and that, while she couldn't bear to refuse him, she longed to wait until your consent could be obtained. Of course I advised her strongly that this was the only possible right course, and she seemed to agree with me."

"Yes, Daisy is very conscientious—that is, she was before this. But she seems to be infatuated with that man! She has at this moment more faith in him than in anyone else, I believe."

"Well, she was glad to get to my room then, at least," said the other woman. "She even wanted the door locked. When I started to go down and tell Mr. Keller she was safe and comfortable for the night with a woman, she begged me to lock the door and *take the key with me!*"

"And yet she says she loves him, when she cannot trust him! And at such a time! Oh, my little girl!"

"Dear friend, the human heart is a curious thing, and the devil has many illusions for deceiving."

"Did you actually go down and talk to that man? What a wonderful heaven-sent friend you proved to be!"

"I did. I'm afraid I rather enjoyed the commission. You must remember I'd been watching him in the train for several hours. While he was courteous and assiduous in caring for her, and did nothing wrong I could put my finger on, I acquired the same feeling toward him that you seem to have. I just could not see how that flower of a girl could have married him. And of course when I talked with your daughter, finding out they weren't married after seeing how he registered, my feelings were anything but lenient toward him."

"I should think so! But, oh, my little girl! What would her father have said if he could have known she'd go through a thing like this!"

"Courage, dear sister. I'm sure God means something lovely to come out of all this."

"How could that possibly be!" exclaimed the mother. "Oh, if she could have been spared any contact with a creature like that! It is so terrible to see her go through such an ordeal. My Daisy!"

"Yes, but, Mrs. Sheldon, think if she didn't have you in this trying time!"

Just then the two women heard the maid answer a ring at the door. Moments later someone was standing in the doorway of the room where they were sitting.

Mrs. Sheldon stood up quickly, dabbing at her wet eyelashes, and crossed the room toward him.

Mary Dunlap glanced up to see a tall young man with his hat in his hand and a question on his face. He had keen gray eyes, a crop of nicely groomed reddish curls and a forthright, dependable look about him.

"Oh, Nelson!" exclaimed Mrs. Sheldon, with relief in her voice. "You came to see Daisy about that committee meeting, didn't you? Why—she—she wasn't feeling very well tonight, Nelson. She's retired. She—had a headache. She asked me to excuse her."

"Daisy not well?" he asked seriously, as if that were an unheard of thing.

"I should have telephoned you not to come," apologized Mrs. Sheldon, "but this friend of hers—this friend of mine—arrived just then, from out of town, and it slipped my mind. Let me introduce you to Mrs. Dunlap, Nelson. Mrs. Dunlap, Mr. Whitney."

"A friend of Daisy's?" said the young man, his serious eyes lighting pleasantly. He stepped forward and grasped Mrs. Dunlap's hand, giving her a swift, searching glance.

"I certainly am!" said Mary Dunlap with a hearty handclasp.

He lingered only a minute or two to leave a message for the daughter about what had happened at the committee meeting. But he gave another keen glance with a warming smile as he left, letting the stranger know that he approved of her and that he understood she hadn't caused the tears he'd seen on Daisy's mother's face.

After he left Mrs. Sheldon returned to her caller.

"Why couldn't it have been that young man?" asked Mary Dunlap with a sigh.

"Oh, if only it could have been!" sighed the mother. "He's the dearest boy! My husband trusted him so. He's been Daisy's schoolmate and companion for years, and yet she could think she's fallen in love with that other creature!"

"There, there, dear friend. I tell you the human heart is a mystery. And a girl at Daisy's age gets odd ideas sometimes. She'll come out of it and be fine and beautiful. You'll see!"

"Oh! I don't know!" sighed the mother. "She's so strange! Not even willing to see Nelson. She thought it was Nelson when you came and rushed away telling me she wouldn't see him or anyone else tonight. I couldn't tell him that, of course. He's been so kind and devoted. And I can see he's terribly worried about this Keller. He looks as if he'd like to fight every time Daisy mentions his name. But, tell me, what did the fellow do when you told him Daisy was going to remain with you for the night?"

"Do? He was fairly insolent. He was furious. He told me to mind my own business. He strode around that parlor like a madman, till I told him Daisy had appealed to me for protection and said she wasn't married to him yet. I told him I'd seen how he registered in the hotel. Then he calmed down a little and tried to smooth things over. He said he'd done that merely to protect the girl and intended to make everything right for her. He even said that perhaps he'd been wrong in doing it, but he'd followed an impulse when he wrote. Oh, you know how a man like that can lie himself out of anything! He even said that if Daisy preferred to be with me, it was all right; but he must see her before she slept and arrange about his telegrams. Of course I saw through that. He knew his influence over her! So I told him she'd asked not to be disturbed and didn't wish to see him again until she was at home with her mother and her mother knew all. He raved at me, but I told him I wouldn't hesitate to call for assistance if he made further trouble. I fancy he didn't care for publicity and withdrew with what grace he could."

"And then?"

"Well, strange to say, we had no further trouble with him. I'd looked up trains and found there was a very early one. Perhaps he was asleep, although I was taking no chances. I decided to stay by till I placed her safely in her mother's care."

"You've been wonderful!" said the mother. "I can never thank you. And I'm glad, too, that you came and told me all tonight. It's been very hard to hear, but it's right that I should know. Only, my dear new friend, I don't know what I'm going to do. I'm terrified at what may yet develop. I'm sure that man won't be easily shaken off. He's probably only waiting till Daisy gets wrought up with anxiety, as she is now, when he knows she'll be wax in his hands. I can't believe he'll give up so easily. He'll know you can't linger here to protect her forever, and, unfortunately, he's not afraid of me."

"My dear, wait until you've heard the rest of the story."

"Is there more?" The mother leaned forward, clasping her frail hands in one another till the knuckles showed white.

"No, dear, don't be frightened," Mary said. "I'll try to be as brief as possible, but I'm sure you should know everything."

"Oh, yes!" implored the mother.

Mary's heart ached for her as she continued the story. "After I left Daisy with you that morning, I later went to New York where I was to be entertained by a Mrs. Oliver whom I'd met a number of times in connection with my public work. She'd often invited me to be her guest and talk over various matters with her, but I'd never been able to arrange a definite date. I arrived at midnight and was taken almost at once to my room, seeing none of the family that night except my hostess. But the next morning at breakfast I was introduced to her two lovely daughters and, a moment later, to her husband who had just arrived on an early train from the West. You can imagine my horror when I looked up to greet him and found that the man Mrs. Oliver was introducing, calling him 'her husband Mr. Oliver,' was the Mr. Keller from whom your daughter had been rescued a few nights before!"

Mary Dunlap told the end of her story rapidly, conscious that her listener was under a heavy strain, and now she looked up with relief that all was told.

But the poor mother had borne all she could. She slumped forward and would have fallen if the caller hadn't put her arms about her and laid her gently on the couch.

"My dear!" she said as she stooped over the suffering woman and patted her gently. "Don't feel so terribly about it. I'm sure this part of the story should be a relief, for it certainly puts that man in a position where he dare not touch your daughter again!"

"But, oh, to have my Daisy mixed up with a man like that!" cried the mother. "I can never lift my head again!"

"Oh, dear, that is a very small part of the whole matter. The main thing is that no harm shall come to the child. No one here knows, of course, and he has promised!"

But a new voice broke forth in the room, clear and cold like a young Nemesis.

"What are you doing to my mother? Have you come here to make more trouble for us? Who are you, anyway?"

Chapter 6

The girl stood in the doorway, her eyes flashing like blue flames. Her delicate profile was outlined against the rich portier, chin lifted, the light catching the glint of the waves in her hair, turning them into gold. The delicate blue of her silk kimono brought out the pearly tint of her skin, a haughty patrician, insolent in her loveliness.

Mary Dunlap looked at her in pity and admiration and with growing amazement. Was this the girl who had melted into tears in her arms but a few nights before and implored her to protect her? How lovely she was even in her frenzy. She made a picture as she stood there in her familiar setting. Poor, misguided young woman! What a hard road she had set her feet to travel, and how soon she must come to humiliation.

"Marguerite!" the mother exclaimed, sitting bolt upright and looking at her daughter sternly, as she hadn't since she was a very little girl. "Marguerite! You forget yourself! Apologize at once to Mrs. Dunlap. She is the best friend you have in this world. She has gone to great inconvenience and expense to save you from an awful calamity!"

The Marguerite of a few days ago would have been crushed to earth by such words from her beloved mother. Not so the girl of that night. She did not even wince. Instead, she drew herself up to her full height and, looking her mother steadily in the eyes, as if their ages had been reversed, spoke with an air of authority that was almost startling.

"No, I am not beside myself, Mother! You don't know what *you* are doing. You've allowed yourself to be blinded by a total stranger. You've swallowed whole the lies she's handed you. Mother, I understand it now. This woman is a rank imposter, employed by others to ruin the reputation of a prominent and successful businessman, in order to extort money from him. Oh, I've heard a lot she's said! Don't try to stop me. Isn't this kind of thing being done every day now? The daily papers are filled with it. Why, even novels are full of plots like that. What about that horrid woman whose latest book is being lauded in every review column? Didn't she make one of her characters boast of being a daughter of Eve to some purpose because she'd told some successful lies about one of her victims? I tell you, Mother, you don't know the world. Times have changed since you were a girl. You think every woman is good, simply because she's a woman and dresses respectably. That's why you're willing to believe all these terrible things about Rufus and why you want me to believe them. Just because a woman has told you. Just ask her how much she's being *paid* to bring about his ruin. Ask her that! Do you suppose she'll be paid whether she succeeds or not? Probably not; that's why she's so persistent, sneaking in to tell tales to you when I'm not here and get you on her side. She's afraid she'll lose her money!"

"Marguerite! Oh, my poor child!" cried the mother in horror. "Oh, Mrs. Dunlap, I beg you to forgive her. She doesn't know what she is saying."

"That's perfectly all right, Mrs. Sheldon. Don't think of it for a moment. I understand."

But the girl's voice broke in scornfully. "I certainly do know what I'm saying. I understand it all perfectly. I can see the plot clearly now. I remember how this woman sat behind us in the cars, no doubt with a purpose, listening to us. She was writing all afternoon. I suppose she took down our private conversation. She probably carries on such business constantly and chooses her victims among those who look as if they'd care about their reputations and have plenty of money to hush up such tales. That's called blackmail, Mother, and I've read a lot about it in the papers. But they're not going to frighten us. Rufus and I will search out this thing to the root and make it impossible for this woman ever to gain in her deadly work on any other good Christian man. It would even be worth sacrificing ourselves if we could do that. It's because people are afraid that they succumb to such things as this. We're not afraid! This woman listened to our plans and discussions and knew just where to get us. If I hadn't been such a fool I'd have understood at the time, and I shouldn't have yielded to the spell she cast over me. She must be a hypnotist. She somehow succeeded in making everything look different from what it really is. But she can't do it again. My eyes are open!"

The two women listened to more such statements as the evening wore on. Mrs. Sheldon was mortified at the way her daughter lashed out at the woman who'd saved her from a life of humiliation. Further, she was alarmed for the sanity of the one who was dearer to her than life—so much so that she roused from her own weakness to try to bring the girl to reason, but to no avail.

Mary stood by helpless, trying to think of something she might say to bring the girl to her senses. At last she leaned over to the mother and said quietly, "Suppose I just go away for the night now. She's excited, and the sight of me only irritates her. If she could get some sleep she might be more reasonable in the morning. No, don't get up. I can find my way to the door. You can telephone if you need me. I'll stay close to my room till I hear from you. And I will pray! Don't despair, dear sister! God is *strong!* Now—I'll just slip away!"

The girl's keen ears caught the last sentence.

"Yes, 'slip away,' by all means! I'm surprised that didn't occur to you before!"

Then, as the door closed behind Mrs. Dunlap, Marguerite began to pace the floor in her fury. Finally, having exhausted herself with her wild words, she flung herself down before her mother with her head in her mother's lap and wept.

"Oh, Mother, that dreadful woman has made me almost crazy! Sometimes I don't know what I'm saying. But I know this, and I mean it. I *know* that Rufus is true to me, and not only to me, but to God. He's very religious, Mother. You ought to hear him talk. And, Mother, I know I love him, *love* him, with my whole *soul!* And I shall forever! No matter how many fiends from the underworld try to make me false to him!"

At the word *love* her sobbing ceased. She sprang to her feet and began to pace up and down the room again. Her voice rose to almost a shriek.

What use was there to attempt further words with one who was surely not responsible for what she said or did? The mother slipped to her knees and began to pray.

A voice of power spoke to her soul, while she was still on her knees, seeking help. It seemed to her that she almost heard the words, "I will bring the blind by a way that they know not; I will lead them in paths that they have not known. I will make darkness light, before them; and crooked things straight."

Oh, the wonderful words! Could there be a human being any *blinder* than her Daisy? How terribly she needed new "paths"! Because of the amazing voice Mrs. Sheldon got through that night and the next morning and was able to persuade her daughter to receive Mrs. Dunlap in the evening and hear from her lips what she had to tell.

Mrs. Dunlap had requested this over the telephone, having decided that the mother was physically unable to endure further strain. But that Christian woman considered the hour spent with Daisy Sheldon as one of the hardest in her life.

Not that Daisy didn't try, at least at first, to treat her in accordance with the rules of propriety. But as the story progressed, the question kept pressing in the narrator's mind: *How shall I convince this girl that I am speaking only truth!* She was used to being trusted implicitly and quoted as unquestioned authority in everything connected with the work to which she'd given her life. Yet this girl listened calmly to the story that had caused her mother's lapse into almost unconsciousness, with a half smile on her lips that deepened into a sneer.

"That's a very strange story, Mrs. Dunlap! Being as well acquainted with Mr. Keller as I am, I don't quite understand how I could be expected to believe it! I'd really like to see a photograph of this mysterious person, to help me figure out how a woman of your discernment could have been so deceived! Of course, you were acquainted with Mr. Keller only briefly, while he is my closest friend."

Could this be the girl who had so recently clung to her, weeping and begging to be shielded from even the sight of the man who was her "closest friend"? How could Mrs. Dunlap keep from giving a second's thought to such a question? But she turned from it and tried again.

"Wait, please," she said patiently, "I must tell you the rest. I've had a longer acquaintance with the man than you've heard as yet. After breakfast, Mrs. Oliver asked him to take me into the library while she attended to other duties. After he closed and *locked* the doors he threw himself on my mercy and begged me not to wreck his household by telling his wife and children what I knew about him. He didn't deny he was the same Mr. Keller I'd held a long conversation with two nights before. In fact, he frankly admitted that you were a 'temptation' to him and that the 'marriage ceremony' was only a joke to relieve your anxieties for being away from your mother longer than you'd planned.

"I'd rather not hurt you by repeating the words he used to describe your wonderful mother and her ignorant prejudice as he called it. He also told me that his friend who posed as a minister for the time being was an amateur actor who had successfully impersonated a clergyman while they were in college; that gave him the idea of a mock marriage to quiet your protests.

"And here's a paper written and signed by this man in which he pledges never to write or telegraph or telephone you or visit you again. It is a paper I went back to secure, after I started on this western trip. The man knows that his keeping this agreement both in letter and spirit is the price of my silence toward his wife and children. His wife is a charming and beautiful woman, and his two daughters are as sweet and charming as you. It seemed terrible to wreck that home, but I wouldn't keep silent unless I felt sure you would be safe forever from him."

Marguerite Sheldon tilted her patrician chin haughtily, a smile of scorn on her lips.

"Mrs. Dunlap," she said, "you certainly are mistress of your profession. You've worked out your evil plot to the last detail. You must have gone to great pains to counterfeit Mr. Keller's handwriting. Perhaps you stole some of his own letters from my handbag to copy while I slept. Of course this remarkable interview is part of the whole scheme. One wonders whether you were cunning enough to concoct it on the spur of the moment or had it prepared if I didn't fall for your story at once? The daily papers are full of such tales of blackmail and the like. Perhaps if my tastes lay in that direction and I'd informed myself better on the ways of people like you, I might have been saved from yielding to your influence which I thoroughly believe to have been hypnotic.

"Of course I might have saved your time by saying all this before I heard you. But my mother was so anxious for me to hear you that I've listened to your remarkable tale with what patience I could summon. But now we've had enough of this farce. I believe in Mr. Keller's honor and integrity as entirely as I did before this insane plot was planned. Until I hear from his own lips that he did not intend to marry me that night and that he is not Mr. Rufus Keller, and never was, I shall not believe one word of this story. And I shall remain as I am now, his promised wife until he comes to claim me."

Before this outburst the baffled woman sat silent, dumbfounded. She had never seen such beautiful faith in such a worthless man. She wasn't troubled over the insults that were flung at her; the situation had become too serious to be thinking of self. The question that appalled her was, how was it possible to save this poor blind child from her own folly? Suddenly she resolved to try one more thing. It seemed the last resort.

"Miss Sheldon," she said, looking straight into the eyes of the angry girl, "will you put this thing to the test? Will you accompany me on the midnight express to New York? I'll take you to call on Mr. Ralph Oliver in his private office, Number—Fifth Avenue, so he may tell you himself he's the Mr. Keller you know so well? He's to be in his office tomorrow morning. Will you go?"

The girl rose in silence and moved swiftly across the room. She opened the door and closed it behind her with a distinct slam.

Chapter 7

Mary Dunlap was left alone in the big beautiful room with the echo of the scornful young words and that slammed door driving into her soul. She suddenly rested her elbow on the arm of the chair in which she sat and dropped her tired head upon her hand. Closing her eyes she prayed, with her soul crying out from the depth of her failure. She'd done her best for this young woman and failed. Now she called upon her Father for sustaining strength, for light, for guidance, for calmness in the midst of despair, for the headstrong blinded girl and for the worn, despairing mother.

Then out of her despair came peace and an awareness that the Father cared more than she did, even more than the stricken mother.

She became conscious of the quiet entrance of that mother, like a sad wraith. Lifting her head Mary tried to smile but failed.

"It was no use!" she said sadly. "She wouldn't believe a word I said."

"Oh, my dear friend!" sighed the mother. "What should I do without you? I've been praying while you were down here. I can't think my little girl will be allowed to go to destruction or lose her mind or anything. She is a child of the covenant. Her father and I dedicated her to the Lord when she was born. He cannot desert us! You don't think He would let her go like this, do you? She is—a church member—of course—and has always seemed—a Christian. Haven't I a right to claim His promises for my child?"

"You certainly have," said the strong hearty voice. "Come, let's kneel down now and claim that promise, 'Where two of you shall agree as touching anything that they shall ask, it shall be done for them of my Father.'"

So the two women knelt hand in hand beside the couch and poured out their hearts in prayer for the foolish girl. At last it seemed that their yearning words must be already spread before the mercy seat with the swift answer on its way; new courage entered the mother's heart.

Upstairs footsteps hurried about for a few minutes, and then silence fell. But if the two petitioners heard them it was only to be thankful they were not the regular measured frantic tread going back and forth all day. Perhaps she was resting at last.

They rose with a peace upon their faces.

"Now," said Mary Dunlap, "it's time you went to bed and slept. We've put the whole matter in the Father's hands, and we can't do anything else till He shows us. Suppose you run upstairs and see if she's all right. Then if she's resting I'll go back to the hotel and let you get to bed, for I'm sure I won't be needed anymore tonight."

"You've been so wonderful!" murmured Mrs. Sheldon. "What would I have done without you? Why not stay here tonight? Our guest room is always ready, and then we can talk things over in the morning."

"No," Mary said decidedly, "it's better for me to be out of the house. The child resents my presence just now and will come to herself twice as quickly if she's alone with her mother. Get a good night's rest, and perhaps she'll see things differently in the morning. Sleep does a great deal toward bringing sane vision."

"Oh, I do hope she's asleep! She never even lay down last night—just walked the floor and talked in that wild frantic way and then cried! I never saw anybody cry like that, so desperate, so resentful! It frightened me! But I can't let you go back to the hotel at this time of night. It must be very late indeed. I'm sure I heard the midnight train go down quite a few minutes ago. It isn't safe for a woman to be out alone so late."

"Nonsense!" Mary said with a laugh. "Nobody would touch me. I've been out at all hours in all kinds of places and shall often be if I live. It doesn't bother me a bit. Come, run up and see if the child is all right and then I'll go. You mustn't lose any more sleep. Can't I just stand here at the foot of the stairs and you wave to me if all is well? Is the night latch on the door? And does that light turn out from above? Then I'll shut the door after me, and you needn't come down again tonight. Good night, dear, brave mother. I'll call you up in the morning and see how the Father is answering our prayer."

Mrs. Sheldon pressed the other woman's hand and then tiptoed upstairs. Her footfalls were muffled in the heavy texture of costly rugs, and Mary Dunlap waited below for her signal, yawning wearily and suddenly realizing she felt very old and tired.

But the footsteps did not return at once. It seemed a long time before she heard Mrs. Sheldon running across the floor above, rushing through the hall and down the stairs with a fluttering paper in her hand. Her face was chalk white in the subdued light of the hall chandelier, and her eyes burned dark.

"She's gone!" she cried, her voice catching in a sob. "She's not there at all. She's gone to New York!" She thrust a paper into Mrs. Dunlap's hand and dropped down on the lowest step of the stair, her face in her hands.

Mary read the paper Mrs. Sheldon had handed her.

> Dear Mother:
>   There is only one thing left for me to do, and that is to go to Number—Fifth Avenue, New York, and prove there is no Mr. Ralph Oliver. After I've done that, I shall go and find Rufus, and we'll be married at once! It is my duty to save Rufus from this terrible plot against his character.

After that we will take care of you. Don't worry. I'll let
you hear from me.

Lovingly,
Daisy

Mary read the letter twice, while Mrs. Sheldon cried softly. Then the elder woman spoke: "I know what you're thinking. You think the Lord hasn't heard your prayer. But you mustn't think that. I heard a great preacher from England once say that we must learn to 'trust Him where we could not trace Him.' If God has been preparing this thing while we were praying and claiming His promise, in some way it is to answer our prayer. Come, let's trust Him and tell Him so."

Right there by the stairs Mary Dunlap prayed, talking to the Lord as if He stood where she could see Him, asking directions for what they should do next.

When the brief prayer was over the mother lifted her head and stood up.

"Daisy isn't used to traveling alone—especially out in the night this way, and to a great city!"

"She's not alone," Mary said. "God is with her!"

Then after an instant she added, "And there's no reason why we shouldn't follow, is there? Wouldn't that be what the Lord would want? When is the next train?"

"Not until five o'clock in the morning," sighed the mother.

"Even so," said the steady traveler, "we won't be so far behind her, and perhaps this was the only way to convince her, to let her see that it's all true. Sister, we've got to trust our Father! There just isn't anything else to do!"

Daisy's mother looked up with a weak smile and said, through trembling lips, "All right!"

"You good little sport!" said Mary and stooped down to kiss her.

"Now," she said, "sit down a minute while we plan. I'll go back to the hotel and pack my grip. It takes just five minutes. Then I'll get all the information we need about the train and order a taxi to come for us, and then I'll come back here. That shouldn't take more than three quarters of an hour. Let me see. It's now quarter of one. I'll be back here at half past. In the meantime, are you strong enough to get together what few things you'll need on the way while I'm gone? And can't you call your maid and give her directions about leaving the house for a few days? You can telegraph her later if you forget anything. Is she trustworthy?"

"She's been with us fifteen years," said Mrs. Sheldon. "She simply takes care of us."

"That's good then. Let's go. Work fast, and be done when I get back so we can get a few winks of sleep. Oh, yes, you've got to sleep or you'll be sick, and that won't do. But you don't need to bother about breakfast. We'll get that on the train. Now I'm off!"

Mary Dunlap was as good as her word, doing all she'd promised to do with a few minor details thrown in. She was back three minutes ahead of her schedule and standing over the poor bewildered mother who was gathering up the things she would need.

"Now," said Mary, peering into the half-packed suitcase, "what do you have in here? Night dress and toiletries? A couple of other dresses, one for daytime and one for evening. Yes, you can't tell what we may run into on this jaunt! Always prepare for any emergency. Two extra dresses will generally do it. A warm kimono, slippers and another pair of shoes, a change of under-wear—that's about all. You'll want to take your pen perhaps and a few extra handkerchiefs. I've done this so much that it's second nature. Sometimes I almost have to live on the cars.

"How about Daisy—did she take anything with her? She certainly didn't have much time. It must have been after eleven o'clock when she went upstairs, and she wrote that note before she left."

"Yes, her suitcase is gone. I don't really know how much is missing. Perhaps she hadn't unpacked it since she came home."

"Did she have money?"

"I don't know how much. She has her own bank account and probably has her checkbook. They know her at the station and would cash her check. That makes me wonder how much money I have in the house. Perhaps Daisy took it. She's always free to go to my drawer when she runs out of money."

"Don't worry about money. I always carry a few traveler's checks, and I asked the hotel to order tickets and chairs for us. They'll come with the taxi in the morning. Now where do you keep your hat and coat and gloves? Is your handbag ready? I want you to lie down now and get some sleep. No, don't lie there and think about Daisy. Just lean back on the Father's promise and relax. Everything is going to be all right!"

So Mrs. Sheldon, ready for her journey all but her dress, wrapped her kimono about her and was tucked up by Mary Dunlap. Surprisingly she went to sleep, worn out with her two nights of vigil.

Mary slept, too, taking catnaps and squinting in between at her wristwatch with the aid of her ever-ready flashlight stowed under her pillow.

At daybreak she slipped down to the strange kitchen and made some good strong coffee. She carried it up and gave a cup to Mrs. Sheldon. And she in-spected the suitcase at the last minute, snapped it shut and carried it down to the door. Mrs. Sheldon gave a few last directions to the loyal maid who had stumbled down from her sleep to say good-bye just as the taxi pulled up at the door.

They were seated in the train for perhaps an hour when Mrs. Sheldon said with a troubled look: "I almost wish I'd asked Nelson to come with us. He's—

so dependable—where Daisy is concerned, and it doesn't seem quite fair to him to run away without a word. He's so—loyal and patient."

"H'm," Mary said thoughtfully. "Was there—any way you could have asked him? Would Daisy have resented your telling him?"

"I suppose she would. No, I don't suppose there was," the mother answered, reversing the order of the questions. "But somehow it seems all wrong not to have him along when we're in trouble."

"Well," said Mary, "if the Lord needs him He'll know how to send him. Don't you fret."

Fortunately both women were exhausted and got some refreshing rest in their chairs while the miles raced along beneath the wheels, and Daisy drew nearer to New York.

What would Daisy do when she got to New York? Her mother couldn't keep the question out of her mind, and yet she couldn't answer it. Oh, what awful experience might she have if she went to that office and met her old lover! A creature as hardened as he would perhaps think nothing of spiriting her away somewhere, so that her mother might never see her again. If she arrived at his office early and found him by himself, he might tell her *any* lie, and in her present state of mind she would believe it.

On the other hand, what if that Mrs. Oliver or her daughters happened to be there when Daisy arrived? What if she said something to her lover that indicated what her relationship had been to him? Would she and Daisy ever live after such humiliation?

The poor mother could not fathom the answer to her painful thoughts and could only pray over and over again in her heart, "Oh, Father, keep her—keep my child from falling." And then like soothing balm the familiar words came to her: "Able to keep you from falling and to present you faultless before the throne—without spot or wrinkle or any such thing." Oh, how blessedly the old verses learned in childhood came trooping to her whirling thoughts, as if the Father were speaking them to her heart, while the train carried her on her way.

The long day was accomplished at last. Both women slept a good deal and talked a little, discovering common interests and speaking of Daisy now and then, of Nelson Whitney, of Daisy's wonderful father and Mrs. Sheldon's girlhood. As night drew on and the lights appeared, the two women felt as if they'd known each other for years and were bound by ties closer even than sisters might have been. Then there was the long night, to be waked through, thinking of the possibilities to come on the morrow.

"Now," said Mary Dunlap, looking at her wristwatch the next morning after they'd eaten breakfast and returned to their section in the sleeper, "it's quarter of nine. We'll be in in three quarters of an hour and take a taxi straight to Fifth Avenue if there isn't time to go to a hotel. Nothing opens in New York much before ten o'clock. Daisy got in last night, but all the offices were closed.

She couldn't have done anything till this morning, and she can't get there much ahead of us. At least if she does she won't see him, for I'm sure he never comes down to the office before ten, and sometimes later. Take heart, sister, and trust the Father. He's managing this business, and I fancy He could have taken care of Daisy even if we hadn't come along. You know He manages a lot of things without us!"

"I know," she said. "I'll try to rest on Him."

And then they drew near to the great city, and the two women put on their hats and coats and sat up ready for action. Who knew what the day held in store for them?

Chapter 8

Nelson Whitney rang the bell of the Sheldon house at exactly quarter past eight the next morning. It was as early as he felt it would be at all courteous to disturb the household, especially as one of the members hadn't been feeling well the night before.

Nancy, the trusted servant for many years, opened the door to him.

"Good morning, Nancy," he said familiarly, for he'd been almost as much in the Sheldon house since childhood as in his own home. "Is Marguerite up yet? I don't like to disturb her, but she was to have some measurements written out for the things she wanted me to get for the hospital fair. I think she's expecting me to see to it this morning."

"Miss Marguerite is away, Mr. Nelson," said Nancy, shaking her head. She'd been with the family too long not to know every time one of the beloved family winked an eye or shed a tear. She felt that things were all wrong just now—what with the idol of her heart crying and carrying on all day and then running away on the midnight train, and her mother leaving at daybreak! It certainly was not right.

"Away?" said Nelson. "Why, she was here yesterday, wasn't she? Her mother told me she was lying down with a headache last evening when I telephoned."

"Sure she was here last evening," said Nancy, glad to share her troubles with someone. "I don't know whatever her mother was thinking about to let her go, and her having headaches and crying all yesterday. But young folks seem to do about as they please nowadays."

Nelson gave her a pleasant grin, but his eyes showed that he was troubled.

"Well, I guess then I'll have to see Mrs. Sheldon. If she isn't about just ask her, please, if Marguerite left any word with her. Or if she's asleep still, just look on Marguerite's desk and see if you find a paper with my name on it. She's likely written it out and left it there."

"Ms. Sheldon's gone too," burst forth Nancy. "She left on the five o'clock with some woman who was here all evening and come back and stayed all night, what there was left of it when they got packed."

Nelson looked up startled.

"Mrs. Sheldon has gone too? And she didn't go with Marguerite? That is strange. There wasn't a death in the family or anything—near relatives in New York perhaps? I believe they have relatives there, haven't they? Perhaps they telegraphed for Marguerite."

"No, it couldn't a been that. All the Sheldons and Hamptons in New York went to Europe a month ago—went for a year."

"Well, it's none of my business, of course," Nelson said with a grave smile that ended with a sigh. "But what in sixty am I going to do about that committee? They'll be in my hair if I don't get those things for tonight, and they told me Marguerite had the list. She probably forgot to say anything to you about it, Nancy, going in such a hurry. Suppose you go up and look around her room and see if you see anything that looks like a list, whether it has my name on it or not."

"Come on in, then," Nancy said and opened the door wider.

Nelson stepped into the hall, glancing toward the open doorway where he'd stood two nights before, talking to Mrs. Sheldon. Who was that other woman? Was she connected with this sudden exodus? He liked her. She seemed to be a true friend. He remembered the twinkle in her eyes, though they had looked serious, as if she was full of sympathy.

How strange it was to have the family go off this way without telling him. He'd always been told of every change from day to day. His life had been so closely twined with theirs; they never even moved a piece of furniture from one room to another without asking him how he liked it in its new place, always joyously consulting him about any action. When they went away he always got their reservations, checked their baggage and took them to the station in his car, that is, since he'd been old enough to have a car. Before that he attended them in a hired taxi.

But the last few months he'd noticed a change. Mrs. Sheldon was the same, but Marguerite had a certain reserve, as if he didn't matter anymore. It was all since that night when the Farr girl brought that Keller fellow with her to their literary club and introduced him to Marguerite. Nelson had heard him calling her Daisy the very first night; Daisy, the name that belonged exclusively to her mother—and him—until that night! After that he studiously called her Marguerite. He wanted no name for his girl that he had to share with that man! He was a villain, that's what he was—a middle-aged man coming in and monopolizing a girl almost young enough to be his daughter! What was he anyway, and what did they know about him? He meant to make it his business pretty soon to find out, if he persisted in coming around.

Then Nancy's voice sailed down the stairway. "Was it a list of flower seeds and bulbs, you meant, Mr. Nelson?"

Nelson walked over to the foot of the stairs and looked up. "No, Nancy, it would be lumber and canvas and curtain material for the stage setting for the cantata."

"Oh," said Nancy, "this ain't it, then. I'll look again."

She walked back into the girl's room, while the young man waited. He shifted his position impatiently, sighing, and something crackled under his foot. A paper! Probably that was the list. Marguerite had left it on the hall table, and it had blown across the floor when the door was opened.

He stooped and picked it up. Yes, it was Marguerite's writing. Probably some directions about color and fabrics. Maybe a bit of a word of apology for going so hurriedly or even a friendly good-bye. His heart was lifted at the thought. His eyes plunged into the midst of the words in the dim light of the hall, searching for that personal word he longed to read. Before he realized he was reading a note addressed to someone else, he had gathered the whole unhappy truth.

For an instant he stood there, the paper shaking in his hand. He was mortified for reading something he shouldn't; yet his heart sank within him for what the brief note revealed.

So then Daisy—Marguerite—had left without her mother's knowledge! She would never have done that a year ago! Something terrible must have happened that she would worry her mother by doing so. And that explained the mother's hasty departure by the next train. Mrs. Sheldon would never allow that without doing something about it. But why hadn't she telephoned him? She would have just a few weeks ago! Oh, and what was that other awful thing the note had said? When she had accomplished her strange mission, whatever it was, trying to prove that somebody did not exist, she was going to hunt up that unspeakable villain Keller and marry him! Could any calamity loom greater than that to Nelson Whitney in his whole bright world that had suddenly gone black?

While he was trying to make sense out of those awful facts, he heard brisk footsteps coming down the stairs. He crushed the paper and buried it deep in his overcoat pocket.

"I can't find it nowheres, Mr. Nelson," Nancy said. "Would you like to go up and look? You might recognize it when I wouldn't."

Nelson sprang up the stairs. "I'll just take a look," he said.

But it was not for the list he wanted to go up. He wanted to look about the room where she'd last been as if its very walls would cry out and give him a clue to go by, some hope for his soul that was wrapped up in the girl he had loved since childhood, the girl about to step off into danger! What could he do about it?

But the room was in perfect order, as always, with nothing about to tell any tales, except her blue sweater, lying on the bed in a heap as if it had suddenly been cast aside. He stood for an instant in the doorway, surveying the room, walked to her desk and bureau glancing over them quickly, and headed back to the door. Pausing beside the bed, he picked up the soft wool garment and pressed it to his cheek, just an instant, like a caress. Dropping it, he left the room hastily and ran down the stairs.

"D'ya find it?" asked Nancy, noting triumphantly that he held no list in his hand.

"No, Nancy, it wasn't there," he said. "Thank you. She must have forgotten it. I'll have to get along the best way I can without it."

"Well, if it turns up when I go to sweep I'll phone you to the office, Mr. Nelson."

"Thank you, Nancy. By the way, they didn't say when they were returning, did they? Or give you an address? I might reach her on long distance."

"No, they didn't say. M's Sheldon, she did say that if they decided to stay mor'na day or so she'd write and tell me what hotel they're in. If she does, I'll phone ya, Mr. Nelson."

"All right, Nancy. Thank you!"

Outside, as he stepped into his car and threw in the clutch, Nelson Whitney knew what he must do. His people were off alone, in possible trouble, and he must be at hand, ready, if they needed him! He must travel to New York and find them.

But how could he find them since each detachment had a headstart and might be lost in New York long before he could get there?

He began to calculate distance and time. Marguerite had a whole night ahead of him, and her mother several hours! When he reached New York they might have already left. Marguerite might already be married. And even if he were there, unless he got there ahead and met their trains, how would he know where they went?

Wait! Hadn't that note mentioned a place where Marguerite was going? He pulled out the crumpled paper and smoothed it, getting the number fixed in his mind:—Fifth Avenue! Well, at least, he knew one place where she intended to go—if there was such a place. Her note implied that she doubted it. But there would at least be the number whether the person whose existence she was seeking to disprove was there or not.

Yes, with only that clue and no chance of getting there on time, he meant to go after her. For what could her mother do? True, she might have more information of her whereabouts than was contained in that note; but even so, she was a woman of another day and generation, a woman used to being cared for and not accustomed to traveling by herself. That other woman had looked capable, of course, as if she might go around the world by herself and have no trouble whatever. But who knew whether that other woman—Dunlap, her name was, wasn't it?—who knew whether she was going all the way to New York or not? Yes, he must go! And there was only one way to get there in time to be of use. Could he do it?

He drove hard to his office, a new office with a new secretary and office boy, new desks and chairs and typewriter, and new clientele. This was a busy day, too, but that couldn't be helped either. His boss in Chicago was not a hard master, and his secretary was efficient and experienced.

He plunged into his morning mail. He must get that out of the way first.

Matilda Herrick, the shell-rimmed secretary, had it all in neat order for him: the new orders, the old customers, the complaints, the letter from the head office in Chicago. He hurried through the piles, giving a word of direction now and then.

"Get these letters ready for me as soon as you can," he said. "I may have to go to New York today. Call up Bainbridge and find out if he's ready to talk business yet. Get Hetherington on the phone and see if he's heard from that order he took yesterday, and send the boy up to my home to get my suitcase. He'd better go as soon as he has those envelopes addressed. There'll be time."

When Matilda Herrick had left his private office he locked his door and slipped to his knees beside his desk. He was a young man who traveled under guidance and went nowhere without orders.

When he stood up from his knees a new look of purpose was etched on his face. He reached for his telephone and called a number.

A hearty voice answered.

Nelson's face lit up with relief.

"Hello, Bert, is that you?"

"Sure is! Hello, Nel. Glad to hear your voice! How's crops?"

"Oh, growing, growing fast. Say, Bert, flying anywhere today?"

"Sure thing. Want to go?"

"If you're going in the right direction. What's your chart?"

"Wherever you say. You never thought you could spare the time to go with me before."

"Happen to be going anywhere within a hundred miles of New York?"

"Flying right to the heart of the city, this afternoon if you'll accompany me. Got a bit of engine trouble to make right. It'll take a couple of hours to fix, then I'm ready. How soon can you start?"

"Anytime after one if things go well here."

"Make it snappy, and we'll paint New York red tonight."

"I'd prefer white, if you don't mind, Bert."

"OK with me, Nel—just so's you go along. Meet me at the field at two o'clock."

Nelson hung up with an awed expression on his face.

"It seems to be in the plan," he said to himself reverently and began to work at several business matters that he knew must be set right before he could honorably leave his own city.

Not a single hitch occurred in the things that must be finished before he left. Every man he called on the telephone was in; every sales report was such that he could give the needed directions concerning them before he went away.

"It's just as if somebody else was working with me to smooth the way," he thought.

The morning hours sped by. Matilda Herrick had the letters ready for signing in plenty of time. Nelson telephoned his mother to ask her to pack his suitcase for a quick trip, and the office boy did all the rest, even accompanying his chief to the flying field and driving the car back to the garage again.

At two-thirty they lifted off into the clear blue sky—Nelson Whitney's first experience in flying.

At first the new sensation occupied his senses. But after he was accustomed to sailing with the clouds and gazing down upon the earth, he began to think of what lay before him in New York. Was this a wild-goose chase? Wouldn't anybody think he was a fool to start off with as little warrant as he had? Wasn't there danger of making his lady forever angry chasing her this way, even if he found her? Wouldn't even her mother have a right to resent it?

And what, pray, was he to do when he arrived in New York, beyond meeting the trains at the station and getting in touch with the people he was trying to help? How could he do that? Just walk up smiling and say he knew they were expected so he met them? He had no real justification for that. Of course he could say that Nancy told him what train they took, but he'd feel like a fool saying that to Mrs. Sheldon. Her keen eyes would see through it, and she might resent his intrusion into her affairs, though she'd always acted as if he belonged in her plans.

And what could he do before her train arrived to keep Marguerite in sight? If he met her train she'd likely be indignant. He couldn't tell her he'd found her note on the floor and read it, although it was addressed to her mother, and that he was here to protect her from whatever evil, real or imagined, threatened her. Assuredly he would meet her train and try to appear as casual as possible, but he shrank from the look of scorn in her eyes. There was no doubt Marguerite would resent his entrance onto the stage at this point. She'd been haughty and independent lately, and it stung him to remember her indifference.

If he failed to make contact with her at the train, if he should hunt up that number on Fifth Avenue and find it there, what would he do? And what if it weren't there? And where did this Keller man live? He was apparently causing all this trouble. Why! He ought to have telephoned somebody and found that out before he left! Here he was thinking he'd done everything up in fine shape and had left out a strategic point. Of course he could telephone back when he got to New York, but a lot of time might be lost.

But wasn't he traveling under guidance? Couldn't He who had smoothed the way thus far manage it so he'd go to the right place and do the right thing? Wouldn't the way open as he advanced? He had put himself under the guidance of the greatest leader in the universe, and there he must trust and not be afraid.

The silver wings that bore him above the earth flew straight on, over wide stretches of the map. Sometimes he wondered when he saw a railroad train creeping along like a small worm on the earth, if he might be looking at the very train in which those he went to protect were traveling. The strange thing was that though he was positive they needed protection he wasn't sure from what. Only in the case of the girl, if she tried to carry out her threat of marrying that man Keller, he knew he must prevent it. It could be nothing short of a calamity for her, to say nothing of her mother and him, if that should ever come to pass. He felt, too, that God was on his side, for hadn't he put himself and his plans in God's hands, willing to be guided, willing to have all plans overturned if they weren't the right thing? And the way had been smoothed before him. Not even the least detail had hindered him from going through the air.

So the silver wings flew on, and in due time Nelson Whitney arrived in New York.

He didn't help his friend paint the town red. Instead he went directly to Pennsylvania Station and got full details of all trains arriving from the West. He learned that Marguerite's train was due to arrive late that evening. He begged off from going with his friend for more than dinner and returned immediately to the station. There he acquainted himself with the various exits of the train and found the best place to watch and wait for her.

It hadn't been hard to discover where the train would come in. He established himself behind the great iron bars just above the train floor, where he could look down upon the disembarking passengers. They wouldn't see him unless they deliberately turned around and looked up. He was near enough, however, to the gate to reach her at once if he should see she needed a friend or was at all hesitant as to which way to turn.

During the long day he planned what he'd say when he met her. He would tell how he called at the house for her list, and Nancy said she went to New York on the midnight train. So when he was invited to fly with his friend to the same city he thought he would meet her train and ask her about the list, in case he returned the next day. That was a reasonable story as well as true, for his friend had many times invited him to fly and told him to call when he could go.

Nevertheless he wished to reconnoiter before he approached her. It was even conceivable that that Keller person might have somehow gotten in touch with her and be traveling with her. His blood boiled at the thought, and he stood for twenty long minutes till the train arrived thinking over what he should do if that were the case. He decided he would in any event go to the gate and speak to Marguerite. It might even be that a face from home might hinder her from doing a foolish thing. At least he'd ask where she was staying and perhaps let her know that her mother was on the way, just casually, as if of course she knew it.

He could judge a great deal from the way she reacted to what he said.

In the meantime, while he mused with not a little anxiety, forgetting for the moment his Guide, the train arrived. People streamed forth like ants, filing up the iron stairs to the gateways. Not one escaped the careful eye of Nelson Whitney, as he stood in his sheltered nook behind a display of train flags and gate signs.

But Marguerite did not appear.

She didn't even ride up in the elevator, which was in full view from his position. He was sure he hadn't missed her, yet a frenzy of anxiety seized him. Perhaps she'd seen him and evaded him while he was looking the other way. *Where was she?* he wondered.

Chapter 9

M arguerite had never visited New York before, although she traveled with her father and mother in other directions. She knew nothing, of course, about the city except what she gleaned from novels.

When the porter of the Pullman car asked her whether she was going uptown or downtown, she looked at him bewildered. Thinking an office building would likely be downtown, she answered after a moment's hesitation, "Oh, yes, downtown. I'm going downtown."

"Then you get out at Manhattan Transfer, lady," said the porter eyeing her questioningly, she thought, because she said downtown at that time of night.

Manhattan Transfer was desolate and empty. Few passengers were traveling so late, and no official seemed to be in charge. Marguerite stood for a few minutes, looking about her, and then wandered up and down, gazing into the distance at the stars and weird lights. Was this the great New York she'd heard so much about?

But at last a train came. A brakeman on the step, swinging a lantern and yelling some unintelligible thing, condescended to listen to her plea.

"Where you wantta go, lady? Uptown or downtown?"

The same mystical question, but she must have answered it all wrong before.

"Oh, I don't know which," she cried, almost in tears, for she suddenly realized her situation at this late hour. "I want to go to a good respectable hotel."

"You go uptown then, lady. Get on the next train that comes by, over on that side of the platform. Be 'long in five minutes now. Take you t' the Pennsylvania Station—good hotel right across the street. All aboard!"

And he swung away, leaving her more alone than ever, for now the windswept platform was empty of the few travelers who had been waiting for this train. Marguerite dared not go in search of any official who might be inside the shelters lest she miss her train.

Thus she arrived at the great station almost an hour later than the train by which she should have come. Emerging into the gloom and climbing the stairs at midnight into the wide upper area, she felt smaller and more alone than when she stood on the high barren sweep of Manhattan Transfer.

The glaring lights and strange clatter of noise at the station frightened her. She might have stood there all night, afraid to venture onto that vast empty floor. But a kindly agent of the Traveler's Aid happened by as she emerged from the iron gate and, noting her hesitation, asked, "May I help you?"

Soon the weary girl was established safely in the fine hotel across the way and told how to get to the desired address on Fifth Avenue in the morning.

One's mind and body cannot continue in a state of extreme emotion without rest. So Marguerite, at last in a quiet room with a luxurious bed and nothing she could do until morning, succumbed to her weariness and fell into a deep sleep.

She fully intended to awaken about seven o'clock, get ready for her errand and try to contact Rufus Keller. She had a good idea where to telegraph him; if she did so, she thought it would only be a few hours before she had word that he was coming to her.

She hadn't traveled enough to know she could leave an order for the hotel desk to call her at seven; even so she'd have thought it unnecessary. For years she had prided herself on her ability to awaken at a set time and never failed to wake up on the minute. Nevertheless, she slept straight past seven, eight, nine, ten, eleven, and never woke up until quarter to twelve o'clock, dazed and confused as to where she was and why.

Meanwhile at ten o'clock Mary Dunlap and Mrs. Sheldon arrived in the city and, with a porter carrying their luggage, made their way through the tiled tunnel and into the Pennsylvania Hotel. There they were given a room one floor below where Marguerite slept her exhausted sleep.

"We'd better not wait for anything," said the mother. She pushed and patted the straggling locks about her temples and headed for the door.

"My dear, you're going to have a cup of coffee before we stir a step," said Mary Dunlap firmly. "I told the boy as we came up in the elevator to have it sent up at once, and it won't take three minutes to drink it. Nothing is doing in New York until ten, and she can't get away at once. You're running on your nerve, and that might give out at the wrong time and spoil everything. There— he's knocking now. Sit down and drink it. Then we'll call a taxi and be there in no time! It's early yet, and I'm positive Mr. Oliver—I mean, Keller—never goes to his office before half past ten."

Through the early morning hours Nelson Whitney hadn't slept. He had lain on the bed, of course, and closed his eyes. He committed himself and his wishes and his girl to the care of One who was infinitely powerful, infinitely able and infinitely willing to bring order out of confusion, and he was resting on that. But he lay there staring into the night.

Suppose he should find that Marguerite had already gone to the other man and that, unworthy though he believed him to be, she was now irrevocably committed to him, for better, for worse? Could he give up his will in the matter, his joy, his very life and his girl to a sorrow he felt was inevitable if she married Keller?

Nelson did not oversleep. He arose far earlier than he'd intended and tried to eat some breakfast; but it was like dust in his mouth. He set out to walk, but the exercise was mechanical. He didn't see the buildings he passed and noticed no one on the street. He was reviewing the morning's probable program, trying to decide what to do first.

If he met Mrs. Sheldon at the train he would be late in getting to Fifth Avenue when Marguerite would likely arrive. If he went to Fifth Avenue first he would be too late to meet the train. He finally decided to find Marguerite rather than her mother, for the mother would communicate with Nancy at home as soon as she was situated in a hotel. If he found Marguerite he could telephone Nancy and have little trouble in locating Mrs. Sheldon afterward.

He easily located the number on Fifth Avenue that was indicated in Marguerite's note. He was somewhat reassured, but also not a little troubled, to find the name "R. H. Oliver, Manager" in gold letters on the rich glass of the heavy mahogany door. What effect would it have on the girl who took this wild midnight journey to prove there was no such person? He pondered this as he sought out the janitor and asked about the opening hour of the offices in that building.

He was still pondering it as he set out to walk a regular beat, up the avenue, across the street, down the avenue, across and back again. He varied it occasionally by a quick detour into one of the side streets where he turned about and returned the other way. He didn't care to be noticed, as he kept his anxious vigil. As the minutes passed into an hour, his heart sank with the fear lest after all he had missed her. Perhaps she came down to the office building ahead of him, or perhaps she looked up the name in the city directory, discovered that it really was there and changed her course. Why didn't he think of that? Yet what else could he have done? He had no other clue and must follow it to its reasonable end.

There weren't many people on that part of the avenue so early, and he had no difficulty in getting a good look at each one. He was fairly certain she couldn't have passed him, so he tramped back and forth like a lion in a cage, not daring to go beyond the limits he set lest she escape him. But now one question haunted him: What connection could there be between this man Oliver and the fellow Keller?

One possibility stole into his troubled thoughts, but he dismissed it as unworthy of a decent man to think about another, even about one he distrusted. Yet again and again it recurred. Had someone been trying to show Marguerite that the man she was infatuated with was unworthy of her? Had she set out to disprove what they told her?

By the time he had tramped nearly two hours away, he wished he could get his hands on this Keller man and give him a good thrashing. He felt more and more confident he deserved it, even though he might not be the unworthy villain his imagination had conjured.

It was still five minutes before the offices would open when he strode back to the building and entered the elevator. He considered staying outside in the street till he saw Marguerite arrive. But she might see him if he came too near and evade him. Most likely she didn't want her friends with her on this expedition; otherwise she would have confided in her mother.

He also considered hiding himself in the hallway, if there were such a hiding place, but rejected that also; if anything was going to happen he wanted to be there to see it. He felt that it was his right to understand the case, since he was going to try to help Marguerite. How else could he know whether or not he might be intruding where even angels should not tread? No, he must be in the office, in a place where she wouldn't notice him, or he might never find out whether he even had a right to try to help her. He must fathom this mystery himself.

He had a bad moment when several young women rushed into the hall and headed for the elevator. Perhaps she was among them. The elevator was certainly not the place he planned to meet Marguerite!

But the girl he sought was not among them; they were obviously secretaries hurrying to their jobs. He sighed with relief as the elevator door closed. The young women stepped out at different floors along the way.

He was glad he was the only one in the elevator when it stopped at the ninth floor. He could get off and take his bearings once more without being observed. Then he noticed that the door of R. H. Oliver's office was standing ajar. With a quickened pulse he hastened down the hall.

Chapter 10

Nelson Whitney pushed the door of R. H. Oliver's office open and stepped inside with an air of quiet triumph. He took a quick look around, half fearful of what he might see.

But no one was there except an elderly woman taking off her hat and coat at the back of the room. She hung them on pegs in a corner, patted her hair into shape before a small mirror and put a last dab of powder on a thin angular nose. He paused and watched her uncertainly.

"Is Mr. Oliver in yet?" he asked as she turned and crossed the room toward him, her folded gloves and a large flat purse in her hand.

"Oh, no!" she said, as if she were surprised he didn't know that. She glanced at the clock. "He never gets down before half past, if he does then."

Nelson gazed around the room once more, as if the girl he sought might be hiding somewhere in the shadows.

"Mind if I wait here?" he asked, ignoring the contempt in the woman's voice.

"Help yourself," she said in a chilly tone.

She unlocked her desk and pulled out a typewriter from some hidden recess. Slipping her pocketbook and gloves in a drawer, she took out a dust cloth and started to polish her desk and clean her typewriter. She seemed to have forgotten someone was present and set to humming a jazzy little radio tune.

This suited Nelson. He deliberately took in every corner of the room, the beautiful furniture and the rich Oriental rug, and selected a dark alcove behind the main door, facing toward the windows on the other side of the room. It was a gloomy corner, formed by the ground glass partition of an inner office that ran out from the main wall ten feet and then down to the back of the room. The angle of these walls would obscure him partially, even from the woman at her desk in the middle of the room. The darkness of the corner would not call attention to his presence.

He drew a carved walnut chair into the right position to give him a view of the room, without being conspicuous, and sat down. After a minute or two he unfolded a morning paper, which he could not possibly read clearly in the dim light, and prepared to hide behind it at the approach of footsteps. Surely he could remain incognito here, for a while at least; none of the people who might play a role in the drama had the slightest idea he was in that part of the country. They would scarcely recognize his shoes and trousers or his hands, and that was all that the paper and the gloom would reveal. He would sit quietly and see what happened.

The secretary finished her morning cleaning and began typing some letters. The minutes ticked slowly by on the magnificent mahogany grandfather clock that stood six feet against the opposite wall between the two high windows. Nelson Whitney began to chide himself for being a fool who had come on a fool's errand. Probably no one he expected would come. Probably the morning would pass by, and the man Oliver would arrive, and he wouldn't know him from any other man, let alone what to say.

For the next five minutes he planned what errand he could have for visiting an unknown man in his office. A perusal of the ground glass door into the hall did not help. It bore over Oliver's name only the legend "Ransom, Oliver, Bates and Company." Nelson didn't know whether they sold bonds or automobiles or insurance. Not a scratch of anything in the room gave him the slightest clue. Only a framed etching of old New York hung on the wall within sight.

Should he say he was waiting for friends who were to meet him there, or tell the man when he arrived that he must have come to the wrong address? He would appear foolish in almost anything he might say; yet he held his ground and sat behind his paper, trying to frame a reasonable excuse for his presence. He might ask if the man wanted to employ a helper. Jack Rector at home was crazy to get a job in New York. Yet what kind of job would it be? Sales? Jack would make a sharp salesman.

The minutes dragged on. The secretary typed incessantly and paid no more attention to him than if he'd been an empty cell, sealed from the roar and rumble of the city noises.

Nelson was still pondering possibilities when at last he heard the clang of an elevator and steps outside the door. His heart stopped, then beat faster; he was certain they belonged to a woman. Had the moment arrived at last? If the girl should see him, would she think he, too, was in league against her and be angry? He withdrew still further into the depths of his paper, and the door swung open, admitting a lady.

The secretary jumped up with an eager smile.

"Oh, good morning, Mrs. Oliver! Aren't you downtown early? Didn't Mr. Oliver come with you? I thought he planned to be in the office this morning. I have some checks for him to sign."

Nelson lowered his paper and saw a woman about forty years old, with a lovely smile and faultlessly dressed.

"Good morning, Miss Flinch," she said pleasantly.

"Why, no, Mr. Oliver and Katherine left earlier. Hasn't he come in yet? He said he'd be here by now. I expected to find him in his office hard at work or ready to chide me for being ten minutes later than I promised. I was waiting for Gloria. She was to drive back with the car and get me; but she telephoned that they had a flat tire and would meet me here. Hasn't she come yet either?"

"No, Mrs. Oliver, but I guess they'll be here presently," said the secretary.

"Of course," said the lady. "Well, I'll just step into Mr. Oliver's office and write a note. I was afraid I wouldn't have time to write it at home, but it really ought to go."

The secretary smiled, and the lady retreated through the ground-glass door of the inner office. The typewriter clicked on.

The clang of the elevator was becoming more frequent now, and more and more footsteps were heard clicking down the marble corridor. Nelson scarcely realized that the hall door had opened again until he heard a woman's clear voice speaking to the secretary.

"Has Mr. Oliver come in yet?"

"No."

"How soon do you expect him?"

"Almost anytime now," said his keeper briskly. "Did you have an appointment?"

"No," the woman said, "but he knows me well."

"He's very busy this morning," interrupted the secretary. "He's been away for three weeks and has a lot of things to attend to. I don't know if he'll have time to see anybody." She glanced sharply at the newspaper and the legs in the dark alcove.

"Don't worry," said the firm, but pleasant voice. "I won't keep him a second. I merely want him to endorse a check for me. I'm a personal friend. I'll just wait till he comes."

The secretary fixed her eyes on the woman, as if she doubted her words, then shrugged her shoulders and continued typing.

Nelson wondered why the voice reminded him of something recent? He lowered his paper and glanced at the woman. Then he saw, standing beside her, a quiet woman with gray hair and a sweet profile he had known all his life. The one who spoke was the woman who was calling on Mrs. Sheldon when he went to see Marguerite! Well, at least he wouldn't have to search for them; here they were.

Now what should he do? Reveal himself to them and make some plan? But no—he heard more footsteps, and the elevator clanged continually now. It wouldn't do to be caught saying good morning to them if Marguerite should walk in. And besides—how would he explain his presence there? Confess he'd read a letter that wasn't intended for his eyes? Strange he'd forgotten to think that out. He'd had all night to plan it but hadn't.

The two women hesitated by the desk, but now Mrs. Dunlap crossed the room to the corner as Whitney stole a glance over his paper.

"Let's sit over here by the window," she said as if she felt quite at home. She whirled the chairs about so they would face away from the room and anyone entering the door.

But Mrs. Sheldon did not follow immediately. She lingered by the desk, a worried look in her eyes.

"My—daughter—hasn't come in yet, has she?" she asked. "She was to—that is, she was expecting—I mean we expected to meet her here."

She looked apologetically toward her companion and then back to the secretary.

"Nobody's been in this morning but that man," said the secretary, pointing to the legs in the alcove beneath the newspaper.

Daisy's mother gave a frightened glance at the alcove without realizing the legs had been a familiar sight in her house. She retreated to the chair Mary Dunlap offered, and the two women sank down quietly with two magazines Mary produced from the window seat. Again the click of the typewriter was the only sound that was heard.

The postman arrived presently and left a stack of mail which gave the secretary a rest from her typing. She flipped through the letters, sorting them into piles.

Many footsteps were heard out in the corridor now, and the three whose hearts were listening for a certain step were not certain at all. The mother started whenever anyone approached the door.

The elevator clanged incessantly. Soon a faltering step came down the corridor, as if the owner had hurried, then hesitated a moment in front of the door. The knob turned slowly.

Nelson knew that step and knew in his heart that she had come. He felt the horror that would be on her face as she discovered the name she'd come to disprove shining golden in the noonday light. The newspaper shook in his hand. He dared to peer around it at the face of the girl he loved.

She stood in the doorway for an instant and swept the room with a glance, not carefully for she was too nervous, nor was she looking for people from home. Nelson sat to one side, almost behind her now, for she was standing in the middle of the room. She scarcely noticed the backs of the two women shrinking into their chairs in the window corner earnestly reading magazines.

She marched up to the desk. "Is this Mr. R. H. Oliver's office?" she asked.

Miss Flinch surveyed her casually before she nodded.

"May I see him at once?" asked Marguerite, growing more certain of herself.

"He isn't here yet."

"Not here?" The catch in the girl's voice could be heard around the room. "How soon will he be in? I've got to catch a train in three quarters of an hour."

"I can't say when he'll be in," said the secretary, turning back to her typewriter. "It might be five minutes; it might be half an hour."

"But you're sure he's coming? This morning?"

"Positive," the older woman replied tersely. "His wife's in the private office waiting for him now. All these people are waiting to see him, and he's awfully busy besides. He's got to sign a lot of letters and meet two men at one o'clock, and he's taking his wife and children off for a holiday. If that isn't a full day I don't know where you come in. But you can sit down and wait if you think there's any chance for you."

"Oh, I won't keep him but an instant. If I can just *see* him!"

The secretary waved her to a chair. "You'll have to take your turn," she warned.

Marguerite glanced around the room again: at the two figures huddled in the chairs by the window, with their backs to her, and at a pair of gentlemanly legs underneath a newspaper. Strangers in a strange land—what could they mean to her but hindrances to the completion of her mission? It was hours later than she intended; she should get out of New York and away to seek her beloved.

She knew her mother would stir up something soon. She was not a woman to sit idly by and see her only daughter lost in the world with an undesirable marriage in the offing. She must catch a train as soon as she saw this man. Of course he wouldn't be the right one. That lying Mrs. Dunlap had merely given the name of someone she knew as a bluff to gain her point. When she saw the man and knew he was a stranger, she would apologize pleasantly, say she must have the wrong address and depart.

Earlier she remembered a way to find Rufus. She'd call that minister friend, the one who was to have married them, and find out how to reach him. The rest would be easy. Then she would leave New York as fast as possible and go somewhere, anywhere—so she couldn't be traced—and then get off and telephone Rufus. She'd meet him wherever he said and be married at once. Perhaps she might even suggest this to the minister friend when she found the address—just say they were going to be married at once, that all difficulties were cleared away or something like that. How fortunate it was that she remembered the name and address of that minister. She'd watched Rufus write out the telegram as he argued, and he wrote Rev. Lee Spencer, D.D., so beautifully. He had a wonderful, bold way of writing that thrilled her to watch—it seemed so masterful!

All these thoughts raced through Marguerite's head as she dropped into a chair near the desk facing the entrance, her eyes fixed on the door so that she might get the first glimpse of the man as he entered.

Mrs. Dunlap almost leaned over toward Mrs. Sheldon to whisper something, but thought better of it. They exchanged lifted eyebrows, and a question formed in their eyes for an instant. Then all at once they heard eager steps rushing down the corridor. The door opened with a swoosh and closed with a bang as a slim pretty girl entered, gasping for breath.

"Oh, Miss Flinch," she said between puffs, "has Daddy—come yet? I've simply—ruined myself running up—all the stairs. I couldn't wait for the—elevator. I was afraid Dad and Mother wouldn't wait for me. Oh—hasn't he—

come yet? Oh, I'm glad! But Muth is here, isn't she? I thought she would be. I telephoned her I had a flat tire, and I had to leave the tiresome old car in a garage away uptown and walk three blocks to get a bus, and then it didn't come forever and an age. The bus service in this town is the limit, isn't it? Did you say Muth was here?"

"Yes, Miss Gloria, she came half an hour ago. She's in your father's office writing a letter."

"Oh, I know. She said it simply had to go or she couldn't go with us. You know, Miss Flinch, it's her birthday, and Daddy came home especially for it. We're going off on a spree. Daddy won't tell us where, but we're going in the new car, and it's to be a surprise party for us all. Muth doesn't even know which way we're going. But I can't think what's keeping Daddy and Katherine.

"You know, Miss Flinch," Gloria lowered her voice with a glance toward the ground-glass partition, "they've gone to get her present. She doesn't know a thing about it, of course. Katherine picked it out weeks ago, and she and I had it put away till Daddy got back. We knew he'd love it for her, and I know it's just what she wants. It's a platinum wristwatch and bracelet with diamonds and sapphires all set around the edge. Oh, it's perfectly darling. She'll show it to you, of course. But I'm just dying to see what she says when he gives it to her. Oh, dear! Why don't they come? I do hope there isn't some stupid old mistake. Perhaps some dumbbell of a salesman sold it to someone else. Wouldn't that be simply unbearable? Maybe they had to hunt around for another. But I never saw any as precious as this one."

"I wouldn't worry, Miss Gloria," said the secretary fondly. "They've likely been delayed in traffic. There! There's the elevator! Maybe they're coming now. Yes, I think that's Mr. Oliver's step."

"Oh, it is! The day is saved!" cried Gloria in her best dramatic voice.

The door opened, and another pretty girl scarcely older than the first entered and behind her a gentleman.

"There, Daddy! You're late yourself. I won the bet, and you've got to pay up! A five-pound box of chocolates! Remember! You promised! And a new pair of slippers for the party! Muth and I've been here a long time—and I had a flat tire, too, and a lot of trouble."

The gentleman stepped in and closed the door, glancing at the legs and the newspaper in the alcove, then toward the window where the two women huddled. Finally he turned toward the desk, where for an instant his two daughters stood blocking him from the view of the girl.

"Now, Daddy," Gloria said, "you've simply got to come into the office and show it to her at once. I can't wait another second. I'm dying to see what she thinks of it. Come in now before Miss Flinch gives you a lot of tiresome checks and letters to sign. Come on, Daddy—it won't take long, and then Muth can enjoy it while she waits."

Gloria caught his hands and pulled him toward the door of the inner office. Just then Katherine moved aside to follow, and the man saw the pale girl. She had risen from her seat.

She spoke eagerly, pleadingly, as if somehow her eyes and her ears had deceived her.

"Rufus! Oh—*Rufus*—I've come—!"

The man's face turned the color of ash. He stopped, frozen. His hands fell limply from his daughter's clasp.

"Go! Go!" he told his daughters. "Go to your mother! I'll come in a moment!"

Something in his voice made the girls obey, though reluctantly.

"What's the matter now?" murmured Gloria impatiently. "Didn't you get it? Didn't he like it, Kath?"

"Yes, and he's crazy about it. I'm sure I don't know what's the matter. Some tiresome old business probably. It's always that way."

As the inner door closed on them, Gloria was heard asking, "What did that girl mean '*Rufus*'?"

Chapter 11

It was Mrs. Dunlap who took command of the situation. She stepped into the picture at the most awful moment when several lives seemed about to fall into chaos.

"Oh, Mr. Oliver," she said in her pleasant, commanding tone, stepping forward with a fountain pen and a bit of blue paper in her hand. She stood exactly in front of the girl and the man. "Good morning! I won't detain you but an instant. I just stopped in to ask if you would kindly endorse this check for me so that I can cash it. I found myself suddenly out of money and near your office, and I knew you would help me out."

She held out the check and pen, and the desperate man reached out for the rope being thrown to him.

He even tried to summon a smile to his stiff lips and a naturalness to his voice as he consented: "Why, certainly, Mrs. Dunlap—I'm—delighted to do anything for you."

His voice was noticeably strained, and his attempt at a laugh was a decided failure. His hand shook as he wrote his name, Ralph H. Oliver, across the back of the check. It was an old blank one which Mrs. Dunlap had carried with her in her purse for several months in case of emergency. That morning she had made it out to herself, signed with her maiden name and endorsed it. But the man who endorsed it again didn't notice whether it was a check or not. He was only grasping for some way to get out of this situation.

By the time his name was written he'd made his decision. He would ignore this girl and leave the room at once, and the building, even if he must emerge through the tenth-story window to the street. Anything, no matter how ghastly, was better than what would probably happen if he remained.

He wheeled around to face Mrs. Dunlap and put Marguerite out of range, as he gave her the check with a trembling hand.

Again the stiff lips wrinkled into some semblance of a smile, and he attempted to be debonair in his manner. "Mrs. Dunlap, I think my wife is in my private office, and she will never forgive me if I don't call her. She'll want to see you if only for a moment. Let me go and call her."

"Oh, I'll call her, Mr. Oliver!" said the secretary eagerly, half rising from her chair.

"No, no, Miss Flinch. I'll call her myself. I want you to get those letters out before the next mail, please. It's imperative. I'll just call her."

"Indeed, Mr. Oliver, I can't wait even a moment," interrupted Mrs. Dunlap. "Tell Mrs. Oliver for me that I'm returning this way in a week or two and I'll call and make an appointment to see her. But now I really must go. I have friends here with me who are in a hurry. By the way, you know them, of course."

She stepped back and turned toward Mrs. Sheldon, who had risen and come forward, her jaw tight, her mouth set in a firm line.

"My friend, Mrs. Sheldon. I think you've already met in her hometown—and Miss Sheldon, her daughter. And now we mustn't keep you an instant."

Nelson Whitney had long ago discarded the newspaper and was on his feet, standing in the shadow of the alcove, with eyes only for the pale girl. When the others stepped in front of her and hid her from view, he walked forward into the light, forgetting he didn't mean to reveal his identity just now. He forgot everything but that his beloved's eyes were suddenly filled with understanding and agony, the beloved lips were trembling, and his girl looked like a white flower stricken and about to fall.

He, too, was wise to the situation. When Mr. Ralph Oliver turned to hand Mrs. Dunlap the endorsed check, the light from the windows fell upon his ashen face, and Nelson recognized him at once as Rufus Keller. The whole dastardly truth burst upon him. For an instant the desire rose up within him to take the scoundrel by the collar and thrash him, or fling him from the room. But a new element entered the scene: the two girls and their mother appeared from the inner office!

The wave of terror that passed over Oliver's face revealed even more to the young man. He saw what sorrow would come to the innocent ones, as well as to his dear girl, if further revelations were made at that moment.

Not for a second would he have hesitated for the sake of the villain—for he deserved every inch of punishment that was coming to him. But even in this crisis it came to Nelson Whitney like a flash that there was One who had said, "Vengeance is *Mine!*" Who was he to judge this cringing soul and bring sorrow to these other trusting ones?

Thus he stopped, just behind the man who had done his best to shatter the joy of at least four lives—and waited. He didn't even know he'd come out of hiding or that his presence would need to be explained. He just stood there as if he were called to a place by some power higher than himself, ready for the moment when he would be needed.

Ralph Oliver was a clever man and a cunning actor; otherwise he couldn't have for so long deceived those who loved him. He was quick to clutch again at the slender rope thrown out to him. He barely acknowledged the introduction, remaining where he was.

"I believe we've met before," he said coldly but politely to Mrs. Seldon and her daughter. "In Winfield, wasn't it? Or one of those little towns out that way? I travel so much and meet so many—"

Nelson Whitney marveled at the assurance that could utter such words so coolly, and then his attention was drawn to Mrs. Sheldon. She had gathered her sweet patrician dignity about her as a garment and seemed to stand two inches taller than her usual height. She looked straight into the eyes of the man who had deceived her only daughter, as if her eyes could say to him what her lips were forbidden for the sake of others to say, and spoke with clear contempt.

"And our friend Mr. Whitney, Nelson Whitney, of Wellsburgh! I think you have met him also, Mr.—*Oliver?*"

It was a masterful stroke and conveyed to the wretched man all that a woman of Mrs. Sheldon's birth and breeding could never have said in words.

Ralph Oliver spun around and faced Nelson, with genuine fright in his eyes. Just a flash and then he turned quickly back and waved toward the three who were advancing eagerly from the office door.

"Here comes my wife now, and my daughters. I knew they'd be delighted to see you. Mrs. Dunlap, will you do the honors and excuse me just a moment? I must send a telegram at once!" he glanced at his watch. "I'd forgotten it."

He turned furtively, reminding Nelson of his dog at home. When reproved for misbehavior, the dog would steal from the room, half crouched, his tail between his legs, stealthily looking back as he slithered out of the room.

So Ralph Oliver slunk from the room into his inner office and locked the door. Mrs. Dunlap's keen ears heard the grate of the key.

Yet, just before he had left them, a clear voice filled the room. "We all really ought to go at once. Nelson and I've been planning to see Grant's tomb and the museum. Will you take me there now, Nelson?"

It was Marguerite, the old sweet challenge of her friendly voice startling him into life once more. It was more than an appeal. It was if she swept back the hands of the clock ten years to their childhood days when they'd planned to see all the wonders of the world together. It had been a long time since she'd appealed to him for anything, and his heart leaped with joy. Take her to the museum? Yes, take her to the world's end if she chose!

He reached her side in two long strides and drew her arm within his. Together they acknowledged the introduction to a scoundrel's lovely wife and daughters. With that Mrs. Dunlap noisily and skillfully covered the retreat of the enemy, the victory in her hands. There was even a lilt in her voice as she told Mrs. Oliver what a dear woman Mrs. Sheldon was; but her heart ached as she watched the anguished mother hold up her head and stand her ground, with her knees doubtless shaking under her.

Mrs. Sheldon took the hand of the other mother and said with a warmth of feeling unusual for such a brief acquaintance: "I've wanted to meet you. I've heard such beautiful things about you, and now I see they are justified."

Nelson Whitney noticed the little gloved hand fluttering on his arm as if in ague. Tenderly he laid his strong hand over it and carried the burden of the conversation as the introduction came their way, leaving nothing for the girl to do but smile.

Then he led his beloved out of that office as soon as the law of politeness allowed.

For an instant he paused beside Mrs. Sheldon. "Is there any special time you'd like for us to meet you at the hotel?" he asked quietly.

But it was Mrs. Dunlap who heard him and handed him a card on which she'd been scribbling.

"Anytime you like," she said in a tone for his ears alone. "Mrs. Sheldon needs to rest, and I'll see that she does. Just ring up the room when you get back and let us know the program. I'll stay till you get back at least."

He glanced at the card. On it was written the name of the hotel and their room number. A smile spread across his face. Here those two good ladies had come straight to the same hotel where he was booked. He had no need to worry at all with such a Guide. Why hadn't he remembered that God was able to work out things without his interference, to make the crooked places straight and the dark things plain in His own good time!

Chapter 12

Moments later, after Mrs. Seldon and Mrs. Dunlap had left too, Gloria turned to her mother.

"I didn't like the way she spoke to you, Mums!" she said. "It was almost as if she felt sorry for you somehow."

"What a strange idea!" her mother said. "I think she is a very charming woman. In fact, anybody Mrs. Dunlap sponsors usually is."

"Yourself included, Mums!" said Gloria. "Come on, Muth. Let's rout out Dad and get started. We're two hours behind schedule now. Kath, you ought to have run things better than this!"

Laughing, they set off to find the beloved husband and father. They found him standing by the window with the sash thrown up, wiping beads of perspiration from his forehead, though the day was crisp and clear.

"What's the matter, dear? Is there any trouble about your business?" asked Mrs. Oliver.

"I—wasn't feeling very well there—for a minute!" the husband replied. "I—felt a little dizzy! I guess—I've been going at it—a little too hard lately. I suppose I'm getting old."

He paused for his loving family to refute this statement, but they only laughed as if it were a good joke.

"I—think I'll—have to cut out—some of this—traveling," he said slowly, taking deep breaths between his words. He still wore the look of a whipped dog—except in his family's eyes.

But at that they shouted a joyous assent. "Then you'd be all ours and not belong to the world at large anymore," added Gloria as the hurrah subsided.

"Come on—let's go!" said Mr. Oliver, turning from them to hide the shame that stole over his face.

"But we haven't given Muth her presents yet," said Gloria, who never forgot anything.

With relief Oliver took the little white box containing the watch from his pocket. With the attention focused upon it, instead of on him, he was even able to make a pleasant little speech in presenting it.

Nevertheless the occasion was no longer the joyous celebration he'd anticipated. Half of his mind was occupied with wondering what on earth that Dunlap woman meant to do next. Did she intend to keep that miserable affair of Daisy hanging over his head like a Damoclean sword the rest of his natural life? If so, he would have no peace anywhere. He would never know when they might walk in and shame him among his friends. Well, he'd been a fool. It was hard to admit it. Perhaps he merely bungled things. But—yes, he felt a good deal of a fool. After all, what was that girl but a pretty pink and white thing—just a passing fancy. Home was best. He would stay at home—unless that obnoxious Mrs. Dunlap haunted his steps. Perhaps it would be as well to go abroad for a year. The business was in pretty good shape now, and the girls would love it. Yes, they would go abroad. He'd broach the subject that very day and speed up arrangements to leave as soon as possible. He couldn't stand any more shocks like this one!

Thus reasoning he grew calm, and the family rode the elevator down to the new car and their interrupted holiday.

On the street Mrs. Sheldon seemed dazed for a moment and put her hand to her head. Her companion caught the gesture and slipped an arm around her.

"My dear, you're going straight back to the hotel and get a good long sleep," she said and raised her other hand to summon a passing taxi.

"Oh, I'm all right," murmured the mother. "Everything is—all right now. At least I hope it is, for a while. Only—what shall I do with Daisy? Her life is broken! My poor little flower of a girl!"

"Don't you believe it!" said the woman who knew life. "God doesn't let even a flower get broken as easily as that. Here, let's get in this taxi, and then we can talk."

She gave the order to the driver and then laid her hand on the stricken woman's arm. "My dear! You should be singing and shouting hallelujah, not mourning. Can't you trust the Father? He's revealed this to your girl to show her that life isn't over because she made a mistake about one wolf in sheep's clothing. Perhaps this came to her to teach her and prepare her for a fuller, wider life than she could have otherwise been prepared for."

"Oh!" the mother sighed. "I wish I could feel that way, but it seems to me we've lost our self-respect. Daisy has lost all the fine dignity and judgment she had and can never lift up her head again."

"She has only lost her cockiness, my dear. She hasn't lost a bit of self-respect. She's made a mistake, yes, and a bad one, but she'll learn to be more careful now, not to trust herself implicitly. She'll learn to pray her way through the difficulties, perhaps, instead of insisting she knows best and demanding her own way. She'll pay more heed to her mother's advice—to her mother's intuition—and not think her own judgment of character is final. We must all experience sharp lessons to teach us to find our guidance in the Lord and our own utter helplessness without Him."

"But I'm so afraid Daisy won't look at it that way. She's such an intense child, so proud and excitable and enthusiastic, and so prone to fall to the depths when the heights have failed her. I'm afraid—Mrs. Dunlap, forgive me, but I'm afraid she may lose her mind! You weren't with her that last night before she went away. You don't realize."

"I realize that underneath are the everlasting arms, dear," said Mary

Dunlap. "God has performed the seemingly impossible for you: He's convinced your daughter of the unworthiness of the man she was determined to marry. He did it in time and before it was too late to save her from the public shame of her own actions. And He can perform like wonders in other ways. Now, dear sister, suppose you just trust in Him. He has said, 'Commit thy way unto the Lord; trust also in Him and He shall bring it to pass.' Couldn't you rest on that this morning and let Him give you a good rest? I'm sure everything will be made plain for you. Now here we are at the hotel."

Mary Dunlap helped her friend up to her room, for she looked as frail as a lily by that time. Then she ordered a nice lunch sent up and convinced her companion to partake.

The troubled mother wanted only to talk about the morning's events; Mary complied but also brought out at every turn the wonders the Lord had performed. Then she inquired about the young man Nelson Whitney.

"I'm wonderfully taken with that young man," she said, pouring a second cup of coffee. "He looks like true blue to me."

"Oh, he is!" said Marguerite's mother. She told of the days—the years—when her girl and this fine boy were growing up together. At last the tension disappeared from the mother's face.

But then she stopped her story with sudden bitterness. "She had all that devotion in a fine young man her own age, and yet she could think she cared for that old slippery beast!"

Mary Dunlap gave an almost girlish giggle. "He is that, isn't he? I keep thinking of his poor wife and daughters, who think he's the salt of the earth. I hope they don't ever have to find it out this side—or at least not till the Lord has made him over. But, dear, don't you think perhaps your child just hadn't awakened to realities yet? Wasn't she more in love with being in love than with the man himself? She was under a strong delusion, as the Bible says, but I'm sure it's been swept away, and just at the right time.

"I'll tell you something. Her hand was on the boy's arm as if she trusted him, and his strong hand covered it tenderly as if she were dearer to him than life. I couldn't help seeing the look on his face as he bent to speak to her from his fine height—she is such a little girl and so sweet.

"Perhaps I shouldn't have seen it and ought to keep it to myself; but it seems to me you have a right to know. She smiled up into his face, such a sweet trustful smile, that I couldn't help feeling that her heart will fly back to him as a refuge now in her trouble. I saw that. Yes, I saw it while you were talking to Mrs. Oliver. I'm sure you have a right to know. And the Lord has let that young man be an instrument of rescue for your girl."

"Oh!" sighed the mother wistfully. "If that could only be, I would ask nothing better of life."

"Don't set your limits, dear! The Lord may have that and even greater blessings yet in store. Now you are going to sleep, and I'm going to sit here at the desk and get some of my correspondence out of the way or I'll be swamped."

Chapter 13

D own on the street Marguerite almost collapsed. A glance at her face showed Nelson that she had reached the limit of her strength. He summoned a taxi and put her in.

"Would you like to go to the hotel and lie down a while?" he asked.

"Oh, no," she said, reaching toward him, "I don't want to be alone now. I can't bear it. I must have someone who belongs. Let's go to some quiet place where we can sit down a little while, or—walk—where there won't be so many people."

She sank back in the seat and closed her eyes, and Nelson gave the order: "Drive to the park, and drive around till I tell you to stop."

He stepped into the taxi, pulled down the shades and drew her head gently over till it rested on his shoulder.

"Now," he said, "just rest there a few minutes and get calm."

At last the tears spilled over onto her cheeks.

"That's all right, dear," he said. "Cry as hard as you can. It'll do you good!"

His voice had an unmistakable lilt to it. He was thinking how she said she wanted to be with somebody who "belonged." Then in her soul she felt that he belonged after all.

Marguerite let the tears have their way for a minute or two, and then she said, "But you don't know what it's all about. I—ought—to—explain."

"Explain, nothing!" said Nelson. "I know all about it."

"Oh! How did you know?" she asked with a perplexed frown. "Did Mother tell you?"

"Never a word," said the young man, pulling a large white handkerchief out of his pocket and unfolding it. "Can't you give me credit for having eyes? When you love somebody, you understand."

He lifted the girl's tear-wet face and wiped it gently with the cool handkerchief.

"Oh, Nelson, you've always been wonderful! And—I—but you won't feel that way about me anymore when you know everything. I've been—so—silly—! And wicked, Nelson! I've been terribly wicked. Oh," she shuddered, "to think that I—got into such an awful mess. Oh, I can't stand myself! How can I live? To think—"

"See here, Marguerite. You're not to think anything about it now. You're just to rest and get over the shock. Later, when you're rested, we'll talk it out."

"But I want to get it over with first," said Marguerite, sitting up. "Indeed I can't rest till you know what a fool I've been."

"All right," said Nelson, "you've been a fool, have you? Well, I love you anyway. Have you had any breakfast? No, I thought not. Well, neither have I. What if we stop somewhere and get some?"

"But I can't go anywhere with my eyes all red," objected the girl, dabbing at them.

"That's all right," said the young man. "We're going to get out pretty soon and walk around the park a little. I think we'll find a fountain or a spring or a lake or something wet. We can mop up and get cooled off, and then we'll go and eat."

"You're always so dear," she murmured.

He bent over and kissed her on the forehead.

"Thank you for that, little one. Now are you ready to get out and find that fountain?"

"Wait," said the girl, her face clouding again. "We can't go on like this, Nelson. We can't even be friends again till I tell you everything. It—chokes me!"

"Out with it then!" said the young man calmly. "But make it snappy. Make a clean breast of it in three sentences."

"Oh, Nelson, I fell in love with that man—a *married* man!"

"That's number one," said Nelson, unperturbed.

"I started to run away with him and get married, without telling Mother!"

"Number two," counted Nelson.

"And—I've been awful to Mother—and to that Mrs. Dunlap—and—and—to *God!* I almost lost my senses!"

"I inferred as much. Now is that all, little one? Shall we get out now and fix up for breakfast?"

She buried her face in the folds of the wet handkerchief and murmured: "Oh, Nelson, you always did take the ache out of things!"

"That's what I'm here for," Nelson said with a smile, "and I mean to keep on. You know you're mine, have been ever since we were children, and I don't intend anything to hurt you if I can help it. Of course if you get sick—mentally or physically or spiritually sick—I'll just have to stand by and help till you get well again. But you're mine, little girl. I want that understood. Now shall we get out and walk a little?"

"But, Nelson—you mustn't. I'm not worthy of a devotion like that—I couldn't let you—"

"We're getting out, driver," Nelson tapped on the glass.

He helped her out and paid the fare. Marguerite stood still in the bright sunshine at the entrance to a park pathway and let the cool breeze blow on her hot cheeks and forehead. She had turned her face away lest the cabman should see that she had been crying. And suddenly a great burden seemed to roll from her.

She expected to find herself desperate, in agony, unable to live longer, when she escaped from that terrible office where she underwent such awful revelations. But now it seemed to her a great relief. The fearful responsibilities that a day ago had lain upon her heart with deathlike heaviness were gone. Her path had been diverted from a dark and perilous way, into brightness and sunshine again.

The only thing troubling her was the shame over her part in the terrible drama that had just been played to the finish. She thought of her foolishness and gullibility, her readiness to fall for the handsome eyes of a man of the world, whose flattery was used merely for his own passing amusement. She came from a long line of respectable and noble ancestors, with a heritage of Christian training and tradition, with a mother such as hers and a father whose memory was enshrined forever in her heart. To think that she had been so easy to deceive!

She started at the thought of how she was arraigning the man who had been her lover—almost her husband, but a few brief days ago! Three hours ago she would have sworn to anyone who asked that she loved him with her whole soul; that life would be worthless without him; that she would cling to him with her last breath though she were separated from him for years; that she would love him and believe him, yes, and even forgive him no matter what others said, no matter what he did.

And now in a few short minutes the cloak of illusion was torn from him and left his shame naked to her view; left him without a charm or virtue; and showed his love to be a mere worthless pretense—for how could he possibly love her when he had so deceived her? How could he dare to bring her a love so dishonored by his own broken vows? For she was not one of those girls who glory in winning a man who belongs to another.

She shivered as she remembered the way he said, "My wife," and, "my daughters," in that familiar married way. If she heard nothing else but that, it would have convinced her.

Then her own words to Mrs. Dunlap returned sharply to her memory: "Unless I can hear him say with his own lips—" Well, she heard him. How terrible it was! Hot irons had seared her heart, and she would never forget.

As she turned toward Nelson she glanced down. There in the path behind him a bit of metal, gold or silver perhaps, gleamed in the sun. It proved to be only a bit of foil wrapping from candy or gum that someone had flung down carelessly in passing. But with the unexplained whimsicalness of such small inanimate things it became for the moment a trinket like a gold and platinum charm the one-time Rufus Keller had worn on his watch chain. During those intimate days she toyed with it lovingly more than once, pleased to think it was her privilege. She even wore it about her neck on a little gold chain for a few days, till she grew alarmed lest her mother should see it, and returned it to him.

Suddenly she recalled he wore it that very morning. She noticed its gleam as he turned away with a guilty look, a look she would never forget. That look tore from her heart the last shred of respect and what she once thought was love for the man. The trinket had twinkled wickedly at her as he turned and pierced her with what she once held so dear.

She caught her breath in a sob as Nelson came alongside her and slipped his hand inside her arm to steady her.

"Oh, how can I ever live? How can I stand it?" she gasped.

"Poor child!" said Nelson sadly. "Do you love him as much as that?"

"Oh, no! Not now!" she cried. "That's gone! But my self-respect is gone too. How can one live without self-respect?"

"That will come back again," said Nelson with a ring in his voice. It was good to hear her say she no longer cared.

She was quiet for several minutes, and he watched her as they walked deeper into the park. Then she lifted her face.

"Nelson, you're wonderful!" she said. "I don't—know—what I should do—without you!"

"Well, you don't have to do without me," said Nelson. "I suppose this is why God sent me down here."

"How did you come, Nelson?" she asked suddenly. "Was it just chance?"

"Nothing in this world is chance, is it, Daisy? But this certainly wasn't anyway. Why, you see, I went to the house to get that list you promised—"

"Oh, I never thought of it again."

"Well, it's of no consequence now," he grinned. "I made up one instead and ordered the things. You'll have to use what there is or get more. But when Nancy and I started to look for the list, your note to your mother was lying right on the floor by the stairs in the lower hall. How it got there I don't know. But Nancy was upstairs, and I didn't have much time, and the note was in your handwriting—so I picked it up and read it. I hadn't gone far before I discovered it wasn't the list, but I couldn't let it go then. I caught a word or two that showed me you were in danger and that your mother must be hunting for you. So I put it in my pocket as Nancy came downstairs and took it with me. If you ask me, I think the Lord left that note there for me to read. I thought you belonged to me enough to give me the right to read it."

Her cheeks reddening, Marguerite tried to recall what she scribbled in that angry note to her mother when she hurried to the midnight train.

"The rest was a cinch," Nelson continued. "I had the address you were going to in your own handwriting. I just had to meet you at the train in New York as it came in—if I could get there ahead of you. Or, failing in that, as I did, I had a second chance of catching you at the office before you went off to marry that villain."

Marguerite shivered at the thought.

"But—how did you get here in time?" she asked. "Why, that must have been rather late in the morning when you found that note. I knew Mother would probably take the early morning train, but I'd hoped to have everything straightened out before she came. But the only other train after you found out is a local, and you couldn't have gotten here even yet—unless you flew. Are you a mystery man?"

"That's exactly what I did. I flew here," said Nelson.

"What do you mean?" she asked, her eyes round with wonder and absent of their trouble for the moment. "Don't tease me, please. I'm so tired."

"I'm forgetting all you've gone through. We'll find that water and then get something to eat. If I remember, it was down this path. I came here once three years ago and thought that someday I'd like to bring you."

A quick turn brought them to a spring gurgling in a granite basin. Marguerite dashed the water in her face and dried it on another clean handkerchief that Nelson produced from his pocket.

"Do you have an unlimited supply of these?" she asked as she emerged from its fresh-smelling folds.

"Very nearly!" he smiled. "Now come on—let's find something to eat."

"But you haven't told me what you meant when you said you flew here."

He noticed that her voice was almost cheerful again.

"Just that," he said, laughing. "I flew. It's the first time in my life, but I would have enjoyed it if I hadn't been so worried about you."

She still looked mystified, so he explained.

"I have a friend who has been coaxing me to fly with him for months, and I never seemed to have time. He has oodles of money and no end of time, so I just made good on a promise I'd given him once and called him. He was game all right and said he was going to New York in a couple of hours. So we came. We got here sometime before your train arrived. By the way, why didn't you come on it?"

"I did," she said, "but I got off at the wrong station, something they called Manhattan Transfer. I had to wait ages before another came along."

"Manhattan Transfer! And you were knocking around that desolate place alone at that time of night? Well, I'll say your angels must have had their hands full taking care of you yesterday. They must be all worn out. I guess that's why I have the job for a little while now. Come—here's a taxi."

She flashed him a smile, and he helped her into the cab with a lighter heart. At least the days of reserve and distance were over between them. She was confiding in him as she used to do. One couldn't expect more than that so soon.

They found a quiet tearoom. Nelson seemed to know just how to manage things, without asking his way anywhere. He put her in a seat where she was sheltered and ordered the items he knew from long years of association that she liked. Deftly, he drew her attention away from herself and the tragic events of the last few days, tempted her to eat and provoked her to laugh. He described his first sensations of flying, telling anecdotes of his aviator friend when they were together in France. He even called her attention to a beautiful white kitten that came purring in to be stroked and fed tidbits. It was nearly three o'clock when they finished their meal. The color was stealing back to the girl's lips and cheeks, and the terror had faded from her eyes.

"Now," said Nelson, consulting his watch, "it's three minutes to three. What do you want to do? Shall we make good our word and go to the tomb and the museum, or shall we save that for another day and go back to the hotel so you can get a good rest?"

"Oh," said Marguerite, the color draining from her face. "I can't go back— yet. But don't let me detain you. I'll—I'll—just wander around a little. I'll go—shopping," she ended with an attempt at briskness in her voice. "You've been awfully good."

"Now, look here, Marguerite. Haven't I known you too long and loved you too well for you to get off any bunk like that on me?" he asked, laughing. "I'm here to take care of you, and what you want to do is what I want to do. What I meant is, are you too tired to take on sightseeing, or are you really interested? Neither of us is in a state to get much intellectual good out of a tomb or a museum, but perhaps I'm mistaken. If you want to, we'll go. But if you're not particular which day we go tombing, suppose we take a lighter expedition. I'll tell you what would suit me. I'd like to take you down to Tiffany's and buy you the prettiest diamond ring we can find."

Marguerite started back in her chair. "Nelson! What do you mean?" she asked, her face a curious study of tenderness and fear.

"I mean just that, Daisy. I think it's high time you had some kind of a safe-guard to wear. I don't want to let you drift around the world unprotected any longer."

"But—Nelson—"

"Yes, I know—you want to tell me that you don't love me—that you couldn't possibly love one man when you've just gotten over caring for another and all that. But I'm going to do this anyway. The chances are, you may someday find you do care a little, and then everything will be all right. But if you don't, why, there are such things as broken engagements. You don't have to marry me if you find out I'm a villain or that you love somebody else better. But you do have to wear my ring for a while anyway. You're not going back home without it. Nobody is going to have a chance— not that dirty crook of a Keller anyway—to say that he threw you over. You're going home engaged to me, Marguerite Sheldon. Whatever you do with me afterward, you're going to have a ring right now! You can take it for all the love I have in the world, if you're willing, or you can take it for just a means of protection for now if that suits you better. Until you've told me you can't love me ever, I'm out to see that we're known as belonging to each other."

There was such quiet strength and tenderness in the way he said these words—so low that they reached only her ears and so full of feeling and earnestness that she could not ignore them or laugh them off.

"Nelson, you feel sorry for me—and you're dear—but you don't need to go to such lengths," she began helplessly.

"Marguerite," he rebuked her, "that's beneath you. You know I never lie! You know I wouldn't say it if I didn't mean it. You know I've loved you ever since I can remember."

She was quiet for a long time, the blush of color dusting her cheeks. At last, lifting her eyes, she spoke: "Nelson, forgive me—I shouldn't have said that. I know what you've always been. But I didn't know till today quite how wonderful you were. I believe you. Your love is the greatest thing the world can ever give me, and I'm sure I don't know what I would ever be without you. I would tell you that I love you, too, only I've been such a fool the last year and a half that I don't even trust myself to say it. It seems cowardly of me to creep into the refuge you offer me, when I have so little to give. A threadbare love that was thrown away on an old married man with grown daughters!"

"That's all right, Daisy," Nelson said, looking at her tenderly. "I understand what you've been through. It's no wonder you distrust yourself, but I trust you, when you get rid of the mists and get back to yourself. We'll be square with each other, and you can trust me. I won't ask you to marry me till you're ready, and not then if you don't love me enough to be happy with me, better than any other man on earth. But I do ask you to wear my ring home and let it be a shelter to you in any complex circumstances that this situation may bring about."

She etched little patterns on the tablecloth with the tip of her spoon. At last she lifted hesitant eyes. "Nelson—have you thought what Mother will think if I do this? Off with the old love and on with the new? Won't she be more horrified than ever at me? Won't she think I'm false at heart?"

"Your mother will jump for joy," said Nelson Whitney. "Take it from me. It would be the happiest moment of her life if she could see my ring on your hand and know you wanted it there."

"So soon—after—"

"The sooner, the better!" said Nelson, wrinkling his face into his nicest smile. "Come! Let's go!"

She followed him in a mixture of joy and doubt. Could it be right for her to be happy like this, when only a few hours ago she had been—

But Nelson was summoning another taxi, and in a few whirls they were entering the great Fifth Avenue store.

When she stepped out again a little while later, after searching among priceless jewels and fragile glass that looked like the breath of a frozen flower, she was wearing his ring on her hand and a deep joy in her eyes that was good to see.

"And now," said Nelson, as he hailed another taxi, "I think we'd better go and find Mother and tell her all about it, don't you? It seems to me she has suffered long enough."

Chapter 14

It was late that evening before mother and daughter were alone at last.

Mrs. Dunlap had responded to a telegram and left on the seven o'clock train for Boston to meet with an important committee on some international work for young women.

Nelson Whitney had attended to her needs as the son of the family might have waited on a powerful ally who had pulled them out of distress. He escorted Mrs. Sheldon and her daughter to a wonderful symphony with a soloist of world reputation and then returned them to the hotel, refusing to remain even for a few minutes because they needed to rest. He accompanied them to the door of their room, kissed Marguerite reverently and then half timidly kissed her mother, saying, "Good night, Mother!" He left both mother and daughter tingling with joy and pride in him. At last the door was closed on the outer world, shutting them in alone together.

The girl hurried to the closet to hang up her coat and hat, feeling a sudden shyness before her mother. She realized then that some things must be cleared between them before she could feel that all was right.

The mother removed her street things slowly, a light of joy in her face. She was thinking of what her new friend said to her that afternoon and of the Bible verse she quoted to her. How swiftly and wonderfully the promise was made good to her. Why, she scarcely awoke from that refreshing sleep into which she had fallen, pillowed on that promise, when the fulfillment knocked at her door in the appearance of Nelson and Marguerite come to show her the ring.

Marguerite was reserved and lovely, almost silent, and they didn't press her to talk much. She was humble and loving toward her mother and toward Mrs. Dunlap; she thanked that goodhearted woman in no uncertain words, though few, and hugged her in a close, seemingly repentant embrace when she left.

But Marguerite hadn't as yet said a word to her mother about the recent events. She let Nelson do the talking, sitting with downcast eyes and a childlike contentment on her face that spoke volumes of reassurance to the two who had waited through the long hours to know how it fared with her.

But now the time had come, and Marguerite knew it, to have it out with her mother.

She stayed in the closet several minutes arranging her things, placing her hat carefully on the shelf and searching in her coat pocket for a handkerchief she thought was there. But at last she came out.

Mrs. Sheldon was taking down her hair for the night; it fell in silver waves to her waist with curls at the ends. The girl watched her mother for a moment, wishing she would begin.

"I don't see how I could have done it to you!" she burst forth all at once. "You are so dear, and here I've led you through all this horrible mess! I don't see how you can ever love me again!"

With one swift movement the mother turned and folded her daughter in her arms.

"My darling!" she said, holding her close.

A long time they stood thus, Marguerite's face hidden in her mother's neck, with the mother's cheek against her daughter's forehead, her hand stroking her hair with caresses that could not be measured or counted or described.

No words passed between them, nor was there any need. Their thoughts were as open to one another as if they had almost been one, so close their hearts seemed to come.

Finally the girl, now forgiven, pulled away and looked at her mother. "Mother, you must think I'm an awful fool. You must think awful things of me—that I let Nelson—that he—that I—so soon after—"

"No, dear, I don't think awful things. I think my girl has been through a bewildering experience, didn't know her own mind and wasn't capable of judging. But I think you've come to your senses again. And I thank God that you have such a wonderful friend as Nelson who is willing to protect you with his love—after all the suffering you have caused him these months. He could not be a greater comfort to me and to you if he were my own son."

"Yes, Mother, he is wonderful!" Marguerite said quietly. "And more wonderful than you know. But you think I let him buy that ring just to protect me from gossips, to let others see that I had not been—a—fool! But I didn't, Mother. I wouldn't do that even to protect you from the shame and disgrace of people finding out what really happened. I wouldn't have unless I loved him.

"And you probably think it can't be true love so soon after I thought I was dying for that other man," she continued. "But it is. I don't think I knew real love before. Why, when Nelson told me how he felt toward me and what I was to him, it opened up a whole new world to me. I didn't know what true love was before. The other seemed like a cheap imitation of it. Nelson's love showed up the other experience. I saw in contrast how selfish Rufus—I mean, Mr. Oliver—was, how all he talked about was having a good time. He didn't seem to care whether I was pleased or not—only to bend me to his will.

"I've been thinking about it all evening," the girl said. "I believe I was just proud to think a man as wise and experienced as I thought he was, had stooped to notice me. I was frantic when I thought I'd lost him. But, Mother, I didn't know the deep sweet joy I feel now in Nelson. I didn't know there was such joy. Truly, Mother—and you know it isn't as if I'd just met Nelson—he's been dear always, since I was a little girl. But he'd never opened this door to his soul before or showed me that he'd put me in his heart. And it has just carried me into heaven, Mother. But I know you think I haven't any right to it—since—since—"

"Yes, you have, my dear. I've watched your face. You're a different girl. You've met the real thing at last and recognized it. I couldn't have hoped it would come to you so soon. I was fearful what might happen to you in the interval, till our new friend showed me that I might trust you with my heavenly Father. And somehow, my precious child, I believe He let this come to you so soon just to show us both how He can heal and how He will lead and save and bless those who trust Him entirely with their lives."

"Oh, Mother!" exclaimed Marguerite. "You are the most wonderful woman in the world. And Mrs. Dunlap is next. What would we have done without her? Suppose I had gone on and had my own way. Suppose I had lost Nelson. Even if the other man hadn't been what he was—what if I had missed knowing how wonderful Nelson is? He's—different. He's *wonderful!*"

"I believe it!" said the mother fervently. "And now let's kneel down and thank God for the wonderful way in which He has led us."

Later, while her mother was preparing for the night, Marguerite took out her little Bible. It always traveled with her, for it was part of the fittings of the bag her mother had given her the Christmas before. She opened it and paused, startled.

"Mother, listen to this," Marguerite said at last. "I opened right to it, Isaiah 42:16: 'I will bring the blind by a way that they knew not; I will lead them in paths that they have not known: I will make darkness light before them, and crooked things straight. These things will I do unto them, and not forsake them.' Mother, that was what He did for me. I was blind!"

About the Authors

Grace Livingston Hill (1865-1947) remains popular more than fifty years after her death. She wrote dozens of books that carry her unique style of combining Christian faith with tasteful, exciting romance.

Isabella Alden (1841-1930), an aunt of Grace Livingston Hill, was a gifted storyteller and prolific author as well, often using her writing to teach lessons espoused by her husband, Gustavus, a minister. She also helped her neice get started in her career as a bestselling inspirational novelist.

If you enjoyed
Grace Livingston Hill Collection #2,
then read:

Grace
Livingston Hill

Collection #1

A romantic collection of four
inspirational novellas including:

Aunt Crete's Emancipation

A Daily Rate

The Girl From Montana

Mara
Isabella Alden